Edinburgh Essays

in Public Law

Edinburgh Essays

in Public Law

edited by
Wilson Finnie
C.M.G. Himsworth
and Neil Walker

EDINBURGH UNIVERSITY PRESS

© Edinburgh University Press 1991
22 George Square, Edinburgh

Distributed in North America
by Columbia University Press
New York

Set in Compugraphic Plantin by
Alexander Ritchie & Son, Edinburgh,
and printed in Great Britain by
Page Bros, Norwich

British Library Cataloguing
  in Publication Data
Edinburgh essays in public law.
  1. Great Britain. Public law
  I. Finnie, Wilson II. Himsworth, Christopher III.
  Walker, Neil 1960 –
  344.102

I S B N 0 7486 0226 7

Contents

Notes on Contributors

Michael Adler has been a lecturer and then senior lecturer in the Department of Social Policy and Social Work since 1971.

T. St John N. Bates was a lecturer and then senior lecturer in the Department of Constitutional and Administrative Law between 1969 and 1985. He is now Clerk of Tynwald (Isle of Man) and Professor of Law at the University of Lancaster.

A.W. Bradley held the Chair of Constitutional Law at the University of Edinburgh between 1968 and 1989. He is now Professor Emeritus and is in practice at the English Bar.

Douglas Brodie has been a lecturer in the Department of Scots Law since 1983.

The Hon. Lord Clyde is a Senator of the College of Justice, the Chancellor's Assessor on the University Court, and Chairman of the Europa Institute.

Terence Daintith was a lecturer in the Department of Constitutional and Administrative Law between 1964 and 1972 and is now Professor of Law and Director of the Institute of Advanced Legal Studies, University of London.

A.G. Donaldson has been a part-time lecturer in the Department of Constitutional and Administrative Law since 1976. He was previously Second Parliamentary Draftsman, and later Director of Law Reform, in Northern Ireland.

K.D. Ewing was a lecturer in the Department of Constitutional and Administrative Law between 1978 and 1983 and is now Professor of Public Law at King's College, London.

Wilson Finnie has been a lecturer in the Department of Constitutional and Administrative Law since 1979

C.M.G. Himsworth has been a lecturer and then a senior lecturer in the Department of Constitutional and Administrative Law since 1974.

Robert Lane has been a lecturer in the Europa Institute since 1983.

Gavin Little has been a research student in the Department of Constitutional and Administrative Law since 1986 and a lecturer in law at the University of Dundee since 1988.

Neil MacCormick has held the Regius Chair of Public Law and the Law of Nature and Nations at the University of Edinburgh since 1972.

Alastair Mowbray was a research student in the Department of Constitutional and Administrative Law between 1981 and 1984 and is now a lecturer in law at the University of Nottingham.

Roy Sainsbury was a research student in the Department of Social Policy and Social Work between 1984 and 1988 and is now a member of the Social Policy Research Unit, University of York.

Neil Walker has been a lecturer in the Department of Constitutional and Administrative Law since 1986.

W. James Wolffe is a solicitor and part-time lecturer in the Faculty of Law.

INTRODUCTION

This book has its origins in a proposal made by Tony Bradley a number of years ago that there should some day be published a volume of *Edinburgh Essays in Public Law*. It would be a book to which he and others closely associated with the study of public law in the Faculty of Law at the University of Edinburgh would contribute but, as the proposal for the book simmered gently, it was suddenly overtaken by Tony's decision to take early retirement from the Chair of Constitutional Law with effect from the end of September 1989.

As now published, the *Essays* reflect two complementary purposes. One is to bring to fruition Tony Bradley's original idea, and the other to celebrate his tenure of the Constitutional Law Chair over the twenty-one years between 1968 and 1989. In pursuit of the second purpose the *Essays* may fairly be viewed as a *Festschrift*, but one having the singular characteristic of containing an essay by the person in whose honour the volume is published! In achieving this hybridity, we believe that not only have we secured for the book one of its most distinguished contributions but we have also been able to adhere more faithfully to the first conception of the *Essays* – of which Tony's own essay would have been an integral part. It is, furthermore, a hybridity nicely redolent of the late twentieth-century phenomenon of early retirement, a retirement which is not the cheerful abandonment of the study but instead the sideways move into a new study which, in Tony Bradley's case, still contains the desk from which *Public Law* is edited and from which a new practice at the English Bar is conducted. *Edinburgh Essays in Public Law* appears not at the end but only part-way through an active life of the teaching, research and practice of constitutional and administrative law.

The period since 1968, when Tony Bradley succeeded John Mitchell in the Chair of Constitutional Law, has been for public lawyers one of great vitality, a vitality captured in successive editions of Wade and Phillips (by the tenth edition, in 1985, Wade and Bradley) on *Constitutional and Administrative Law*. The re-evaluation of public law doctrine and theory has been a standing characteristic of a period which has seen so much ideological and institutional change.

1

The year 1968 lay at the mid-point of the second Wilson Government. The European Communities were little-known territory for most British public lawyers, much less well known than the lingering rules of the British Empire and Commonwealth. In that Commonwealth the 1960s was the decade of independence, especially in Africa (including Tanzania where Tony Bradley taught during 1966–67) but also (from 1965) the early part of the UDI era in what was then Southern Rhodesia. The Commonwealth had yet to experience the impact of the Immigration Act 1971, the constitutional crisis in Australia in 1975 and the repatriation of the Canadian constitution in 1982. Meanwhile, domestic politics in 1968 had still to encounter the explosion of violence in Northern Ireland and the termination of the Stormont system of government, and the waxing (up to the Scotland and Wales Acts 1978) and waning of official interest in devolved government in Great Britain. The party was barely over in the unreorganised system of local government; the first ombudsman had only just taken office; the 'new' select committees were a decade away. The European Convention on Human Rights was of little significance and domestic Bills of Rights and even debates about Bills of Rights were for foreigners. In the heartland of administrative law, *Ridge v Baldwin* (1964) and *Padfield v Minister of Agriculture* (1968) were features only recently added to what seems, in retrospect, to have been a bleak landscape.

During the years from 1968, Tony Bradley was not only a witness to the constitutional developments which occurred but was also one of the period's most active and articulate analysts. His contribution to maintaining Wade and Bradley as the leading student text and his editorship, from 1986, of *Public Law* have been mentioned. His devotion to administrative law led, among a wide range of other writing, to a highly influential memorandum for the Scottish Law Commission on *Remedies in Administrative Law* (1971), and then to the *Administrative Law* title for the *Stair Memorial Encyclopaedia of the Laws of Scotland* (Volume 1, 1987). He wrote widely on the liability of public authorities, on ombudsmen, and on the impact on United Kingdom law of the European Convention on Human Rights and of the European Community. Concern for the protection of the rights of individuals affected by official action provided much of the motivation underpinning Tony's work and this led not only to his interest in fairness in administrative practice but also to a wider interest in the protection of civil liberties. His article on 'The Role of the Ombudsman in Relation to the Protection of Citizens Rights' ([1980] CLJ 304) is perhaps the most prominent published manifestation of this overlapping interest. He took a great interest in (and in 1988 organised an important conference in Edinburgh on) the Canadian Charter of Rights and Freedoms. With this, he combined a practical interest through his close association, over a number of years, with the Scottish Council of Civil Liberties.

This combination of scholarly interest and practical engagement was also evident in other areas. Tony was a member of the Wolfenden Committee on Voluntary Organisations which reported in 1978, and later on two Committees on Local Government in Scotland (Stodart reporting in 1981 and Montgomery in 1984). He served for many years as a Chairman of Social

Security Appeal Tribunals, a reflection of a keen teaching and research interest in welfare law. He gave great encouragement to socio-legal work in that and related fields.

An important characteristic of Tony Bradley's work in Edinburgh, already reflected in this brief summary, was his determined legal bilingualism. An English legal education never stood in the way of a fluent familiarity with the Scottish legal system. The Wade and Bradley text (despite its primary commercial orientation towards the English student market) became fully sensitive to the needs of Scottish students. Tony's more specialised contributions on Scots administrative law and the Scottish institutions of government provide more substantial evidence of this facility. It was perhaps the discipline of comparison between the home-based legal systems which provided the foundations upon which was built Tony's wider enthusiasm for comparative work. His extensive contacts with public lawyers in Commonwealth jurisdictions, the United States and Western Europe are a testimony to his work in this field, whether at comparative law symposia, summer schools or conferences. Long before the political changes in the last year, Tony Bradley had established contacts with liberally-inclined academies in Eastern Europe.

In addition to his teaching, research and writing, Tony Bradley was tireless in the administrative contribution he made both in Edinburgh and beyond. He was Head of the Department of Constitutional and Administrative Law during the whole of his term in Edinburgh and was Dean of the Faculty of Law between 1979 and 1982. He was a founding promoter of the Administrative Law Group of the Society of Public Teachers of Law, locally active in the Royal Institute of Public Administration and served on committees of the Social Sciences Research Council (and ESRC) and of the University Grants Committee.

However much Tony Bradley's energy, enthusiasm and intellectual integrity continue to be applied in the next phase of his professional life in London, they are already greatly missed in Edinburgh and it is in appreciation of Tony's Edinburgh years that the sixteen essays which join his own in this volume are offered. The essayists are all people who, as present or former members of or as students in the Department or in other ways associated with public law at the University, have worked with Tony Bradley. They were offered only the gentlest editorial guidance as to subject-matter but we have been gladdened to find that, whilst a comprehensive review of contemporary public law was neither sought nor achievable within the bounds of a single volume, we have drawn together original contributions over a wide field. Loosely grouped under the headings 'Constitutional and Legal Theory', 'Institutions', 'Rights', and 'Administrative Law', none of the essays strays far from the public law concerns of Tony Bradley. His own masterly treatment of the ECHR is nicely complemented by Keith Ewing's differently angled essay on the role of the Judicial Committee of the Privy Council as a human rights court for the Commonwealth. More specifically focused pieces on the protection of rights and liberties are provided by Wilson Finnie, who compares Scots and English law on public order, and by Douglas Brodie on political strikes. The theme of procedural protection looms large in the contributions of Alastair Mowbray (on private sector ombudsmen) and Roy Sainsbury (on social security appeals), which are joined in the 'Administrative Law' group by an illuminating essay on the limits of the supervisory jurisdiction by James Clyde. The significance (however unhelpfully) given to a public/private law distinction drawn in England need not, he argues, be adopted in Scotland. Another original trans-Border comparison is drawn by James Wolffe in his essay on the Crown and the Prerogative, whilst Gavin Little focuses on Scotland alone to discuss the singular administrative law jurisdiction of the sheriff.

The collection opens with four essays pursuing broader themes in public law. Michael Adler re-examines ideas of justice, discretion and poverty earlier pursued in 1975 in a book jointly edited by Tony Bradley and himself and, in so doing, provides a perspective on recent changes in welfare law which sets in broader context the more detailed treatment by Sainsbury. St John Bates's essay is also concerned with the theme of institutional change and with how this may be profitably analysed by public lawyers. Terry Daintith and Neil Walker, in different ways, grapple with the thorny problem of the relationship between public law and politics.

Loosely grouped under 'Institutions' are an original and stimulating commentary by Neil MacCormick on the Scottish National Party's proposal, dating from 1977 but still relatively unknown, for an independence constitution and a highly topical discussion by Robert Lane of the possibilities of an independent status for Scotland within the European Community. These are joined by Chris Himsworth's essay on political autonomy in local government and an intriguing foray into the mysterious history of parliamentary draftsmen by Alfie Donaldson.

To all those contributing essays we would like to extend our profound thanks for, in the first place, undertaking to contribute at comparatively short notice and, despite the pressures of other work, managing to take editorial deadlines fairly seriously. In addition we would like to record our thanks to our Departmental Secretary, Margaret Penman, whose prodigious efforts assisted the project throughout.

We are painfully conscious of the many areas in public law which cry out for examination by essay but which have escaped unconsidered in the present volume, and also of the fact that, by reasons of constant change within the field, as the late John Mitchell observed, 'there is no right time to write a book on Constitutional Law'. We comfort ourselves with the thought that, all contributors being in good health, we reserve the right, in due course, to trouble them for a second offering.

Constitutional and Legal Theory

Justice, Discretion and Poverty: A Reappraisal*

Michael Adler

A. Introduction

Fifteen years ago, Tony Bradley and I organised a conference on Supplementary Benefit Appeal Tribunals (SBATs) and edited a book based on the conference proceedings *Justice, Discretion and Poverty* (which, for convenience, will sometimes be referred to as JDP).[1] Since Tony and I often discussed the possibility of organising a follow-up conference on Social Security Appeal Tribunals (SSATs), it seemed appropriate in this volume to review, with the benefit of hindsight, the arguments we put forward and the approach we adopted in *Justice, Discretion and Poverty*; to assess the significance of subsequent changes in policy; to indicate what can be learned from the experience of the last fifteen years; and to suggest how I now think the subject should be approached.

B. The Approach Adopted in JDP

Justice, Discretion and Poverty was 'primarily concerned with the standards of justice which characterise the administration of discretion towards poor people'.[2] To the extent that the book focused on SBATs as a forum for handling disputes between claimants and officials, justice was seen as something external to the administration of the Supplementary Benefit scheme.

Although Tony and I asserted that 'the effectiveness of a class of tribunals cannot be judged in isolation from the scheme of administration with which it is associated'[3] and emphasised that 'SBATs must be judged as part of the social security system',[4] and although we included in the book a previously published analysis of the discretionary powers within the Supplementary Benefit scheme,[5] we did not take our own advice very seriously. Pointing out that there was more criticism of SBATs at that time than of any other tribunals, we preferred to judge them as tribunals. Thus, we made numerous references to the three criteria for assessing the justice inherent in tribunals advocated by the Franks Committee[6] (openness, fairness and impartiality) and tended to ignore the questions of justice inherent in the day-to-day administration of the Supplementary Benefit scheme.

Evidence for this approach can be found in the final chapter of *Justice, Discretion and Poverty*, where we outlined a strategy for reform. We indicated[7] that there were four possible approaches to the reform of SBATs:

1. The existing system of tribunals could have been made to work better, e.g. by recruiting better chairmen and members and by introducing a programme of training.
2. Structural changes to the existing system could have been introduced, e.g. the administration of the tribunal system could have been made independent of the Department of Health and Social Security (DHSS) and a second-tier appeal tribunal could have been introduced.
3. An integrated system of tribunals for all social security benefits could have been set up or, alternatively, the jurisdictions of National Insurance Local Tribunals (NILTs) and the National Insurance Commissioners (NICs) could have been expanded to hear Supplementary Benefit cases.
4. The place of Supplementary Benefit within the social security system and of discretion within the Supplementary Benefit scheme could have been reviewed with a view to reforming the statutory framework of the Supplementary Benefit scheme.

We concluded that the first approach would have been quite inadequate but, at the same time, backed away from the fourth approach on the grounds that it raised issues of social policy which went beyond the problems inherent in the operation of the tribunal system. Although we did not exclude the third approach, we focused on the second. Thus, we advocated:

1. That it should be possible to appeal from an SBAT to a second-tier appeal tribunal whose published decisions would provide authoritative guidance on points of law to SBATs and to staff administering the Supplementary Benefit scheme.
2. That responsibility for SBATs (and NILTs) should be transferred from the DHSS to an independent Social Security Tribunal Service (SSTS) which would have been responsible for the selection and training of members and chairmen and the employment and training of tribunal clerks.
3. More advice and assistance relating to appeals.

C. The Aftermath of JDP – Subsequent Developments in Policy and Practice

Within ten years, the first and second of the recommendations outlined above had both been implemented. Following research carried out for the DHSS by Professor Kathleen Bell,[8] which also recommended the appointment of legally qualified chairmen to SBATs (in the short run) and the eventual integration of Supplementary Benefit and National Insurance appeal tribunals, the government embarked on a series of reforms of Supplementary Benefit appeal procedures. By 1985, when Tony Bradley published his review of social security adjudication[9] the position was as follows:

1. There was a common (three-tier) system of lay adjudication and the independent statutory authorities (comprising adjudication officers (AOs), Social Security Appeal Tribunals (SSATs) and the Social Security Commissioners (SSCs)) were responsible for almost all social security benefits. The main exception was housing benefit, which is administered by local housing authorities and from which the only right of appeal is to a Housing Benefit Review Board made up of councillors appointed by the local authority.[10]
2. An independent Presidential system had been introduced in which the President is responsible *inter alia* for the selection and training of legally qualified chairmen and lay members of SSATs and for the employment and training of tribunal clerks.
3. A new statutory authority, the Chief Adjudication Officer (CAO), had been set up to monitor standards of adjudication within the day-to-day administration of social security, to provide advice and guidance to adjudication officers, and to prepare the Department's submissions to the SSC where claimants appeal against decisions of an SSAT.[11]

The third of these provisions is a particularly novel and important one, not least because the Chief Adjudication Officer has confirmed that first-instance decision-making is not particularly good, because such a small proportion of initial determinations, probably no more than 1 in 100, are the subject of appeal[12] and because anecdotal and impressionistic evidence suggests that the decisions of SSATs have relatively little direct effect on the day-to-day decisions of adjudication officers. Of course, that is not to deny that the existence of SSATs and the possibility that a claimant might appeal may effect the decisions of adjudication officers indirectly, e.g. by making them more careful and conscientious than they would otherwise be.

It is clear that there have been many changes in social security adjudication in the fifteen years since the publication of *Justice, Discretion and Poverty* and that these changes realised, and in some cases went beyond, the recommendations we made in the book. However, this should not give rise to complacency, since social security adjudication today still contains a number of disturbing features:

1. Although the selection and training of members and chairmen are now the responsibility of the President and Regional Chairmen of SSATs, it would appear that selection hardly exists and training is not nearly as extensive as it should be or as imaginative as it could be. Research which Carol Jones and I recently carried out for the Scottish Consumer Council[13] indicates that, although tribunal members now represent a broader cross-section of the community than was previously the case, it is very uncommon for persons who are recommended not to be appointed and, once appointed, for members not to be reappointed. Members can sit without having undertaken any training and attendance at training sessions is not compulsory. Moreover, the training is infrequent and rather conventional in its content and approach. In both these respects, the SSATs' record was much less impressive than that

of the District Courts and Children's Panels with which they were compared.

2. As Hazel and Yvette Genn have recently shown in their report for the Lord Chancellor's Department,[14] advice and representation are still only available to a small proportion of claimants who could benefit from them. There were lower rates of representation before SSATs (12%) than before Industrial Tribunals (58% applicants and 73% respondents), Mental Health Review Tribunals (65%) or at hearings before Immigration Adjudicators (90%). Since representation has a substantial effect on outcomes – in SSATs, specialist representation increased the rate of success from 30% to 48% – this must be a cause for concern.

3. The most recent report of the Chief Adjudication Officer[15] indicates that there have been no reductions in rates of error in adjudication. Faults (whether of substance or procedure) are to be found in 30% of all decisions.

4. The Chief Adjudication Officer is only concerned with the decisions made by officials in their role as adjudication officers and not at all with decisions which staff (sometimes the same staff) make as officers of the Secretary of State. The Secretary of State's powers have recently been reviewed by Martin Partington[16] but we know very little about the ways in which they are exercised; they are not subject to external scrutiny by the CAO or any other body. The decisions made by local authority staff who administer housing benefit are likewise not subject to external scrutiny.

5. The establishment of the Social Fund in 1988 resulted *inter alia* in a very substantial curtailment of the jurisdiction of the independent adjudicating authorities, since the majority of appeals (96,375 out of 165,307 appeals heard by SSATs in 1987) concerned single payments but, except in the case of maternity and funeral grants and cold weather payments, Social Fund payments have been removed from the jurisdiction of the independent adjudicating authorities. Decisions at first instance are taken by Social Fund Officers, who may exercise discretion but are expected to follow Departmental directions and guidelines.[17] Dissatisfied claimants can no longer appeal to an independent tribunal but may apply for administrative review by DSS local office management and thereafter to a Social Fund Inspector in one of the DSS Regional Offices. (There is also, of course, the possibility of an application for judicial review.) Social Fund Inspectors, like Social Fund Officers, are Department of Social Security officials although they are appointed by and accountable to a Social Fund Commissioner who monitors their work and reports annually to Parliament on the quality of their decision-making.[18]

D. Learning from the Past

At this point, I should like to return to *Justice, Discretion and Poverty*. Although Tony and I took a rather cautious stance at the time, we were soon overtaken by events. Noting that DHSS staff frequently used their discretion to deny payments to claimants and thus deprive them of their entitlements, many welfare rights workers and organisations began to advocate a reduction in the extent of discretion within the Supplementary Benefit scheme as well as a strengthening of the appeal system. In this they were joined by David Donnison and the Supplementary Benefits Commission (SBC), who argued that the much larger caseloads, the changing composition of the claimant population (in particular, the substantial increase in the number of unemployed persons and single parents claiming Supplementary Benefit) and the greater assertiveness of claimants made it impossible to exercise discretion in a humane and sensitive manner.[19] The Labour Government set up a review of the Supplementary Benefit scheme which concluded[20] by advocating, *inter alia*, a new statutory framework in which regulations were to replace administrative discretion. Arguing that DHSS staff and appeal tribunals used their discretion to make payments to claimants who did not really need them and were 'playing the system', the incoming Conservative Government accepted the arguments for reducing the extent of administrative discretion and introducing statutory rights to what later became known as single payments (for the purchase of essential items which claimants could otherwise not afford) and additional requirements (designed to meet the higher recurrent expenses of claimants with additional needs). Adopting a 'top-down' strategy, the Government hoped that rights to single payments and additional requirements would curb the generosity of staff (and tribunals) and strengthen their resistance to the blandishments of fickle and unscrupulous claimants; adopting a 'bottom-up' approach, welfare rights activists hoped that rights to single payments would ensure that more claimants received their full entitlement.[21] Thus, for entirely opposite reasons, the Government and the welfare rights lobby found themselves supporting the same strategy.[22] However, it is important to stress that neither side advocated a rights strategy for its own sake and both did so for instrumental reasons.

For a short while following the passage of the Social Security Act 1980, it looked as though the Government would achieve its objectives, since the number of single payments fell quite dramatically; but, after a year or so, it began to rise again. The rise proved quite remorseless and was met by a series of cuts in the items which could be provided through single payments.[23]

This development illustrates very well another issue which we failed to take on board, namely the relationship between procedural and substantive justice, i.e. between process and outcome. It would appear to be the case that the independence of the appellate machinery and the responsiveness of appeal tribunals to the claims of appellants were partly responsible for the cut-backs in single payments. The large number of appeals relating to single payments generated a substantial additional workload for DHSS offices and the appeal tribunals as well as considerable extra expenditure.[24] Certainly, Ministers and civil servants have often argued that aggressive and irresponsible welfare rights advocacy contributed to the downfall of single payments and, to the extent that this is true, this would clearly detract from the achievements of increased welfare rights activity.[25] But whether or not this is true, it raises the important issue of the relationship between procedural and substantive justice, i.e. between administrative and social justice.

In *A Theory of Justice*, John Rawls argues that just outcomes can be achieved through the adoption of fair procedures.[26] Such a conclusion might suggest that procedural justice is a necessary and sufficient condition for the achievement of substantive justice. However, closer inspection of Rawls' argument shows that this is not the case. If procedural justice is concerned with process, i.e. with means rather than ends, while substantive justice is concerned with outcomes, i.e. with the ends themselves, then it is clear that only one of the three principles for judging the basic institutions and laws of a society which, according to Rawls, would be chosen by rational individuals in the so-called 'original position' is concerned with procedural justice. While the principle that offices and positions should be open to all under conditions of fair equality of opportunity (the principle of equal equality) is solely concerned with process issues, the other two principles, namely that each person should have an equal right to the most extensive total system of equal basic liberties compatible with a similar system of liberty for all (the principle of equal liberty) and that social and economic inequalities are to be arranged so that, subject to the 'just savings' principle they are of the greatest benefit to the least advantaged (the difference principle) are both clearly concerned with outcomes. Is it the case, then, that procedural justice is a necessary albeit not a sufficient condition for the achievement of substantive justice? Common sense might suggest that this is the case inasmuch as procedural safeguards may be required to ensure that the intended outcome is attained. However, the relationship between procedural and substantive justice is unfortunately complicated by the fact that trade-offs are often made between the one and the other. Thus procedural safeguards may be strengthened in order to ensure greater fidelity to the aims of the legislation while the substantive outcomes which, in this case are comprised of criteria of eligibility and levels of entitlement to benefit, are actually reduced. In such circumstances, who is to say whether the lot of the claimant is actually improved? In a powerful critique of the strategy we advocated in *Justice, Discretion and Poverty*, Prosser conceded that it was 'tempting to see the matter as one of equality: because the rich have proper judicial protection for their property rights ... this should be extended to the poor'.[27] However, he was in my view clearly correct to conclude that 'if legality is seen in isolation from the social and economic circumstances on which it is based, it can be merely an "empty procedural device" serving to legitimate social organisation by giving an appearance of formal equality without providing substantive rights'.[28] Although procedural justice is intrinsically important and, as Galligan effectively demonstrates, procedural rights are not simply parasitic on what he calls 'primary rights',[29] their relationship to primary or substantive rights is still a matter of considerable importance.

Recent policy changes in social security raise other important issues too. The introduction of the cash-limited Social Fund referred to above, dispensing loans on a discretionary basis and without the possibility of appeal to an independent tribunal, provides further evidence, if such is required, of the Government's instrumental approach to issues of rights and discretion in relation to social security. However, it is not just to be understood as an almost foolproof defence against financial or administrative pressure or as the Government's answer to aggressive advocacy, since it also has important ideological connotations, attempting as it does to undermine the so-called 'culture of dependency' by forcing claimants to stand on their own two feet.[30] This is also the case for the unprecedented catalogue of cuts in social security provisions for the unemployed which are clearly intended to discourage so-called 'voluntary unemployment', encourage work incentives, and, likewise, to attempt to subvert the 'dependency culture'.[31]

The Social Fund cannot be viewed in isolation since it was introduced as part of a wide-ranging set of reforms to the social security system following what the Secretary of State at the time referred to as 'the most substantial review of the social security system since the Beveridge Report'.[32] In particular, it needs to be considered alongside the introduction of Income Support, since the two schemes together replaced the Supplementary Benefit scheme. Of particular importance here was the replacement of additional requirements which sought, to a limited degree, to tailor Supplementary Benefit payments to the needs and circumstances of individual claimants by a set of premiums payable 'automatically' to certain dependency groups. This change necessarily involved gainers as well as losers. Claimants who qualified for premiums, e.g. the disabled and claimants with families, gained at the expense of those who did not, e.g. the unemployed and claimants without children. At the same time, claimants who had not previously been in receipt of additional requirements gained at the expense of those whose Supplementary Benefit had included extra payments for heating, laundry costs, the costs of special diet, etc. Although the former category probably included some claimants who should have received additional requirements but, for whatever reason, did not do so, the latter included most of the claimants in greatest need.[33]

The final topic which I should like to refer to here is the Operational Strategy, the largest single computer application in Western Europe, which is intended to revolutionise the administration of social security.[34] The replacement of Supplementary Benefit by Income Support was made possible by the Operational Strategy and the design of the Income Support scheme assumed that manual assessments of entitlement would soon give way to assessment by computer. More generally, the Operational Strategy involves the harnessing of information technology to a 'top-down' strategy in order to improve administrative efficiency and solve a number of administrative problems. However, as Roy Sainsbury and I have recently pointed out,[35] information technology does not have to be used in this way in that it could equally well be linked to a 'bottom-up' strategy, e.g. by providing comprehensive welfare benefits information for claimants and other members of the public. But, to the extent that the administration of social security represents a compromise between competing bureaucratic, professional and juridical forms of organisation, and to the extent that each of these in turn is associated with a distinctive conception of administrative justice (see below), the Operational Strategy is bound to affect the justice inherent in the administration of social security and not merely the efficiency of the administration.

E. Looking to the Future

The upshot of all this is that, if I were ever to organise a sequel to *Justice, Discretion and Poverty* I would do it rather differently. This is in part because the context has changed. SSATs in 1990 do not attract the level or intensity of criticism that SBATs attracted fifteen years ago, although the inadequacy of the arrangements for reviewing Social Fund decisions is certainly the subject of considerable scorn and derision. But it is also, in part, because socio-legal studies of administrative law have developed enormously in the intervening period. Thus, if I were to organise another conference or edit another book with the same title, it would differ from the first one in a number of important ways:

1. It would not focus exclusively on appeal procedures but would address the justice inherent in the whole corpus of administrative decision-making in social security. This is not merely because claimants can no longer appeal to a tribunal against the decision of a Social Fund Officer, for a new edition of *Justice, Discretion and Poverty* would clearly have to include a critical appraisal of the procedures for administrative review of such decisions. It is, I think, for even more important reasons. By focusing on judicial review and references to the various ombudsmen, administrative lawyers sometimes give the impression that 'justice' is something external to the administrative process. However, applications for judicial review and references to the ombudsman are invoked relatively infrequently and, in any case, it is not clear how much impact these decisions actually make on routine day-to-day decision-making. Similar arguments apply to a focus on appellate decision-making. Although the number of appeals to Social Security Appeal Tribunals and the number of Social Fund reviews are both quite substantial, they constitute only a relatively small percentage of first-instance decisions.[36] Moreover, their impact on routine day-to-day decision-making would appear to be relatively slight, while evidence from the Chief Adjudication Officer and the Social Fund Commissioner suggests that error rates are uncomfortably high.[37] Thus, I would wish to adopt an alternative approach to 'justice' which recognises this as something intrinsic to administration and focuses on the justice inherent in routine administrative decision-making. One such approach which I find particularly helpful is to be found in Jerry Mashaw's book *Bureaucratic Justice*.[38] At one level this book is simply a case-study of the American Disability Insurance scheme but, at another level, it provides an analytic approach to administrative justice which has wide general application.

Mashaw started out by looking at criticisms of the Disability Insurance scheme. It was not particularly popular and was criticised for all sorts of shortcomings. For example, it was criticised for failing to provide adequate management controls, for failing to provide a good service to its clients, for failing to ensure 'due process' and to respect the rights of its clients. Mashaw argued that these criticisms reflected different normative conceptions of the Disability Insurance scheme, i.e. different views of what it could and should be like. In fact, these criticisms corresponded to three normative models or ideal types of organisation; to the model of the organisation as a bureaucracy; as a profession; and as a legal system.

Mashaw defines the justice of an administrative system in terms of 'those qualities of a decision process which provide arguments for the acceptability of its decision'.[39] Since the three normative models of organisation which he identifies are each associated with a different set of organisational characteristics, it follows that there must be three different conceptions of administrative justice, one associated with bureaucracy, another with professions and a third with the legal system. Mashaw contends that these three models are 'competitive' but not mutually exclusive.[40] Thus, they can and do coexist with each other, although the more there is of one, the less will there be of the others. The importance of this particular insight is that it enables us to see that the implementation of social security is best understood as a compromise between bureaucratic, professional and legal system imperatives and should not be judged by any single set of evaluative criteria – in particular, by those associated with the legal system. Rather, the task should be to understand what trade-offs have been made, in particular contexts, between the different models of organisation and to determine, in those particular contexts, whether different trade-offs might be more appropriate.

2. It would be a mistake to focus exclusively on the Social Fund. This is in part because the Social Fund has taken over only some of the functions of the now defunct Supplementary Benefit scheme. Most of its functions have been taken over by the Income Support scheme and, to the extent that recipients of Social Fund grants or loans must be in receipt of Income Support (or Family Credit), the new Income Support scheme should certainly fall within our remit. However, I would wish to take the argument to embrace a concern with the entire social security system. This is in part because claimants are often in receipt of several benefits simultaneously, and because the outcomes of claims for one benefit frequently carry with them implications for entitlement to other benefits. Clear illustration of this is provided by the decisions of adjudication officers in the Department of Employment on disqualification from Unemployment Benefit which automatically entail a reduction in entitlement to Income Support.[41] However, it is also because of the insights which can be derived from comparative studies, i.e. from comparing the different procedures and standards of adjudication which apply to different social security benefits. In fact, I would go further in advocating a greater commitment to comparative study by including within our remit an explicit comparison between the administration of social security in Britain with that of other countries with which Britain can be compared. Thus, it would follow that our new project would embrace the whole range of first-instance decisions taken by adjudication officers, Social Fund Officers and officials acting on

behalf of the Secretary of State;[42] second-instance decisions taken by SSATs and Social Fund Inspectors; Commissioners' decisions, court decisions and decisions of the Parliamentary Commissioner for Administration;[43] as well as the monitoring activities of the Chief Adjudication Officer and the Social Fund Commissioner.

3. It would not be appropriate to focus, as we did last time, on problems associated with the exercise of discretion. Without wishing to deny the importance of such problems,[44] it should be realised that problems may equally be encountered with the enactment of rules and with the enforcement of rights. Rules, discretion and rights correspond to the three models of organisation outlined above: rules are associated with bureaucracy, discretion with the professions and rights with the legal system. Just as trade-offs are made between the models of administrative justice associated with each of these models of organisation, so trade-offs must also be made between rules, discretion and rights. The arguments for and against each of these concepts can be set out and the circumstances in which each is likely to work best identified. Thus, rules are intended to lead to greater consistency in decision-making and to ensure that like cases are treated alike. However, they can lead to excessive rigidity unless they are frequently revised, and to extreme insensitivity if they do not take into account significant differences between individuals. At the same time, they can also confer a great deal of power on an organisation and foster a passive approach from those who have to deal with it. On the other hand, discretion allows for greater flexibility and enables unlike cases to be treated differently. Thus it facilitates greater creativity, although decisions do rather frequently reflect the moral judgements of decision-makers. In addition, discretion can confer a great deal of power on individual officials and foster an undesirable degree of dependency. By and large, rules are often associated with generalist and fairly low-status administrators, and, in a social security context, tend to work best when coverage of benefits is fairly comprehensive and levels of benefits reasonably generous. Discretion, on the other hand, is usually associated with high-status professional groups who have undergone an appropriate course of training, e.g. doctors and social workers, and works best when decision-makers are trusted to promote the well-being of claimants.

By comparison with rules and discretion, rights foster a greater sense of independence among claimants in that they call for independent procedures for arbitration in the case of disputes between two parties. On the other hand, they are often criticised for promoting an undesirable degree of litigiousness and for giving too much power to the individual right-holder. Rights are associated with the involvement of lawyers and other para-legal workers who adopt an adversarial approach, i.e. one based on conflict and in a social security context tend to be invoked when the authorities cannot be trusted to promote the interests of claimants. Since rules, discretion and rights all have something positive to offer and all have certain negative connotations, the task must be to establish, in a particular context, whether the right balance has been struck and, if not, what a better balance might be.

4. Since there are substantive as well as procedural components of justice and since claimants are at least as concerned with what they receive as with the manner in which they are treated, it would be necessary to explore the relationship between procedural and substantive justice, i.e. between administrative and social justice. The latter has at least two dimensions in that it invites a comparison between the incomes of social security claimants and those who derive their income from other sources, in particular from employment, as well as a comparison between the incomes of different categories of claimants and an assessment of the ways in which the social security system is able to respond to some states of dependency but not to others. I have in mind here a study of the extent to which the rules and regulations governing eligibility as well as the levels of entitlement provided by the social security system conform to public perceptions of fairness among recipients of social security and among the public at large. In this connection, I would also envisage a study of the acceptability of the trade-offs which have been made between procedural (administrative) and substantive (social) justice.

F. Conclusion

All this might seem like a very tall order. It would certainly be far too much for any one person to take on alone. However, it is important to remember than when Tony Bradley and I discussed the possibility of a follow-up to *Justice, Discretion and Poverty* we had in mind a conference that would of necessity be considerably larger than our first one, and another book based on the conference proceedings. Many more people (lawyers as well as social scientists) are now interested in these problems and would be in a position to contribute to the proceedings. The project is certainly feasible and would, in my view, be highly desirable. If it ever comes to fruition, Tony, I hope you will find the time to come.

*A draft of this essay was presented at the Annual Conference of the Socio-Legal Studies Association held at the University of Bristol on 9–11 April 1990. The author would like to record his thanks to a number of people in the audience for their helpful comments.

Notes

1. M Adler and A W Bradley (Eds) *Justice, Discretion and Poverty* Professional Books (1975).
2. *Ibid* 1.
3. *Ibid* 207.
4. *Ibid* 207.
5. R Wilding 'Discretionary Benefits' (1972) 3 *Social Work Today* 5, reprinted in M Adler and A W Bradley *op cit* note 1 *supra* at 55.
6. *Report of the Committee on Administrative Tribunals and Enquiries (Franks Report)* Cmnd 218 (1957) para 25.
7. M Adler and A W Bradley *op cit* note 1 *supra* at 213.
8. K Bell *Research Study on Supplementary Benefit Appeal Tribunals: Review of Main Findings, Conclusions, Recommendations* HMSO (1975).

9.   A W Bradley 'Recent Reform of Social Security Adjudication in Britain' (1985) 26 *Les Cahiers du Droit* 403.

10. M Partington and H Bolderson *Housing Benefit Review Procedures: a Preliminary Analysis* Brunel University (1984) and R Sainsbury 'Social Security Appeals: in need of Review?' in the present volume.

11. R Sainsbury 'The Social Security Chief Adjudication Officer: the First Four Years' [1989] PL 323.

12. In 1986–87, there were 14,710,000 new and repeat claims for benefit and 130,000 appeals were heard by tribunals. However there were substantial variations in the proportion of new and repeat claims for different benefits which led to appeals. For further details, see *Social Security Statistics* HMSO (1983).

13. C Jones and M Adler *Can Anyone Get on These? A Study of Systems of Appointment and Training of Justices of the Peace and Members of Social Security Appeal Tribunals in Scotland* Scottish Consumer Council (1990).

14. H Genn and Y Genn *The Effectiveness of Representation at Tribunals* Lord Chancellor's Department (1989).

15. *Annual Report of the Chief Adjudication Officer for 1987–88 on Adjudication Standards* HMSO (1989).

16. M Partington *The Secretary of State's Powers of Adjudication in Social Security Law* (SAUS Working Paper) University of Bristol (1990).

17. See, in particular, R Drabble and T Lynes 'The Social Fund: Discretion or Control?' [1989] PL 297.

18. See H Bolderson 'The Right to Appeal and the Social Fund' (1988) 15 *Journal of Law and Society* 279; R Drabble and T Lynes *op cit;* and T Mullen 'The Social Fund: Cash Limited Social Security' (1989) 52 MLR 64.

19. See, in particular, D Donnison 'Against Discretion' (1977) *New Society* 534 and D Donnison *The Politics of Poverty* Martin Robertson (1982).

20. *Social Assistance: a Review of the Supplementary Benefit Scheme* DHSS (1978).

21. The terms 'top-down' and 'bottom-up' are usually used to describe two contrasting approaches to policy implementation. See, for example, P Sebatier '"Top-down" and "Bottom-up" Approaches to Implementation Research' (1986) 6 *Journal of Public Policy* 21. For an application to the study of policy making in social security, see M Adler 'Lending a Deaf Ear: the Government's Response to Consultation on the Reform of Social Security' in R Davidson and P White (Eds) *Information and Government* Edinburgh UP (1988).

22. For an alternative view, see D Bull 'The Anti-Discretion Movement in Britain: Fact or Phantom?' [1980] *Journal of Social Welfare Law* 65.

23. Following the 1980 changes, there was a short-term drop in the number of Single Payments from 1.1 million in 1980 to 0.8 million in 1981. After that the numbers rose sharply: by 1982 the number of Single Payments had exceeded its pre-1980 level and by 1986 it had risen to 4.7 million. For a fuller discussion, see J Bradshaw 'The Social Fund', *Yearbook of Social Policy 1986–87* Longmans (1987) 31. Changes in the Single Payment regulations introduced by the Supplementary Benefit (Miscellaneous Amendments) Regulations 1986, SI 1986/1259, resulted in a substantial reduction in the number of Single Payments, which fell to 2.7 million in 1987. For a discussion of these changes, see R Cohen and M Tarpey *Single Payments: the Disappearing Safety-Net* (Poverty Pamphlet 74) Child Poverty Action Group (1988).

24. Although, in 1985 Single Payments still accounted for only 5 per cent of total expenditure on Supplementary Benefit, they represented one third of all Supplementary Benefit decisions. See *Report of Social Security Advisory Committee* Cmnd 9836 (1986). In addition, almost half the appeals were concerned with Single Payments. Again, for a fuller discussion, see J Bradshaw *op cit* note 23 *supra*.

25. The thin spread of welfare rights workers throughout the country makes it extremely unlikely that they were directly responsible for the increase in

the number of Single Payments. However, they probably contributed to the emergence of a 'rights culture' among claimants. Of greater importance were changes in the composition of the claimant population, in particular the increase in the number of unemployed persons and single parents claiming Supplementary Benefit. For an assessment of the achievements of the welfare rights movement, see T Prosser *Test Cases for the Poor* Child Poverty Action Group (1983).

26.   J Rawls *A Theory of Justice* Clarendon Press (1972).

27.   T Prosser 'Poverty, Ideology and Legality: Supplementary Benefit Appeal Tribunals and their Predecessors' (1977) 4 *British Journal of Law and Society* 39.

28.   *Ibid* at 60.

29.   D J Galligan 'Rights, Discretion and Procedures' in C Sampford and D J Galligan (Eds) *Law, Rights and the Welfare State* Croom Helm (1986) and, more generally, D J Galligan *Discretionary Powers: A Legal Study of Official Discretion* Clarendon Press (1986).

30.   These claims were articulated very clearly by the Rt Hon John Moore MP Secretary of State responsible for Social Security from 1987–89. See, in particular, J Moore 'The Future of the Welfare State', *Address to CPC Conference*, London, 26 September 1987 (unpublished).

31.   A B Atkinson and J Micklewright 'Turning the Screw: Benefits for the Unemployed' in A B Atkinson (Ed) *Poverty and Social Security* Harvester Wheatsheaf (1989) 125.

32.   2 April 1984 H C Debs col 653 (per Rt Hon Norman Fowler MP Secretary of State for Social Services).

33.   The Government's estimates of gainers and losers can be found in *Reform of Social Security: Technical Annex*, HMSO 1985. See also R Berthoud 'New Means Tests for Old: the Fowler Plan for Social Security' in *Yearbook of Social Policy 1986–7* Longmans (1987) 7.

34.   *Social Security Operational Strategy: a Framework for the Future DHSS* (1982).

35.   M Adler and R Sainsbury 'The Social Shaping of Information Technology: Computerisation and the Administration of Social Security', paper presented at JRMT Social Security Workshop, London School of Economics, 23 February 1990. This paper is to be published in M Adler, C Bell, J Clasen and A Sinfield (Eds) *The Sociology of Social Security*, Edinburgh University Press (forthcoming, 1991).

36.   Between April 1988 and March 1989 there were 106,337 requests for reviews of Social Fund decisions relating to discretionary payments. These corresponded to approximately 20 per cent of refused applications. In the same period there were 2,954 requests for reviews by Social Fund Inspectors. For further details see *Annual Report by the Secretary of State for Social Security on the Social Fund, 1988–89* Cm 748 (1989).

37.   Cm 748 *op cit* note 36 *supra* and *Annual Report of the Social Fund Commissioner for 1988–89 on the Standard of Reviews by Social Fund Inspectors* DSS (1990).

38.   J L Mashaw *Bureaucratic Justice* Yale UP (1983).

39.   *Ibid* 24.

40.   *Ibid* 34.

41.   N Wikely 'Unemployment Benefit, the State and the Labour Market' (1989) 16 *Journal of Law and Society* 291.

42.   No reference has been made here to medical adjudication within the social security system or to decision-making by local authority staff. The former is important in relation to disability benefits, the latter is central to the administration of housing benefit. Both could well be included within the scope of the new project.

43.   *Justice, Discretion and Poverty* contained a chapter on the Parliamentary Commissioner for Administration. See M Partington 'Social Security and the Parliamentary Commissioner' in M Adler and A W Bradley *op cit* note 1 *supra* at 155.

44. Two classic contributions to the debate on this issue are still worth reading.
     See K C Davis *Discretionary Justice* University of Illinois Press (1971) and
     R M Titmuss 'Welfare "Rights", Law and Discretion', (1971) 42 *Political
     Quarterly* 113. See also R Baldwin and K Hawkins 'Discretionary Justice:
     Davis Reconsidered' [1984] PL 570.

Constitutional Dodos: Approaches to Constitutional Analysis*

T. St J.N. Bates

A. Introduction

Those who are most inclined to consider constitutional development, in particular institutional development, come to the task with a variety of advantages and handicaps. The academic commentator may have time, and may be capable of taking a broad view, but will have limited direct access to contemporary information on political and institutional development. The political or civil service practitioner will usually have less time, will often adopt a narrower view, but comes with contemporary knowledge and expertise. Although views are expressed to the contrary,[1] it would be foolish to suggest that only the practitioners, and not the commentators, contribute to the development of the constitution; analysis, whether by commentator or practitioner, may also make a significant contribution.[2] For the commentators to overcome their handicaps by drawing on the advantages enjoyed by the practitioners, or indeed vice versa, has always been fraught with difficulty. For the academic commentator a balance has to be struck between drifting into journalism without the merit of being truly contemporary and offering an analysis based on inaccurate or outmoded constitutional information. There is inevitably a continual search for means of analysing constitutional development on the basis of publicly available information which will have a value and relevance not only to other commentators but also to practitioners. It is for this reason that the reader is led to the admittedly much used analogy of the dodo.

It will be recollected that the dodo lived on the island of Mauritius. It had become heavy with a powerful bill and strong legs but had lost the power of flight in the safety of its predator-free island. It fell an easy prey to marauding sailors and was unable to compete with pigs and other introduced livestock. It became extinct in about 1681.[3] It had adapted, but it had adapted to an environment free of predators and competitors. When more vigorous competition was introduced the dodo was not equipped to survive; it had neither the resources nor the adaptability to do so. The interaction between dodo and human was crucial and no doubt Mauritius would have been a more complete place had seventeenth-century sailors possessed late-twentieth-century environmental sensitivities.

21

Various factors have influenced and encouraged this Darwinian consideration of constitutional development. The first is a perforce close observation of recent constitutional development in the Isle of Man. The Isle of Man is a dependency of the Crown and the Crown remains responsible for the conduct of its foreign relations, for its defence and, ultimately, for its good government. In other respects the island enjoys a high degree of autonomy. As might be expected, the relationships between its institutions differ somewhat from those that prevail within the United Kingdom and in recent years these relationships have undergone change. Two aspects of the relationship between the Legislature and the Executive may serve as illustrations.

The first is the process of nominating the Chief Minister and his Ministers. The Chief Minister is appointed by the Lieutenant Governor after his nomination has been approved by the majority of Members of Tynwald.[4] Until recently he in turn presented the names of the nine Ministers of the Council of Ministers, the cabinet, *en bloc* to Tynwald and their appointment similarly required Tynwald approval.[5] Casual ministerial vacancies followed a similar procedure.[6] The Chief Minister's nominations were not always successful[7] and at a certain stage of the procedure there was the possibility of nomination from the floor of Tynwald; in such circumstances the successful candidate would have been imposed on the Chief Minister as one of his Ministers. Now, following the Westminster practice, the Ministers are appointed by the Lieutenant Governor acting on the advice and with the concurrence of the Chief Minister.[8] The ministerial system was introduced into the Isle of Man in 1986 to replace what was, in effect, a nineteenth-century board system. A consequence of this is that a limited convention of collective responsibility has developed within the Council of Ministers. In response to the development of collective responsibility there has now emerged an informal back-benching grouping. There is thus, out of a historically apolitical legislature devoted to consensus politics, the possible beginnings of a party system.

The second aspect is the development of the legislative programme. Government Bills come to the Speaker of the House of Keys. Formally, he determines which Minister of the Keys will take the Bill through the House and also, in practice, when it will have its first reading.[9] Theoretically, he could substantially reduce the success of a Bill and the speed with which it is enacted by giving it to a less competent member and delaying its introduction. In practice, he will usually accede to the advice of the Minister of the Department most closely associated with the Bill on which Member should be invited to take it, and respond to any view expressed by the Council of Ministers on the urgency of bringing the Bill before the House.

These illustrations are not intended to suggest that the Isle of Man's constitutional relationships are more effective than those of the United Kingdom, by whatever criteria effectiveness is judged. They merely serve to demonstrate an evolutionary process in a constitution in which the relationship between the institutions of the state has not yet tilted decisively in favour of the Executive, although no doubt the evolution will be in that direction. It is not claimed that the Manx system is significantly better. Indeed, there is very little evidence that, for example, the scrutiny of legislation is markedly more effective in the House of Keys than it is in the House of Commons.

A second factor leading to a Darwinian consideration of constitutional development is a striking modern consensus, across the political spectrum, of the underlying problems which beset the British constitution. This may be illustrated briefly by three examples. The first is the thesis of Professor Nevil Johnson contained in his book, *In Search of the Constitution.*[10] Professor Johnson is an Oxford politics don with particular knowledge of both German and British politics, and with previous experience as a Treasury civil servant, who would, I think, describe himself as right of centre. He complains of the theory of the 'Crown in Parliament' as one which inevitably leads to the fusion of Executive and Legislature and the dominance of the Executive. He complains of a lack of principle in the constitution and cites as an illustration the development of civil liberties through historical necessity rather than on the basis of principles which balance the rights of the individual as against the needs of the State. His solutions are, variously, a Bill of Rights or a written constitution. Secondly, there are the views of Professor David Marquand, in his remarkable book, *The Unprincipled Society.*[11] Professor Marquand is a Professor of History and Politics who was previously a Labour MP and an official of the European Communities, and was a founder member of the Social Democratic Party. He also, as the title of his book suggests, complains of a constitution devoid of principle. He finds unsatisfactory Anglo-American political philosophies which are dependent on enlightened self-interest coupled with altruism (which he wittily describes as Thomas Hobbes six days a week and Bob Geldof on Sundays), and just as unsatisfactory the more abstract interest of the individual for the community as espoused by Rawls. He has many concerns. One of them is that an emphasis on parliamentary sovereignty in the constitution means that sovereignty cannot easily be shared. Another is that political philosophies, from Hobbes to Rawls, based on the interests of the individual do not take sufficient account of the role of the State and are increasingly difficult to sustain in an interdependent world. The solutions he offers are devolution upwards to the European Community, which is in a sense obligatory, and devolution downwards. My third example is a book of essays, by writers who can fairly be described as left of centre and are in the main lawyers, edited by Cosmo Graham and Tony Prosser and enviably entitled *Waiving the Rules: The Constitution under Thatcherism.*[12] The theme of the authors is the profound and, in their view, perhaps irreversible constitutional change since 1979. This change, they claim, has been facilitated by a 'stateless society' in which the notion of the State has not been developed, and by the doctrine of the sovereignty of Parliament coupled with an unwritten constitution which demands that there should be shared expectations of the objectives to be achieved if the constitution is to work and the public sector is to be regulated. The nature of the book, reflecting perhaps the nature of lawyers, is that the authors do not really offer firm solutions to the dilemmas which they pose. There is a commonality of complaint in all these writings that constitutional theory, in particular the doctrine of parliamentary sovereignty, has become detached from the development of the principles and institutions of the constitution.

The third and final factor leading towards our Darwinian analogy is an apparent marked and disturbing decline of interest by public lawyers in the institutions of the state and in analysis of their workings and development. It may be that with increasing specialisation such matters are now to be primarily the concern of the political scientist. Certainly, public lawyers seem to experience greater difficulty than the political scientist in finding techniques for bridging the gap between the commentator and the practitioner. The consequences of this are unfortunate. A modern work on Whitehall, which although anecdotal is well researched, has few footnote references to the work of public lawyers.[13] A major recent work on Parliament, although one of the co-authors is a distinguished public lawyer, has a bibliography which lists only five books by public lawyers.[14] To take a single Parliamentary example, evidence appears to be invited or offered much more rarely by public lawyers than by political scientists to the House of Commons Select Committee on Procedure.

These various factors might at least suggest that academics, and in particular those that are public lawyers, may earn the criticism levelled at constitutional commentary that it is 'a realm of quasi-legal necromancy in Britain. It is performed on a mist-shrouded academic plateau by a specially-evolved breed of academic lawyer philosophers, whose totemic lore is remote from everyday politics. An ancient goat-track connects it with Westminster'.[15] Flowing from recent developments in the constitution of the Isle of Man, a consensus among commentators on the weaknesses of the British constitution and the decline of analysis by public lawyers, or at least an apparent decline in an appreciation of its importance, three types of emphasis which may be used to test analysis of constitutional development are offered below. Although all of the approaches have been considered before, perhaps they have not previously been a primary focus of constitutional analysis.

B. Human Resource Analysis

Constitutional studies make various assertions about the functions of institutions and actors within the constitution. The extent to which such assertions have a basis in reality can, to a degree, be measured by an analysis of the human, and no doubt other, resources devoted to the function. In its cruder forms, human resource analysis will be a very imperfect indicator; even in a refined form, it will be hard pressed to take account of individual efficiency and informal use of human resources. While such matters cannot be discounted, at the very least human resource analysis may stimulate reassessment. The dodo as a bird may have laid claims to be an aviator, but once its small useless wings were identified its claims would at least deserve re-examination.

Something of the value of human resource analysis may be illustrated by applying it to two familiar constitutional issues.

1. The personal prerogatives of the Crown

Here, the question which may be asked is: what do the human resources devoted to the exercise of the personal prerogatives of the Crown reveal about the nature of their exercise?

It is only a few years ago that interest in the personal prerogatives of the Crown was largely focused on the appointment of the Prime Minister and the dissolution of Parliament.[16] Then there seemed a real and immediate prospect of the emergence of a third political force in the United Kingdom and these particular prerogatives and their exercise were a matter of practical contemporary concern.

In both cases, the prerogative power left to the Sovereign is a residual one. The election of party leaders has, in most circumstances, determined who should be invited to form an administration, and the Sovereign will normally accept the advice of the Prime Minister on a dissolution of Parliament. Indeed, the Crown probably has no power to refuse such advice where the Prime Minister has a clear majority in the House of Commons.

As far as the appointment of a Prime Minister is concerned, there may be situations where the Sovereign would be expected to take initiatives. For example, if a Prime Minister died in office, or were too ill to continue, it might be necessary to make some interim arrangement, prior to an election of a new party leader, and the Sovereign might be involved. Normally a deputy party leader would receive the interim appointment as Prime Minister but there might be no such deputy or the deputy might not be in Government or might be a peer; alternatively, there might be dissension within the party forming a Government or within a coalition Government. Again, it might be that no party has a majority after a General Election, and there might be deadlock in the House of Commons over who should form a Government. If a coalition Government were emerging it might be on the basis that it is led by a person other than a leader of any party within the proposed coalition. There are no doubt other situations where the Sovereign may exercise discretion but perhaps the constitutional significance is not as great as has sometimes been suggested. In all the situations mentioned, the discretion open to the Monarch is probably no more than to invite those most immediately involved to continue their discussions.

The discretion left to the Monarch in refusing a dissolution of Parliament is of a slightly different character. It is generally considered to be controlled by some rather unhelpful guidelines. The received and most quoted view is perhaps that expressed by Sir Alan Lascelles in a letter to *The Times* under the pseudonym 'Senex' in 1950, which followed his earlier briefing prepared for King George *VI*, after taking political and official soundings. In the letter, Lascelles suggested that the Sovereign could constitutionally deny a dissolution to a Prime Minister if the following conditions were satisfied:

(a) the existing Parliament is still vital, viable and capable of doing its job
(b) a general election would be detrimental to the national economy
(c) the Monarch could rely on finding another Prime Minister who would carry on the Government, for a reasonable period, with a working majority in the House of Commons.

It may be that this letter and the conditions outlined in it were a product of a particular debate and have been accorded undue deference. The first condition is virtually meaningless. How does the Sovereign judge whether a Parliament is still 'vital' or 'viable'? If this means that there is still the possibility of forming a Government with a workable majority it replicates the third condition and any other interpretation would tend to undermine democratic principles. Again, how is the Sovereign to judge whether a Parliament is 'capable of doing its job'? Is the Sovereign to be asked to define what the job of Parliament is? What means does the Sovereign have of judging the capability of a Parliament even if its job can be defined? Is the Parliament to be compared with previous Parliaments or with its own performance in, say, the last parliamentary session? Some might even suggest that, on certain criteria, Parliament has not been capable of doing its job for at least two centuries.

The second condition appears in hindsight to be too restrictive. Prior to his letter to *The Times*, Lascelles had prepared a memorandum on the question of refusing a dissolution of parliament for the King and had consulted widely amongst politicians in the course of its preparation.[17] The state of the national economy was, of course, a particular concern at the time, when post-war reconstruction was taking place. However, why should refusal of the dissolution be limited to a situation where a general election would be detrimental to the national economy? The test might equally well be that the general election would not be detrimental to the safety of the realm or to the social fabric of society.

The third condition may, in part, be a reflection of Sir Alan Lascelles' previous experience. He was Secretary to the Governor General of Canada from 1931 to 1935. This was only a few years after Viscount Byng of Vimy had an unfortunate constitutional experience in respect of the dissolution of the Canadian Parliament when he was Governor General; no doubt, knowledge of this experience influenced the young Lascelles in his time in Canada and thereafter. Certainly the condition requires a series of political value judgements to be made and is of singularly little value to a Sovereign faced with responding to advice from the Prime Minister of a coalition Government which is fragmenting.

When these residual powers of the Sovereign are looked at in terms of human resource analysis the advice available to the Sovereign is inadequate. In the case of the dissolution of Parliament, where does the Sovereign seek advice when there is no advice, or only conflicting advice, from politicians; or if the Sovereign is minded not to accept the advice of the Prime Minister? Although the Royal Household is quite extensive it does not provide the sort of advice needed in the circumstances. Of course, the Queen does have personal legal advisers and she could perhaps seek guidance from that quarter. However, her personal legal advisers are not constitutional lawyers. This also has implications for the adaptability of the Crown in giving advice. In 1974, when Mr Heath found that he did not have an absolute majority after the general election and intended to spend a weekend exploring the possibilities of forming a coalition, both Mr Heath and the Palace appear to have sought advice in a rather haphazard manner from a variety of constitutional lawyers. The vulnerability of the Crown in such circumstances is evident also in the advice available to the Monarch as Head of the Commonwealth and, in relatively recent times, in respect even of her Christmas message to the Commonwealth.

The implication may be that the Sovereign is not equipped for what is the occasional exercise of these various discretions and that either the Sovereign should be so equipped or, as far as possible, the discretions removed elsewhere. If the test of the appointment of a Prime Minister is whether he or she can command a majority in the House of Commons, perhaps the Sovereign should not speculate on the matter but have it put to the test. Why should it not be put to the House as a motion of advice to the Sovereign that X be appointed? The motion will satisfy the traditional test if it is successful. If it is not successful a motion can be put to the House in respect of another candidate. To those that suggest that it cannot be done, let it be pointed out that it is done in the Isle of Man.[18]

Similarly, there is perhaps no insuperable problem of making a dissolution of Parliament depend upon a motion of advice passed by the Commons, or both Houses, rather than on the advice of the Prime Minister or, as some constitutional experts would have it, the Prime Minister in Cabinet. This is perhaps more desirable than the Sovereign having formal access to limited constitutional advice.

2. *Parliament and the enactment of primary legislation*

Here, the question is what do the human resources devoted to the parliamentary function of enacting primary legislation reveal about the exercise of that function?

Westminster spends a substantial amount of its time on primary legislation. In recent sessions, when some sixty or so statutes have been enacted, the House of Commons has spent four hundred to five hundred hours in debate on the floor of the House and five to six hundred hours in Committee; the House of Lords has spent some six hundred hours considering primary legislation. This represents approximately 30 per cent of the time on the floor of the Commons and is now approaching 60 per cent of the time on the floor of the House of Lords. To put it another way, in recent sessions Westminster has spent on average about an hour per page in the consideration of primary legislation.

This time does not appear to be spent to good effect. Most successful amendments are moved by Ministers, although the issues behind them may have been originally raised as Opposition amendments. When a Government has a good working majority it is rare for it to modify a principle of a Bill. In a study of three of the sessions between 1967 and 1971, Professor John Griffith could only identify sixteen occasions when Government modified a principle of a Bill in committee, which is the time it is most likely to happen.[19] Government Bills rarely fail to be enacted. In the 1983-87 Parliament, leaving aside hybrid Bills which could be continued, only 5 of 198 Government Bills failed to get Royal Assent, perhaps the most noteworthy example being the Shops Bill 1985-86.[20] The parliamentary scrutiny of Bills is undertaken by Members, even in Committee, with a rather less than comprehensive knowledge of the substance of the Bills before them, and it is not consistent scrutiny. The proposals from the House of Commons Procedure Committee to ameliorate this have had a very limited effect. Special standing committees were introduced but now find little favour with the Government, whose approval is effectively required in order to use them. Repeated attempts to provide a formula to timetable Bills from their introduction has also proved unsuccessful. Parliament continues to be a place where those in Opposition seek to put time pressure on the Government to obtain rare legislative and other concessions; legislation is merely a by-product of the political power struggle.

This is, of course, all well known. Legislation is envisaged and drafted in consultation with a variety of interest groups before its first reading. Serious scrutiny and subsequent successful Opposition amendments in Parliament are not a normal pattern of events. Both with respect to primary legislation and delegated legislation we have passed to what the political scientists describe as 'post-parliamentary democracy' and what has been described by Lord Hailsham, in a more dramatic and less sophisticated manner, as 'elective dictatorship'.[21]

Applying human resource analysis to the question, whether the role of Parliament is described as legislative or simply legitimating legislation, Parliament has few resources allocated to it for the task. First, although parliamentary clerks do draft amendments for Members and some clerks have legal qualifications, it is extraordinary that in neither House is any lawyer employed to assist Members to draft amendments. It is true that a grant of £200 towards the drafting of their Bills is made to those Private Members who are successful in the ballot.[22] However, that is the limit of the formal assistance available, unless the Private Member's Bill has Government support.

The stock explanations for this curious phenomenon are two:

(a) It is said that it would be extremely expensive to duplicate the staff of the Office of Parliamentary Counsel. Alternatively it is argued that it would be impossible to expect draftsmen to draft Bills and also to draft amendments which might be inimical to the Bill; however, this is precisely what happens in the US Senate.

(b) It is also said that it does not matter than an amendment is not professionally, or even adequately, drafted. If the amendment has merit, the argument runs, it can be tidied up by the draftsmen later. This is clearly not a sustainable view. The merit of a badly drafted amendment may not be apparent and the substance of such an amendment may be avoided by a Minister who is able to comment adversely on the quality of its drafting.

Secondly, the number of lawyers employed in both Houses is, I believe, five or possibly six,[23] three of whom devote their time to delegated legislation or European Community legislation. Their number may be compared with the number of lawyers in the civil service. Leaving aside the Fiscal Service and the Crown Prosecution Service, there are about a thousand lawyers in the civil service.[24] Even allowing for the fact that only a certain proportion of the thousand are concerned directly or indirectly with legislation, from a parliamentary standpoint this is a poor ratio of resources. The figures certainly do not suggest that parliamentarians are interested in the form of legislation and its technical implications. They may, of course, obtain limited advice on the policy of legislation within the Palace of Westminster, in particular from the House of Commons and House of Lords Libraries. However, even here there is a lack of resources and a certain lack of adaptability. Although there are some specialist librarians who provide an excellent service for Members of both Houses there is relatively little specialist support for Members.[25] Certainly, the clerks in both Houses still remain generalists in the Northcote-Trevelyan tradition, perhaps more so than in the civil service.

This lack of resources and ability to adapt is reflected in the manner in which legislation now comes to Parliament. Governments are increasingly cavalier with regard to the Bills presented to Parliament. In 1983, the then first Parliamentary Counsel, Sir George Engle, made courteous allusion to this disturbing state of affairs.[26] The situation has possibly deteriorated since then. The lead time between a draftsman receiving instruction and the Bill being ready for presentation for first reading is being steadily reduced. Bills are becoming longer and covering more disparate matters, because for procedural reasons there is an effective numerical limit on the number of Bills which can be enacted in a parliamentary session. The solution is, therefore, to include more in each Bill even if the result is a loss of coherence. Some of these elements may be found, for instance, in the Children Act 1989, a fairly typical mixture of new law, re-enactment of previous provisions and some substantial amendments over quite a wide range of child law. The time available for drafting the Children Bill was alleged to be twelve weeks from start to finish; the Bill would have been drafted by one senior and one junior draftsmen who, of course, would not have been family law specialists. It is not surprising that very substantial Government amendments are tabled to major Bills in their passage through Westminster; a practice commonly referred to as 'legislating on the hoof'. The Children Bill received its second reading in the House of Lords on 6 December 1988[27] and the first list of marshalled amendments was tabled three days before the beginning of its consideration in committee on 19 December.[28] In that marshalled list were amendments in the name of the Lord Chancellor who was taking the Bill. Ten days after the second reading there were amendments, many no doubt consequential amendments, in the name of the Lord Chancellor to nineteen of the clauses and three of the schedules of the Bill. Later in the same session, there were complaints in the House of Lords when a large number of Government amendments were tabled to the Local Government and Housing Bill 1989 shortly before they were due to be considered by the House.[29]

These are not merely isolated examples. In the 1979-83 Parliament, the annual average of Government amendments to Government Bills tabled in the House of Lords was 1106; in the 1983-87 Parliament, it was 1609; in the years 1987-89, it had risen to 2668.[30] In the 1989 spill-over sittings, the

House of Lords spent 20 hours over 6 days considering 1100 Commons amendments to four Bills.[31]

The concern of the House has been such that the Lord Privy Seal has undertaken to examine the number of Government amendments tabled after a Bill has been introduced into the House of Lords. The House of Commons, of course, faces similar problems. For instance, 183 Government amendments were tabled on the first sitting of the committee in the Commons considering the Housing Bill 1988.

Thus, analysing the human resources, at least in terms of lawyers, available to Parliament in the exercise of its function of enacting primary legislation would perhaps reinforce the view that the British constitution may be aptly described as drifting towards a post-parliamentary democracy.

C. Adaptability

Not only did the dodo lack resources for survival, it also had a limited capacity to adapt and eventually became extinct. Perhaps fortunately, the institutions of the state do not expire so rapidly because they generally have the capacity and opportunity to adapt somewhat more easily when faced with predators and competitors.

Assessing the adaptability of institutions is another means of constitutional analysis. It is obviously related to human resource analysis but it may be viewed as a less mechanistic analytical technique. Evidence of the adaptability of an institution to changed constitutional circumstances may be a means of reference to the extent to which the institution is an actor in the changed circumstance. It may, in effect, be a means of establishing the role which the institution does, rather than should, play. The extent and nature of the adaptability of the institution may also be a means of assessing the feasibility of imposing rules upon the institution, or expecting it to assume them.

Establishing evidence of adaptability of institutions would create many methodological difficulties if it were simply an exercise in measurement, but perhaps poses less acute problems if it is seen as a more descriptive analysis. In any event, this may in some instances be the more practical emphasis. Exercises in human resource analysis of executive functions would be considerably more complex, and for the academic more difficult, than human resource analysis of the limited aspects of monarchical and parliamentary functions considered above. Even determining the existing human resources of the civil service is not easy; it is dependent, for instance, on how legalistically a civil servant is defined.[32] However, something of what might be achieved by comparative assessment of institutional adaptability may be illustrated by quite a brief comparative examination of institutional response to UK membership in the European Communities.

Institutional response to membership of the European Communities

(a) **Executive response**
The executive had responsibility for negotiating the terms of UK membership in the Communities over a period of years and had immediate responsibility for negotiating the terms of the Treaty of Accession in 1972.

Consequently, it is not surprising that institutional response of the executive to Community membership was rapid and in some forms, such as in Cabinet committees, pre-dated membership.[33] Following membership, there was a need for the executive to develop institutional structures in order to formulate strategies in respect of Community developments, to co-ordinate individual Departmental approaches to Community policy and legislative initiatives and to resolve inter-Departmental conflicts of interest flowing from these initiatives. It was also necessary to monitor Departmental implementation of Community directives, and in some instances to co-ordinate legal argument before the Court of Justice. These activities must be conducted with an awareness of the diplomatic relations between the United Kingdom and other Member States and also, as the external affairs competence of the Community expands and its commercial activities have an increasing international significance, with non-Member States. It is also conducted with a consciousness of domestic, political and parliamentary implications. Something of this is reflected in the institutional response to Community membership.

Identifiable structures were established in the Cabinet Office. At an early stage the European Unit was created. It was later renamed the European Secretariat to reflect a more permanent establishment and it is one of six secretariats in the Cabinet Office. Parallel structures have been created in the Foreign and Commonwealth Office. To the extent that the Departmental co-ordination and monitoring roles can be demonstrated to be located in the Cabinet Office, the academic commentator can gauge by this institutional response the relative weight placed by the executive on Community affairs and the broader implications of diplomatic relations with the other Member States. More may perhaps be gauged from the demands for a substantial reduction in the numbers of civil servants within the Diplomatic Service and for the amalgamation of the Home Civil Service and the Diplomatic Service, and the executive response to their demands.[34]

Similarly, at Departmental level the redistribution of resources in response to Community membership may evidence the level of departmental involvement in Community affairs and the nature and extent of Cabinet Office co-ordination and monitoring of the Departmental involvement. To take a simple example, each Department has civil servants who are responsible for Departmentally-related Community documents and, for instance, the number and seniority of civil servants in a Department with such an immediate responsibility may in itself be revealing. In summary, the speed, nature and extent of ascertainable Executive response to Community membership may reveal something of the constitutional and functional importance of its involvement with Community affairs.

(b) Judicial response

This Executive response may be compared with the judicial and legislative response. Once the UK became a member of the Communities, Community law became a matter of direct and indirect concern for the judiciary in the United Kingdom. One example of direct involvement, and perhaps the most immediately apparent, was the procedure under article 177 of the EEC

Treaty, by which domestic courts and tribunals refer questions of Community law to the European Court of Justice for a preliminary ruling. In early judicial[35] and extra-judicial[36] pronouncements the senior judiciary in England indicated the danger of inferior courts exercising the power to make Article 177 references. However, in a comparatively short period references were being made by inferior courts and tribunals; discouraging extra-judicial pronouncements were not heard and there was some movement away from judgements proposing a restrictive approach to references. The judiciary adapted to this functional relationship with the Community relatively quickly, and was no doubt encouraged to do so by commercial and professional pressures. Admittedly, other, more theoretical, rather than institutional, issues have not been resolved as completely or as speedily; the relationship of Community law to domestic primary legislation might be cited as an illustration.

An example of an issue of Community law which has an indirect concern for the judiciary in the United Kingdom is the approach to legislative interpretation. The approach of the European Court of Justice to interpretation relies more on the policy which it considers should be achieved and certainly on a more teleological approach to the legislative text than that taken by British courts.[37] English courts have accepted that Community texts should be interpreted in accordance with Community canons of interpretation[38] but have not been noticeably enthusiastic in adopting these canons in interpreting other than Community texts.

Such an analysis may move the commentator to some tentative conclusions about the adaptability of the judiciary. It might be suggested, for instance, that the judiciary shows greater adaptability at an institutional level than in respect of fundamental constitutional principle, and less adaptability when faced with alternative judicial technique.

(c) Parliamentary response

Finally, analysis of the way in which Parliament adapted to Community membership would also perhaps be revealing. Unlike the Executive and the Judiciary, Parliament has no functional role in a Community context, in the sense that the Community legislative process proceeds independently of deliberations at Westminster. Parliament does have a domestic functional role in holding the Executive to account for its policy towards the Community and for its decisions and actions within the Community.[39] Bearing this in mind, it would perhaps not be surprising to find that the response of parliament to Community membership has been a rather stately one. Due to the difficulties of achieving cross-party co-operation on an issue which divided both the Conservative and Labour parties, there was no formal consideration at Westminster of the parliamentary implications of Community membership until the United Kingdom had become a Member State of the Communities.[40] No procedural responses to Community membership were introduced until sixteen months after membership. For some time thereafter, parliamentary scrutiny of draft Community legislation revealed limited awareness of the Community legislative process. Equally, scrutiny of the implementation of Community directives by delegated legislation, the most common manner of implementation, took, and to some degree continues to take, relatively little account of the genesis of such delegated legislation.[41]

Furthermore, the pace of Parliamentary response to institutional and procedural developments within the Community has not noticeably increased. Only in November 1989 did the House of Commons Select Committee on Procedure report on possible reform of procedures for scrutinising draft Community legislation,[42] although the need for reform became acutely apparent as a consequence of the Single European Act,[43] on which negotiations were concluded in February 1986 and which entered into force on 1 July 1987.[44]

D. Balance and Interaction

No doubt, in the seventeenth century the future of the dodo could have been analysed most penetratingly not by an analysis of its physical resources or its capacity to adapt to changed circumstances but by observing the interaction between it and human beings. In the sphere of constitutional analysis, the *balance* between institutions of the state is familiar territory for the theorist and commentator, but the functional *interaction* of the institutions, which is perhaps the means by which separation of powers theories may best be tested, does not attract the same degree of consistency of attention from public lawyers. Greater attention to the interaction of institutions might lead commentators to place more emphasis on the increased rigour in exercising its powers demonstrated by an institution, or on its heightened awareness of its constitutional role, rather than simply its accretion of power, as a factor in constitutional change and development.

Accretion of power is perhaps the manner in which we characterise historical constitutional development; increased rigour and heightened awareness is perhaps a more useful approach to contemporary constitutional development. Examining the accretion of power may be an adequate analytical approach for lawyers in respect of the Stuarts, the Commonwealth and Protectorate, or the twentieth-century corporate state. It is less adequate in respect of judicial activism in the European Court of Justice, the European Court of Human Rights or, in a purely British context, judicial activism in areas of administrative law. Increased rigour in the exercise of its powers, or a heightened awareness of its constitutional role, may be viewed with unqualified equanimity if an institution is viewed singly, but this view may be qualified if it is examined in relation to others. Indeed, although administrative lawyers are perhaps more conscious than most of the wider consequences of the legal principles which they develop, an illustration from administrative law may serve to demonstrate the value of placing emphasis on the interaction of institutions.

Executive responses to judicial review of prerogative powers

Just as it would be surprising if strategies were not formulated in Whitehall to meet the consequences of, for example, the decisions of the European Court of Human Rights as they affect UK Executive action, it would be equally surprising if there were not a similar Whitehall response to the considerable domestic development of judicial review. Some of the strategies of a direct nature would be expected and approved of by lawyers: more attention to correct procedure, to giving reasons, and so on. Some, of a less direct nature, might be disapproved of, because one cannot expect the executive to depart the field when confronted with a dynamic development from the judiciary.

Judicial review of prerogative power may be taken as an illustration; it has been well charted but perhaps some of the developments may be mentioned. Before November 1984, although there were dicta that suggested modification of the law,[45] courts in the United Kingdom were taken to be able to determine the existence and extent of the prerogative power, and some related matters, but not generally to be competent to review the merits of the exercise of an admitted prerogative power.

There followed a judgement of the House of Lords in *Council of Civil Service Unions v Minister for the Civil Service*[46] (the GCHQ case). This case concerned availability of judicial review to challenge the procedural propriety of an instruction, and subsequent certificates from Ministers which removed from the staff in GCHQ the right to belong to a trade union and to have access to industrial tribunals. The majority (Lords Scarman, Diplock and Roskill) held that reviewability depended on the justiciability of the subject matter, not on the source of the power exercised, whether that be statute or prerogative. The minority (Lords Fraser and Brightman) left this question open. For the majority it was thus possible to review the exercise of prerogative power on the grounds, in Diplock terminology, of: (a) illegality (error of law) (b) irrationality (unreasonableness) and (c) procedural impropriety (natural justice and procedural fairness). However, there was unanimity that although the staff at GCHQ had a legitimate expectation of being consulted before their trade union rights were removed (and they were not consulted) the decision not to consult was based on national security which, it was held, was a consideration which overrode requirements of procedural propriety.

Lord Roskill's judgment is perhaps not the best example of precision in judicial law-making. He indicated some of the prerogatives which 'as at present advised' he did not think would be amenable to review by virtue of their subject matter. They were a curious assortment: the making of treaties, the defence of the realm, the prerogative of mercy, the grant of honours, the dissolution of Parliament and the appointment of Ministers, 'as well as others'.[47] Lord Roskill observed that 'it is our legal history which has enabled the present generation to shape the development of our administrative law by building on but unhampered by our legal history' (sic).[48] However that may be, there is no doubt that the GCHQ case has shaped the law in respect of judicial review of prerogative power.

Subsequently, in *R v Secretary of State for Foreign and Commonwealth Affairs, ex parte Everett*,[49] the Court of Appeal held that the prerogative act of the issue or renewal of a passport, and presumbly the withdrawal of one, is reviewable. In *R v Director of Government Communications Headquarters, ex parte Hodges*[50] the Divisional Court held that a decision to withdraw a person's positive vetting status in the interest of national security was not reviewable as to reasonableness but was reviewable as to procedural propriety because the procedures did not directly involve national security. The case arose in consequence of an annual review of a GCHQ employee who in the review revealed his homosexual orientation and gave a full account of his sex life on request. A note was taken of the review and he was refused access to it when he sought it on appeal against his subsequent withdrawal of positive vetting status. He was given written reasons for the decision which was taken but not access to the full notes which were made at the time of his annual review. Although the court was following the GCHQ case in this decision it may have extended the scope of review where there are considerations of national security.

These few cases demonstrate a fairly swift extension of judicial review which constrains Executive action and contain more than a hint of the possibility of further development, particularly as, until recently at least, there was little discernable rationale as to which prerogative powers were reviewable.[51] It might not be altogether surprising if the Executive were to be encouraged to respond to this development. For instance, civil libertarians have congratulated themselves on the success of a campaign to place a part of the security services on a statutory basis and this success is reflected in the Security Service Act 1989 which places MI5 on a statutory basis. However, other considerations may also have prompted this legislation. It may be a reaction to the development of judicial review of the prerogative powers under which the security services would otherwise have continued to operate. Although statutory powers are reviewable, at least the Executive may reduce the possibility of review in the terms of the statute, a strategy which would be denied to them if the security services operated wholly under prerogative powers.[52]

E. Conclusion

Tawney once observed that 'a commonplace characteristic of Englishmen is their power of sustained practical activity, and their characteristic vice is a reluctance to test the quality of activity by reference to principles. They are incurious as to theory, take fundamentals for granted, and are more interested in the state of the roads that in their place on the map'.[54] The modest proposals set out here for alternative emphasis in analysing constitutional development may well be open to such criticism. However, the reformulation of domestic constitutional principle must await a comprehensive analysis of constitutional development which would incorporate the consequences and implications of UK membership of the European Communities. The techniques of constitutional analysis suggested here may contribute to that.

After so many years of Community membership it is certainly time that Community law and institutions ceased to be examined as if they were novelties. However, it is perhaps only now that a mature evaluation can be reached of the domestic constitutional developments which can and should flow from Community membership. For instance, the debate about the future membership of the House of Lords might usefully include comparison with the Economic and Social Committee of the EEC and

Euratom. Determining the membership of the House of Lords by reference to various professions and activities is an attractive idea which was espoused by the late Professor John Macintosh and it might be made more attractive by suggesting that constitutional links could be developed between a House of Lords with such a membership and the Economic and Social Committee.

On a broader front, consideration of the institutions of the State in a purely domestic context may offer some immediate practical conclusions but is unlikely to reveal more fundamental institutional relations. The danger is that in the fury of debate the participants overlook the fact that the object of the debate is fast diminishing.

The legislature is a case in point. The legislative supremacy of Parliament, save in a high theoretical sense, can hardly be seriously maintained in the face of Community membership. Furthermore, the substantive areas which fall within the Community competence continue to show a capacity for growth. In that context, while upward devolution is obligatory, downward devolution simply has less to devolve. Years ago, a brief analysis of Schedule 10 to the Scotland Act 1978, which listed the groups of matters to be devolved and not devolved to the Scottish Assembly and Executive, demonstrated that of the twenty-five groups of devolved matters seventeen would then be affected by existing and proposed Community law.

Community institutional development also suggests that the scrutiny of Community policy and legislation at Westminster has a decreasing utility. A consequence of the Single European Act is that an individual Member State is unlikely to be able to exercise an effective veto on a wide range of draft Community legislation. Consequently, a resolution in Westminster that the Government should oppose a draft legislative proposal in the Council of Ministers will have less significance both within the Community and domestically.

Similarly, Community legal developments have resulted in the extension of domestic judicial review to prerogative powers being deprived of a certain significance. A number of prerogative powers, reviewable or not, are absorbed by Community developments. The issue of passports is now reviewable domestically, but their issue is to a degree controlled by Community law[54] and to that extent reviewable in Community law. Lord Roskill in the GCHQ case considered the making of treaties to be an unreviewable prerogative power, but national capacity to enter into treaties is being absorbed by the European Community and the treaty-making capacity of the Community is reviewable in Community law[55].

As the dodo discovered, the factors which lead to the most dramatic change in circumstances may not be indigenous, but may be those introduced by others from off the island.

*An earlier version of this essay was delivered as a Clydesdale Bank lecture at the Faculty of Law, University of Glasgow, in January 1989. The author writes in a private academic capacity.

Notes

1. E.g. 'Constitutional theory always has and always will emerge from the hard facts of politics rather than from the text-books of professors': Leading article, *The Times* 24 December 1985, quoted in the frontispiece of J.A.G. Griffith, M. Ryle and M.A.J. Wheeler-Booth *Parliament: Functions, Practice and Procedures* Sweet and Maxwell (1989).

2. The study by S E Finer 'The individual responsibility of ministers' (1956) 34 *Public Administration* 377, affected thinking on that subject; in other areas of public law S A de Smith *Judicial Review of Administrative Action* Stevens & Sons (various eds) has had a significant influence on judicial thinking and the development of the law.

3. See generally the entry R.K. Murton 'Columbiformes' in *Encyclopaedia Britannica* (15th ed, 1983) vol 4,936.

4. Constitution (Executive Council) Act 1984 s1 (as substituted by the Constitution (Executive Council) (Amendment) Act 1986 s1).

5. Constitution (Executive Council) Act 1984 s2A (as substituted by the Constitution (Executive Council) (Amendment) Act 1986 s1).

6. *Ibid* s 2A(9).

7. The nomination of Mr Gilbey, MHK, as Minister for Industry in 1988 was unsuccessful: 101 *Report of the Proceedings of Tynwald Court,* T1280 – 1, 20 April 1988.

8. Council of Ministers Act 1990 s 3.

9. *Standing Orders of the House of Keys,* SO 37, provides that the business of the House 'shall be ordinarily that set forth in an agenda, prepared by authority of the Speaker' and no other business shall be considered unless by virtue of a resolution of the House, supported by an absolute majority of its members.

10. N. Johnson *In Search of the Constitution; Reflections on State and Society in Britain* Pergamon Press (1977).

11. D. Marquand *The Unprincipled Society: New Demands and Old Politics* Johnathan Cape (1988).

12. C. Graham and T. Prosser (Eds) *Waiving the Rules: the Constitution Under Thatcherism* Open UP (1988).

13. P. Hennessy *Whitehall* Secker & Warburg (1989).

14. J.A.G. Griffith, M. Ryle and M.A.J. Wheeler-Booth *Op cit* note 1 *supra.*

15. T. Nairn *The Enchanted Glass: Britain and its Monarchy* Radius (1988) 362.

16. In addition to the standard constitutional law textbooks these matters are explored in G. Marshall *Constitutional Conventions: the Rules and Forms of Political Accountability* Clarendon Press (1986) at 19 – 53 and, more briefly, in C.R. Munro *Studies in Constitutional Law* Butterworths (1987) chs. 3 and 8.

17. For the terms of the briefing and the letter to *The Times* of 2 May 1950 see J.W. Wheeler-Bennett *King George VI: His Life and Reign* Macmillan (1965) at 773 – 5. The text of the letter is also to be found in G. Wilson *Cases and Materials in Constitutional and Administrative Law* (2nd ed) CUP (1976) at 22 – 23.

18. See note 4 *supra.*

19. J.A.G. Griffith *Parliamentary Scrutiny of Public Bills* Allen & Unwin (1984).

20. These figures are drawn from a careful analysis by Professor Gavin Drewry in M. Ryle and P.G. Richards *The Commons Under Scrutiny* Routledge (1988), Ch. 7.

21. Lord Hailsham *The Dilemma of Democracy: Diagnosis and Prescription* Collins (1978).

22. T.St.J.N. Bates 'Drafting Private Members' Bills' [1986] *Stat L R* 45 – 6.

23. There are two counsel and an assistant counsel to the Chairman of Committees in the House of Lords; there are two Speaker's Counsel and an assistant to Speaker's Counsel in the House of Commons.

24. An analysis of the statistical information publicly available will be found

in G. Drewry and T. Butcher *The Civil Service Today* Basil Blackwell (1988) at 66–67.

25.   For brief descriptions of the House of Commons services to members see J.A.G. Griffith, M. Ryle and M.A.J. Wheeler-Booth *op cit* note 1 *supra* at 156–7, and M. Ryle and P.G. Richards, *op cit* note 20 *supra* at 45–49. For a professional view of the services provided in both Houses, see D. Englefield, *Parliament and Information* Library Association (1981).

26.   Engle '"Bills are made to pass as razors are made to sell"': practical constraints on the preparation of legislation' 1983 *Stat L R* 7.

27.   6 Dec 1988 H.L. Debs cols 487–540, 1130.

28.   *Ibid* col 1130.

29.   9 Oct 1989 H.L. Debs cols 11–14.

30.   21 Nov 1989 H.L. Debs cols 12–13. The contemporary record is probably held by the 784 Government amendments tabled in the House of Lords to the Financial Services Bill 1986, which had the consequence of a small informal Group being appointed by the Leader of the House to consider its procedures. Unfortunately, they were unable to suggest a resolution to the difficulty. See further, M.A.J. Wheeler–Booth 'The Report by the Group on the Working of House of Lords, 1987' (1988) LVI *The Table* 41.

31.   12 Feb 1990 H.L. Debs col 1093–8. The four bills were the Football Spectators Bill, the Companies Bill, the Children Bill and the Local Government and Housing Bill.

32.   For the problems associated with defining civil servants see G Drewry and T Butcher *op cit* note 24 *supra* at 13–30.

33.   For a description of Cabinet committees with European Community functions see P. Hennessy *The Cabinet* Blackwell (1986) at 27.

34.   See, for example, Central Policy Review Staff, *Review of Overseas Representation* London (1977); Second Report, House of Commons Select Committee on Foreign Affairs, *Foreign and Commonwealth Office Organisation* H C 511 (1979–80).

35.   See, e.g. *H.P. Bulmer Ltd v J. Bollinger S A* [1974] Ch 401.

36.   See, e.g. Lord Diplock (1972) *Journal of Association of Law Teachers* 3; Lord Denning *'Forward Into Europe' Pt I The Times* 2 Jan 1973; Lord Hailsham, speech to magistrates, extract appended to Home Office Circular No. 149/1973 (CS 18/1973).

37.   An interesting example of this is found in Case 294/83, *Parti Ecologiste 'Les Verts' v European Parliament* [1987] 2 CMLR 343.

38.   See, e.g. *Litster v Forth Dry Dock & Engineering Co Ltd (in receivership)* [1989] IRLR 161.

39.   T.St.J.N. Bates 'Scrutiny of Administration', in M. Ryle and P.G. Richards, *The Commons Under Scrutiny* Routledge (1988); T.St.J.N. Bates, 'The Scrutiny of European Secondary Legislation at Westminster' [1975–6] *E L Rev* 22.

40.   The House of Lords Select Committee on Procedures for Scrutiny of Proposals for European Instruments was appointed on 20 December 1972, and the House of Commons Select Committee on European Community Secondary Legislation was appointed the next day, but they held their first meetings on, respectively, 23 and 24 January 1973.

41.   See T.St.J.N. Bates 'Models of Scrutiny' in *Proceedings of the Third Commonwealth Conference on Delegated Legislation* London (1990).

42.   Fourth Report, House of Commons Select Committee on Procedure, 'The Scrutiny of European Legislation' H C 622–I and II (1988–89) and see further Cm 1081 (1990).

43.   Cmnd 9758 (1986).

44.   The European Single Act was incorporated in United Kingdom domestic law by the European Communities (Amendment) Act 1986.

45.   In, for example, *R v Criminal Injuries Compensation Board, ex p Lain* [1967] 2 QB 864.

46.   [1985] AC 374.
47.   *Ibid* at 418.
48.   *Ibid* at 417.
49.   [1989] AC 1014.
50.   *The Times*, 26 July 1988 (QB).
51.   A public, or public law, element in the decision for which review is sought may be the criterion. See, for example, *R v Disciplinary Committee of the Jockey Club ex p Massingberd – Maundy, The Times* 3 January 1990 (QB); *R v Derbyshire County Council, ex p Noble,* [1990] *IRLR 332 (CA).*
52.   *Attempts to exclude judicial review in a comprehensive manner still occur in modern legislation. See, for example, the Local Government Finance Act 1987 s 4(6).*
53.   *R.H. Tawney The Acquisitive Society* G. Bell & Sons (1922) 1.
54.   See, for example, E C Directives 68/360, Arts 2(2), 10; 73/148, arts 2(2), 8.
55.   For a consideration of the treaty-making capacity of the Communities and some of the implications for the treaty-making capacity of Member States see T.C. Hartley *The Foundations of European Community Law* (2nd ed) Clarendon Press (1988) ch. 6.

Political Programmes and the Content of the Constitution*

Terence C. Daintith

A. Introduction

Over more than a decade, the United Kingdom has been ruled by a government, of an avowedly radical tendency, ready to make large claims and set major objectives: rolling back the frontiers of the state, accentuating individual initiative. Not only the promises, but also the performance, of this government display a genuinely substantial shift in position from pre-existing policies and institutions, much greater than that effected by the series of post-1951 Conservative governments which remained in power for longer than Mrs Thatcher has yet achieved. One measure of the difference is that while Mrs Thatcher is certainly not the only Prime Minister of recent times to achieve eponymy, only in her case do the terms built on her name – Thatcherite, Thatcherism – connote a commitment to a programme, even an ideology, as opposed to a personal affiliation. The policies of the government are of course presented as a matter of major political, economic, and social change, which together will produce or perhaps have already produced a significant alteration of national attitudes, a rebalancing of public life around a new fulcrum of individual, as opposed to collective, responsibility. Whatever we may think of it, this is a large and ambitious project, of which a large number of elements have already been put in place: containment of public spending; a large reduction in the burden of direct taxation, especially at the upper levels; restriction and legal control of trade union power; wholesale dismantling of the public sector of the economy; a new and more constricting financial basis for local government; and so on. It would be surprising if such a radical scheme had no constitutional implications; indeed, in any country with a detailed written constitution, it is likely that some elements of the Thatcherite scheme would have been subject to constitutional challenge or would have required constitutional amendment. In such a country, some – doubtless not all – constitutional implications of Thatcherism would be clear-cut, identifiable and measurable in terms of the formal documentation of the constitution.

Such is not the case with us. We do not have a written constitution. Let me here interpolate, as an Englishman who taught public law in Scotland almost as long as Tony Bradley, if with far less distinction, that I am well

41

aware of the constitutional claims made for the Acts of Union. But the Acts, if they are to be regarded as constitutional in design and intent, represent a moribund constitution, not a living one. We are left with the question of how to measure the impact of Thatcherism on an unwritten constitution; of how we set about understanding what has changed, what is in danger, what stands firm. This is not, of course, a new question. There have been other 'isms' in public life before Thatcherism. Past 'isms' have posed a similar problem in terms of the monitoring of their constitutional effects: much of Dicey's later work, for example, was done against a background of concern about the (to him) negative constitutional effects of the collectivism promoted by the Liberal Governments of the first decade of this century.[1] Since that time, inter-war protectionism, post-war Keynesianism, and 1960s corporatism have each left a distinct constitutional mark, though none of these, I suspect, registered as strongly with constitutional law scholars as Thatcherism is registering today. Before going on to consider why, and to discuss the problem of measuring the effects of these movements in constitutional or public law terms, a word or two might be said about these 'isms' as such.

To talk about Keynesianism, corporatism, and so on is of course to use a kind of shorthand which involves attributing to a single coherent movement or ideology a variety of causes and events in political, economic and social development. In practice the course of development is rarely so tidy, and events can often not be unproblematically described as effects of given ideologies. On the first of these points, we should note how events spill over from the supposed period of ascendancy of the ideologies they are supposed to reflect; they crop up afterwards through institutional inertia;[2] they also frequently appear as isolated forerunners or harbingers of the movement they represent. Although quite a lot of Thatcherite things occurred during the tenure of the Heath Government of 1970-74, including greater competition in banking,[3] legalisation of industrial relations,[4] and a more market-oriented approach to the stimulation and location of industrial investment,[5] it just happened that enough non-Thatcherite things happened thereafter (especially, perhaps, counter-inflation policy)[6] to make us lose sight of them. On the second point, the indeterminacy of the relationship between ideology and event, a large degree of choice can be seen to be available in relation even to major and central political programmes. Were the large-scale nationalisations of the late 1940s an expression of Socialist ideology, of political inspiration; or a Keynesian exercise in investment planning and regulation? Both and neither would appear to be the answer. The constituency for nationalisation was clearly drawn from among supporters of both types of ideas:[7] yet the structures chosen for the enterprises created, and the rules under which they were required to operate, descend in direct line from corporatist structures of the inter-war period, such as the London Passenger Transport Board and the Central Electricity Generating Board, castigated by Socialists as 'State capitalism' at the time of their creation.[8]

The fact that one cannot really speak with precision of the impact of ideologies is not of great importance to my argument. My concern is rather with the problems of measuring the significance for the constitution of the substantive political programmes to which we give such shorthand titles as Thatcherism. This may seem to be rather a surprising thing to worry about. Surely the effects on constitutional law of the different parts of the Thatcherite programme are relatively clear? We can point, for example, to a solid mass of legislative enactment inspired by the ideology and political objectives of this government and effecting major changes in public law: one need only mention the privatisation programme, and changes in the central-local government relationship, to ground this point.[9] And it may not be much more difficult to identify the rather less visible changes which take place through alterations of administrative regulation or practice that, for example, regulate government's behaviour towards its own employees, its decision-making structure in Cabinet, or its administrative structures more generally. All this is perfectly true, so long as we regard our public law as a series of discrete topics, separated both functionally, by reference to the area of government referred to – provision of central or local public services of different kinds, government–Parliament relations, judicial review – and conceptually. In identifying such changes we are, however, not *necessarily* doing more than to register the fact of alteration of an element of law or practice. There is an additional step involved in measuring the constitutional import of a political programme which engenders such alterations, a step which demands a normative evaluation of the change by reference to constitutional requirements. My argument in this paper is that while the form of our constitution makes this a difficult step, the style of constitutional law scholarship exacerbates the problem. A new type of constitutional law writing is needed if we are to be able to judge programmes like that of Thatcherism in constitutional terms.

B. The Style of Public Law Literature

At the origin of the difficulty, in my view, is the prevailing descriptive and eclectic mode of writing about the United Kingdom constitution and public law.

The absence of a written document means that authors enjoy a wide choice of material: none has yet to my knowledge argued for the inclusion in the field of constitutional law of Dicey's famous example of the Dentists Act (just as entrenched a piece of legislation, for him, as the Act of Union)[10] but there seems nothing, in principle, to require its exclusion. Within this indeterminate field the approach taken is one of description of the practices of government. Such description mixes historical development, current practice (or, more often, practice of some years back), relevant legislative and other rules, and relevant judicial decisions, in an effort to convey to lawyers, in a vocabulary they can understand, what actually happens in the discharge of the relevant aspect or branch of government. While what happens (or might be expected to happen) is often expressed in the form of legal rules (whether of a statutory or common law nature), the normative emphasis of the writing is weak. Changes are recorded as they happen, and new practice is absorbed into the account without a great deal of discussion of its compatibility with existing rules or principles. Where sufficiently

important changes occur and are not reversed, the constitution may be said
to be changing, much in the way that one might record a townscape as
changing, as old buildings come down and new ones are built, as roads are
rerouted and public space rearranged. There is little sense of tension between
what the constitution requires, and what is actually done. Most of all, there
is no sense of any obligational structure in the constitution or in different
parts of it, a hierarchy of rules of different levels, of different degrees of
generality, and with different sources, which governmental practice must
either fit within, or lawfully (or, if you prefer, constitutionally) change.
Put briefly, constitutional lawyers do not write like lawyers about the
constitution; they write like pragmatic political scientists.

I am aware that this is a grave charge to level against one's profession
and one which should not be made without supporting evidence. Space
precludes the multiplication of examples, and it does not seem unfair to
select a single case of recent writing by a constitutional lawyer, one whose
excellent reviews suggest that it does embody an acceptable and
representative approach to constitutional law scholarship.[11] This is Rodney
Brazier's *Constitutional Practice* (1988), a work covering the 'high'
constitutional ground of government, Parliament and the constitutional
position of the judiciary. Brazier starts by suggesting that he is interested
in 'divining the meaning of the British constitution'.[12] This implies that
the task is 'to identify the hands in which power lies and to set forth the
institutions and procedures through which it is exercised'.[13] This task
could be interpreted as one of pure description of political power and practice
– in which case the charge of doing political science rather than law would
be amply justified – or as including, or indeed emphasising, analysis of
the rules by which power is defined and structured. Brazier encourages us
toward the latter view by going on to say that 'wherever possible the
approach is prescriptive. The aim is to explain in any particular situation
what may and should appropriately be done'; and in contentious cases, to
suggest 'ways forward which are in keeping with my perception of the spirit
of the constitution'.[14] So far, so good, though the appearance of words like
'appropriately', 'ways forward', and 'spirit' should offer a faint warning.

When, however, Brazier comes down to detailed analysis of constitutional
questions we find that he is much more interested in prescribing practical
solutions for difficult cases than in exploring the bases and scope of the
principles and rules that generally apply. Thus, in writing of the choice
of a Prime Minister, Brazier devotes only a page to a bald statement of the
principles (or are they rules?) governing such a choice, and fifteen pages
to describing the possible application of one of them (that the choice should
fall on the elected leader of a party) to a variety of more and less problematic
circumstances. The conclusion of this discussion is that the choice of Prime
Minister, even in the absence of a hung Parliament, cannot always be pre-
determined by the electoral decisions of the relevant party; in certain
circumstances the Queen necessarily retains some power (and obligation)
of choice.[15] Somewhat similar conclusions flow from his analysis of the
prerogatives of dissolution of Parliament, refusal of assent to legislation,
and dismissal of a government.[16] In each case Brazier can imagine

circumstances in which the Queen could, and should, act otherwise than in accordance with the advice of her Ministers.

Though Brazier's presentation is rich in example and use of precedent, in normative terms it is impoverished by his failure to imagine any question other than that of when, if ever, the Queen may exercise her 'legal' powers. In answering this question in terms of what action would, in given hypothetical circumstances, best protect democracy and a non-political monarchy, he moves directly from individual cases to general values, and passes in silence over the possibility that there might exist constitutional rules by reference to which we might judge the conduct giving rise to issues of royal residuary power: rules, that is, binding on the government, on the Prime Minister, on the political parties, on Parliament itself, as well as on the Queen. Brazier clearly does not believe that such rules cannot exist: thus he tells us that the person to be chosen as Prime Minister 'should' be able to command a majority in the House of Commons, 'must' be a Member of Parliament, 'must not' be a peer, and 'must usually' be the elected leader of his or her party.[17] Yet he appears to assume that all these rules only bind the Queen at the moment of decision as to the appointment of a Prime Minister, even though many of the 'difficulties' which might provoke the need for a decision on her part arise from the behaviour of the political parties. The possibility that these constitutional rules may likewise bind the political parties is not considered; yet if it is correct that the Prime Minister must be the leader of his or her party it would appear to be a breach of the constitution for the party deliberately to put itself in a position where its leader could not satisfy one of the other constitutional requirements.

Similarly with such questions as dissolution or refusal of assent, Brazier never argues the issue of whether a request for a dissolution, or the passage of legislation to gerrymander constituencies or extend the life of Parliament, might constitute a breach of constitutional rules by government or the two Houses of Parliament, though he clearly has views about the propriety of such actions.[18] The omission is in objective terms curious, first because Brazier does sometimes think normatively,[19] and second because the case for royal intervention must be immeasurably stronger where it appears as a response to breach of identifiable constitutional rules than where it only translates a different view of the requirements of democracy.

Whether this omission is curious or not, Brazier is by no means alone in leaving underdeveloped the ground lying between broad constitutional values and the details of constitutional practice. Few constitutional lawyers since Dicey have cultivated it.[20] Instead the preference has been to accept, as the constitutional rule book, essentially what Dicey left to us – Parliamentary sovereignty, the rule of law and the law-convention distinction – while devoting much time and effort to empirical demonstrations of the breach, non-application or changing content of these principles. Yet as McAuslan and McEldowney point out, those rules and principles have themselves been taken so much for granted 'that for many years they have not been thought worth discussion in the legal literature'.[21] Our consequent normative poverty seriously inhibits our capacity for critical discussion of major political and economic change. When Thatcherism or Keynesianism, or whatever other 'ism', produces major social or political change all the constitutional lawyer is equipped to do is to apportion its manifestations among the historical and functional categories of his scheme of writing, and to set them alongside pre-existing practice and continuing rules. Some aspects of practice in the field will be seen to have changed, some to have been left unaffected; some rules may have been replaced, others may have been wholly or partially emptied of content, others will appear unscathed. The constitutional significance of change is hard if not impossible to grasp because we have no sense of the location of its effects in a normative constitutional structure. Thus in relation to the Thatcher Government's mass of legislation on local government finance, it is possible either to describe in detail the way the consequent regime differs from the rules it replaces (and to express these changes in legal terms) or to say that it effects a massive change in the financial character of local government in local-central relations; but neither of these seems a significant statement of constitutional law. What I am arguing is that the tradition of our literature simply disables us from making such statements; we have not formulated the twentieth- as opposed to nineteenth-century principles with which the recent legislation comes into conflict or which it purports to displace or modify.

C. A Utopian Critique?

I can foresee two types of objection to the critique just developed; doubtless there are others as well. The first complains of unreality or utopianism; the second of ignoring recent changes and developments in constitutional law scholarship. I take these in turn.

My critique will be utopian for those who believe that, in the nature of our constitution, there can be no practical alternative to the kind of constitutional discourse we presently practise. How, this argument runs, can one talk about hierarchies of norms governing different parts of governmental practice when our constitution reduces to the principles – arguably contradictory in any event – of parliamentary sovereignty and the rule of law? If parliamentary sovereignty means what it says, then there is no room for any specifically constitutional hierarchies of norms, only for the formal hierarchy common to the whole of United Kingdom law which has parliamentary legislation at its apex; and there is certainly no room for any constitutional principles, since the maintenance of any rule, principle or body of practice is wholly contingent upon parliamentary abstinence from its alteration.

In my recollection of teaching constitutional law in Scotland, this sort of argument – or a dim sense of its outlines – was at the root of difficulty with and disquiet about the subject experienced by many students. Such students did not, in discussion, deny the existence of the subject – after all, they needed it for their degree – but they were troubled by their perception that much of its material, so unlike that encountered in the rest of their studies, was non-legal, disconnected from courts and law reports, while the remainder – the statutes regulating local authority functions, for example, or the cases on police powers – though undoubtedly legal, had little that was distinctively constitutional about it.

A sophisticated version of this attack, directed at those, like Michael Elliott, who have sought to discuss relations between local and central government in terms of what is or is not constitutional,[22] is to be found in Malcolm Grant's contribution to *The Changing Constitution*.[23] Grant properly and helpfully distinguishes between the descriptive and normative uses of the word 'constitutional' and points to the unfortunate tendency of authors 'to move suddenly and confusingly from one to the other'.[24] He goes on to argue that in the presence of a *Grundnorm* of parliamentary supremacy, and without any entrenched constitutional statement of local government functions or judicial review of legislation, the epithet 'unconstitutional' is no more than 'an expression of unease; a code-word indicating disquiet with a destabilising intervention'.[25] Elliott's attempts to formulate 'constitutional' propositions about central-local relations, such as that 'a transfer of functions from one tier to another or from one tier to a hybrid body should take place only if it can be demonstrated that the possibility of holding power exercisers to account will be no worse given the transfer than it is under the existing system',[26] founder on their 'straight, unavoidable conflict' with 'the principle of unlimited parliamentary power'.[27] Such 'constitutional propositions' can only be descriptive, therefore, of existing practice and values. Moreover they *should* only be descriptive; Grant fears 'an unhappy process of inductive reasoning in which description unconsciously becomes translated into norm, and in which constitutional "conventions" are invented to serve the political arguments of the day'.[28]

Grant is writing only of local-central relations, but there seems no reason why such fears as these should not be felt about *any* area of public activity or power, not excluding those occupied by 'recognised' constitutional conventions. Are all normative uses of the words 'constitutional' and 'unconstitutional' just dangerous and self-deluding cant, a devide for hiding from ourselves the fact that, as F. F. Ridley argues,[29] we simply have no constitution, and must look for quite different means of controlling governments like the present one, with its strong radical and authoritarian characteristics?

Is it really the case that our constitution is one of 'minimal normative content', a structure based on aristocratic manners which can no longer operate because the newly powerful middle class does not share them and cannot understand them?[30] The radical and authoritarian characteristics of the Thatcherite enterprise, its widely-noted tendency to the centralisation of public power,[31] have sharpened the expression of such views, but they are not new. It was in 1963 that John Griffith coined the phrase 'if it works, it's constitutional' and urged us to tear up the pages in our text books labelled 'conventions'[32] (though why stop at those pages?).

To demonstrate, in detail, that this is an unduly hopeless view of our constitution as a system of norms requires precisely the kind of writing that I am here urging, and for which I suggest some promising starting points later in this essay. In general, however, it seems to me that the approach is marked by a highly positivistic and Austinian view of legal obligation, which looks for formality of expression and certainty of sanction as the touchstones of normativity, and couples this with an implicit demand for some kind of entrenchment as the mark of a truly *constitutional* rule. Work in legal theory over the last few decades has shown the narrowness of this conception, pointing to functions of law to which sanctions are of small significance, such as facilitation of private arrangements, the creation of expectations or the symbolic expression of values, and showing the pervasive interdependence of formal law with informal or private normative structures.[33] Some of this theory is reflected in recent writing by constitutional lawyers, which needs to be examined in the context of a second possible objection.

D. An Anachronistic Critique?

It might be objected that the complaint here formulated is an outdated one, not because of changes in the constitution itself but because of the appearance in recent years of this new type of constitutional law scholarship – more rigorous, more political, more reform-minded – which largely responds to the kind of concerns articulated here. Certainly it is true that there is exciting new writing on the constitution now being done, unusually, by lawyers, mostly either grouped in Sheffield (Lewis, Harden, Prosser, Graham)[34] or forming a kind of diaspora from Warwick (McAuslan, McEldowney, Partington, Loughlin).[35] The vigour and persistence of the radical project of Thatcherism appear to have jolted constitutional lawyers such as these into an unusual intensity of feeling on their subject, giving rise to reflection which, equally unusually, pays explicit heed to the political origins of the changes to which they are reacting. Admittedly the professional consciousness – or perhaps conscience – of academic public lawyers has also been pricked by the need to celebrate the hundredth anniversary of Dicey's *Law of the Constitution*; nonetheless, the preoccupation with the political springs of constitutional change informing that work was not necessarily to be expected from the Diceyan centenary project (as the cooler tone of the Jowell and Oliver volume on this shows)[36] and is not easily paralleled in writing from the earlier years of this century – even from periods in which comparable political and economic change was occurring. What works in public law have explicitly registered the consequences of this century's earlier 'isms', such as Keynesianism or corporatism?

This new writing is of considerable inherent interest, not least because it also represents a more vigorous and certainly more self-conscious attempt by public lawyers to be explicit about their theoretical premisses in constitutional writing than we have hitherto seen. It has also offered the unusual and entertaining spectacle of public argument about social and political theory among British public lawyers.[37] Times *do* change. Yet despite its positive feaures, I feel that this literature does not, for reasons which differ according to its style and purpose, fill the normative gap which, I have argued, exists in British constitutional law writing. Again, to avoid generalisation, I will concentrate my comments, this time on McAuslan's recent work, including his inaugural lecture at the London School of

Economics, 'Public Law and Public Choice',[38] and on Harden and Lewis's widely reviewed book, *The Noble Lie*.

McAuslan's writing effectively demonstrates the problem to which my argument is directed. Over the decade he has articulated a consistent hostility to Thatcherism and its constitutional effects from (or by reference to) a variety of different theoretical bases: collective consumption theory (1983), legitimacy theory (1985), public choice theory (1988). While these theoretical perspectives – and particularly the critique of public choice theory and its mode of application in the United Kingdom – have been in varying degrees illuminating, they take us only a short distance in the direction of constructing, or reconstructing, the constitution that Thatcherism is said to be damaging. In writing of legitimacy, McAuslan starts by complaining of the 'open-endedness' of constitutional arrangements; 'the difficulty of knowing whether a practice or non-practice is or is not "constitutional"' (the word apparently having normative significance here).[38] In consequence, he finds no middle ground of constitutional critique of government behaviour between detailed listing of ministerial illegalities on the one hand[40] and on the other an accusation (buttressed by detailed evidence) of 'a contempt for or at least an impatience with the principles of limited government',[41] viz., fair and equitable administrative practice, recognition of the rights of political opposition and dissent, compliance with constitutional conventions and adequate means of redress about governmental action affecting one.[42]

The critical analysis is further refined in his inaugural lecture, where he contrasts the new administrative values grounded in public choice theory – such as value for money, rule-based, 'controllable' consultative procedures, and management through contract – with 'our fundamental principles [of] openness, fairness and impartiality and their institutional manifestations'.[43] While this permits a more systematic presentation of examples and the identification of a *trend* in constitutional change it is still not adequate to ground a constitutional evaluation of the new policies and machinery which could distinguish where they are consistent with existing constitutional norms (as must sometimes be the case) and where they are not. Openness, fairness and impartiality are concepts far too broad and indefinite to carry this burden. The missing dimension is some lower-level normative expression of principle which will relate a general requirement, such as that of openness, to the circumstances of particular types of governmental tasks.

Before exploring the feasibility of working in this 'missing dimension', I should say a word about *The Noble Lie* and about which values are to be identified as fundamental. *The Noble Lie* is an important work which is deeply critical both of existing constitutional arrangements and of the traditional style of constitutional scholarship, which it sees as constrained by positivist and intuitive modes of thought.[44] As a substitute it offers the theoretical platform of immanent critique, a critique, that is, 'which seeks to identify the major claims or beliefs of a group or order ... and ... first to examine the logical inter-relationships between the various claims to control for consistency [and second] to examine the relationship between claim and reality – to set the exposed beliefs against the empirical world.'[45] This leads Harden and Lewis to examine current constitutional practice against the British people's immanent expectations of a system of open and accountable government. Their general argument is that the constitution signally fails to deliver on these principles, so that far-reaching reforms, and changes of approach, are required. In coming to this conclusion they conduct a thorough examination of current governmental practice ('empirical mapping', in their terms), measuring it against these desiderata and finding it wanting, but spending little time on identifying existing constitutional norms and assessing its consistency with them. Since it is an important part of their argument that these norms themselves (for example the principle of ministerial responsibility and rules deriving from it) may no longer be consistent with immanent expectations, the omission can hardly be criticised; it is the fact that Harden and Lewis, like McAuslan, do little or nothing to fill the lacuna in scholarship – which they might perhaps call 'normative mapping' – that bothers me.

Their approach may also mean, of course, that their baseline for criticism is not the constitution itself but what it ought to be; indeed it is hard to connect the reasoning through which Harden and Lewis arrive at a fundamental claim to openness in government – which McAuslan also espouses – with any process of historical development in the British polity. For Harden and Lewis, there must be 'an essentially open system *at all times* if the elective exercise is to make democratic sense *at any time*'.[46] Representative democracy, in other words, necessarily implies open government. The fact that they make out a strong case for this proposition[47] does not mean that there necessarily exist any constitutional norms that are expressive of this principle of openness; indeed I would argue that the general tendency of existing norms is to support a 'closed' administration. This may imply that the constitution is incoherent; or that it is not based on representative democracy as Harden and Lewis understand it, but expresses some other logic; or that Harden and Lewis are wrong. Whichever explanation we choose, we can see that immanent critique is as liable to lead us away from positive constitutional norms as it is to identify them for us.

E. What could be done?

Important as the work of McAuslan and of Harden and Lewis is, it does not displace the need for effort to be devoted to a task which is logically prior to such reformist and critical projects. This is the task of developing a vocabulary and system for talking about our constitution in normative terms – in terms of constitutional obligation. It seems essential to try to find out what the constitution *is*, and to express that knowledge in the form of principles, rules, and exceptions to rules. That, in considerable measure, is what Dicey did – albeit not with such formalism as in his work on the Conflict of Laws – and it is because no-one has had the vigour or clarity of mind to do it since that his intellectual vessel, though a rotting and barnacle-encrusted hulk, is the one in which we are still all forced to sail. The fact that some of what Dicey wrote was wrong when he wrote it, and much more is wrong now, has had far less effect that it should have, essentially because of the power of his codifying method and confidence of statement.

It may be objected that this is hardly the century of confidence nor, for that matter, of codification. Perhaps the two things go together. I do not think we should be daunted, if only because we are almost out of this century anyway. But there are other more concrete grounds for arguing that notwithstanding the objections rehearsed earlier, this task can be tackled.

Some attempts in this direction have been made and do not seem to me to be pointless or laughable. Principles of good administration have been promulgated in a variety of places, including the Committee of Ministers of the Council of Europe, and are reviewed with approval by no less a body than the JUSTICE-All Souls Committee on administrative law.[48] The formulation of such principles expressing accepted (as opposed to desired) administrative behaviour would seem quite feasible. An active discussion has been engendered, revolving around the question of what use the courts could make of such principles, and whether they should be expressed in statutory terms or as a 'code of guidance'. An alternative approach, closer perhaps to the British penchant for explicitly inductive reasoning towards rules, might be to seek to build such principles from the already voluminous case-law of the Parliamentary Commissioner for Administration and his ever-growing family of ombudsmen.[49]

This latter technique has in fact been consistently used over more than a century for the purpose of building up principles and rules for the conduct of public expenditure, through the combined efforts of the Comptroller and Auditor-General, the Public Accounts Committee of the House of Commons, and the Treasury. In large measure, the Treasury's rule book on government accounting[50] converts into operating practice the key principles derived from a century of 'jurisprudence' of the Comptroller and the Committee, rendered (up to 1969) into a two-volume Epitome of their respective reports.[51] Together, Epitome and rule book provide the working principles, rules, sub-rules and exceptions which articulate one aspect of the general constitutional principle of parliamentary supremacy: that is, the requirement of legislative (and not merely parliamentary) consent to public expenditure. The fact that these requirements may be breached without causing governments to fall or Ministers to be sued[52] does not disqualify them as possible sources of constitutional obligation capable of creating procedural and substantive barriers, both within government and for government, to the pursuance of desired courses of action. They deserve a better fate than to be dismissed by Harden and Lewis as 'more about the Treasury's desire to ensure its own control over central government departments, than about facilitating open scrutiny and debate',[53] a monocular view which leads them to play down normative constraints in this field. Thus it is true that a Treasury minute was used 'instead' of legislation to establish the University Grants Committee in 1919.[54] What could have been added was that this was a highly exceptional procedure which had regularly to be defended – on grounds of academic freedom – against Treasury and Public Accounts Committee criticism over the whole period until its reversal in 1988.[55] Likewise, McAuslan, while drawing welcome attention to the significance for public lawyers of Audit Commission and National Audit Office reports,[56] ties their current activity too closely to the importation of public choice ideas and neglects the continuing evolution of principles of government financial accountability that have brought these bodies to their current concern with value for money audit within a framework in which other, more 'primitive' concerns – such as legal and administrative regularity – have passed beyond controversy and into the corpus of working rules.

These examples suggest that public decision-making based consistently (though not necessarily explicitly) on 'constitutional' values (such as fairness in administration or democratic control of expenditure) can generate statements of principles and rules with real normative effect, which deserve to be treated as potential constitutional norms. This work of *prima facie* identification does not, of course, exhaust the task I am outlining. The strength of such potential norms needs to be assessed, and there is plenty of room for argument about how this should be done: what part should be assigned to empirical, even quantitative, work on compliance, what part to structural criteria such as the political strength of the institutions interested in adherence to the norms, or their degree of commitment to ensuring such adherence; how one may relevantly demonstrate the constitutional equivalent of the requisite *opinio juris*. Beyond this, if we are to talk in terms of hierarchies of constitutional norms, the connections need to be systematically traced between broad values, general principles, and operating rules.

These investigations will not, of course, always lead to results palatable to those who look for normative strength in our constitution. Michael Elliott's effort in 1981 to identify constitutional principles of central – local relations[57] was harshly judged by the course of subsequent events, and it would now take an even braver constitutionalist to find any governing principle for this field beyond *realpolitik*. The conscientious search for a structure of constitutional obligation might well show that we possess no reliable rules (i.e. with a broad consensus of bindingness) over quite large and important areas of public life, or that some rules or principles to which all pay lip-service are in fact hopelessly indeterminate. Elsewhere we may find that genuinely well-accepted rules point in unattractive directions – away from openness and accountability, for example. But we need to make these discoveries, because until we do we can point convincingly neither at directions for reform nor at areas of outstanding constitutional beauty where the government's political lumberjacks should not be allowed to go. It is, I would argue, a part of the responsibility of those who call themselves constitutional *lawyers* to try to discuss government behaviour in terms of a coherent structure of obligation and not just of random departures from inchoate values.

In a different sphere from ours, we should recall that a good deal of the intellectual efforts of international lawyers goes into the business of identifying and formulating customary international law rules, in circumstances of policing and enforcement which are certainly no more propitious than those applying to the behaviour of governments in the United Kingdom. Supposed rules may be criticised or ignored, denied or flouted, but still the work goes on and appears to produce effects among the subjects of international law, whether in shape of the actual emergence of accepted new rules, of changes in patterns of argument or the weakening of old rules and categories. If international lawyers think this expenditure of intellectual energy is worth it, why don't we?

The international law analogy may be helpful in a second respect. An interest in identifying and refining customary rules of international law in no way impairs the enthusiasm of international lawyers for the elaboration of treaty regimes for the formal regulation of inter-State relations where this is feasible and appropriate. Parallel efforts towards the identification of customary law rules and the creation of conventional ones may be witnessed in a variety of areas: the one activity does not exlude the other. Similarly, the normative mapping of the existing constitution need not exclude a commitment to projects for the formal enactment of constitutional principles, whether within the framework of a Bill of Rights, through the enactment of the European Convention on Human Rights, or more generally. Indeed it can serve such projects by drawing attention to the points at which the enactment of formal rules would represent the creation of quite new norms as opposed to the formalisation and reinforcement of existing ones. And pending the possibly distant day on which any of these formal changes is brought into effect, the informal but systematic elaboration of the normative structure of our constitution, through scholarly research consolidated by open academic and political discussion, could by itself do much to promote, among the people of the United Kingdom, that awareness of the proper organisation of public life and of their place within it which it is one of the prime functions of a written constitution to inculcate.

*Glasgow must share with Edinburgh the responsibility for bringing forth this essay; many of the thoughts in it were first expressed at a Clydesdale Bank Public Lecture in the University of Glasgow in December 1988. I am grateful to Professor Martin Loughlin for offering me that opportunity.

Notes

1. See R.A. Cosgrave *The Rule of Law: Albert Venn Dicey, Victorian Jurist* Macmillan (1980) chs 8 and 9.
2. On corporatist devices appearing under Thatcherism see I. Harden, 'Corporatism without Labour: The British Version' in C. Graham and T. Prosser (Eds) *Waiving the Rules: The Constitution under Thatcherism* Open UP (1988) at 36–55.
3. See Bank of England *Competition and Credit Control* (1971).
4. Industrial Relations Act 1971.
5. See, for its legislative expression, the Investment and Building Grants Act 1971.
6. See V. Korah 'Counter-Inflation legislation: whither Parliamentary sovereignty?' (1976) 92 LQR 42.
7. See E. Eldon Barry *Nationalisation in British Politics* Jonathan Cape (1965).
8. E. Davies *'National' Capitalism* Gollancz (1939).

9. For demonstration see the contributions of Norman Lewis and Malcolm Grant to J. Jowell and D. Oliver (Eds) *The Changing Constitution* (2nd ed) Oxford U P (1989) at 219–272.

10. A.V. Dicey *Introduction to the Study of the Law of the Constitution* (10th ed by E.C.S. Wade) Macmillan (1959) at 145.

11. See [1989] CLJ 549 (R. McCorquodale, who states (550) that 'the most refreshing aspect of the book is that ... there is ... little attempt to propound definite rules of constitutional law'); (1989) 105 LQR 332 (R. Blackburn); (1989) 40 NILQ 459 (B. Hadfield).

12. At i. R. Brazier *Constitutional Practice* Clarendon Press (1988).

13. *Id.*

14. *Id.*

15. At 22.

16. Ch 8.

17. At 8.

18. At 150–158.

19. See at 155 for royal action on 'legislation' passed without proper formalities, at 156 on a test for what 'justifies' royal insistence on a dissolution, and at 157 assuming there are 'rules' forbidding government to carry on after loss of a vote of confidence.

20. For an exception, discussed below, see M. Elliott *The Role of Law in Central–Local Relations* SSRC (1981).

21. In P. McAuslan and J. McEldowney (Eds) *Law, Legitimacy and the Constitution* Sweet & Maxwell (1988) at 7.

22. *Op cit* note 20 *supra*.

23. In Jowell and Oliver (Eds) *op cit* note 9 *supra*, at 247–272.

24. At 253.

25. *Id.*

26. *Op cit* note 20, *supra* at 97.

27. *Op cit* note 9, *supra* at 254.

28. At 255.

29. F.F. Ridley, 'There is no British constitution: a dangerous case of the Emperor's clothes' (1988) 41 Parliamentary Affairs 340.

30. L. Siedentop, 'Thatcherism and the constitution' 26 Jan–1 Feb 1990 TLS at 88, 99.

31. See e.g. Grant *op cit* note 9 *supra*.

32. J. Griffith, Comment [1963] PL 401.

33. See for example R. Summers, 'The technique element in law' (1971) 59 *Calif L Rev* 733; P. Nonet and P. Selznick, *Towards Responsive Law* Harper & Row (1978); B. Bercusson, 'State and private ordering' in T. Daintith (Ed) *Law as an Instrument of Economic Policy: Comparative and Critical Approaches* (1988), at 359–420; Symposium on the Public–Private Distinction (1982) 130 *U Penn L Rev* 1289–1608.

34. Main works are I. Harden and N. Lewis *The Noble Lie* Hutchinson (1986); T. Prosser 'Towards a critical public law' (1982) 9 JLS 1; C. Graham and T. Prosser (Eds) *Waiving the Rules: The Constitution under Thatcherism* Open U P (1988).

35. See in particular *Law, Legitimacy and the Constitution op cit* note 21 *supra* edited by McAuslan and McEldowney with contributions by *(inter alia)* Partington and Loughlin (hereinafter 'Legitimacy'); P. McAuslan 'Administrative law, collective consumption and judicial policy' (1983) 46 NLR 1; P. McAuslan, 'Public law and public choice' (1988) 51 MLR 681 (hereinafter 'Public choice'); M. Louglin, *Local Government in the Modern State* Sweet & Maxwell (1986).

36. *Op cit* note 9 *supra*.

37. In M. Loughlin's review article on *The Noble Lie*, 'Tinkering with the constitution' (1988) 51 MLR 531, and Harden and Lewis's rejoinder thereto, (1988) 51 MLR 812.

38. See references at note 35 *supra*.
39. 'Legitimacy', at 12.
40. *Ibid* at 28 – 32.
41. At 13.
42. At 11.
43. 'Public choice' at 699.
44. At 20.
45. At 10.
46. At 9.
47. Ch 9.
48. *Administrative Justice – Some Necessary Reforms* (1988), ch 2 and apps 6a, 6b and 7.
49. Cf. a work by two political scientists, R. Gregory and P. Hutchesson, *The Parliamentary Ombudsman* RIPA (1975), esp chs 8 and 9 and also Alistair Marbray's contribution to this volume.
50. H.M. Treasury, *Government Accounting* (3d ed, 1986, with supplements).
51. Epitome of Reports from the Committee of Public Accounts, vol I 1857 – 1937 (1937 – 38) HC 154; vol II 1938 – 1969 (1969 – 70) HC 187.
52. But as this essay was being written, the Divisional Court reviewed, at the request of hospital consultants, the legality of expenditure by hospital authorities in anticipation of the passage of new legislation – finding it to be lawful, under their existing powers; *R v Secretary of State for Health and others, ex parte Keen*, The Independent, 22 Feb 1990.
53. *The Noble Lie* at 99.
54. *Ibid* at 162.
55. By the Education Reform Act 1988.
56. *Public choice* at 696.
57. *Op cit* note 20 *supra*.

The Middle Ground in Public Law

Neil Walker

A. Introduction

In reviewing H.W.R. Wade's attempt to identify and ground a set of *Constitutional Fundamentals* in the 1980 Hamlyn Lectures, Tony Bradley observed that the increasing polarisation in British politics had precipitated a similar transformation in public law. In turn, he suggested that, just as minds were becoming increasingly focused on attempts to bridge the gulf in the wider political sphere, so also the question must be posed, 'how may the middle ground in the politics of public law best be occupied and organised?'[1]

As an exercise in diagnosis, Bradley's views, while strongly resonant with the contemporary political and intellectual climate, undoubtedly harmonise even more closely with the views of the vast army of commentators on British government and politics today, including the ranks and divisions of public lawyers. Views may diverge radically as to the long-term roots of political polarisation, but against an immediate backdrop of a decade of neo-liberal Conservative Government and an opposition fragmented, within and between parties, over a broad spectrum of socialist and social democratic positions, only the most perverse would doubt the phenomenon itself.[2] Further, there is agreement that the shock-waves within the wider political culture are connected, through fault-lines which run deep in our institutional history, with fissures and dislocations within the narrower territory of public law. These fault-lines are seen to provide channels of causality which flow in both directions – the institutions of public law, hinged on the permissive idea of parliamentary sovereignty, providing a framework which encourages political polarisation, and this schism in turn encouraging orientations towards and developments within public law which reflect these polarities.[3] Public lawyers have thus come to doubt the stability and adequacy of our constitutional heritage, but the effect of common recognition of these local tremors on the academic seismograph, rather than to promote the espousal of common solutions, has been to stimulate a body of critique and a flow of reform proposals which in their diversity and lack of common points of reference closely mirror the condition of the wider political realm. Opinions differ radically as to whether the traditional

Diceyan triumvirate of the rule of law, parliamentary sovereignty and constitutional conventions, even in revised form, remain adequate to the needs of the public realm;[4] whether a remodelled second chamber, proportional representation, the reorganisation of local government, devolution, federalism, or any of the mooted variants of independence provide appropriate vehicles for the articulation of sectional or territorial interests in a new institutional framework;[5] whether fundamental liberties of a negative and positive nature require the protection of an entrenched Bill of Rights;[6] whether the development of administrative law has been systemic or ramshackle, and whither destined now;[7] whether the mixed economy, in its contemporary mode, requires a new mix of facilitative and regulatory models;[8] and, as an overarching theme, whether to trust and how to mobilise the various actors on the constitutional stage, judges, politicians, administrators, or even 'the people' – themselves conceived of in a wide variety of ways – as the preferred agents of change and as more or less significant components of a restructured totality.[9]

Later, the bare bones of these remarks will be fleshed out; the arguments in terms of which the historical connections between political fragmentation and problems within public law tend to be substantiated will be more fully elaborated, and the manner in which the ensuing debate amongst public lawyers is structured will be assessed. If, however, we concentrate for the moment on the skeletal framework supplied by Bradley's comments, its starkness alerts us to a central and obvious irony within the domain of public law, and to a deep-rooted paradox which underpins this. The academic community remains united only in its judgement that the extant legal framework is 'wearing out'[10] and is no longer adequate to the needs of our modern polity, in its acceptance of its own internal division and diversity in response to these inadequacies, and in its recognition of the significant implication of political factors in this state of affairs. In this concord over discord, the last-mentioned factor, the sense of the pervasive but in certain respects pernicious influence of political considerations upon public law, represents a focal point for concern, providing not only a significant explanatory key – briefly sketched above – to the tensions and fragmentations within public law inquiry, but also a formidable impediment to attempts to repair these fractures and counteract these centrifugal tendencies.

This conundrum flows from the fact that the complex interdependence of the two realms is not merely a historical datum, and one which has become more deeply etched in recent experience, but is also supported by a number of other more resilient themes. First, the idea of interdependence contains a fundamental conceptual truth. Thus, even if we offer provisional definitions of our two core ideas in terms sufficiently general to command widespread assent, a degree of overlap may be seen necessarily to obtain between the respective referential domains of politics (conceived of as the struggle – focused particularly, if not exclusively, upon the competition of political parties through public fora and within state institutions – 'over the organisation of human possibilities'[11] towards certain substantive individual and collective ends) and of public law (conceived of as 'the framework and principles of law that govern the exercise of state power').[12] Secondly, there is the oft-remarked absence of a 'state tradition'[13] in British intellectual life, and the consequential dearth of analytical means of sufficient subtlety and incisiveness to account for the nature and limits of this overlap. The anti-metaphysical tendencies exhibited in the various strands of British analytical philosophy have spawned a 'radical, demystifying nominalism',[14] impatient of holistic ideas such as that of 'the state', and of attempts to dignify such a notion with the attempt to locate in its entrails 'a coherent pattern of authority'.[15] Thirdly, this absence of an independent stream of critical thought on the idea of the state finds its parallel in mainstream political discourse, which tends to eschew a meta-politics of inquiry into the legitimate foundations of the public realm and concentrates instead on first-order questions about 'the control and distribution of economic largesse'.[16] Fourthly, this marginalisation of reflective thought on the general grounds and conditions of political authority is further encouraged by the institutional conditions of political life, and in particular, by the governing idea of parliamentary sovereignty which excuses our transient political rulers from the discipline of addressing a higher order of state theory and constitutional principle, if only as a strategic imperative.[17]

The combination of these various elements – on the one hand, the theoretical considerations, the interlocking of the signified territories of our two core ideas of public law and politics on the relatively unexcavated site of 'the state'; and on the other hand the operant conditions of public life, the existence of a historically developed pattern of interpenetration unalleviated by the presence of symbolic or practical means of retaining or resurrecting a firm sense of differentiation – invites the danger that the territory of public law become entirely subsumed within the territory of politics. In a context where their objective influence has rendered problematical, and is seen to have rendered problematical, a particular sphere of social or institutional life, political considerations and modes of argument have threatened to become endemic, and the possibility of distinguishing between necessary and contingent strands in the overall network of connections has tended to become obscured. This is most obvious where the conceptual overlap is most pronounced, as with the privatisation programme of the last decade, which has involved the simultaneous redefinition of the conditions of ownership and distribution of various social utilities at the political level, and at the level of public law, of its most basic models of public accountability, and, arguably, even of the very boundaries of its proper remit.[18] However, even where the analytical connection is less strong, political factors persistently infiltrate or are seen to infiltrate. New controls on local government are read as the emasculation of particular brands of local politics, and even of particular politicians.[19] Bills of Rights are attacked or defended in terms of the 'semi-permanent choices between the conflicting interests of citizens'[20] which they would enshrine, or the ideological predilections of their judicial guardians.[21] Zealous attempts to restrict the freedom of speech of ex-members of the security service are derided as attempts to offset political embarrassment.[22] 'Authoritarian'

extensions of police powers and of penal discipline are criticised as the thick
end of the wedge of economic liberalism.[23] Even the assumption,
consistent with the weight of constitutional authority, of a largely non-
interventionist stance in the repatriation of the Canadian Constitution, is
viewed as a form of connivance with the federal government in the
continuing denial of the rights of the indigenous Indian population.[24] The
point here is not to evaluate these various critical claims, but rather to
identify them as setting a strident tone for debate beneath which the
contemplation of the materials of public law on any other terms tends to
become submerged.

The crux of the matter is that the more the problems of public law are
seen to be politically rooted, the more likely the thrust of the critiques and
solutions articulated in its name will tend to be political in nature also, or
to be interpreted as politically inspired. But if this drift is accepted, does
it not lead inexorably to the conclusion that attempts to transcend politically-
grounded divisions within public law and public law inquiry will be thwarted
by the very conditions of their origin? Within such an emerging scenario,
if public law's fate is to become politics writ small, its reproduction of the
disorder and dissension of the latter realm cannot be viewed as a mere
historical contingency, the product of a particular conjunction of events,
but instead becomes indelibly fixed as a reflection of its epiphenomenal
status.

If this prospect is unpalatable to many, the political dimension cannot
simply be ignored in the hope that it will go away. The opposite reflect,
which would deny the complex interdependence between public law and
politics and assert an artificial separation of the two realms, poses a number
of comparable threats for public lawyers. First, it may encourage a self-
denying ordinance, a commitment to the exposition of the black-letter of
public law without critical perspective – a tentative treading of the
uncontroversial shallows for fear of losing one's bearings in deep political
waters. But even here, the promise of fidelity to the *terra firma* of the text
which, for example, is implicit in the writing of many case-notes and reviews
of new legislation, is suspect. The very label of commentary or exegesis
under which many such exercises trade evokes something beyond mere
reportage, '*something* more, whether this "more" is an evaluation or a
meaning not apparent on the surface'.[25] Evaluation and constructive
critique require critical premisses, and so the more ambitious the
commentary the more likely that this or that general conception of the
optimal 'organisation of human possibilities' – this or that set of political
concerns – may be at work in moulding these premisses or otherwise be
congruent with them. In turn, if discursive barriers are nevertheless
obdurately retained, two further dangers are courted. On the one hand,
such retention may lead to the uncontrolled exploitation of the goods of
public law in the political market-place, the tools and concepts forged or
finessed in the workshop of disinterested expertise being exposed for sale
without condition to the highest political bidder and invoked in aid of ends
not anticipated by their academic craftsmen and fine-tuners.[26] On the
other hand, disingenuousness may be encouraged amongst the exponents

of public law themselves, a reluctance to articulate the political commitments undergirding particular positions and the presentation of the intellectual products which flow from these positions in neutral, 'legalistic'[27] wrapping.

Thus, separatism may consign the public lawyer to an unduly minimalist role, or to the position of naive political handmaiden, or to a posture of false modesty. However, a keener awareness and more candid articulation of the political dimension may open the floodgates and reduce public law to the status of a mere instrument, albeit a self-conscious instrument, of political concerns and projects. Accordingly, both separatist and integrationist tendencies threaten the prospect of public law as an autonomous field of inquiry with its own salient contribution to make to the understanding and development of public life.

Is it possible, therefore, to trace another path for reflective inquiry into public law to follow which avoids these twin pitfalls, which neither ignores nor uncompromisingly embraces politics but, rather, specifies the terms of the relationship between the two realms in such a manner as to gain for the former a direct but critically constructive purchase on the latter? Can we conceive of public law inquiry as something more than the attempt at value-neutral descriptive mapping of certain categories of rules and of the course of their emergence and implementation, but something other than a discourse of argumentation which is but a pellucid cover for political debate? It is this possibility (if I may take the liberty of reading between the rather sparse lines of a book review) which I believe Tony Bradley had in mind when advocating a middle ground in which could be pursued a politics of public law irreducible to politics, and it is with the examination and evaluation of the potential of such a project that the remainder of this essay is concerned.

B. The Search for the Middle Ground

On what grounds might this project proceed? As a matter of intuition and practical endeavour, public lawyers may be committed to the 'specialness'[28] of their perspective on public life and the distinctiveness of their input to the debate on the virtues of the political order, but this commitment is itself no guarantee of epistemic authority. It may simply be a naive act of faith, or, viewed more cynically, a statement of occupational self-interest. To adapt a well-known formulation of Richard Rorty's, it may express the immodest claim to know something about the proper conduct of public life which nobody else knows so well.[29] It may harbour an aspiration which is either fundamentally misconceived, or even if theoretically attainable, placed beyond our present cognitive grasp. Thus, the idea of the middle ground – the suggested *leitmotif* of such a project – may be no more than a beguiling metaphor, destined to beg the very questions that it is intended to resolve. However, even if it eventually leads to a *cul-de-sac*, the middle ground nevertheless provides a suggestive point of departure.

Neither the notion of the middle ground, not its extension – metaphorical or otherwise – the middle way, denote a singular, still less a precise object of reference. Instead, their usefulness in the present context lies in the fact that they allow us to focus upon a set of overlapping ideas, each of which contributes to the claim of 'specialness', and each of which must be evaluated against counter-claims which purport either to confound or to set limits upon the possibility of the critical engagement of public law with matters political. By considering and evaluating these ideas cumulatively, it is intended to develop a framework of inquiry which addresses with some precision the possibilities, difficulties and limitations inherent in the idea of public law as a distinct critical and evaluative project, and which, incidentally, may illuminate the strengths and drawbacks of some recent attempts to traverse similar terrain.

Specifically, the middle ground provides a point of reference for a set of more or less ambitious standards of critical and normative consensus within public law, ranging from the utopian endeavour to specify the 'one best way' – a set of principles and forms of institutional design which provide a blueprint for an ideal public law – to the more modest stipulation of common criteria in terms of which debate might proceed and certain common themes might emerge and be deployed in the critical enterprise. However, as well as directly signifying an idea of shared normative orientation – of the *substantive integrity* of public law inquiry – the conception of the middle ground also presupposes its *formal integrity*. That is, unless the concerns of public law and public lawyers are in some more fundamental sense *sui generis,* and certain basic criteria of separate identity and internal coherence adhere to public law inquiry and provide it with a recognisable intellectual *form* then it is impossible to conceive of how it may generate a critically constructive body of knowledge *vis-à-vis any* other domain. Thus, although the attempt to estabish a warrantable notion of the middle ground and to settle the boundaries of this terrain more or less ambitiously requires its own form of argumentation, this is necessarily informed by the orienting framework provided in the elaboration of the idea of formal identity. In this sense, the specification of an idea of formal integrity is an indispensable, if insufficient precondition of the development of a conception of substantive integrity. And in order to perform this necessary building-block function, the idea of formal integrity must both be sufficient unto itself, and also be not inconsistent with the possibility of generating a conception of substantive integrity.

Accordingly, in searching for the middle ground it is with the question of form that we must first concern ourselves. But before we do so one final introductory point should be dealt with. It is not claimed that the conceptions of formal integrity and substantive integrity developed in the following pages represented ideas which are already present even in semi-elaborated form in the relevant literature. As suggested, their main value is a heuristic one, as tools through which the middle ground may be constructed and its viability tested. By the same token, however, if the intellectual world which they purport to represent were entirely counterfactual, the point of this exercise would be lost, for in these circumstances it would be difficult to retain any sense of genuine correspondence between the internal logic of such an approach on the one hand and the real problems and aspirations of public lawyers and the actual state of public law on the other. Rather, it is mooted that the argumentative model constructed does indeed extrapolate from the existing practice of public law and the live concerns of public lawyers, but that in so doing it draws upon central themes which are implicit rather than explicit in this enterprise, and extracts from them their best and most constructive sense rather than their only plausible meaning. Accordingly, as an exercise in immanent critique and reconstruction, the proof of the pudding remains in the eating, but its ingredients are necessarily home-grown.

C. The Idea of Formal Integrity

In what sense, then, if at all, can we conceive of public law as displaying an integrity of form, and in such a manner as to sustain the possibility of its attaining a substantive integrity *vis-à-vis* the political domain? Initially, this matter is best approached defensively, since just as it is suggested that there is a close relationship between these two ideas conceived of positively, so also this same connection has been postulated in negative terms and must be challenged. Thus, the thesis that public law has, in substantive terms, begun to reflect closely the divergences and dissension within the wider terrain of politics, has been advanced in tandem with correspondingly gloomy prognostications concerning its formal integrity. In reviewing some recent attempts to map changes in constitutional law and theory in the century which has passed since the first publication of Dicey's seminal *Introduction To The Study Of The Law Of The Constitution*,[30] W.T. Murphy argues that the increasing intrusiveness of substantive political concerns has led to disciplinary fragmentation, with public law seemingly destined 'to become a *mélange* of this and that ..... with no organising principles or thematic unity', its 'academic culture increasingly adrift in a sea of non-referentiality'.[31]

It is unarguable that public law, as an enterprise embracing critical and normative concerns as well as descriptive ones, has scanned far and wide in its search for appropriate conceptual tools of trade. But if political science, history, sociology, organisational theory, economics and moral and political philosophy[32] are all grist for the contemporary public lawyer's mill, then how is it possible to view the compound which emerges from this endeavour as a distinctive blend, as something other than the untidy aggregation of its disparate parts? In order to avoid this conclusion, and Murphy's pessimism, it is necessary to challenge the implicit connection between interdisciplinarity and incoherence.

1. The lessons of political theory: the allure of the lion's den

The supply of this corrective demands a detour into the domain of general political theory. At first glance, this may appear to place us in uncomfortable proximity to the lion's den, for if political theory is conceived of in a broad sense as the *locus* of considered, critical and constructive reflection on what is relevant to and takes place in the world of politics, and if our aim is to ground an idea of critical distance from this domain of polarised values, then this might seem to be the last place to seek out the necessary anchorage.

Shortly, the question of whether such a culpable link between political theory and politics as is implied in the previous sentence can in fact be traced will be addressed. However, even if we assume for the moment that political theory is fraught with the same tensions and incompatibilities as the arena of practical politics, to reject as dangerous or irrelevant any form of attention by public lawyers to the basic premisses underlying its methods of inquiry on this count alone is to confuse form and substance, and also to lose sight of the fact that the aim of critical distance is not hermetically to seal off public law from matters political, but to work out appropriate terms of engagement with the latter domain.

If, therefore, we are prepared to grasp this nettle, we may discern a fundamental methodological unity embracing the concerns of public lawyers and political theorists, and these shared methodological protocols, as well as providing basic materials from which the formal coherence of public law may be wrought, also suggest certain guidelines in terms of which the relationship between the normative concerns of the two domains of inquiry might be worked out. To defend these propositions, we may turn to the work of Martin Hollis who, in an articulate exposition of a broad conception of political theory once thought moribund,[33] describes the anatomy of his subject thus:

> In telling us whom to obey and how to live, political theories have traditionally tackled three sorts of questions. Firstly there are questions of quasi-fact about how men are constituted and how societies function .... Secondly there are those of normative analysis which anatomize the concepts of the theory in a way that has implications for social ethics .... Thirdly there are questions of praxis meant to show how theory is to be put into effect .... The three categories of question are not wholly distinct – indeed one aim of an ingenious theory is to interweave them – and they amount together to a way of finding how men interact, how they should interact and how they can come to interact for the best.[34]

Implicit within this formulation is the notion that the formal scope and coherence of political theory in the grand sense should be defined not with reference to the received categories favoured by academics and their academies, which may owe as much to historical accident, institutional convenience and professional jealousies as to anything else, but with reference to the 'human cognitive interests'[35] which underscore committed involvement in the political domain. Specifically, the interest in 'critically-emancipatory self-reflection'[36] – or, more prosaically, in gaining understanding of how social formations and their attendant institutional apparatuses operate and have operated in order to discover how they might operate better and how this change might be brought about – provides the linchpin of the theoretical enterprise. Formal integrity is thus secured by recognising the normative commitment to an improved social and political order as axiomatic, and by linking analyses of the existing social order and its transformative potential to this objective. Such a project necessarily transcends conventional disciplinary boundaries, while continuing to respect and draw upon the products of thinkers working within the parameters set by these boundaries. Thus, work within the descriptive social sciences, the applied disciplines of social administration and public administration, and the speculative utopian projects of moral and political philosophy may be viewed as corresponding to the discrete parts of Hollis's tripartite design – understanding, praxis and reconstruction – and provided such endeavours are not myopically pursued, but are informed by an awareness of the potential of a wider enterprise, they may be viewed as its indispensable component parts. In sum, political theory, conceived of in this holistic sense, is necessarily interdisciplinary in form, reflecting 'the "lived interdisciplinarity" of all collective life'[37] which constitutes its domain of inquiry.

If we map the concerns or 'cognitive interests' of public lawyers, a similar topography emerges, although this may be conceived of on a number of different scales, ranging from the microscopic to the macroscopic. Microscopically, as indicated earlier, public lawyers are often concerned with the minute dissection of the authoritative texts of the lawmaker, whether the legislator, the administrator or, more commonly, the 'epicentral judges'.[38] These descriptive concerns are closely shadowed by normative concerns, which at their most modest – and again such modesty is most apparent in the face of wisdom from the bench – are committed to the extraction of the best viz., most consistent and coherent sense from the relevant texts. And here at the sharp end of what has emerged historically as a 'participant-oriented discipline',[39] the concern with matters of *praxis* is in turn inseperable from these normative concerns, for the moment of *praxis* consists in none other than the articulation of a particular normative commitment, conceived of as a persuasive address to future lawmakers and those who plead before them.

Where it confines its attention to or near this microscopic extreme, the form of public law inquiry, although distinctive, is dangerously truncated. The opportunity, at the level of *praxis*, to address powerful actors within a common frame of reference encourages a tailoring of normative concerns to a cosmetic style. And to adapt further Rorty's aphorism to the terms of debate *within* such a self-referential community, this style threatens to produce little more than a set of exhortations to refine and express more satisfactorily what is already 'known better' than by any outsider, even although, as has been poignantly observed, the theoretical proximity of the commentator to the fray may unduly flatter him, the advice which flows from his fideist orientation being rarely heeded.[40] Thus, whether manifest in an implicit conformism which in turn may invite the manifold dangers of the separatist tendency, or in the explicit if creatively more indulgent affirmation of the type endorsed by Ronald Dworkin,[41] observers of public law who subscribe exclusively to this microscopic vision tend to be drawn towards a restrictive endorsement of the 'legal system as given',[42] and for precious little tangible return.

By contrast, at the macroscopic level, we may identify a wider canvas for public law inquiry which permits the same formal depth of perspective; a set of quasi-descriptive concerns, a set of normative concerns, and a set of concerns with matters of *praxis*, locked together in a more expansive framework which gains definition from its direct *correspondence* with the three-tiered formal structure of political theory. The implication, as a matter of 'institutional fact',[43] of legal phenomena in general, and of those legal phenomena which are associated with public law in particular, in historical and contemporary social formations cannot be doubted, however diversely these phenomena are thereafter analysed. It follows, since the point of departure of questions of general political *praxis* is the here and now, that the materials of public law must also be addressed at this level. Finally, any rounded normative projection must perforce be concerned with the fate of public law institutions, since these are generally and increasingly judged to have a continuing role even in utopian designs or, if this is not so, their normative limits and the conditions of their 'withering away' must still be specified.[44]

Within this more expansive framework, public law inquiry is not fettered by the normative imperatives of the existing legal framework. Further, as its referential domain is not confined to any of the discrete levels which provide the conventional focus for the various specific disciplinary concerns within the study of human cultures, institutions and possibilities, but instead spans the entire range of concerns of the master framework conceived of as political theory, it follows that the study of public law must follow the interdisciplinary lead of the latter. Hybridity should not be viewed pejoratively, but rather as a necessary consequence of the panoramic focus of public law study. And just as with political theory, although the development of the field as a whole within an integrated pattern may depend upon the relationship between the various strips, and in particular, upon the ascription of ultimate priority to the normative commitment to an improved public law as an organising principle, the ploughing of narrower furrows may continue to provide the staple work of public lawyers. Indeed, one significant aspect of the integrated pattern which may be gleaned from this wider perspective is the degree of fit between the microscopic and the macroscopic. Studies on the former level may simply provide a necessary 'scaling down' of commitments generated on the latter level in order to take account of immediate concerns and developments. They may thus be viewed as a progression from more general principles rather than as the beginning and end of public law inquiry, with all the problems that this entails.

Accordingly, as well as providing the rudiments of a sense of formal identity which transcends conventional disciplinary boundaries, such a conception of the formal depth of public law inquiry, by placing centre-stage a sense of normative commitment which is not mortgaged to the existing legal and political order in any of its general or particular respects, remains compatible with the possibility of the generation of a conception of substantive integrity. However, we have as yet provided only a partial definition of what constitutes public law's formal integrity, and one which is entirely drawn from political theory. Accordingly, the leonine threat remains imminent, for in endorsing the formal design of the cage, the threat remains that we become entrapped by the dangers which it contains. Besides the idea of formal *depth*, which provides a necessary element of continuity with political theory, what is required is a conception of the formal *breadth* of public law study which differentiates it significantly from the former, for unless this is possible, the form of public law will be seen as isomorphic with that of political theory. If public law is placed in bondage to political theory in this sense, and if, as suggested above, political theory retains the propensity to reproduce the divisions of *realpolitik*, the integrationist paradox threatens to reassert itself, and to occlude the possibility of a middle ground upon which a conception of substantive integrity might rest.

And despite the ambitions of writers such as Hollis, profound and widespread scepticism does indeed remain as to the capacity of political theory to generate conceptions of the good life which will command the general affirmation which is absent in the sphere of applied politics. The 'interweaving' of its three elements, even in the most 'ingenious' theoretical hands, seems incapable of producing a definitive ethics of the public realm. For the most part, this scepticism rests upon a seemingly immovable pillar of conventional wisdom in the human sciences, the idea of the logical impossibility of deriving an 'ought' from an 'is'.

To begin with, the discovery of what 'is' cannot be entirely free of 'ought' considerations. At the very least, the very act of value reference, of choosing what is worthy of study, incorporates judgements of the comparative significance of certain ideas and syndromes as crucibles of human possibility.[45] More centrally, to analyse how men interact and how they may come to interact, it is widely held, can never tell us how they should interact.[46] This does not mean that the warrantability or otherwise of social scientific statements is irrelevant to the acceptance or rejection of normative judgements. Many such judgements are indeed dependent upon the persuasiveness of discrete scientific claims. For example, the normative appeal of economic liberalism depends upon the sociological validity of claims that economic rewards and sanctions provide and have provided major indices of human endeavour, just as the strength of a Marxist ethics of social ownership depends upon a persuasive characterisation of capitalist social formations as embracing a significantly inegalitarian pattern of ownership and control of the means of production. In neither case, however, is the relevant judgement *entailed* by the scientific conclusion. Similarly, scientific tests may also be more directly relevant in evaluating the substance of certain normative claims, namely those which themselves embrace consequentalist chains of reasoning as extended forms of justification, most notably in the cases of utilitarian theory and democratic theory. However, even if the conditional predictions involved in these consequentialist chains can be persuasively grounded, this still does not provide independent confirmation of the value of the underlying principles which trigger these chains.

Further, if we enlist considerations of *praxis* in the attempt to ground value judgements within the wider framework of political theory, through the assumption that 'ought implies can',[47] although in principle this provides another limiting condition, its potential tends to be dissipated by the claim that criteria of possibility in the social sciences are inordinately difficult to ground in a value-free manner. Unlike the rigorously dichotomous tests of possibility/impossibility which may be generated in respect of natural scientific theorems, it is argued that such tests in the social sciences focus instead on the grey shades of relative plausibility, and in so doing do not expel but merely conceal value judgements, the 'unthinkable' and the 'undoable' tending to collapse into one another. For example, the idea that socialism cannot be generated from a capitalist socio-economic formation may on close examination be seen to rest on evaluative modes of argument. On the one hand, it may rest on the belief that such a transformation is fundamentally incompetent as it runs counter to certain basic human drives and expectations, which itself involves a value judgement as to the identity of this unimpeachable core. On the other hand, it may be grounded in the view that the means to such a change, namely the wholesale expropriation of private productive property rights, themselves require such inordinate violence to be done to existing patterns of social relations as to be beyond legitimate contemplation, which involves a test of disproportionality which again rests on the value ascribed to the ends which are at stake.[48]

It is in the light of this formidable set of caveats that holistic endeavours within political theory must be viewed. Insofar as such attempts continue to purport to close the gap between 'is' and 'ought' and thereby to supply incorrigible conceptions of how humans might find good reasons to live together, whether, for example, as with Hollis's own variation on an older theme of philosophical anthropology, through the articulation of certain essential, timeless properties of human agency,[49] or through a more emergent conception of normativity such as is contained in Habermas's idea of a universal pragmatics mediated through a developing communicative rationality,[50] in the final analysis such arguments rest upon external metaphysical guarantees whose own credentials cannot be grounded. In terms of their own proselytising ambition, therefore, such projects are bound to fail, as they are ultimately only as convincing as the articles of faith on which they rest, which themselves do not command general assent. Accordingly, viewed against these exacting standards, political theory seems destined to continue to embrace incommensurable conceptions of how men should interact, and thus to strike a note of disharmony which matches the discordant sound of 'ends colliding'[51] in the active domain of politics.

Against this pessimistic backdrop, the differentation of the formal framework of public law inquiry from holistic political theory in terms of its analytical breadth, assumes an even greater urgency as a prerequisite of the generation of a conception of substantive integrity.

2. *The limited government thesis*

One obvious and popular candidate for this distinguishing role is the idea of limited government. Implicit or explicit in the perspective adopted by many public lawyers is the idea that the *corpus* of public law has traditionally been concerned with restraints on government power and that 'constitutionalism'[52] – a loose label with which the normative concerns of public lawyers tend to be dignified – is about setting proper limits to the authority of the state, and in the particular case of the contemporary Western democracies, to the status accorded to the wishes of the absolute or relative majority from which the state purports to derive its authoritative credentials.

Such a functional conception holds a surface attraction in respect both of its historical credentials, and by virtue of its resonance with our present problematic – that is, through the terms in which it isolates the formal concerns of public law and the direct manner in which it endeavours to draw a normative message, a putative notion of substantive integrity, from these concerns. Historically, 'the deep roots of constitutional theory lie in the middle ages'[53] and in particular, in the struggle within feudalism against the absolutist tendencies of the sovereign power, the idea of limited government emerging in opposition to these tendencies. Today, many of the themes which have engaged modern public lawyers from Dicey to the authors of Charter 88[54] and provided the formal scope of their inquiries – individual rights, the separation of powers, the federal distribution of power, judicial review of legislative and executive acts, the idea of responsible government – are construable as correctives to the untramelled power of an indivisible sovereign. In turn, the idea of constitutionally limited government lays ostensibly persuasive claim to the mantle of a critically honed middle ground in that it announces a principle which is relevant to the operating philosophies of government, yet not reducible to the normative concerns of any particular operating philosophy.

Yet these claims do not stand up to close examination. Ideas of limited government today are either politically skewed or hopelessly vague. As to the first of these possibilities, certain theoretical perspectives which would define the *scope* of government power narrowly are not themselves neutral between different conceptions of the *political aims* of government. In particular, what Norman Barry terms 'agency'[55] based theories of the public realm, which suppose that the 'state does not have any authority or legitimacy by virtue of its objective features but only if it is successful in meeting individual demands',[56] tend to generate highly restrictive notions of the legitimate sphere of government activity. Whether conceived of in the awesome form of the Leviathan or in the more homely image of the night-watchman, the agency state has a heavy burden to discharge in justifying the collective ends to which it might be directed and the public goods which it might sponsor against the need to respect the mandate of each subject agent. In consequence, any ambition on its part to venture beyond the provision of certain basic protective services which secure the conditions of peaceful coexistence for all, and the pursuit of a form of welfare economics tied to the Pareto criterion, which disallows individual deprivations in the service of net collective gains,[57] threatens to take it beyond its proper remit. There is thus no or little space within such a framework to pursue directly or indirectly redistributive policies, even if their purpose is to adjust for inequalities of power and resources which arise from the activities of agents in the free-zone of civil society and the market place.

Of course, even on its own terms the coherence of such a vision is decidedly vulnerable, its presuppositions of rational egoism casting doubts upon the capacity to produce any viable notion of the state and, even if somehow instituted, upon the likelihood of such a state displaying other than a self-interested and self-propagating authoritarianism.[58] Further, even enthusiasts of such a conception would acknowledge that, as a matter of fact, 'government in Britain has never, even at its smallest, been the minimum state of classical liberal doctrine'.[59] 'A century and more of interventionism has built up needs and expectations which must be addressed'[60] and has homologated a more complex and more expansive idea of state authority. However, even if in a contemporary paradoxical manifestation of this mis-fit between claim and reality, a government committed to 'rolling back the frontiers of the state' has been required, in the short and medium term at least, to take two steps backward before taking one step forward, the presuppositions of agency theory continue to inform certain anti-collectivist political projects in a 'rough-and-ready sense'.[61] In turn, such a subjectivist notion of the state, in its rejection of robust forms of collectivism, must perforce embrace various devices of self-limitation, including a strong role for at least some of the traditional principles and mechanisms of constitutional limitation.

If the strength of this affinity between certain atomistic conceptions of the social compact and the idea of constitutionally limited government suggests a tendential bias of the latter towards the former and in favour of the political aims which the former embraces, then the alternative currency of limited government as a more general concept, and the non-exclusive nature of the link between this wider notion and particular constitutional limits, suggests the opposite danger of extreme indeterminacy. Set free from its special frame of reference, the description of government as limited is redundant, since government in the modern state is by definition limited. And the attempt to ground limited government in this polysemic sense as the defining characteristic of constitutionalism does not depend on the status of the concept of limited government as the determinate product of any deep-rooted constitutional theory, or even of any substantive political theory, but instead simply rests on a further extension of the above tautology, the invocation of any mechanism or set of mechanisms of constitutional control necessarily implying affirmation of some conception of government, and some conception of its limits. Conceived of thus, the relationship of particular constitutional limits to particular political projects can be only an instrumental one, of means to ends, and although partisans of the minimal state might prove more enthusiastic raiders of the constitutional arsenal, the advocates of any other conception of the state short of unqualified autocracy, which provided the crude opposite in terms of which the limited government thesis originally defined itself, will retain an interest in some such weapons of containment. Within this lax framework, the definitional boundaries of the idea of limited government are unlimited, its rationale free-floating and its import context-dependent, and just because the connection between constitutional limits and political morality or any other 'special' morality which adherents of this vacuous conception of limited government espouse is a contingent one, they may become acutely exposed to the charge of political expediency. This is especially so where, as is often the case, the notion of limited government is used as a weapon of critique rather than as a tool of self-regulation. Constitutionalism *qua* limited government may become the lament of the politically dispossessed, a means of focusing on particular political targets, general themes of constitutional limitation being invoked as blunt instruments to brand as excessive – as "beyond constitutional limits' – unfavoured policies of an incumbent government.[62]

The idea of limited government, therefore, cannot deliver us onto the middle ground. Its posited distinction between scope and substance is insufficiently well-founded to sustain a notion of public law's substantive integrity. But if the substantive concerns of public lawyers are not with questions of limited government, which provides a resilient and pervasive theme within the literature, then where are they situated? If no other location can be found, then the failure of the idea of limited government to bear the necessary conceptual weight may simply signal the impossibility of finding the middle ground. However, it is contended that the wish to retain the middle ground within our sights may be reconciled with the continuing significance of the notion of limited government within a wider conception of the formal breadth of public law which incorporates, but is not exhausted by, the idea of restraint on public power. The pursuit of this argument involves taking a step backwards. Rather than positing an idea such as limited government as an assumptive category – a notion guided by an intuition as to public law's proper function – we should delve deeper into the distinctive anatomy of public law rules in order to secure a more stable grounding from which this or other such functional imperatives might emerge.

C. The positive core and its implications

This wider conception of the form of public law, it is argued, is both analytically more rigorous and also more suggestive of the manner in which the nature and problems of public law inquiry are generally viewed. Analytically, it rests upon a compelling, if rudimentary, framework for identifying the necessary ambit of the enterprise in formal terms; in turn, the heuristic value of this framework may be demonstrated by its capacity to provide an optic through which the historical predilections of British public lawyers may be comprehensively grasped and the terms of their present concerns more clearly discerned.

The analytical foundations are to be found in a source already alluded to, in MacCormick's analysis of law as 'institutional fact' which, drawing upon long traditions in jurisprudence and in analytical philosophy more generally, forms the bedrock of his institutional legal positivism.[63] Against the natural lawyer's belief that the existence of valid laws depends on their satisfying particular moral values, he asserts the essentially socially derived nature of *ius positivum* and argues that what lends a degree of precision to the definition of law within this conception sufficient to marginalise the role of moral choice in the basic processes of legal discovery is the fact that these foundational social processes are themselves in a significant sense rule-orientated. That is, they generate institutional facts, propositions 'whose truth depends not merely upon the occurrence of acts or events in the world, but also upon the application of rules to such acts or events'.[64] As socially grounded rules, the social dimension consisting in forms of general acknowledgement which embrace cognitive, if not necessarily volitional elements,[65] these institutional facts exhibit properties which allow them to cohere in a structure of mutual recognition and accommodation, most persuasively depicted in the Hartian idea of the union of primary and secondary rules, with the secondary rules, and in particular the ultimate rule of recognition, providing determinative criteria for the identification of the primary rules of legal obligation.[66] In other words, the socially embedded articulation of rules within a systematic hierarchy produces a generally endorsed formula for identifying law, and a starting-point for legal analysis which is prior to application of discriminatory evaluative criteria on the part of the analyst.

This starting-point provides a baseline from which, as part of a secondary and now more stably grounded phase of inquiry, functional analysis may proceed in respect of law and its various branches. While in his general jurisprudence MacCormick investigates these matters in some depth, as regards public law – the framework and principles of regulation of state power – his views remain largely undeveloped beyond a somewhat cursory adoption and adaptation of a received distinction between rules with constitutive functions and those with regulative functions.[67] However, this distinction remains an extremely suggestive one, in that it alerts us to a dimension of public law which is missed, or at least obscured, by the advocates of the limited government approach. It suggests that public law is as much concerned with *empowerment* as with *restriction*, that it constitutes the public realm as well as setting limits on it. Nor is this true only in the narrow sense of the rule of recognition providing an ultimate enabling device, necessarily constitutive, from which a panoply of legal restrictions upon an independently conceived state flow. Rather, rules in their constitutive as well as their regulative mode are implicated at every level of public law, whether, to take some recent examples, this relates to adjustments at the macro-level of parliament and the courts, as with the simultaneous constitution and regulation of a National Audit Office,[68] or to a new procedural framework for judicial review;[69] or to innovations at the intermediate level of administrative regulation, as with the introduction of the community charge[70] and self-governing schools;[71] or to particular accretions upon existing middle-range institutions, as with new powers of detention prior to arrest for the police.[72] In all these cases, creation and limitation have proceeded hand in hand, and indeed their mutual articulation reflects the methods by which rules in general and law in particular necessarily recognise and treat their objects of reference.[73] The act of constitution already provides a limiting frame of reference, while the act of regulation presupposes a thing to be regulated. And further, to test the strength of this proposition against its apparently limiting case, even where this act of regulation is of a thing constituted independently of and prior to law, then, at least in the case of a species of law emanating from a theoretically omnicompetent sovereign, it does not follow that law's constitutive function is thereby superannuated, or reduced to secondary importance. Thus, to take the example of two such entities, the Prime Minister and, at a somewhat lower profile, the Security Service, that their recognition in and regulation through law post-dated their creation does not mean that no such constitutive function was in their case available to law, but only that it was performed implicitly, both in the decision not to terminate at any prior point and in the silent endorsement supplied by the eventual act or acts of regulation.[74]

This examination of the posited sources of public law suggests the essential inadequacy of conceiving of the constitution and public law generally as 'an addendum *to* a State',[75] and also of constitutionalism as 'something "attached" to a State, the State being an entity which by its nature desires more power and therefore needs controlling',[76] as in the limited government thesis, however alluring such images might have been in the particular circumstances of the early development of constitutional theory. Rather, existing systems of public law are *deeply implicated within* the sets of concrete mechanisms and relations which give sociological credence to the idea of a state, providing its juridical foundations and a significant means of defining and regulating its authoritative scope. This, in turn should be mirrored in the form of public law inquiry, which ought therefore to be concerned with the operation of the state in a more generic sense, in terms not only of its *limitations* but also of its *capacities*. And, in a manner consistent with this wider definition of its formal breadth, it follows that public law inquiry in its normative dimension should also have a twin focus – negative and positive, concerned to ensure both that legislative and administrative authority are adequately *controlled*, and that legislative and executive policy is generated, implemented and administered under conditions of optimal *effectiveness*.[77]

If we return to the origins of the present sense of intertwined crisis in public law and politics, we can see how this thematic pair – limitation and capacity, constraint and effectiveness – do indeed provide a more rounded framework within which the tenor of such concerns may be articulated. It will be recalled that one common critical strand underlying this mood is a general perception that the state of British politics has 'slipped beyond the explanatory grasp, and the control, of the established constitutional theory'.[78] Since 'we had our overt revolutions early',[79] before the development of the modern democratic, interventionist state, our governing constitutional doctrines and mechanisms have become chronically maladapted to contemporary political imperatives. In particular, the events of 1688-89, the establishment by the newly sovereign Parliament of the conditional monarchy of William and Mary, although hailed as an end to the royal despotism of the Stuarts, may in retrospect be seen to have provided a bridge to other, and in the final analysis, equally pernicious forms of absolutism.

To be sure, in the institutional setting of the late seventeenth and the eighteenth century, the principle of the legislative supremacy of parliament was closely calibrated with the notion of the 'balanced constitution'.[80] First, the constituencies within Parliament – King, Lords and Commons – constrained one another in a dynamic power equilibrium. Secondly, the evolution of a discrete and exclusive legislative power 'independent of the will of an executive King'[81] provided the organising principle underpinning the functional separation of powers of the three organs of government – legislature, executive and judiciary. Under the system of conciliar government, the promulgation, execution and interpretation of laws had been to some extent collapsed together within a single forum of power.[82] For its part, the new Parliament, constrained internally by its procedures and heterogeneous composition but empowered externally, had both an interest in ensuring that its hard-won legislative prerogatives would not be marginalised by a continuing executive hegemony and would be fully and faithfully recognised by a judiciary which owed its allegiance only to the law, and the capacity to ensure that these aims were in fact advanced. Thus, the power of the executive was harnessed and checked by the principles of parliamentary control of the raising and spending of money and of limitation of Crown prerogative,[83] and, upon the development of a independent power-base among the King's ministers during the eighteenth century, by the developing doctrines of individual and collective ministerial responsibility to Parliament.[84] Similarly, the doctrine of judicial independence flowered fully during the eighteenth century.[85]

Of course, if balanced it was, the eighteenth century constitution was very delicately poised. It did not rest on the broad shoulders of the *demos*, but rather, revolved around a narrow axis of elite concerns, its precarious accommodation of the interests of monarchy, aristocracy and the new entrepreneurial class representing the very embodiment of 'oligarchic whiggery'.[86] Nevertheless, it was a constitution *built* for oligarchy rather than for democracy, and the gradual advent of a system of representative government after 1832 challenged, and, in time, confounded its inner logic. By late Victorian times, the broadening of the franchise had begun to stimulate the growth of mass political parties and so to provide the framework for the modern Westminster model of government:

> According to the Westminster model, the electorate transposed its authority to the party possessing majority status in the House of Commons. The authority was in turn deposited with the cabinet, the members of which were both individually and collectively responsible for departmental administration and for government policy. So long as the Prime Minister and cabinet could retain the confidence of a majority of MPs, then most of its proposals would be enacted and its position would be maintained by the public's consent conveyed to the membership of the Commons.[87]

The theme of parliamentary supremacy, rather than the centreplace of a subtly crafted *rapprochement* of powerful, if narrowly conceived, interests, thus became a vehicle for executive control and a link in an attenuated chain of representation, providing the formal 'imprimatur of an ultimate electoral sanction'.[88]

However, this radical transposition of function and meaning of the core principle of the constitution was not itself enough to ground the claim of maladaptation. The British constitution could still provide a role model for constitution-builders in the post-Second World War era. Indeed, as recently as the 1960s, for many commentators,[89] although by no means all,[90] strong executive-led government continued to offer more benefits than disadvantages, and within this analytical prism the concern with both effectiveness and proper limits was refracted. On the credit side, strong government allowed the terms of the electoral mandate to be fully implemented, satisfying the demands of the received theory of representation and avoiding the oscillations, prevarications and unprincipled solutions of compromise politics. On the debit side, the dangers of majoritarian tyranny implicit within this scenario were avoided through cultural controls. The spirit of 'Club Government'[91] pervaded the corridors of Westminster and Whitehall, providing an adequate surrogate for a more formally entrenched system of constitutional checks. The political order was bound together in its respect for certain common rules and standards by a powerful solvent of virtue and prudence. Institutional morality combined with a common strategic awareness of the transience of Government and the inevitability of Opposition to provide certain outer constraints upon political action. And where transgressions were threatened, the boundaries were policed by the permanent guardians of the public conscience, the independent civil service and the judiciary, with the general public, itself yoked to the limited yet tangible values of the post-war consensus, providing a rather more distant critical audience in the galleries.[92] Continuing approbation of the ageing constitutional order thus depended not upon its intrinsic merit, but upon two fragile contingencies: on the one hand, its enduring capacity to deliver the goods – to respond more adequately to the weight of electoral interests than could any other arrangement; and on the other, the continuing self-restraint of the major actors within the 'great game'[93] of adversarial politics. A proper balance between effectiveness and constraint was thus seen as precariously maintained, but a change in either state of affairs could put the account-book into red.

It is against this background that the widening political polarisation in the 1970s assumes significance. In particular, because the posited causal connection here is most direct, there is agreement across a broad spectrum that this shift has crucially affected the second contingency mentioned above, and in this way has exposed the anachronisms and inadequacies of the present constitutional order.[94] The period in question saw the erosion of a Keynesian social democratic consensus which had united the main strands of political opinion in their repudiation of the stark 'dichotomies of market versus state; capital versus labour; private enterprise versus public ownership; personal freedom versus social justice'.[95] Common commitment to the demand management, planning and fiscal mechanisms necessary to retain full employment and a robust safety-net of social welfare provision foundered against the rocky configuration of economic stagnation, inflation and rising material expectations. During the administrations of Heath, Wilson and Callaghan, the final 'hands-on'[96] phase of Keynesianism, a crisis of institutional faith took hold and fed on itself. The state's role as an economic actor widened just as the legitimating philosophy upon which such activism was predicated became more vulnerable. The economic dimension of the crisis of 'ungovernability' became enmeshed with its socio-political and ideological dimensions. The regulation of trade union power, the Ulster problem, the increasing diversity of patterns of political allegiance according to region and the incipient separatist tendencies thereby triggered in Scotland and Wales all helped to focus attention more keenly upon the weakness of government's grasp on the levers of political consent, while the ever more insistent search amongst the mainstream political classes for alternative socialist and conservative governing ideologies revealed a fracturing of political self-confidence which was both a microcosm of the wider legitimation crisis and an additional contributory factor.[97]

In this volatile environment, the informal framework of rules and practices which buttressed the constitutional superstructure is widely perceived to have given way under the accumulated strain. Both the objective conditions of political life and the new creeds which have emerged from these conditions are seen to have stimulated the polarisation process and diluted that morality of the public sphere which was concerned to balance the interests of all groups against the particular wisdom of the majority constituency of the day. Within the policy-making process, the Royal Commission has been remaindered,[98] the Green Paper has assumed a glossier veneer[99] and Parliament's own agenda has become enslaved to a 'railway timetable' more constrictive than Balfour ever imagined.[100] As regards policy output, one significant regulatory motif of this change has been the accelerated development of a 'bureaucratic – administrative'[101] conception of law committed to the engineering of particular substantive ends, at the expense of the *Gesellschaft* model,[102] with its focus on the individual as bearer of formally equal legal rights and duties within a predictable framework of social interaction. The increased use by the executive of its residual prerogative powers, of open-ended discretionary powers under statute, of delegated legislation for primary purposes, and of a *dominium*[103] whose connection to any recognised conception of legality is tenuous have all borne witness to this challenge to the dominant paradigm of a system of universal, perceptible norms.[104] And where the *Gesellchaft* model has been retained or even reinvigorated, such has been its content and directive focus in many cases, as with legislation in the fields of police powers,[105] the prevention of terrorism[106] and social security rights,[107] that it too is seen to have challenged minority rights and interests. All in all, although the extent to which it has developed and the identity of its most manifest pathologies are viewed differently, the theme of 'elective dictatorship'[108] has become widely subscribed to.

Further, if we examine the flip-side of this coin, there has also developed considerable, if less widespread, scepticism as to the continuing salience of the argument from effectiveness. The strength of 'strong' government may also be its weakness. The crux of this argument, which has been set out in cogent terms most recently in the writings of David Marquand[109] and Paul Hirst[110] is that the more that particular administrations – of whatever political orientation – take advantage of their exclusive control over the formal machinery of government, 'the more they weaken both the broader processes sustaining democracy and also ultimately their own base of support'.[111] On one level this is a direct consequence of elective dictatorship, in that even a minimal level of acquiescence on the part of the disadvantaged and dispossessed under such a regime may no longer be guaranteed.[112] More broadly, if unwilling to accommodate a wider range of interests than is embraced by their particular electoral constituency and if unable to command the support of these interests, governments may lack the perspective and the wherewithal to generate long-term outcomes which are satisfactory by reference to *any* recognised criteria of political effectiveness. Successive administrations may attempt to outbid one another and, in contributing to a dangerous spiral of false expectations, assume significant roles in the long-running 'tragedy of the state'.[113] Quadrennial 'political business cycles'[114] may be out of kilter with economic imperatives dictated by regional, or even global patterns, and the prospects of cultivating a 'developmental state'[115] – primed to maximise the potential of productive forces on a national level – may remain unattainable in the absence of the steadfast co-operation of key producer and consumer groups. On such a reading, a more pluralist set of institutions and cultures is viewed as an inescapable practical imperative of modern politics, rather than as the main ingredient of political fudge and compromise.

Thus, from a rudimentary positivist base-line we have at last gained a wider and fuller understanding of the formal integrity of public law inquiry – in terms of its breadth as well as its depth – and, in turn, of the way in which the mechanisms of public law relate to the present state of the public realm, and of the necessarily binocular focus of public lawyers' agendas for debate and reform. However, it may seem that in swearing fealty to an appropriate conception of the scope of public law and an attendant comprehensiveness of perspective, we are thereby merely confirming the entailment of the normative concerns of public law to the estate of politics. For notions of the proper limits of majoritarian rule, of the conditions of effective government, and of the appropriate balance between the two, hinge upon the content attributed to the key terms within this formula and the relative weight to be accorded to them, all of which matters are the very stuff of political controversy. Indeed, the infiltration of political factors appears inescapable even in respect of the argument, referred to above, which purports to resolve the third and cumulative question of balance uncontentiously by proposing that there is no incompatability between the need for respect for minority rights and the demand for effective government and thus no competing interests to weigh, since this simply relocates the burden of analysis more firmly within the domain of the first two questions, the definition of the precise nature of the competing interests themselves.

Therefore, (and unsurprisingly, given the general orientation of positivist analysis) viewed in terms of its normative implications, this cautious grounding of the form of public law inquiry in terms of its posited sources reveals much in the way of questions and little in the way of answers. At best, our conception of the formal breadth of public law inquiry produces a *reworking without remainder* of the perennial themes of modern politics in terms of the juxtaposition of ideas of limitation and effectiveness, and the requirement for an optimal trade-off between the two. Public lawyers must therefore continue to address, albeit in reordered manner, all the grand issues of political theory, and cannot simply hive off a discrete set of these, as in the unfounded promise of the limited government thesis. Does this fuller conception of the form of public law inquiry hold out any possibility of generating a conception of its substantive integrity? In order to pursue this question we must join the two formal aspects of public law inquiry within a single framework of analysis. Is there anything in the modest reordering of political debate, which is supplied by our conception of its formal breadth, to suggest a means of developing the relationship between the 'is', the 'ought' and the 'can' of political theory within the corresponding framework of public law inquiry, which represents our understanding of its formal depth, such as to generate a conception of a normative middle ground for public lawyers?

D. Towards the Middle Ground: The Idea of Substantive Integrity

If this task is approached at the most ambitious level in terms of the specification of a determinate 'ought' – the 'one best way' of a public law utopia – then it is bound to fail. *Ex hypothesi* an ideal public law is a public law in an ideal society, and so necessarily presupposes and is harnessed to a political philosophy which embraces this latter vision. In other words, its adumbration requires a prior specification of the Good Society, and since, as we have argued, such a notion is both essentially contested and a product of holistic political theory, no generally persuasive or autonomous conception of the middle ground can be generated at this exalted level, and no amount of reordering of the central questions of politics can avoid this conclusion. And just as exercises in eschatology accord logical priority to questions of general principle, so they must also grant them epistemic priority. The idea of law in the Good Society is not merely a derivative conception, but even in such modest terms, it is also inevitably a shadowy and unspecific one, its precise articulation escaping the broad sweep of the utopian imagination. If they are to be tailored to adorn the occasion, then until the great day comes, the details of the regulatory principles and norms of public life, and the techniques and skills by which the public lawyer elaborates these, must for the most part be held in reserve.

These conclusions are reinforced if we examine the relationship between the actual and the ideal in this context. The is/ought barrier appears no less unassailable than in the domain of political theory generally. In one recent ambitious attempt to forge links between the two, Ian Harden and Norman Lewis have argued that there is a set of immanent expectations and beliefs within our cultural traditions as to what the constitution is intended to represent, and that if these are adapted to the changing conditions of the public realm, a revised conception of the rule of law which emphasises the twin ideals of openness and accountability emerges as a model framework for public law.[116] However, as they themselves acknowledge,[117] there are certain limitations inherent in this argument – the definition of what 'is' and the derivability of 'ought' from 'is' – which reflect those which attend holistic endeavours within political theory.

As to the first of these, if we move beyond the stable pedigree provided by the positive core of the legal form to the penumbra of beliefs within which a normative conception of the rule of law might be located, then the moral deveopment of such a promiscuous notion is bound to, and does, reveal a complex and contested lineage.[118] And if we seek some common theme within this fragmented genealogy, then we realise a conception of the rule of law either so 'thin'[119] – as in the idea of the rule of law as encapsulating the values of 'predictability and freedom from arbitrariness'[120] – as to be incapable of generating robust normative conclusions, or so abstract – as in Harden and Lewis's own conception of the rule of law as speaking 'to a belief in the kind of polity which seeks to subordinate naked power and to elevate civic order and rational progress'[121] – as to be compatible with a vast array of different normative conclusions.

Proceeding to the second objection, even if we settle on certain beliefs, whether in respect of the rule of law or of other more specific themes and institutions within the constitutional landscape, as commanding significant historical and contemporary support, their normative status may be dubious. Such beliefs may have an ideological currency, embracing forms of meaning which do not flow from common recognition of the conditions of a 'veridically transparent'[122] social order, but which instead are subject to more or less conscious forms and techniques of distortion and are thus shaped to sustain particular relations of domination.[123] To take but one example, Walter Bagehot's thesis,[124] recently updated in certain of its aspects by Tom Nairn,[125] that the constitution may be viewed as an 'efficient' engine operating under a 'dignified' wrapping, suggests the operation of various such ideological processes. By a process of dissimulation,[126] the pomp and ceremony of a monarchy which retains token constitutional significance in several respects may obscure more profane and less palatable relations of authority, while by means of reification, the transitory Golden Ages of Parliament and even of Cabinet Government may be viewed as 'permanent, natural, outside of time',[127] rather than as superseded by arguably less accountable and ratiocinative structures. Further, even if we can distinguish the genuinely ideational roots from the ideological foliage, the popularity or efficacy of certain legal ideas and arrangements in particular institutional contexts provides no security for their general ethical value. To return to the home ground of Harden and Lewis, the 'transcendental rationalism'[128] through which they project an ideal conception of the rule of law inevitably outstrips the context of historical inquiry, and necessarily involves 'laying bets'[129] on hunches which can never be definitively tested. Nor should this surprise us, for, having failed to square the circle, we have travelled its full circumference to return to the unavoidably indeterminate theme of the Good Society.

What if we focus instead upon the idea of *praxis*, the relationship of law to practical political possibilities? Viewing law's ambit in terms of the twin perspective provided above, are we able to locate in the 'can' of public law inquiry, and in the manner in which it relates to the 'is' and the 'ought', some more modest conception of its substantive integrity? If we take this question a stage further, as the point of departure of the 'can' is an immediate conception of the 'is', viewed not in terms of deep historical roots, but in terms of the historical present, is there anything in the relationship between, on the one hand, the matrix of concerns in terms of which we have cast the contemporary problematic of public law, namely the reconciliation of the demands of effective and limited government in the particular conditions of the 1990s, and on the other, the various ultimate purposes with which public law might be associated, which suggests some core of commensurable substantive concerns and of common normative commitment for public lawyers?

Earlier, a significant objection to the possibility of hiving off 'can' from 'ought' matters in social and political theory generally, and of according independent significance to 'can' considerations as suggesting feasible limits upon 'ought' conceptions was referred to, namely the impossibility of addressing questions of possibility in a manner which does not itself contain normative assumptions, however well hidden. But does it follow that just because questions of possibility are informed by notions of the ideal, the answers suggested to these questions of possibility have no reciprocal causal significance in the process of determining the particulars of the ideal? Such a conclusion only follows, it is suggested, if the questions of possibility are themselves framed and answered, as is indeed often the case within political theory, in a *critical* and *general* manner. That is, if questions of possibility, informed by particular ideal normative assumptions, are directed towards questioning the means of realisation of the general socio-political projections favoured by rival ideal normative assumptions, then they add nothing to our understanding of ideal normative limits in general beyond what is already presupposed within the framework which they critically employ. If such critical inquiries conclude that rival conceptions are not feasible, as might well be the case given that these rival conceptions might involve assumptions about human nature and the plausible dynamics of social change which are other than those endorsed by the critic, then this merely flows from the application by the critic of his or her own incommensurate assumptions within the domain of *praxis*. If, alternatively, it is concluded that such rival conceptions are feasible, this implies nothing about their desirability, and similarly will not challenge, displace, refine or extend the different normative presuppositions of the critic. Indeed, if he or she fails to 'discover' a feasibility-trap early – and here the connection between the critical and the general nature of the answers sought and found arises – the critic will be disinclined to do the work of his or her opponents for them, and to develop in assiduous, and perhaps limiting detail, the particular practical route which his or her opponents, from their own premises, ought to pursue.

But such detailed questions of *praxis* may also be addressed *within* the framework of a particular political theory. Under such circumstances, normative assumptions infuse issues of *praxis* more explicitly, yet, paradoxically, these are the very circumstances in which their consideration holds out the promise of influencing conceptions of the ideal in a limiting way. In asking what are the plausible means of bringing about what they already value, political theorists, having thus bracketed off general questions of principle, will look to the details of transformation, and in encountering and attempting to overcome difficulties in this area, may refine and modify their conception of what ought to be. In other words, where the stance of the political theorist is not critical and general, but *committed* and *specific*, the sovereignty of his or her conception of the good may be subjected to meaningful, if limited, challenge. At this point, questions of public law re-enter the frame, since part of this detailed inquiry will be concerned with the conditions of transformation of the massive detail represented by the institutional facts of law. The 'limits of the law'[130] as a tool of social engineering may be viewed as more or less significant, and indeed, as with Pashukanis and his followers,[131] even the general form in which it is presently known may be seen as antithetical to a particular utopian ideal – in their case, a socialist one – but the general efficacy of law as a steering mechanism, as one of the most powerful tools available within modern society for the conscious pursuit of social purposes, cannot be denied or ignored.[132]

Furthermore, in thinking about the transformative potential of law within their various frameworks of aspiration, not only do the exponents of various different perspectives have to grapple with the same raw material, but also there is no necessary reason why the rules and principles that they affirm and the legal techniques which they posit as the hypothetical vehicles of their various ambitions should not in some respects coincide. Although law must be a logically derivative notion within their ideal scenarios, this does not necessarily mean that they will disagree over the basic form that such laws might take, or even over the substance of particular laws in the short, medium or even long term. What is axiomatic from a utopian perspective is that law should be functionally subservient to the vision in question, and although certain theorists would posit a strict homology between function on the one hand and form and substance on the other – and again Pashukanis's insistence on the exclusive correspondence between the commodity form of capitalism and a particular legal form is instructive here[133] – this correspondence thesis is not generally subscribed to. Thus, for example, at the level of general principle, with only minor exceptions the various components of the procedural threshold provided in Lon Fuller's 'inner morality of law'[134] – generality, promulgation, prospectivity, clarity, non-contradiction, possibility, constancy and congruence – have been recently affirmed, without reference *inter se*, by the exponents of three distinct political visions: by a liberal, Joseph Raz;[135] by an advocate of Habermas's communicative rationality, David Sciulli;[136] and by adherents to Gewirth's transcendental deontology, Deryck Beyleveld and Roger Brownsword.[137] To take a more concrete example, the ranks of supporters and critics of the enactment of a general Bill of Rights in the classical tradition in the UK have in recent times been drawn from 'oddly mixed ideological groups',[138] and in particular, the days of the knee-jerk, if not the considered, socialist dismissal of such a conception are long gone.[139]

However, if the demands of various political theories remain 'ought-led', and if these theories remain significantly divergent, then the above instances appear not as harbingers of genuine consensus within the domain of public law, but merely as examples of the contingent concurrence of interests.

Unless *praxis* considerations can be seen to impose a common discipline and a common modifying influence upon different utopian perspectives, and more specifically, to generate a set of frameworks for the articulation of the contribution of public law which themselves display common attributes, then the idea of the substantive integrity of public law inquiry remains chimerical, the vision of the middle ground a mere crossroad.

It is in attempting to conceive of such an overlapping frame of reference that our reordering of the pivotal questions of politics within the framework of public law assumes a heuristic value. If public law inquiry in its normative mode is concerned with adumbrating the conditions of an effective polity, the appropriate limits upon any such teleological conception, and the attempt to reconcile these two aims, through a medium which, relative to other devices of social organisation, carries significant potential, then in both cognitive and practical terms, it provides an important focus for testing in a rigorous manner the adequacy of all political theories in terms of considerations of *praxis*, and for alighting on whatever common ground these various positions are bound to concede. An attempt will be made to demonstrate this by means of a brief examination of some of the questions of *praxis* which arise in the evaluation of the two political theories, or classes of political theory which underpin our contemporary political debate, liberalism and socialism, and of why and how, in grappling with these questions within their own respective domains, liberals and socialists might be drawn towards elements within one another's scheme of thought, and to common legal structures as a means of articulating this convergence.

To begin with, there is the issue of effectiveness. Indeed, efficacy is surely the axis around which considerations of matters of *praxis* revolve. What obstacles stand in the way of any attempt to attain an ideal standard of liberalism or socialism in the real world, and how might these be overcome? As regards the first, the core of the liberal vision is the creation of conditions whereby the value of individual autonomy may be maximised and the sovereignty of individual choice respected and protected against the imposition of some externally derived conception of the good.[140] In crude terms, the efficacy of the liberal project is vulnerable both to internal threats and to external threats. Internally, and this is the standard argument against the economic liberalism of the Conservative government of the last decade, if liberalism is concerned to celebrate the value of individual autonomy, the consequence of allowing free rein to those with an abundance of essential or inherited possessions, attributes and opportunities, and in particular, of eschewing a principle of directive redistribution, might be a somewhat empty feast for those denied the knowledge or wherewithal similarly to indulge themselves.[141] Externally, there is the problem of dealing with individuals who do not themselves adhere to liberal beliefs. How does the liberal protect and develop liberal institutions against the dogmatist for whom such institutions are movable obstacles?[142] And if a defensive framework is constructed, what degree of robustness is permitted without these protective institutions displaying such disrespect for the views of the dogmatist as to no longer merit the appellation 'liberal'?[143]

As regards socialism, the core of its vision is the egalitarian belief in the socialisation of the means of production so as to provide the optimal economic conditions for the self-actualisation of all members of the community, individually and in co-operation.[144] In terms of *praxis*, this is also vulnerable to both internal and external threats. Internally, if social ownership involves the dismantling of the free market in individual productive property rights and its replacement by a planning mechanism, the co-ordination of this planning mechanism threatens to vest disproportionate power in the hands of the few, and thus to create a new political class, or *nomenklatura*, which may both be unresponsive to changing patterns of demand[145] and exhibit a self-serving propensity to sustain conditions of inequality analogous to those which subsist under capitalism.[146] Externally, the question arises as to how socialism is to address and defend itself against those individuals who perceive their existential promise to be obstructed by socialist institutions, and who, if not actively resistant, may be unmotivated to contribute to the creation of the collective abundance of resources without which the socialist ambition will be diluted and the legitimacy of the system exposed to more general threat.

Now, it is immediately apparent that these questions of political effectiveness also have a strong ethical dimension. In considering whether these two utopian visions are feasible, we inevitably generate a set of parallel moral inquiries, since these practical obstacles, by their very nature, compel us to address difficult choices in their negotiation, and thus to decide in a more detailed way what our utopian conceptions are prepared to countenance and what they entail. In turn, these questions may be felicitously presented in terms of the second element within the matrix of normative concerns of public lawyers, namely the stipulation of the proper limits of the political conceptions which inform the public realm by reference to the claims of those who would be disadvantaged by it, that is, both internal victims and external victims. Internally, to what extent are liberals prepared to sacrifice even the modest opportunities of some for the sake of the unbridled want satisfaction of others, and to what extent are socialists prepared to countenance the risk of a new form of domination of the many by the few in the process of dismantling an old form? Externally, to what extent are the advocates of either system, both of which purport to represent conceptions of the general good,[147] prepared to defend it against those whose aspirations are incompatible with its premisses and its consequences? In addressing these questions, we alight upon a first sense in which considerations of *praxis* draw the partisans of different ideal conceptions closer together. As the external victims of either system may well be advocates of the other, and as the putative internal victims of each system may be protected by principles drawn from the other – in the case of liberalism, a redistributive principle, and in the case of socialism, guaranteed voting rights, rights of freedom of expression, freedom of assembly etc. – in the detailed elaboration of its practical and moral mission each system, in order to keep faith with its promise of respect for the interests of all, must perforce countenance incorporation of aspects of the other.

Further, although the practical questions are mirrored by moral questions in this fashion, it should not be thought that the difficult decisions referred to above always resolve themselves into zero-sum choices. And this is where the third normative concern of the public lawyer intrudes, and assumes an independent significance, for, as was suggested when we considered the arguments of Marquand, Hirst and others in respect of the strong government thesis as it applies to our contemporary polity, the relationship between the practical efficacy of a particular political project and a limiting respect for the aspirations of others may be more than one of simple trade-off. External victims may also be external predators, or the potential sources of ideas and resources of value to the exponents of the system. Thus, quite apart from the moral arguments set out above, liberals may have good, prudential reasons to respect socialist views and socialists may have good, prudential reasons to respect liberal views. Accordingly, we come upon a second sense in which questions of *praxis* reveal common ground between advocates of different utopian visions.

If we transpose onto the institutional context of public law these considerations of morality and prudence which we have generated by means of addressing a set of normative questions which themselves emerge from our understanding of the general form of public law, we can see their central relevance in providing a form of mediation between the concerns of advocates of different ideal conceptions. If we return to our two examples, Fuller's inner morality of law may be perceived as a means by which social relationships are grounded in a relatively stable and predictable framework and by which a degree of accountability of law to legal subjects is retained. In turn, these values may be viewed as providing rudimentary protections against internal and external victimisation. So also with a Bill of Rights, growing bipartisan agreement on its value, together with continuing disagreement as to whether it should be constitutionally entrenched,[148] and whether extended to embrace social and economic rights,[149] provides a concrete instance of attempts to resolve the matrix of concerns described above within the framework of public law.

And these are not isolated instances, for it is argued that consideration of matters of *praxis* within the framework of normative concerns suggested for public lawyers and in respect of the institutions of public law inevitably draws out questions of morality and prudence along the lines suggested above. Although considerations of space preclude the development of this argument, irrespective of the particular ideal conceptions between whose terms the debate is structured, and regardless of the dimension of public law upon which the debate is focused, public law suggests itself as a prime site for the interlocking of the concerns of divergent normative enterprises and the negotiation and accommodation of convergent themes. For example, studies with regard to the relationship between rules and discretion,[150] the proper balance between adjudicatory and other techniques of decision-making within public fora,[151] the nature of the territorial distribution of legal authority within the state,[152] and the very definition of the boundaries of public law and public law rights,[153] have in each case served to enhance our understanding of the significance of legal choices of institutional design in the detailed moral and practical elaboration of diverse political projects, and of the complex intertwining of operational commitments which may result from this.

Are these arguments sufficient to establish a conception of substantive integrity, a middle ground for the politics of public law upon which projects within the more general domain of politics may be made subject to critical appraisal? There remain three related caveats to such a conclusion. In the first place, the combination of matters of prudence and matters of substantive morality operating at the margins of holistic normative enterprises might be seen to offer a somewhat thin gruel with which to feed such a conception of the normative project of public law. Secondly, in a technical sense at least, such a project still seems to be led by the concerns of mainstream politics and general political theory. If there is a middle ground upon which public lawyers may address common normative concerns then, on the above reading, it is not the starting point of their various journeys, but rather a second-stage destination to which they are expeditiously drawn. Thirdly, what potential exists for the critical edge of such a project to make an incisive mark upon the real world of politics? The portents are not good. In our contemporary politically polarised environment, which provided a point of departure for this essay and its consistent backdrop, the lessons of praxis – of prudence and of a self-limiting ecumenical morality – seem well-hidden, sometimes, above all, from public lawyers themselves.[154]

Let us take the first two objections together. In combination, they amount to the claim that all that has been established is the need for a *modus vivendi* between exponents of different comprehensive conceptions of the good life, including their adherents within public law, rather than a genuine 'overlapping consensus'.[155] Such a *modus vivendi* is ultimately founded upon the imperatives which flow from the different comprehensive conceptions and so is limited by the terms of these conceptions. Accordingly, where an impasse is reached in terms of the demands of these different conceptions, it contains no self-propagating dynamic in terms of which such an impasse may be resolved. To return to the example of Bills of Rights, in the last analysis many socialists baulk at the idea of a firmly constitutionally entrenched basic framework of classical rights, as they believe that such rights presuppose and sustain a particular conception of the social world, as a place of limited altruism and resources, which is antithetical to their ideal conception.[156] Accordingly, although a structure of liberal rights may be accommodated in the short or medium terms for reasons of self-defence or compromise, in the long-term it is expendable.[157]

Without wishing to understate the significance of the difficulties posed by this general argument or its specific exemplar, such an argument ignores the apparently paradoxical fact, suggested by John Rawls, that many people do not hold to their absolutist conceptions absolutely.[158] That is, although many people espouse life-projects, which, if finessed within the workshop of political theory, might be presented as comprehensive docrines, these are not the terms on which they are in matter of fact held. This is at root a sociological claim. It corresponds with, and is causally linked to the wider premise that few, if any, actually existing societies correspond closely to the design of an absolutist conception; they are essentially hybrids. In turn, the 'implicated self',[159] the human agent within such a society will tend to develop allegiances to the hybrid institutions extant within such a society, including the hybrid institutions of law. Accordingly, if we move from the 'top-down' orientation of high political theory to the 'bottom-up' orientation of everyday experience, we can begin to see how the idea of an overlapping consensus might become more firmly grounded and 'develop an allegiance to itself'.[160] If, however, this shift is too pronounced there are dangers here too, of uncritical endorsement of prevailing social arrangements and, more specifically – to recall an earlier theme – of tacit acceptance of 'the law as given', critical distance being thereby relinquished or reduced to an article of bad faith. To avoid these dangers, a balance must be struck, and in appraising existing institutions both deductive and inductive frames of reference must be joined within the one perspective. To develop the sociological lead in the context of public law inquiry, public lawyers may and should be 'implicated selves' in a double sense, both in the general sense as members of society, and in a special sense dictated by their continuing involvement with and critical reflections upon the institutions of public law, and in particular by their pursuit of the arguments from prudence and a self-limiting morality – the tentative foundations of the middle ground. Thus, in terms of the combination of the general and special role positions of its putative exponents, the foundations of the middle ground might become less precarious, and it also may begin to engender 'an allegiance to itself', a fundamental point of departure for some public lawyers. And if it remains a mere staging post for others, then public law inquiry is none the worse for that, since the continuing exposition of absolutist conceptions from committed positions will provide a corrective against the development of a complacent insularity and corrosive conservatism within the middle ground.[161]

Finally, we return to the question of political efficacy. The extent to which public lawyers, whether domiciled there or not, can develop the middle ground in such a manner as to have some influence on the agenda of practical politics is a question easier to pose than to resolve. Certainly, although their success may depend on a host of factors other than their own efforts, if they can avoid the problems of separatism and integrationism in the manner indicated, they may develop the *cognitive* capacity to make an independent contribution. Perhaps their best prospects lie in the long and less direct route, in their potential influence within the domain of political theory. For it follows from the above analysis that just as the formal and substantive integrity of public law inquiry lies in its modest reorganisation of the concerns of general political theory within its own special domain, so also the best prospects for general political theory lie in an equivalent internal reordering of priorities, with greater emphasis upon questions of political *praxis* and the lessons that may be learned from these. As John Dunn has argued, political theorists must learn to focus more clearly on 'the structural propitiousness of the socio-political context within which [their] values must be actualized'.[162] They must set at the centre of their concerns 'a theory of prudence – a theory adequate to the historical world in which we *have* to live'.[163] The litmus test and abiding legacy of the development of a defensible conception of the middle ground within public law may lie in the contribution which it makes to this project.

Notes

1. A.W. Bradley (1981) 1 *Legal Studies* 329 at 332; reviewing H.W.R. Wade *Constitutional Fundamentals* Stevens and Sons (1980).
2. Two of the best reviews of the wider literature on the causes, nature and consequences of the polarised development of British politics in the post-war era are D. Held *Political Theory and The Modern State* Polity Press (1989) esp ch 4 and A. Wright 'British Decline: Political Or Economic?' (1987) 40 *Parl Affairs* 41. Within public law studies, the theme of political polarisation has also been taken up by various writers. See e.g. P. McAuslan and J.F. McEldowney (Eds) *Law, Legitimacy And The Constitution* Sweet & Maxwell (1985) ch 1; C. Graham and T. Prosser (Eds) *Waiving The Rules: the Constitution under Thatcherism* Open U P (1988) ch 1; M. Foley *The silence of constitutions: Gaps, 'abeyances' and political temperament in the maintenance of government* Routledge (1989) esp ch 5; R. Holme and M. Elliott (Eds) *1638 – 1988: Time for a New Constitution* Macmillan (1988); N. Johnson *In Search Of The Constitution: Reflections on State and Society in Britain* Pergamon Press (1977).
3. The sources referred to in note 2 *supra* are relevant here. See in particular M. Elliott 'Constitutionalism, Sovereignty and Politics' in R. Holme and M. Elliott (Eds) ch 2.
4. E.g., contrast the essays in R. Holme and M. Elliott *op cit* note 2 *supra* with the approach taken in P. Norton 'The Glorious Revolution of 1688 – 1988: Its Continuing Relevance' (1989) 42 *Parl Affairs* 135.
5. For discussion of arguments for and against a reformed second chamber see e.g. B. Hadfield 'Whether and Whither The House of Lords' (1984) 35 NILQ 313. For discussion of electoral reform proposals, see e.g. D. Butler 'Electoral Reform' in J. Jowell and D. Oliver (Eds) *The Changing Constitution* (2nd ed) Oxford U P (1989) 371. For discussion of the relevance of constitutional principles to the reorganisation of local government, see M. Grant 'Central – Local Relations: The Balance of Power' in J. Jowell and D. Oliver (Eds) *ibid* 247. As regards the wider question of the territorial reorganisation of the British state, this theme has most recently arisen in a constitutional context in terms of the evaluation of claims for a Scottish Parliament, as a result of the launching of 'A Claim of Right For Scotland' in 1988, and the subsequent emergence of a Constitutional Convention to pursue the implications of this document. For text and discussion, see O.D. Edwards *A Claim of Right For Scotland* Polygon (1989).
6. For recent concise statements of the arguments for and against a British Bill of Rights, see N. Lacey 'Are Rights Best Left Unwritten?' (1989) 60 *Pol Q* 433 and G.W. Jones 'The British Bill Of Rights' (1990) 43 *Parl Affairs* 27.
7. For contrasting views on the systematic quality of our administrtive law and its possible future development, see H.W.R. Wade *Administrative Law* (6th ed) Clarendon Press (1988) esp ch 1, and D. Galligan 'Judicial Review and the Textbook Writers' (1982) 2 OJLS 267.
8. See e.g. N. Lewis 'Regulating Non-Governmental Bodies: Privatization, Accountability and the Public – Private Divide' in J. Jowell and D. Oliver (Eds) *op cit* note 5 *supra* 219.
9. What is at issue in such discussions, implicitly or explicitly, is the relationship between public law and particular conceptions of democracy. For recent notable attempts to analyse and evaluate our framework of public law in terms of democratic theory, see A.H. Birch 'The Theory and Practice of Modern British Democracy' in J. Jowell and D. Oliver (Eds) *op cit* note

5 *supra* 87; C. Harlow 'Power from the People? Representation and
Constitutional Theory' in P. McAuslan and J. McEldowney (Eds) *op cit* note
2 *supra* 62; P. Hirst *After Thatcher* Collins (1989) ch 2. For an interesting
comparative study between the United Kingdom and the United States within
the same framework of inquiry, see R.S. Kay 'Substance And Structure As
Constitutional Protections: Centennial Comparisons' [1989] PL 428. See
also, more generally J. Elster and R. Slagstad (Eds) *Constitutionalism And
Democracy* Cambridge U P (1988).

10. Lord Hailsham 'Elective Dictatorship' *The Listener* 21 October 1976.

11. D. Held *op cit* note 2 *supra* 1.

12. This definition is adopted by the sponsors of The Public Law Project, which
was launched in February 1990 with the aim of making assistance in matters
of public law more widely available to members of disadvantaged groups.
Its prospectus, from which this definition is drawn, was published from its
offices in the Institute of Advanced Legal Studies of the University of London
during that month.

13. K. Dyson *The State Tradition in Western Europe* Martin Robertson (1980).

14. *Ibid* 200.

15. *Ibid* 199.

16. M. Elliott *op cit* note 3 *supra* 30.

17. *Ibid* 31.

18. N. Lewis *op cit* note 8 *supra*.

19. As with regard to the abolition of the largely socialist-controlled metropolitan
county councils under the Local Government Act 1985. See e.g. S. Leach
and G. Stoker 'The Transformation of Central – Local Government
Relationships' in C. Graham and T. Prosser (Eds) *op cit* note 2 *supra* 96 at
106 – 109.

20. Lord McCluskey *Law, Justice and Democracy* BBC Books (1987).

21. J.A.G. Griffith *The Politics of the Judiciary* Fontana (3rd ed 1985) esp ch 9.

22. The legal, political and academic controversy surrounding the *Spycatcher*
affair is the most significant case in point. For a general overview, see the
debate between Watt and Lustgarten in the pages of *The Political Quarterly*;
D.C. Watt 'Fall-Out from Treachery: Peter Wright and the *Spycatcher* case'
(1988) 59 *Pol Q* 206; L. Lustgarten 'Learning from Peter Wright: A response
to D.C. Watt (1989) 60 *Pol Q* 222; D.C. Watt 'Learning from Peter Wright:
A reply' (1989) 60 *Pol Q* 237. See also *Attorney-General v Guardian Newspapers
(No. 2)* [1990] AC 109.

23. See e.g. P. Wiles 'Law, Order and the State' in C. Graham and T. Prosser
(Eds) *op cit* note 2 *supra* 153; A. Norrie and S. Adelman '"Consensual
Authoritarianism" and Criminal Justice in Thatcher's Britain' (1989) 16 JR
of *Law and Society* 112.

24. Canada Act 1982. See the Second Reading debate in the Commons, 17
February 1982 H C Debs cols 292 – 370 and in particular the comments of
Mr Bruce George MP at col 347. For contemporary dicussion of the wider
constitutional issues see the series of reports by the House of Commons Select
Committee on Foreign Affirs; First Report HC 42 (1980 – 81); Supplementary
Report HC 295 (1980 – 81): Third Report HC 128 (1981 – 82).

25. W.T. Murphy and S. Roberts 'Introduction' to special issue entitled 'Legal
Scholarship In The Common Law World' (1987) 50 MLR 677 at 679.

26. For example, the orthodox doctrine of the legal sovereignty of Parliament,
whose continuing strength is in some part due to the sustained weight of
academic opinion (see e.g. A. Bradney 'Parliamentary Sovereignty – A
Question of Status' (1985) 36 NILQ 2) runs in tandem with a political
conception of parliamentary sovereignty – 'the idea that there is a final and
absolute authority in the political community' (F.H. Hinsley *Sovereignty* (2nd
ed) Cambridge U P (1986) – and this convergence may not be lost on those
who wish to defend this political conception for particular political ends.
Thus the idea of parliamentary sovereignty, with its dual signification, has

loomed large in the arguments recently presented by the Conservative Government against unqualified acceptance of the expansionist claims of the European Communities. See e.g. the address given by the Prime Minister at the opening of the academic session 1988 – 89 of the College of Europe, in Bruges (November 1988).

27. For discussion of the idea of legalism see J.N. Shklar *Legalism* Harvard U P (1964). As regards the charge of disingenuousness, this is frequently laid against Dicey, it being argued that his idea of the rule of law is inextricably bound up with his anti-collectivist and anti-interventionist political preferences. For recent discussion see J. Jowell 'The Rule of Law Today' in J. Jowell and D. Oliver (Eds) *op cit* note 5 *supra* 3; J.F. McEldowney 'Dicey in Historical Perspective – a Review Essay' in P. McAuslan and J.F. McEldowney (Eds) *op cit* note 2 *supra* 39; P.P. Craig 'Dicey: Unitary, Self-Correcting Democracy and Public Law' (1990) 106 LQR 105.

28. M. Elliot *op cit* note 3 *supra* 26 and 30.

29. Philosophers, to whom he attributed the imperialist claim to know 'something about knowing which nobody else knows so well', were the butt of Rorty's original criticism: Rorty *Philosophy and the Mirror of Nature* Basil Blackwell (1980) 392.

30. E.C.S. Wade (Ed) Macmillan (1959).

31. Book Review [1986] PL 641 at 643.

32. Thus Murphy claims that public law 'has become an umbrella covering a range of quite heterogeneous and unrelated specialisms' *ibid* 641. The influence of political science and philosophy, of history and, to a lesser extent, sociology is present in the collections by J. Jowell and D. Oliver, *(op cit* note 5 *supra)* and P. McAuslan and J.F. McEldowney *(op cit* note 2 *supra)* which he reviews. As regards economics, the recent influence of public choice theory within constitutional thought, particularly in the United States, is reviewed and its future prospects assessed by P. McAuslan 'Public Law and Public Choice' (1988) 51 MLR 631. As regards organisational theory see e.g. W.M. Evan 'Administrative Law And Organisation Theory' (1977) 29 *Jl of Legal Education* 106.

33. See I. Berlin 'Does Political Theory Still Exist?' in *Concepts and Categories: Philosophical Essays* Oxford U P (1950) 143.

34. M. Hollis *Models Of Man: Philosophical thoughts on social action* Cambridge U P (1977) 1 – 2.

35. The language is that of Karl-Otto Apel 'Types of Social Science in the Light of Human Cognitive Interests' in S.C. Brown (Ed) *Philosophical Disputes in the Social Sciences* Harvester (1979) 3. More generally, the concepts referred to here and in note 36 *infra* reflect Apel's allegiance to the Frankfurt School of critical theory, and in particular, to the significance accorded by this intellectual movement to cognitive processes as well as material processes within the dynamics of social transformation. Similar language and similar ideas are utilised by the leading contemporary exponent of critical theory, Jurgen Habermas. See e.g. J. Habermas *Knowledge and Human Interests* Heinemann (1972).

36. Karl-Otto Apel *ibid* 6.

37. D. Held and A. Leftwich 'A Discipline of Politics?' in D.Held *op cit* note 2 *supra* 243 at 246.

38. W.T. Murphy and S. Roberts *op cit* note 25 *supra* 679.

39. R.B.M. Cotterrell 'English Conceptions Of The Role Of Theory In Legal Analysis' (1983) 46 MLR 681 at 682.

40. W.T. Murphy and S. Roberts *op cit* note 25 *supra* 687.

41. See most recently his *Law's Empire* Fontana (1986). Ch 10 offers a specific application of his general theory to constitutional cases.

42. C.M. Campbell 'Legal Thought And Juristic Values' (1974) 1 *Br Jl of Law and Society* 13, 22.

43. N. MacCormick 'Law as Institutional Fact' (1974) 90 LQR 102; reprinted

in N. MacCormick and O. Weinberger *An Institutional Theory of Law* D. Reidel (1986) 49.

44. The idea of the withering away of state and law no longer attracts much support amongst socialist lawyers. For discussion and exemplification of this development see C. Graham and T. Prosser (Eds) *op cit* note 2 *supra*, esp ch 10; (1988) 15 *Jl of Law and Society* No 1 (special issue on 'Law, Democracy and Social Justice' R. Cotterrell and B. Bercusson (Eds)); P.Q. Hirst *Law, Socialism and Democracy* Allen & Unwin (1986).

45. For discussion of the nature of the distinction between value reference *(Wertbeziehung)* and comprehensive value judgement *(Werturteil)*, with particular reference to the work of Max Weber, see R. Aron *Main Currents in Sociological Thought 2* Penguin (1967) 193 – 202. Further, if it is recognised that the generation of sociological 'facts', quite apart from its dependence upon an initial value reference, cannot thereafter proceed on the basis of an empiricist correspondence thesis but is instead theory dependent, additional questions arise as to whether the explanatory premises of the general theoretical framework utilised are themselves necessarily value-laden. For a forceful rejection of such a conclusion see R. Keat *The Politics Of Social Theory* Basil Blackwell (1981).

46. See R. Keat *ibid* chs 1 and 2. The argument advanced in this paragraph draws from Keat's discussion. See esp 44.

47. *Ibid* 45.

48. *Ibid* 46.

49. *Ibid* esp chs 7 – 9.

50. See esp J. Habermas *Theory of Communicative Action* vol 1. *Reason and the Rationalisation of Society* Heinemann (1985). For an excellent overview see J.B. Thompson *Studies in the Theory of Ideology* Polity Press (1984) ch 8.

51. I. Berlin *op cit* 149.

52. See e.g. C.H. McIlwain *Constitutionalism And The Changing World* Cambridge U P (1939 reprinted 1969); M.J.C. Vile *Constitutionalism And The Separation Of Powers* Clarendon Press (1967); J. Elster and R. Slagstad *op cit* note 9 *supra;* A. Vincent *Theories of the State* Basil Blackwell (1987) ch 3.

53. A. Vincent *ibid* 84.

54. The Charter 88 campaign is administered from the premises of *New Statesman and Society*, in whose pages the text of the Charter was first published on 2 December 1988. By September 1990 the campaign was known to have attracted some 22,000 subscribers.

55. 'The State and Legitimacy' in A. Phillips Griffiths (Ed) *Key Themes in Philosophy* Cambridge U P (1989) 191.

56. *Ibid* 194.

57. For a conception of the state as the provider of basic protective services see e.g. R. Nozick *Anarchy, State and Utopia* Basic Books (1974) 113 – 115. For discussion of the Pareto criterion see N. Barry *op cit* note 55 *supra* 196 – 197, referring to the work of the Italian economist Vilfredo Pareto: see esp V Pareto *The Mind and Society* Harcourt, Brace (A. Livingston (Ed) 1935) vol 3 946 – 947.

58. *Ibid* 197 – 198.

59. J. Gray *Limited Government: A Positive Agenda* IEA (1989) 21.

60. *Ibid* 22.

61. *Ibid* 21.

62. See e.g. W.T. Murphy *op cit* note 31 *supra* at 64; Murphy returns to this theme in a review of M. Foley *op cit* note 2 *supra* in (1990) 53 MLR 274 at 275; see also M. Elliott *op cit* note 3 *supra* 29 – 30. It is a tribute to the allure of the limited government thesis that one of the writers explicitly criticised by Murphy for endorsing the limited government thesis, Patrick McAuslan (see esp McAuslan and McEldowney *op cit* note 2 *supra* 8) provides a much more sophisticated and rounded conception of the public domain and of the nature of the concerns of public lawyers vis-à-vis this domain

in his other work; see in particular P. McAuslan 'Administrative Law, Collective Consumption and Judicial Policy' (1983) 46 MLR 1.

63. A number of MacCormick's essays on the theory of institutional legal positivism are collected in N. MacCormick and O. Weinberger (Eds) *op cit* note 43 *supra*. See in particular 'Law as Institutional Fact' 49–76.

64. *Ibid* 51.

65. MacCormick himself emphasises the importance of volitional elements; see 'Law, Morality And Positivism' *ibid* 127–144 esp 131–132; see also N. MacCormick *Legal Reasoning and Legal Theory* Clarendon (1978) 275–292.

66. H.L.A. Hart *The Concept Of Law* Clarendon (1961) 77–96.

67. Within his general jurisprudence 'Law As Institutional Fact' *op cit* notes 43 and 63 *supra* represents his most detailed analysis. For his application of this framework to public law see 'Institutional Morality And The Constitution' in N. MacCormick and O. Weinberger (Eds) *op cit* note 43 *supra* 171–187 esp 181–182 where he draws explicitly upon the work of John Rawls and John Searle. His equation of constitutive and regulative rules with primary and secondary rules in this passage seems oversimplistic in the light of his more complex analysis in 'Law As Institutional Fact'.

68. National Audit Act 1983.

69. For Scotland sees Act of Sederunt (Rules of Court Amendment No 2) (Judicial Review) 1985, SI 1985/500, inserting Chapter IV Section 14 Application for Judicial Review RC 260B. For England and Wales see Supreme Court Act 1981 s31(1).

70. For Scotland see Abolition of Domestic Rates Etc. (Scotland) Act 1987. For England and Wales see Local Government Finance Act 1988.

71. For Scotland see Self-Governing Schools Etc. (Scotland) Act 1989 Part I. For England and Wales, and the institution and elaboration of the idea of the grant-maintained school, see Education Reform Act 1988 Part 1 ch 4.

72. For Scotland see Criminal Justice (Scotland) Act 1980 ss 2–4. For England and Wales see Police and Criminal Evidence Act Parts IV and V.

73. The work of John Searle, although innovative in the field, sets up a rigid distinction between constitutive and regulative rules; J. Searle *Speech Acts* Cambridge U P (1970) 33–42; Although MacCormick himself does not question the precise terms of this general distinction (see references in note 67 *supra*) it is interesting to note that theorists working within jurisprudence and sociology have separately arrived at the conclusion that such singular descriptions of rules are not apt, but that individual rules instead tend to exhibit *both* constitutive and regulative functions. Within jurisprudence see O. Weinberger 'The Role of Rules' (1988) 1 *Ratio Juris* 224 at 234–235. Within sociology see A. Giddens *The Constitution Of Society* Polity Press (1984) 17–25.

74. For the office of Prime Minister see e.g. Chequers Estate Act 1917, Ministerial and other Salaries Act 1975. For the Security Services see Security Service Act 1989; see also W. Finnie 'The Smile on the Face of the Tiger' (1990) 41 NILQ 64.

75. A. Vincent *op cit* note 52 *supra* 78.

76. *Ibid*.

77. Despite the traditional strength of the limited government approach, the alternative dual-pronged approach is nevertheless not without significant historical support amongst those engaged in public law inquiry, as P.P. Craig reminds us in his recent analysis of the constitutional writings of Jeremy Bentham. P.P. Craig 'Bentham, Public Law and Democracy' [1989] PL 407 esp at 412 and 417.

78. J. Dearlove and P. Saunders *Introduction to British Politics: Analysing a Capitalist Democracy* Polity Press (1984) 81.

79. J.D.B. Mitchell 'The Cause and Effects of the Absence of a System of Public Law in the United Kingdom' in W.J. Stankiewicz (Ed) *British Government in an Era of Reform* Collier Macmillan (1976) 27.

80. For discussion see M.J.C. Vile *op cit* note 52 *supra* ch 1; P. Vincent *op cit* note 52 *supra* esp 98 – 100.

81. M.J.C. Vile *op cit* note 52 *supra* 26.

82. For discussion see e.g. C.R. Munro *Studies in Constitutional Law* Butterworths (1987) ch 8 59 – 66; E.C.S. Wade and A.W. Bradley *Constitutional and Administrative Law* Longman (10th ed 1985 by A.W. Bradley) 50.

83. Bill of Rights 1689 Articles 1, 2 and 4. Claim of Right 1689.

84. For discussion see e.g. E.C.S. Wade and A.W. Bradley *op cit* note 82 *supra* ch 7.

85. See in particular Act of Settlement 1700 Art III.

86. D. Marquand *The Unprincipled Society* Fontana (1988) 177.

87. M. Foley *op cit* note 2 *supra* 98.

88. *Ibid* 99.

89. See e.g. the discussion and references cited in Foley, *ibid.*

90. An obvious case is that of Marxism with its general suspicion of 'bourgeois' versions of representative democracy. For a very readable assessment of the development within the English tradition of Marxist thought in respect of the state and other themes see P. Anderson *Arguments Within English Marxism* New Left Books (1980). Another significant critical tradition is that of English pluralism which reached its apogee in the 1920s when the writings of such as Laski, Cole and Figgis exerted their greatest influence. For extracts from these writings and overall assessment see P. Hirst (Ed) *The Pluralist Theory of the State: Selected Writings of G.D.H. Cole, J.N. Figgis and H.J. Laski* Routledge (1989).

91. D. Marquand *op cit* note 86 *supra* ch 7.

92. See e.g. B. Crick 'Sovereignty, Centralism and Devolution' in R. Holme and M. Elliott (Eds) *op cit* note 2 *supra* 57-80.

93. *Ibid* 57.

94. See e.g. M. Foley *op cit* note 2 *supra* 99 – 100; A. Wright *op cit* note 2 *supra*.

95. D. Marquand *op cit* note 86 *supra* 19.

96. *Ibid* 45.

97. *Ibid* 52 – 62; P. Hirst *op cit* note 2 *supra* 39 – 51.

98. The last Royal Commission to be set up was the Royal Commission on Criminal Procedure in February 1978. Chaired by Sir Cyril Phillips, its Report is published as Cmnd 8092 (1981) HMSO.

99. For example, in relation to local government finance, compare the truncated, polemical style of 'Paying for Local Government' – the Green Paper which preceded the introduction of the community charge (Cmnd 9714 (1986)) with the more sober, analytical approach of the Layfield Report – the previous major review of policy in this area which was produced a decade earlier (Cmnd 6453 (1976)).

100. D. Miers and A. Page *Legislation* (2nd Ed) Butterworths (1990) 69. For critical discussion of the extent to which present parliamentary procedures relating to legislation and control of public spending favour the incumbent government see e.g. the respective essays by G. Drewry and A. Robinson in M. Ryle and P. Richards (Eds) *The Commons Under Scrutiny* Routledge (1988).

101. A.E – S. Tay and E. Kamenka 'Beyond Bourgeois Individualism: The Contemporary Crisis in Law and Legal Ideology' in E. Kamenka and R. Neale (Eds) *Feudalism, Capitalism and Beyond* Edward Arnold (1975).

102. *Ibid* Tay and Kamenka concede that elements of *gesellschaft* law and bureaucratic-administrative law may coexist within the one legal system. See further D. Nelken 'Is There a Crisis in Law and Legal Ideology?' (1982) 9 *Jl of Law and Society* 177.

103. T. Daintith 'Legal Analysis of Economic Policy – I' (1982) 9 *Jl of Law and Society* 191 at 215.

104. For general discussion of recent trends in this direction see P. McAuslan and J.F. McEldowney (Eds) *op cit note 2 supra* ch 1.

105. Criminal Justice (Scotland) Act 1980; Police and Criminal Evidence Act 1984.

106. Prevention of Terrorism (Temporary Provisions) Acts 1974, 1976, 1984 and 1989.

107. The Social Security Act 1980 witnessed a shift in the direction of a rights-based model, which in turn was to some extent reversed by the Social Security Act 1986. For a particularly instructive discussion of the rights *versus* discretion debate in the light of earlier legislation in this field see T. Prosser 'The Politics of Discretion: Aspects of Discretionary Power in the Supplementary Benefits Scheme' in M. Adler and S. Asquith *Discretion and Welfare* Heinemann (1981) 148–170.

108. Lord Hailsham *The Dilemma of Democracy* Collins (1978) esp ch 20.

109. D. Marquand *op cit* note 86 *supra.*

110. P. Hirst *op cit* note 2 *supra.*

111. P. Hirst *ibid* 63.

112. For instance, many attempts to explain the urban disorders of the 1980s have focused upon the cumulative effect of political and economic marginalisation. See e.g. J. Lea and J. Young 'The Riots in Britain 1981: Urban Violence and Political Marginalisation' in D. Cowell *et al* (Eds) *Policing The Riots* Junction Books (1982) 5–20.

113. H. Wilkie 'The Tragedy of the State' (1986) LXXII 4 *Archiv für Rechts-und Sozialphilosophie* 455.

114. A. Wright *op cit* note 2 *supra* 45.

115. D. Marquand *op cit* note 86 *supra* 13.

116. I. Harden and N. Lewis *The Noble Lie: The British constitution and the rule of law* Hutchinson (1986) esp 11. See also N. Lewis 'Public Law and Legal Theory' in W. Twining (Ed) *Legal Theory and Common Law* Blackwell (1986) 99–114 at 108.

117. This acknowledgement is more clearly made in subsequent discussion of *The Noble Lie* in the pages of the *Modern Law Review* than in the text itself. See the review by M. Loughlin 'Tinkering With The Constitution' (1988) 51 MLR 531 followed by the authors' rejoinder; I. Harden and N. Lewis 'The Noble Lie: A Rejoinder' (1988) 51 MLR 812 at 815.

118. M. Loughlin *op cit* note 117 *supra* 547–550.

119. R.S. Summers 'The Ideal Socio-Legal Order. Its "Rule of Law" Dimension' (1988) 1 *Ratio Juris* 134; see also the critical response by N.B. Reynolds 'Comments on Robert Summers on the Rule of Law' (1988) 1 *Ratio Juris* 263.

120. R.S. Summers *ibid* 160.

121. *The Noble Lie op cit* note 116 *supra* 19.

122. J. Dunn *Rethinking modern political theory* Cambridge U P (1985) 125.

123. See e.g. the work of J.B. Thompson on developing a theory of ideology closely yet subtly linked to the wider analysis of relations of domination within society. See esp *Studies in the Theory of Ideology op cit* note 50 *supra* ch 3. In this text Thompson identifies three main modalities through which ideological processes operate – legitimation, dissimulation and reification (see esp 130–131). In a later article he suggests fragmentation (of meaning) as a fourth modality. J. Thompson 'Language and Ideology: a framework for analysis' (1987) 38 *Soc Review* 516 at 521. Legitimation appears to be a general category within which the other modalities may be subsumed. Dissimulation and reification are dealt with in the text. The process of fragmentation of meaning is not of direct relevance to the present argument, as we are here concerned with the ideological currency of relatively clearly formulated ideas (i.e. ideas capable of providing a sense of the core meaning of the constitution) which are in social circulation rather than with the ideological implications of ideational themes which themselves lack a clear apparent meaning, and indeed whose ideological potential rests on that very fact. However, given the unsystematic foundations of our constitutional order the idea of fragmentation of meaning is clearly of more general relevance in understanding the ideological dimension of the British constitution. This area has recently been explored in an imaginative manner by M. Foley

through his development of a theory of constitutional abeyances. M. Foley *op cit* note 2 *supra*.
124.   *The English Constitution* Fontana (1963 RHS Crossman intro).
125.   *The Enchanted Glass: Britain and its Monarchy* Radius (1988) esp ch 4.
126.   J.B. Thompson *op cit* note 50 *supra* 131.
127.   *Ibid.*
128.   I. Harden and N. Lewis 'The Noble Lie: A Rejoinder' *op cit* note 117 *supra* 816.
129.   *Ibid.*
130.   See e.g. N. Luhmann 'The Self-Reproduction of the Law and its Limits' in G. Teubner (Ed) *Dilemmas of Law in the Welfare State* De Gruyter (1985).
131.   E.P. Pashukanis *Law and Marxism. A General Theory* Ink Links (1978 C. Arthur Ed). A useful and largely supportive overview of Pashukanis's work is provided by R. Kinsey 'Marxism and the Law' (1978) 5 *Br Jl of Law and Society* 202.
132.   The theory of legal autopoeisis recently developed by Niklas Luhmann and Gunther Teubner, *inter alios*, has attracted a great deal of interest within socio-legal studies generally as a perspective which, while rejecting a crudely instrumentalist stance, retains a significant co-ordinating role for law within the highly differentiated framework of modern society. See G. Teubner 'After Legal Instrumentalism? Strategic Models of Post-Regulatory Law' (1984) 12 *Int Jl of the Sociology of Law* 375 – 400; reprinted in amended form in G. Teubner (Ed) *op cit* note 130 *supra*. See more generally the essays in this collection and in G. Teubner (Ed) *Autopoietic Law: A New Approach to Law and Society* De Gruyter (1988).
133.   *Op cit* note 131 *supra*.
134.   L. Fuller *The Morality of Law* Yale U P (rev ed 1969) ch 2.
135.   J. Raz *The Authority of Law: Essays on Law and Morality* Clarendon Press (1979) ch 11.
136.   D. Sciulli 'Foundations of societal constitutionalism: principles from the concepts of communicative action and procedural legality' (1988) XXXIX *Br Jl of Sociology* 377.
137.   D. Beyleveld and R. Brownsword *Law as a Moral Judgement* Sweet & Maxwell (1986) ch 7. For a more recent elaboration of their general position see D. Beyleveld and R. Brownsword 'Normative Positivism: The Mirage of the Middle-Way' (1989) 9 OJLS 463. The general thrust of Gewirth's position is set out in A Gewirth *Reason and Morality* Chicago U P (1978).
138.   G. Marshall 'Power And Liberty In The Anglo-American Constitution' (1989) 40 NILQ 213 at 220.
139.   A landmark study in 'taking rights seriously' from a socialist perspective is T. Campbell *The Left and Rights* Routledge (1983). A fine example of a considered rejection is R. Bellamy 'Liberal Rights and Socialist Goals' Unpublished Paper delivered to the Fourteenth World Congress of the International Association for Philosophy of Law and Social Philosophy University of Edinburgh 17 – 23 August 1989.
140.   Recent outstanding works in the liberal tradition include M.J. Sandel *Liberalism and the Limits of Justice* Cambridge U P (1982); R. Dworkin *A Matter of Principle* Oxford U P (1985) esp chs 8 – 11; J. Raz *The Morality Of Freedom* Clarendon Press (1986).
141.   See e.g. K. Graham 'Liberalism and Liberty: the Fragility of a Tradition' in A. Phillips Griffiths (Ed) *op cit* note 54 *supra* 207 at 213 – 215.
142.   See e.g. K. Graham *ibid* 215 – 216; B. Barry 'How Not to Defend Liberal Institutions' (1990) 20 *Br Jl of Political Science* 1.
143.   See e.g. the anarchist critique of liberalism set out by R.P. Wolff *In Defense of Anarchism* Harper and Row (2nd ed 1976).
144.   See e.g. B. Crick *Socialism* Open U P (1987).
145.   See e.g. F.A. Hayek *Rules and Order* Routledge 1973.
146.   See e.g. M. Krygier 'Weber, Lenin and the reality of socialism' in E.

Kamenka and M. Krygier (Eds) *Bureaucracy* Edward Arnold (1979) 61.

147. See e.g. D. Held *op cit* note 2 *supra* ch 5 esp 163–167.

148. See the discussions in R. Bellamy *op cit* note 139 *supra*; N. Lacey *op cit* note 6 *supra*; Lord McLuskey *op cit* note 20 *supra*; L. Lustgarten 'Socialism and the Rule of Law' (1988) 15 *Br Jl of Law and Society* 25 esp 31–32.

149. See e.g. L. Lustgarten *ibid*; R. Bellamy *ibid*; T. Campbell *op cit* note 139 *supra*.

150. Consider e.g. Dennis Galligan's penetrating analysis of the relationship between different conceptions of the scope and purpose of state power on the one hand and the continuing requirement for balance between rule-based and discretion-based manifestations of such power on the other; D. Galligan *Discretionary Powers: A legal study of Official Discretion* Clarendon Press (1986) esp ch 2.

151. Consider e.g. the definitive study by L. Fuller 'The Forms and Limits of Adjudication' (1978) 78 *Harv L R* 353. See also J. Jowell 'The Rule of Law Today' in J. Jowell and D. Oliver (Eds) *op cit* note 5 *supra*.

152. Consider e.g. David Marquand's analysis of the resonance of the 'ideology of centralism' with a variety of different visions within our existing political culture and the equally wide-ranging potential appeal of certain suggested forms and techniques of dispersal of power; D. Marquand 'Regional devolution' in J. Jowell and D. Oliver (Eds) *op cit* note 5 *supra*.

153. Consider e.g. Peter Cane's examination of the various boundaries within our system of law between public and private dimensions and of how this 'complex set of distinctions' (at 78) may be viewed from the perspective of different political theories; P. Cane 'Public Law and Private Law: A Study of the Analysis and Use of a Legal Concept' in J. Eekelaar and J. Bell *Oxford Essays in Jurisprudence* 3rd Series Clarendon Press (1987) 57–58.

154. The charge of failing to address seriously questions of *praxis* is one which, for example, has been levelled against exponents of the limited government thesis. See note 62 *supra* and accompanying text. See also Michael Elliott's criticism of suggestions such as that of G.W. Jones that administrative structures operating outwith the ambit of direct ministerial control should be wound up, as having 'an air of almost pathetic unreality' in the prevailing political climate. M. Elliott *op cit* note 3 *supra* 27; commenting upon G.W. Jones 'An Answer: Stand up for Ministerial Responsibility' (1987) 65 *Public Administration* 87.

155. J. Rawls 'The Idea of an Overlapping Consensus' (1987) 7 OJLS 1.

156. See e.g. N. Lacey *op cit* note 6 *supra*; R Bellamy *op cit* note 139 *supra*; S. Lukes 'Can a Marxist believe in Human Rights?' (1982) 1 *Praxis International* 334.

157. N. Lacey *op cit* note 6 *supra* 40.

158. J. Rawls *op cit* note 155 *supra* 18–19.

159. P. Selznick 'The Idea of a Communitarian Morality' (1987) 75 *Calif L R* 45 at 451.

160. *Op cit* note 155 *supra* 23.

161. It should be emphasised that many theorists who view the middle ground as a staging post nevertheless take questions of *praxis* very seriously. The search for concrete mechanisms of political advancement is a pervasive theme throughout the recent socialist writings on law cited in note 44 *supra*. In a similar vein, their assiduous attention to the specification of an ideal conception of the rule of law notwithstanding. Harden and Lewis devote considerable space to questions of immediate institutional redesign. See *The Noble Lie op cit* note 116 *supra* esp chs 8–10 and 'The Noble Lie: A Rejoinder' *op cit* note 117 *supra* 816.

162. J. Dunn *op cit* note 122 *supra* 154.

163. *Ibid* 189.

Institutions

The High Priests of the Mystery:
A Note on Two Centuries of Parliamentary Draftsmen

A.G. Donaldson

A. By way of preamble

The words in the first part of the title have been applied to the exponents of parliamentary sovereignty.[1] Here the phrase is used to describe the practitioners of another art, the drafting of parliamentary bills by lawyers in official posts, who may be regarded as using their skills in the exercise of sovereignty.[2]

As for the second part of the title, the reference to drafting is to be construed as including work done by parliamentary counsel or parliamentary draftsmen, however designated. The latter term has the advantage of relating to the three jurisdictions in the United Kingdom as well as those outside it. For convenience, the rules as to gender enshrined in Brougham's Act and the Interpretation Acts are used to include those female lawyers who were or are members of the drafting offices, a development which commenced over half a century ago.[3] They are the high priestesses of the mystery, equal in skill and learning. On another point of interpretation, a liberty has been taken with the definition of time, for the two centuries in the title cover an extra two decades.

By way of a purpose statement, this note does not purport to examine in detail the drafts produced by the draftsmen. Rather it seeks to give an impressionistic survey of the organisation of drafting, together with some references to those who did the drafting, progressing from quill pen to word processor.

B. The first of the few

The extended two centuries run from 1769, with a natural division at 1869, but it is worthwhile to cast a backward eighteenth-century glance. By 1752 Robert Yeates, a Commons clerk, was being paid an additional allowance 'for drawing up and preparing sundry bills to be laid before the House' and in 1759 he was additionally appointed a Treasury clerk 'to do all the Parliamentary business'. Yeates's position was summed up in Lambert's work *Bills and Acts* (on legislative procedure in eighteenth-century England) as 'effectively the first Parliamentary Counsel to the Treasury', doing all the Treasury drafting.[4] That lower case 'f' is significant, for although

Yeates was not of Parliamentary Counsel he was obviously a parliamentary draftsman and as such he is clearly one of the forerunners of the present-day draftsmen.

First on the nominal roll was Danby Pickering, barrister, bencher, Reader and Treasurer of Gray's Inn, whose edition of the *Statutes at Large* is both a source of knowledge and a pleasure to handle. In 1769 he turned from editing statutes to drafting them, being appointed by the Lords Commissioners of the Treasury 'to do the parliamentary business of this office performed by the late Mr Yeates with a salary of £600 a year'.[5] (Another appointment for parliamentary work was that of a Parliamentary Agent to the Treasury.) As the first Parliamentary Counsel to the Treasury, Pickering heads the list in Sainty's *Treasury Officials 1660–1870*.[6] There is a short entry for Pickering in the *Dictionary of National Biography*, but it concentrates on his editing of legal works and makes no mention of his position as Parliamentary Counsel.[7] Nevertheless, he started the first century of Parliamentary Counsel, leading up to the 1869 inauguration of the Office in its present form.

Pickering held office for over eleven years, being succeeded on his death in 1781 by Francis Hargrave. Hargrave had in 1772 'attained considerable prominence at the bar in the *habeas corpus* case of the negro, James Somersett'.[8] Like his predecessor, Hargrave was a prolific legal author and editor, and in 1788 he ventured to publish some anonymous views on the Regency question. Lambert suggests that this publication may have led to his leaving office, but also suggests that his duties as Parliamentary Counsel did not rank highly among his tasks.[9]

The third Parliamentary Counsel was William Lowndes, a friend of Pitt the Younger. Lowndes succeeded Hargrave in 1789; he did not lay down his drafting pen when he was appointed Chief Commissioner of Taxes in 1798, but continued to draw Bills, though after Pitt's death in 1806 he confined himself to tax and Irish Bills. Thus he was first Counsel and then draftsman, but in the former office he had asked for assistance for forthcoming work, that very natural plea easily recognisable by draftsmen.[10] The request was granted and so began a lengthy career in the drafting of Treasury and other Bills.

The appointee was William Harrison, then a special pleader under the bar, who was in work for several years without salary and to have the reversion of Lowndes's post when the latter became chairman of a board. (Had Sir Walter Scott learned of this arrangement he could have drawn an analogy with his clerkship in the Court of Session.) Thus it happened that Harrison became Parliamentary Counsel to the Treasury in 1798, holding office until his death in 1841. Ilbert, in the chapter on 'Preparation of Acts' in his *Legislative Methods and Forms* was somewhat dismissive of Harrison's work, but he drew on the 1833 *Report on House of Commons Offices and Fees*[11] to summarise something of Harrison's work. Harrison said that he had drafted tax and Army Bills before the French Revolution and had been called to the bar in 1800, but because of the pressure of public business had been forbidden to go on circuit. By the time he gave his 1833 evidence his duties were to draft all Treasury Bills, but he had drawn bills for the Foreign Office, the Colonial Office and the Home Office as well; he was also Law Clerk to the War Office. An interesting part of his evidence was his description of his work, which is an early (if not the first) example of its kind: 'I receive the Minute of Instructions from the Chancellor of the Exchequer; I put the Minute into heads, with details for revision and approbation, and I then prepare the Bill; and I attend meetings with the Law Officers, at his house, in consultations, not legal, but official consultations'.[12]

There is also a fuller exposition of Counsel's duties. It came from Sir Thomas Tomlins, a member of the Inner Temple who in 1801 became counsel to the Chief Secretary for Ireland and parliamentary counsel to the Irish Chancellor of the Exchequer.[13] When the Irish exchequer was abolished in 1816 Tomlins became an Assistant Counsel attached to the Treasury 'with special responsibility for Irish business and a salary of £400 per year',[14] a position which he held until 1831. Tomlins's description of his duties is a pointed one. As set out in Parris's *Constitutional Bureaucracy* they are classified as drawing government and revenue Bills; settling Bills prepared by departmental counsel or officials; advising on the necessity of introducing Bills; preparing resolutions for the introduction of revenue Bills; attending the progress of his Bills 'from the first introduction into Parliament to the final passing', and preparing committee and other amendments; and advising on the construction of the statute and common law, including similarities and differences between the Irish law and that of Great Britain. The enumeration of duties concludes with what was surely a heartfelt cry: 'Answering in writing or verbally (and immediately) all questions and references relating to any point of law on any subject whatever.'[15] Add to this description the need to be in attendance during sessions at a moment's notice, and generally to be ready to be speedily sent for; a six- to eight-hour day during the session, and drafting during the recess; the preparation of an annual index of the statutes in force in Ireland and of the sessional report on expiring laws,[16] and it will be seen that Tomlins did not have an idle pen. Indeed, the tenor of his description may well sound familiar to later ears.

So much for this brief sketch of Parliamentary Counsel to the Treasury in their first incarnation, which lasted from Pickering's appointment in 1769 to Harrison's death in 1841. The period cut a swathe through British history, but for over seventy years the Treasury was served by only four Parliamentary Counsel, of whom Harrison set a record for longevity in drafting. But the arrangements were to change and the reincarnation of Parliamentary Counsel was not to take place for over a quarter of a century.

C. The Interregnum

Ilbert thought that Harrison's office fell into abeyance about 1837, at a time when the Home Secretary was responsible for the most important government legislation,[17] but Sainty chronicles the new arrangements for drafting Treasury Bills by saying:

On the death of the then holder in 1841 the office was discontinued and in 1842 it was provided that the work of drafting bills for the

Treasury and a number of other departments should be undertaken by the Parliamentary Counsel to the Home Office. The Home Office Counsel remained the principal government draftsman until 1869 when the office of Parliamentary Counsel to the Treasury was revived.[18]

As this quotation indicates, the 1842 arrangement was a measure of centralisation. An indication has already been given of Parliamentary Counsel drafting Bills other than for the Treasury. As for departmental drafting, Parris points to James Stephen, counsel to the Colonial Office and the Board of Trade, drafting a Truck Bill and one on clergy salaries; and to William Gregson at the Home Office, who assisted with the 1832 Reform Bill. But Parris also points out that after the 1842 arrangements others outside the Home Office were involved in drawing Bills. For example, the Counsel to the Speaker, James Booth, helped to draft the 1845 Clauses Acts; and in 1849 Romilly, the Attorney-General, was superintending the drawing of a Public Health Bill for London.[19] So the 1842 system did not entirely supersede the work of departmental draftsmen. As to that, Sir James Fitzjames Stephen provided an example of the work of his father at the Colonial Office when called upon to draft an Act relating to the slave trade: 'The act 5 Geo. 4, c.113 was drawn by my father, and was dictated by him in one day and at one sitting. It consists of fifty-two sections, and fills twenty-three closely printed octavo pages. Many of the sections are most elaborate.'[20]

Again, the *Dictionary of National Biography* records of Stephen that:
When abolition (of slavery) became inevitable, he was called upon to prepare the measures passed in 1833. Unless it could be drawn at once the abolition might be postponed for a year. He therefore on this occasion (and on one other only) broke the Sabbath; and between the noons of Saturday and Monday dictated an elaborate bill of sixty-six sections.[21]

Clearly the drawing of Bills, then as now, could necessitate personal sacrifices on the part of the draftsman.

D. The state of the statute law

For a quarter of a century, from the 1830s to the 1850s, there was a burst of activity in general consideration of the statute law. To veer a little from the chosen course of this note a brief look at this activity will show how it developed in parallel with the work of the official draftsman; indeed, there are some parallels between the personalities involved. This aspect of the statute law forms part of a series of activities which has been traced back at least as far as Francis Bacon and which has not yet ended.

Taking the relevant bodies chronologically, there was the Royal Commission which Brougham instigated in 1833 to digest the statute and common law relating to crimes, and to consider consolidation of other branches of the law. Then there was the Select Committee on Public Bills, reporting in 1836 with important evidence. Between 1845 and 1849 another Commission worked on the criminal law, producing a digest, and a report on criminal procedure. To assist Cranworth in his project for a comprehensive Code Victoria a Statute Law Board was constituted in 1853 and reported on revision and consolidation, being succeeded in 1854 by a Statute Law Commission consisting mainly of judges and law officers and reporting in the next five years on consolidation, the scrutiny of Bills, the classification of statutes and the registration of statutes in force. Finally in this sequence came the 1857 Select Committee, set up to consider the 1854 Commission's second report so far as it related to the improvement of 'the Manner and Language of Current Legislation'. Thus the twin concerns of these various bodies were the revision and consolidation of the statutes, and the language of the statute law.[22]

Three men associated with these bodies show something of the work involved. The first was Henry Bellenden Ker, whose career was epitomised by Sir Cecil Carr in *A Victorian Law Reformer's Correspondence*. Ker,[23] a Lincoln's Inn conveyancer and a friend of Brougham, sat on the 1833 Commission whose work Brougham introduced as a Bill in 1845. Giving evidence to the 1836 Committee he urged consolidation to improve drafting style and the use of full-time draftsmen. As a member of the 1853 Statute Law Board he preferred consolidation to revision, and recommended scrutiny of Bills in Parliament. Ker was the sole paid commissioner on the 1854 Commission, which also reported in favour of scrutiny, and in giving evidence to the 1857 Select Committee he dealt both with statutory language and the need for scrutiny. Given his assistance to Cranworth with legal Bills, and his drafting of Bills dealing with the Privy Council, Ker justly deserved the title of Victorian law reformer.

A second figure, an attorney with an interest in legislation, was Arthur Symonds, who was rescued from the obscurity of the Parliamentary papers by Sir Cecil Carr in an article on 'The Mechanics of Law-making',[24] using the title of a work which Symonds published in 1835. This examined legislative style and proposed practical remedies, such as uniform language, short sentences and single-proposition paragraphs, and, especially, an Interpretation Act.[25] Symonds was another witness before the 1836 Select Committee and in 1838 laid before Parliament papers on the drawing of acts and the use of uniform language. He worked on the classification of Private Acts for the Board of Trade but fell out with his collaborator, James Booth, who went on to produce the 1845 Clauses Acts. But, like Ker, Symonds was concerned with the particularities as well as the generalities of the statute law.

Thirdly, there was George Coode, an Inner Templar, who was a sub-commissioner of the 1853 Statute Law Board, preparing papers on consolidation, and who gave evidence to the 1857 Select Committee. The remit of legislative language was appropriate, for fifteen years previously Coode had written his paper on 'Legislative Expression' incorporated in the 1843 report of the Poor Law Commissioners on Local Taxation. For Coode, legislative expression depended on the legislative sentence, composed of the legal subject, the legal action, the case confining the legal action and the operative conditions for the legal action. This basic analysis would produce more well-expressed provisions, since it was based on ordinary English and could therefore be easily understood.[26] A feature of Coode's work is its capacity to survive, for it went from a separate London edition in 1845 through editions in Philadelphia and Nova Scotia to current reprints in the standard Canadian work on legislative drafting and in a work on conveyancing drafting.[27]

In sum, it was the work of these bodies and of law reformers such as these which paved the way for the Statute Law Revision Acts, the *Statutes Revised* and those indispensable weapons in the draftsman's armoury, the *Index to the Statutes* and the *Chronological Table of Statutes in Force*.

E. The chief priest

Reverting to the sequence of official draftsmen, the interregnum at the Home Office lasted from 1841 to 1869, during which period there were three Home Office Counsel. J.E.D. Bethune left in 1848 to become legal member of the Governor-General's Council at Calcutta. He was succeeded by Walter Coulson, who had a connection with the statute law reform bodies just described in that he was a member of the 1854 Statute Law Commission and gave evidence to the 1857 Select Committee.[28] But for the present purpose the outstanding name was that of Coulson's successor in 1861, best known in the latter part of the nineteenth century and afterwards as a master draftsman. He was Henry Thring.

The first-hand evidence for Thring's interest in drafting and his experience of it comes from the introduction to the second edition of his *Practical Legislation*.[29] His classical education fostered his interest in language and after he became a member of the Inner Temple in 1845 he apparently preferred legislation to conveyancing. He read the work of Coode and of others, concluding that Bills might have a degree of uniformity, that the arrangement of clauses could be made logical and that 'the form of expressing the enactments might also be made the subject of regulation'. In 1850 he tried his prentice hand on a Colonial Bill and, after drafting the Bill for the 1853 Succession Act, was able to put his drafting principles into practice in the Merchant Shipping Act 1854, arranging the clauses logically and drawing them in accordance with Coode's views. So it was no tyro who became Counsel to the Home Office, starting a career of which he said 'for the remainder of my official life I was occupied almost entirely in preparing legislation'.[30]

Ilbert says of Thring's stay at the Home Office that he 'appears to have drawn all the most important measures of his time', which is certainly in keeping with the 1841 arrangements.[31] And Thring gives an example of something mentioned earlier in this note, the occasional need for very quick drafting. This arose with the Bill for the Representation of the People Act, where Thring had commented unfavourably on a draft and was then instructed by Disraeli on Thursday, March 14 that the Bill was to be entirely redrafted and to be ready for Saturday, March 16. Thring's account continues:

> Accordingly next day I took the Bill in hand, and working with two shorthand-writers from ten to six, I completed it. The Bill was printed during the night and was laid before the Cabinet on Saturday. It was considered on Monday by Mr Disraeli; he personally instructed me

in the matter and the Bill was circulated to the House of Commons on Tuesday.'

Even allowing for the fact that in the previous year he had drafted a Franchise Bill which did not become law, this was, as Thring aptly described it, a *tour de force*.

In 1868 Thring was appointed to the newly-created Statute Law Committee by Lord Cairns, thus commencing his lengthy membership. But an even more important appointment was in store for him the following year.

F. Parliamentary Counsel Office

The previous paragraphs have provided some hints at the need to reorganise the arrangements for drafting Government Bills. Counsel at the Treasury, the various departments and the Home Office had all been involved, together with other members of the bar, but there was need for change. Ilbert summarised the position thus:

> It was found that as the number of Bills increased, different Departments employed independent counsel to draw their Bills, while other Bills were drawn by Departmental officers without legal aid. This system, or want of system, was far from satisfactory. The cost was great; for barristers employed 'by the job' were entitled to charge fees on the scale customary in private Parliamentary practice. There was no security for uniformity of language, style, or arrangement, in laws which were intended to find their place in a common Statute Book. Nor was there any security for uniformity of principle in measures for which the Government was collectively responsible. Different Departments introduced inconsistent Bills, and there was no adequate means by which the Prime Minister, or the Cabinet as a whole, could exercise effective control over measures fathered by individual Ministers. And lastly, there was no check on the financial consequences of legislation. There was nothing to prevent any Minister from introducing a Bill which would impose a heavy charge on the Exchequer, and upset the Chancellor of the Exchequer's Budget calculations for the year.[33]

The arrangement devised by Robert Lowe, Gladstone's Chancellor of the Exchequer, for the drafting of government Bills was the creation of a central office responsible to the Treasury and thus to the Chancellor of the Exchequer and to the Prime Minister as First Lord of the Treasury. So it was two months after Lowe's entering the Cabinet that he and Gladstone signed the minute constituting the Office of the Parliamentary Counsel to the Treasury, so that on 8 February 1869 Thring became the Parliamentary Counsel. The name had been revived, the function had been extended and the new line of succession had begun.

The 1869 minute instituted a familiar pattern of activity. Parliamentary Counsel were to be full-time, being prohibited from private practice. They were to settle departmental Bills, and draw and settle other government Bills as the Treasury might require, acting on written instructions sent by heads of departments through the Treasury. The remit did not extend to Scottish and Irish Bills, though as matters turned out there was a variation on this theme. Counsel could be required to advise on Bills and Acts which they had drawn, and to report on Private Members' Bills, but they were dispensed from attending parliamentary committees. The legislative word and its creation were to predominate.

Before turning to the Office in its reincarnation, mention of Scotland and Ireland prompts a reference to some parallel developments in those jurisdictions.

G. Scotland and Ireland

The 1975 Renton Report on *The Preparation of Legislation* summarised the developing drafting of Scottish Bills by suggesting that prior to the Union of 1707 this work was done by the Lord Advocate and the Lords of Session, and that from the Union until 1871 drafting was done *ad hoc* by private practitioners.[35] Other hands at work were those of the Crown Agent and the Solicitor-General for Scotland. For instance, when Henry Cockburn became Solicitor-General for Scotland in December 1831 he was immediately summoned to a Cabinet committee on Scottish parliamentary reform. That his pen was usefully employed is shown by the statement that when the draft of the Scottish Reform Bill was completed the following September it was 'mainly Cockburn's handiwork'.[36]

Then, in 1871, two years after the Parliamentary Counsel Office was set up, a Parliamentary Draftsman for Scotland was appointed, but the post lapsed after four years, so that private practitioners were still involved. Other drafting was done by the Legal Secretary to the Lord Advocate, but the holders of this post varied from Lord Advocate to Lord Advocate, and Scottish Bills tended to be drafted by officials in the Scottish Office. (Also, Scottish Bills had to be scrutinised by Parliamentary Counsel.) The drafting arrangements were rationalised in 1925 when Sir Marshall Millar Craig, the then Legal Secretary, became draftsman, thus giving the Scottish Parliamentary Draftsmen and Lord Advocate's Legal Secretaries their present status and function.[37]

As for Ireland, the shade of Sir Thomas Tomlins has already been evoked. Another Irish draftsman was Hugo Marmaduke O'Hanlon, who became Counsel to the Irish Office shortly after the Union with Ireland in 1801 and who gave evidence to the 1836 Committee on Public Bills, supporting the use of lawyers as draftsmen, defending the existing drafting style as aimed at clarity and precision, but favouring classification and short titles.

Then at some point before 1866 a Draftsman of Bills was appointed to the Office of the Chief Secretary for Ireland; he had five successors. The draftsman's duties, stated in 1876 and later expanded, included the preparation and adaptation of government Bills relating to Ireland, the preparation or examination of amendments, and attendance in Parliament on Ministers in charge of Irish Bills 'during their second reading and every subsequent stage'.[38] The link with Parliamentary Counsel was set out in detail:

> It is of great importance that uniformity of practice in the preparation of bills or amendments should be followed by the draftsman of the Irish Office and the gentlemen who perform the same work for other departments of the Government. The draftsman therefore will be in

constant communication with these gentlemen in order to secure this agreement, and will, in the course of such communication, have due regard to the superior position and authority of Parliamentary Counsel.[39]

Given this formal basis the relationship between counsel and draftsman developed – and continues – harmoniously, as may be instanced by the fact that the last holder of the office of Draftsman of Bills to the Irish Office, Sir Francis Nugent Greer, was appointed in 1908, continued his association with the Parliamentary Counsel Office after the passing of the Government of Ireland Act 1920 by becoming a member of it.

The constitutional changes in the 1920 and 1922 period brought out the need for new drafting arrangements. The government of Northern Ireland recruited Arthur Scott Quekett (who was knighted in 1922), who had been Inspector of Bills for the Local Government Board for Ireland, and who had published some of his academic researches in administrative law. In addition to his drafting work on Northern Ireland and Westminster Bills Quekett published a commentary on Northern Ireland's constitution.[40] His twenty-five year tenure of office as Parliamentary Counsel founded what is now the Office of the Legislative Draftsmen in Belfast.

In the newly-constituted Irish Free State the government employed for its drafting Arthur Matheson, a Chancery practitioner at the Irish Bar, who was the founding father of the Office of the Parliamentary Draftsman in Dublin.[41] (There is a possible parallel between the Dublin draftsmen, whose office is linked with the Attorney General, and the Scottish draftsmen in the Lord Advocate's Department, in that both come under the aegis of a law officer.)

H. To the end of the reign

Something of the work of the Parliamentary Counsel Office can be gleaned from some pieces of anecdotal history, both selective and illustrative. The recurring Irish theme is due to the fact that the political and financial implications of some Irish bills brought them within the scope of Parliamentary Counsel's work.[42]

In the first year of the Office's existence Thring had to draw the Bill for the disestablishment of the Irish Church; he subsequently gave a sketch of his experience of working with Gladstone:

Mr Gladstone's was the most constructive intellect with which I was ever brought into contact and also the most untiring in its devotion to its subject. He understood and revised every word of a Bill and even settled the marginal notes. Once only had we any discussion as to the arrangement of a Bill. I wished to put in one short clause at the very commencement, a sentence disestablishing the Irish Church. Mr Gladstone disapproved and I was about to accept his instructions when Lord Granville interfered, saying, 'Had you not better pay attention to the draftsman's suggestions?' Whereupon Mr Gladstone gave way and the proposed clause appeared at the beginning of the Bill.[43]

Thring contrasted Gladstone's approach with that of Disraeli, saying of the latter's management of the Bill for the Representation of the People Act

1867 (Thring's *tour de force*) that ' [h] e seemed to have an intuitive perception of what would pass the House of Commons, but he cared nothing for the details of a Bill, and once satisfied with the principle of a Bill, he troubled comparatively little about its arrangement or its construction.' Here the draftsman's self-critical responsibility must be even greater than usual.

Thring gave another example of working with Gladstone on mainly verbal instructions for the Bill for the Irish Land Act 1870, where the draftsman did not hesitate to say 'This will not do', whereupon Gladstone 'would then stand up and make me a little speech urging his view of the case; I then replied shortly till the point was settled'. Except possibly for its description of the length of the discussions this could be applied in principle to the drawing of almost any Bill.

Thring was made KCB in 1873 and in the following year, perhaps by way of light relief, he published in the *Quarterly Review* an article on simplification of the law in which he urged the revision and consolidation of the statutes and proposed the creation of a Privy Council for Law, to superintend the reform of the law, but not its administration. (Ninety years later the constitution of the Law Commissions was in line with Thring's general ideas.) It was in this article, later printed separately, that there appeared the frequently quoted phrase that 'Bills are made to pass, no less than the razors mentioned by the poet were made to sell.' More than a century was to pass before the phrase was identified and elucidated by one of Thring's successors, as will be mentioned later. And in 1875 Thring gave evidence to the Select Committee on Acts of Parliament, of which Robert Lowe (the founder of the Parliamentary Counsel Office) was a member. The Office had been in existence for a mere six years, but Thring would presumably have agreed with the Committee's conclusion that the drafting style had improved, with arrangement of clauses, sub-division into parts and increased simplicity and clarity of language, and with the general statement that 'the difficulty is, and always will be to reconcile together the symmetry of legislation on the one hand with the independence of Parliament on the other', a fair summary of the draftsman's dilemma.

With the publication of *Practical Legislation* in 1879 Thring put into permanent form his instructions to draftsmen used in the Office with its four-fold division into 'getting up the subject', arrangement, the composition of sentences and the formal provisions of Acts. Much has been written since about drafting and by draftsmen in different jurisdictions but this is a landmark.

A final extract from Thring's reminiscences illustrates another feature of drafting time: not the short day, but the long years. As he put it:

> The Army Act of 1881, like the siege of Troy, took ten years before it was brought to a conclusion. Instructions were given to me by Mr Cardwell in 1867; a Bill was prepared but was not proceeded with; in 1872 the subject was revived and a complete scheme was prepared for consolidating the Mutiny Act and the Articles of War. This scheme was partially considered by the War Office in 1873. It was then again laid aside till 1877 when a short interval of discussion occurred, after which it was once more shelved until 1878, when a select committee

was appointed to consider the Bill. This committee gave a general approval to the Bill, and in 1879 an almost identical measure was at last introduced into Parliament and passed.[44]

The fact that the explanatory documents alone came to 1067 folio pages gives some indication of the time, space and energy required by this piece of legislation.

The relationship between the Office and the Irish Office is illustrated by events succeeding the murder in 1882 in the Phoenix Park, Dublin, of the Chief Secretary for Ireland, Lord Frederick Cavendish, and his Under-Secretary, T.H. Burke. On the evening of May 11 the Home Secretary, Sir William Harcourt, introduced a Prevention of Crimes Bill for Ireland, to constitute judicial tribunals sitting without juries, and to extend the powers of arrest and search. The background to this piece of speedy legislation was set out in a note by Lord James of Hereford:

> The Bill of 1882 was designed, and on the stocks, during the month of April. I saw F. Cavendish as to some of its details almost immediately before his starting for Ireland. As Chief Secretary he discussed with me the provisions the Bill should contain. On Sunday, May 7, 1882, when the news of F. Cavendish's murder became known, I went to see Harcourt. He begged me to see that the drawing of the Bill was hurried on. About 2 o'clock I went to the Irish Office, and found the Irish Attorney-General hard at work on the Bill. The first draft of it was then in print. No doubt F. Cavendish's death tended to affect the subsequent framing of the Bill. Harcourt came upon the scenes. T and J were called to the assistance of the Irish draftsmen, and no doubt the Bill was rendered stronger in consequence of the events of May 6.[45]

The names in the cast list for this drafting drama are easily identified. The author of the note, Sir Henry James, was then Attorney-General. The Attorney-General for Ireland was William Moore Johnson, who in the following year became a judge of the Queen's Bench Division in Ireland. The Irish Office Draftsman at the time was W.F. Cullinan, who published an edition of the *Irish Statutes Revised*. The identity of 'T' does not require much detection, while 'J' was Jenkyns, the Assistant Parliamentary Counsel. In such a crisis this was more than a meeting of minds; it was a collection of drafting skills.

In 1886 Thring retired, full of years and honours, most notably the peerage which was conferred on him. (This distinction, rare among well-known actors, is so far unique among draftsmen.) In his retirement he was not divorced from the statute law, being active on the Statute Law Committee. His almost jaunty appearance in a 1893 *Vanity Fair* cartoon shows someone who was neither withered nor condemned by lengthy dealings with the statutes.

Jenkyns was Thring's successor as the Parliamentary Counsel, having been Assistant Parliamentary Counsel since the Office was founded. Just as Thring, in his last year of office, had been involved with Gladstone's first Bill for Irish Home Rule, so Jenkyns was concerned with the second Home Rule Bill in 1893, and there is some evidence of his acuity and

assiduity. In the previous year he advised on the Cabinet consideration and
the circulation of the draft; in 1893 he hoped that Gladstone 'would spare
himself; his speeches roused the Opposition, and raised unnecessary points';
John Morley, the Chief Secretary for Ireland, described how, when the Bill
was in the Commons, Jenkyns, Rigby (then Solicitor-General) and he would
wrestle with clauses, and how Mr Gladstone would 'pick up the paper of
amendments, put on his glasses, make up his mind in the twinkling of an
eye with little thought of outlying consequences from a concession here,
a refusal there.' After Jenkyns' death Morley wrote to Ilbert a lengthy tribute
containing the following phrases:

a consummate master of his trade

His vast experience had given him an acute insight into the points which
might be raised against you in the House . . .

I have seen him more than once stand against Mr Gladstone's driving
power (which was no joke) . . .

His powers of toil were immense, his industry unflagging . . . [H] e
was using an active, vigorous, and searching mind all the time.

[H] is cheerfulness of accost, his unsparing energy, and his supreme
competency in each of the thousand matters in hand, gave perpetual
animation to the company of the most admirable of civil servants.[46]

An outsize tombstone or a large memorial plaque would be needed to record
these sentiments, but in view of the comments often made about draftsmen
it is worth noting this piece of posthumous praise.

After Jenkyns' death in 1899 the third holder of the office of Parliamentary
Counsel was Courtenay Peregrine Ilbert, without whose extra-statutory
writings several of the propositions in this essay would lack authority. He
had assisted Thring with the Bills for the Statute Law Revision Act 1881
and the Civil Procedure Act 1883, and had then gone as legal member of
the Governor-General's Council at Calcutta, where he had been engaged
in the preparation of legislation. On his return he became Assistant
Parliamentary Counsel to Jenkyns at the end of 1866.[47] (His KCSI in 1895
was the first Indian knighthood conferred on a member of the Office, the
second being Sir John Rowlatt's KCIE for his work on the Indian
Independence Act 1947.) Whereas Thring's tenure was seventeen years and
Jenkyns' thirteen, Ilbert's tenure was a short three years. Having published
his *Legislative Methods and Forms* in 1901, in the following year he left the
Treasury and went to Whitehall to become Clerk to the House of Commons.
Yet he did not lose interest in his work as draftsman, for he combined it
and his experience as Clerk in his Carpentier Lectures at Columbia
University, which he published in 1914 under the title *The Mechanics of
Law Making*.

Drawing to some extent on his earlier work, Ilbert dealt comprehensively
with his subject (which, as Sir Cecil Carr pointed out, had the same title
as Arthur Symonds' 1835 publication). In outlining the duties of a
government draftsman he explained about the conferences on a Bill at which
ministers, officials and the draftsmen were present, and where the
draftsman's concern was with more than legislative language, for he had

to provide the statutory background and to ask awkward questions. He said, 'I look back on some of those conferences as some of the most interesting and instructive experiences of my life'. Again, he described in detail a day in the life of a draftsman during the committee stage of a Bill, painting a picture which is still easily recognisable. Also, he argued that the creation of the Office had resulted in an improvement in the form of statutes.[48]

But Ilbert's greatest drafting achievement was the Interpretation Act 1889, of which he said:

> I was responsible for drafting this Act . . . . It embodies the definitions in Brougham's Act, and adds a great many other definitions and general rules of construction. I framed it on purely empirical lines. I got my clerks to make comprehensive lists of the numerous definitions to be found in Acts of Parliament, selected those which had been found by experience to be convenient and therefore had passed into common use, touched some of them up here and there where I thought them capable of improvement in form, and embodied them in the new Act. I believe the Act has been very useful, and it has certainly tended to uniformity of language. Special definitions are still often necessary, though in my opinion they should be sparingly used. But a vast number of special definitions which have been repeated again in particular Acts have disappeared from the modern English statute book.[49]

Obviously Ilbert was justly proud of his monument, which survived him by more than fifty years until it was replaced by the Interpretation Act 1978.

I. The next century

This bird's-eye view must be taken from a greater height to scan the drafting arrangements of the twentieth century, classifying them (in an attempt to apply the logic of Thring's principles) by mentioning the draftsmen, some of the evidence these draftsmen gave to official bodies and some of their extra-statutory writings. Given the numbers and the decades the scanning bird must have a selective eye.

The starting point is 1902, when Ilbert left the Office and Sir Mackenzie Chalmers, who had been Assistant Parliamentary Counsel since 1899, succeeded him. Chalmers's connection with the statute law had started earlier, around 1880, when Lord Herschell (as he became) encouraged him in drafting, the result being the Bills of Exchange Act 1882. As counsel to the Board of Trade he worked on the Bankruptcy Act 1883 and as a county court judge he worked for six years on the Bill for the Sale of Goods Act 1893. Then, like Ilbert, he had a three-year spell in the Viceroy's Council in India before entering the Office. His monumental drafting was done outside the Office, and his stay as its head was short, for he left after a year to become Permanent Under-Secretary at the Home Office, where he produced the Marine Insurance Act 1906, the third in the trinity of Chalmers's Acts.[50] After Chalmers, came Sir Arthur Thring (who might be thought of as 'Thring the Nephew' were it not impossible to think of 'Thring the Uncle')[51] and he was followed in 1917 by Sir Frederick Liddell. Next in line was Sir William Graham-Harrison who had joined the Office in 1903 as Assistant Parliamentary Counsel to Arthur Thring.

He was seconded to the National Insurance Commissioners in 1912 and became solicitor to the Customs and Excise in 1913, devising the Trading with the Enemy Act 1914. He rejoined the Office in 1917 as Second Parliamentary Counsel to Liddell, whose place he took in 1928.[52] Both in office and in retirement he expressed views on the statute law which are next to be considered.

J. Views official and unofficial

In giving evidence to the Donoughmore-Scott Committee on Ministers' Powers, Graham-Harrison dealt with the origins of delegated legislation and pointed out that the Lord Thring had favoured this legislative tendency as a proper way of drawing Bills, and that the principle had been followed in the Parliamentary Counsel Office.[53] He put his views on this branch of administrative law into a separate publication. Then in 1931 he gave evidence to the Select Committee on Public Business dealing with the following points:

On attaching draftsmen to Committees:

> I do not think we could turn out much more than we are doing now, with our present staff. I should like to say that nothing is more difficult in the world than to get people to come to my office. It is highly specialised and extremely unpopular.

On the reason for this:

> Because it is slavery.

On his working week:

> One begins at 10 to half-past, and one cannot make a single engagement for the evenings of Monday, Tuesday, Wednesday and Thursday. I have to work on Friday, and the only time I get for thinking about anything without interruption is Saturday. I have to work on Sunday too during the session.

On the difficulties of recruitment:

> One talks to one's friends down at the Temple and Lincoln's Inn and sees if they have anyone at all likely . . . . I have had enormous difficulty in getting anybody who is competent. I have a very good staff now, but it was very difficult to get them, and I could not get them at all until I told the Treasury that I must have more money to pay them . . . . I have two men from quite large practices. I do not think they like it very much now they have come.[54]

Recruitment and remuneration can be perpetual problems, and the workload and its pace may not vary, but the reference to slavery is a real *cri de coeur*.

In his retirement Graham-Harrison did something surely rare if not unique when he took a brief for the petitioner in a Privy Council case on the constitutionality of a Northern Ireland statute.[55] And in 1935 he addressed the annual meeting in Exeter of the Society of Public Teachers of Law on 'An Examination of the Main Criticisms of the Statute Book and of the Possibility of Improvement'.[56] Here he drew heavily on the report of, and the evidence given to, the 1875 Select Committee on Acts of Parliament before which Thring (his predecessor at six removes) had been a witness.

He both rehearsed and discussed these documents, using them to expound his views on such topics as drafting assistance for committees, explanatory memoranda, the Interpretation Act 1889, statute law revision and the *Statutes Revised*, consolidation, referential legislation, the scope of amendments and interpretation. This comprehensive survey concluded by alleging that drafting had improved somewhat since 1875; that drafting defects were exaggerated and the difficulties of drafting under-estimated; and that draftsmen were not infallible and the Office was too small. It appears that, released from the slavery of drafting, Graham-Harrison was prolific in expressing his views on the statute law.

K. 'In on the Act'

Overlapping Graham-Harrison by a couple of years was a then junior member of the Office who has provided first-hand evidence of the working of the Office from the early 1930s to the early 1950s. Sir Harold Kent, as he became, left the Office in 1953 to become Treasury Solicitor but his days as Parliamentary Counsel must have been close to his heart for in 1979 he published his experiences under the apt title *In on the Act*, with the subtitle *Memoirs of a Law Maker*. His two decades coincided with the reigns of four heads of the Office, and his cameos of the men and women with whom he worked give a fascinating picture of life in the Treasury, Old Queen Street and Old Palace Yard. There are succinct and pointed descriptions of the drafting of various Bills and the subjects range from the Abdication crisis through Emergency Powers (Defence) to post-war nationalisation. There is an appendix, 'Chapter and Verse', of individual instances, giving a commentary on the documents. It would be tempting to include in this note an anthology of extracts from the book, but that would not do it justice. It was stimulating to review,[57] and a pleasure to give it more than one Second Reading.

L. Before and after the Second World War

The eighth head of the Office, from 1934 to 1937, was not promoted from within. Sir Maurice Gwyer had been Treasury Solicitor and editor of Anson's *Law and Custom of the Constitution* (in reverse order) and had been involved in the Dominion discussions which led to the passing of the Statute of Westminster 1931. In the Office he was concerned with the Bill for the Government of India Act 1935, so that when he left in 1937 to become Chief Justice of the Indian Federal Court he took with him knowledge of what the 1935 Act was meant to mean. This may have been a mixed blessing, for it has been said that some of his judgements may have been influenced by that knowledge.[58]

Gwyer's successor was Granville Ram, who had become Third Parliamentary Counsel in 1922 and Second Parliamentary Counsel in 1929. He discharged faithfully the dual functions of drafting and administration, expanding the Office, establishing the consolidation branch in 1947, producing Consolidation Bills and earning the tribute of having brought order out of chaos.[59] Like Graham-Harrison he addressed the Society of

Public Teachers of Law, taking as his title 'The Improvement of the Statute Book'.[60] He included a description of the work of Parliamentary Counsel ('seldom seen and never heard') in the making of a statute ('forged on the anvil of the draftsman's table'), and of the working of the Office, touching on the difficulty of recruiting suitable candidates and mentioning that his three immediate predecessors (Liddell, Graham-Harrison and Gwyer) had been Fellows of All Souls. He gave details of a Bill's drafting stage ('its pre-natal history'), and of the methods of providing information to Parliament, arguing that post-Bill memoranda might not be 'calm, impartial and judicial in tone'. His description of a draftsman's day was like Ilbert's but he adds that if such days were the rule the draftsman's 'life would be a short one'. He referred to his special interests of statute law revision and consolidation, and ended by appealing to the law teachers for their help in the improvement of the statute book. This was a credo delivered with conviction.

Sir Allan Ellis was First Parliamentary Counsel from 1947 to 1953, a period covering the Indian Independence Act 1947, the Parliament Act 1949 and a new instalment of the intricacies of nationalisation and denationalisation, the Iron and Steel Act 1953. Then, until 1956, came Sir John Rowlatt, whose Indian Independence Act earned him his KCIE, a deserved distinction but one not usually awarded to a Whitehall-based official. Sir Noel Hutton's period of office was longest, from 1956 to 1968, and for the first time in the history of the Office his KCB was elevated to a GCB, at a time when Hutton was described as 'the hinge of government'. Like others, he went to the Law Commission when he retired and, emulating Brougham and Ilbert, drafted the Interpretation Act 1978.[61] Another public duty he performed was to sit on the Renton Committee on the preparation of legislation, assessing the evidence of his two immediate successors (Fiennes and Stainton); he was quoted in the report, and entered a note dissenting from the proposal that explanatory notes be printed opposite sections in Acts, which he thought would cause difficulties in construction.[62] The report's quotation came from one of Hutton's extra-statutory writings, an article on 'Mechanics of Law Reform'[63] (a title with an echo of Symonds and Ilbert) in which after outlining the task of drafting he stated that 'a Law Reform Bill is . . . . a breath of fresh air to a draftsman' and developed the concept of 'legislative audiences' (propounded by the United States authority on drafting, Reed Dickerson), the parliamentary one seeking general purpose and effect, and the legal one looking for specific answers to specific questions: 'One wants a picture and the other wants a Bradshaw'.[64] The drafting of law reform Bills is easier, Hutton stated, because the legislative audience for them is not a dual one: 'Whereas bills are made to pass as razors are made to sell, this particular razor can be designed to shave.' Also, courts may assume that a law reform Act means what it says, and the pressure on parliamentary time may be less. Hutton illustrated his propositions with detailed discussion of the drafting problems arising with the Law Reform (Miscellaneous Provisions) Act 1934 and the Occupiers' Liability Act 1957, commenting on the court decisions interpreting the Acts. This article was innovatory in the literature of legislative drafting. Hutton had more than a British audience for his views, for in 1971 he attended a conference in the United States on legislative drafting, contributing a paper on English drafting practice and participating in the general discussion. This was a method of spreading the legislative word.

Hutton's successor in 1968 was Sir John Fiennes, who had been Second Parliamentary Counsel from 1956. In 1965-66 he inaugurated the system of seconding members of the Office to the Law Commission to work on law reform and consolidation Bills. (Also, Fiennes figured in an analysis of drafting style by a later Lord Chancellor.)[65] In 1971 he gave evidence on the form and preparation of Bills to the Select Committee on Procedure.[66] Then he gave evidence to the Renton Committee on some fundamental points.

On Bills in Parliament:

> One of the jobs of the draftsmen is to present changes in the law to Parliament in a debatable form. You have to arrange a Bill, be it a new Bill or an amending Bill in a form in which it is capable of rational debate in the House all through its stages . . . .

On the length of sentences:

> Shorter sentences are easier in themselves, and it would probably help overall to have them shorter, but of course you are then faced with having to find the relationship between that sentence and another sentence two sentences away, which, if you have it all in one sentence, is really done for you by the draftsman.

On the time for drafting:

> There was one occasion, on a Finance Bill, when I sat down on a Sunday at home and rewrote a whole Part of a Finance Bill. It went to the printer on Monday night, and the text was handed in at tea-time on Tuesday. The Revenue never saw the final version of that until the Bill was published.[67]

That was surely Fiennes's *tour de force*.

Fiennes's successor in 1972, Sir Anthony Stainton, also gave evidence to the Renton Committee, being mentioned in the report by office rather than by name. On two of Fiennes's points he expressed similar views: the draftsman should aim at short sentences, but the price to pay might be more cross-references with longer sections and more sub-sections. And he said of the pressure of time,

> the pressure makes it difficult for the drafting team to prepare material to help in understanding the Bill when it first appears. Even drafting an Explanatory Memorandum may be a considerable task for a big Bill. The preparation of the occasional White Paper by way of giving more detailed explanations of the text can be a burden so great that it interferes with the main object of getting the Bill right.[68]

Throughout the report Stainton's views on the range of the statute law are chronicled, from elaboration and purpose statements to numbering and italics. This was a diligent and meticulous discharge of one of the draftsman's non-drafting duties.[69]

M. The post-war entrants

Stainton's three successors, Sir Henry Rowe in 1977,[70] Sir George Engle in 1981 and Sir Henry de Waal (the present incumbent) were all post-war recruits to the Office and in the last dozen years they have contributed a cumulative total of some ninety years' drafting experience. They have seen a number of changes, such as the assistance given to Commonwealth jurisdictions and, nearer Whitehall, the exposition of legislative drafting to administrators on training courses. (A succession of members of the Office have been welcome external examiners for university courses in legislation.) A development far outside the walls of that neat building at 36 Whitehall was the foundation, during the Commonwealth Law Conference in Hong Kong in 1983, of the Commonwealth Association of Legislative Counsel, of which George Engle was founder-president.[71] Also, the flow of extra-statutory publications continued.[72] An important example was the contribution to *Halsbury's Laws of England* of the title *Statutes*,[73] learned in scope and authoritative in style. Then in 1986 there was a Franco-British conference on British and French Statutory drafting,[74] the contributors and the audience alike being distinguished. The contributors from the Office were the First and Second Parliamentary Counsel (George Engle and Henry de Waal), and Christopher Jenkins and Edward Caldwell, of Parliamentary Counsel. Between them they dealt with the British legislative system and the form and style of legislation, consolidation and codification, and summarised the themes of the conference. In this was more than an *entente cordiale*, it was an *aggiornamento*, caused by a further piercing of the veil shrouding the mystery.

N. Thring's razors

But, whatever developments there were in drafting and its discussion the solution of one mystery stands out: the identity of the poet Thring had in mind when he wrote of Bills being meant to pass as razors are made to sell. In an address to the Statute Law Society in 1982 (itself an event worthy of note) George Engle outlined his researches and gave his conclusion that the reference was to Peter Pindar, an eighteenth-century satirical lyricist, one of whose odes told of a razor seller who never thought his wares would shave but that they would sell.[75] Over a century after Thring's jocular reference a combination of literary and legal ingenuity had solved the puzzle. Truly Thring was justified of his successor.

O. The last clause

This note has no short title, but it has employed chronology, biography and bibliography in an arrangement of other men's flowers.

Notes

1. R.F.V. Heuston *Essays in Constitutional Law* (2nd ed) Stevens & Sons (1964).
2. In *Harrison v Tew* [1990] 2 W L R 210 at 220; [1990] 2 All E R 321 at 329; Lord Lowry linked parliamentary sovereignty and legislative supremacy with their exercise in considering the replacement of an inherent jurisdiction by a statute, citing E.C.S. Wade and A.W. Bradley *Constitutional and Administrative Law* (10th ed) Longman (1985).
3. The alternative description of 'legislative counsel' was suggested by Peter Graham CB, Second Parliamentary Counsel, at the 1986 Jamaica meeting of the Commonwealth Parliamentary Association; (1987) *The Loophole* 7.
4. Cambridge U P (1971) 45 at 67–68; and see D.L. Rydz *The Parliamentary Agents: A History* Royal Historical Society (1979) 34.
5. S. Lambert *op cit* note 4 *supra* at 68; and see Rydz *op cit* note 4 *supra* at 37.
6. Athlone Press (1972) 99.
7. Compact ed Oxford U P (1975) 1661. (Subsequent references to *DNB* are to this edition.)
8. *DNB* 896; *Somersett v Stewart* (1772) 1 Lofft 1; 98 ER 498.
9. *Op cit* note 4 *supra* at 69.
10. *Ibid* 70.
11. 1833 HC xii.
12. Sir C.P. Ilbert *Legislative Methods and Forms* Clarendon Press (1901) 80–83.
13. *DNB* 2095.
14. J. Sainty *op cit* note 6 *supra* at 99.
15. George Allen and Unwin (1969) 173.
16. *Ibid* 174.
17. *Op cit* note 12 *supra* at 83.
18. *Op cit* note 6 *supra* at 99.
19. *Op cit* note 15 *supra* at 173–174.
20. *A History of the Criminal Law of England* Macmillan (1883) iii 256 n 3.
21. 1993; and see L. Radzinowicz *Sir James Fitzjames Stephen* Selden Society Lecture, Bernard Quaritch (1957) 3.
22. Ilbert *op cit* note 12 *supra* at 51–59.
23. Selden Society Lecture, Bernard Quaritch (1955).
24. (1951) CLP 122--136.
25. F. Bowers, 'Victorian Reforms in Legislative Drafting' [1980] 48 *Tijdschrift voor Rechtsgeschiedenis* 329–348. For a summary of this article see [1982] *Stat L R* 119–121.
26. Bowers *op cit* note 25 *supra* at 340–342.
27. The publishing history started with the 1843 Report and was followed by a separate London edition in 1845. Then came a Philadelphia edition in 1848 and a second London edition in 1852. After a gap of nearly a century a photo-offset version of the Philadelphia edition was produced in Halifax, Nova Scotia, in 1947. Currently the text appears as an appendix to E.A. Driedger *The Composition of Legislation and Legislative Forms and Precedents* (2nd ed), The Department of Justice, Ottawa (1976) and as Appendix A to S. Robinson *Drafting: its application to conveyancing and commercial documents* Butterworths (1980).
28. See Parris *op cit* note 15 *supra* at 176.
29. John Murray (1902). The sub-title, like that of the original 1879 version, included the words 'The Composition and Language of Acts of Parliament' but added 'and Business Documents'.
30. *Ibid* at 4–5.
31. *Op cit* note 12 *supra* at p 83. For a tribute to Thring's work at the Home Office see Lord O'Hagan K.P. *Occasional Papers and Addresses*, London (1884) 57–58.
32. *Op cit* note 12 *supra* at 83; see also Parris, *op cit* note 15 *supra* at 178.
33. *Op cit* note 12 *supra* at 83–84; see Parris, *op cit* note 15 *supra* at 177.
34. Ilbert *op cit* note 12 *supra* at 84–85.

35. Cmnd 6053 (1975) 6.
36. *DNB* 398.
37. See generally Lord Mackay of Clashfern 'The Drafting of Government Bills affecting the Law of Scotland' [1983] *Stat LR* 69 – 70. An example of outside work in the early 1900s was that of Aeneas J.G. Mackay, a former professor of constitutional law and history and a retired sheriff-principal, who prepared the pre-Union Scottish Acts for revision (*DNB* 2770). See also A.J.G. Mackay, 'The Art of Legal Composition', (1887) 3 LQR 326 – 328; 'Some General Rules of the Art of Legal Composition' (1888) 32 *Journal of Jurisprudence* 169 – 182, reprinted in S. Robinson *Drafting: its application to conveyancing and commercial documents* Butterworths (1980) Appendix B.
38. Bowers *op cit* note 25 *supra* at 343 – 344.
39. *Notes on Estimates 1920 – 1921;* R.B. McDowell *The Irish Administration 1801 – 1914* Routledge and Kegan Paul (1964) 77. On private draftsmen see J.F. McEldowney 'Legislative Drafting in the Nineteenth Century: A Case Study – the Juries Act (Ireland) 1871' [1981] *Stat L R* 161 – 173; and see A. Dowling 'The Genesis of Deasy's Act' (1989) 40 NILQ 53 – 63.
40. See Sir Cecil Carr's introduction to Quekett *The Constitution of Northern Ireland Part III,* HMSO (1946). Parts I and II were published in 1928 and 1933 respectively. In the 1932 Report of the Donoughmore–Scott Committee on Ministers' Powers (Cmd 4060) at 25 – 26, an extract was quoted from Quekett's article on local government and devolution in (1918) 34 LQR 357. See also 'The Action of Parliamentary Sovereignty upon Local Government' (1919) 35 LQR 163 and 'Devolution: Some Recent Precedents' (1921) 37 LQR 363.

    Quekett's publishing precedent was followed by his successor but one, W.A. Leitch CB, who produced *A Handbook on the Administration of Estates Act (Northern Ireland) 1955* Incorporated Law Society of Northern Ireland (n d). He co-authored 'A Commentary on the Interpretation Act (Northern Ireland) 1954' (1955) 11 NILQ 45 – 180 and wrote other articles on legal subjects.
41. For a description of the work of the Dublin draftsmen by one of Matheson's successors see Gerald McCarthy 'Legislation—its Preparation and Enactment' in F.C. King (Ed) *Public Administration in Ireland Vol III* Browne and Nolan (1954) 1 – 14.
42. Sir C.P. Ilbert *The Mechanics of Law Making* Columbia U P (1914) 66.
43. *Practical Legislation* 6.
44. *Ibid* 9 – 10.
45. G.W.E. Russell *Fifteen Chapters of Autobiography* Nelson (n d) 246 – 248.
46. H. Hutchinson (Ed) *Private Diaries of Sir Algernon West GCB* John Murray (1922) 81 – 82, 163; Lord Morley *Recollections* Macmillan (1917) 359, 361 – 362. See also [1986] *Stat L R* 65 – 66.
47. *DNB* 2712.
48. *Op cit* note 42 74 – 76, 83 – 84, 88.
49. *Ibid* 118 – 119.
50. *DNB* 2560.
51. A schoolboy visitor to Thring's home, who later became a prominent literary and theatrical figure, recalled in his memoirs how Thring had cured him of unpunctuality with the 'intimidating query: Is he always late for everything at school?' J. Speaight *The Property Basket: Recollections of a Divided Life* Collins and Harvill Press (1970) 35. The point is not blunted by the description of Thring as 'Clerk to the Parliamentary Council'.
52. *DNB* 2663.
53. Cmd 4060 (1932) p 24; see *Practical Legislation* 45 – 46.
54. (1931) HC 161 171 – 172.
55. *In re a Reference under the Government of Ireland Act, 1920 and s. 3 of the Finance Act (Northern Ireland) 1934* [1936] AC 352.
56. [1935] JSPTL 9 – 45.

57. [1980] *Stat L R* 181–192.
58. *DNB* 2673.
59. *DNB* 2673; see R.F.V. Heuston 'Lord Chancellors and Statute Law Reform' [1988] *Stat L R* 7-8.
60. (1947–51) 1 JSPTL (NS) 452–459.
61. For the evidence to the Joint Select Committee see (1977–78) HL 200–I; HC 543–I. For the joint report of the Law Commission (No. 90) and the Scottish Law Commission (No. 53) see Cmnd 7235 (1978).
62. Cmnd 6053 (1975) 59, 160.
63. (1961) 24 MLR 18–31.
64. F.R. Dickerson (Ed) *Professionalising Legislative Drafting* American Bar Association (1973) 110–119, 136–137.
65. Lord Hailsham of St Marylebone, 'Addressing the Statute Law' [1985] *Stat L R* distinguishing between the drafting of 'K' and 'F'.
66. See Second Report – *The Process of Legislation* (1970–71), HC 538, Minutes of Evidence 200–205, and Appendices to the Minutes of Evidence 322–327.
67. Cmnd 6053 (1975) 39, 64 and 39 respectively.
68. *Ibid* 39.
69. See Sir Henry Rowe's obituary tribute to his immediate predecessor in *The Guardian* 11 Nov 1988.
70. Earlier in his career he had produced a valuable survey of State drafting services in the USA.
71. See [1983] *Stat L R* 43–44: see also G. Engle 'The Legislative Process Today' [1987] *Stat L R* 71–76, a paper presented to the 1986 Jamaica meeting of the Association.
72. Francis Bennion, who had two spells in the Office, has produced numerous works, ranging from *The Constitutional Law of Ghana* Butterworths (1963) to *Statutory Interpretation* Butterworths (1984) and *Statute Law* (3rd ed) Longman (1990).
73. (4th ed) Butterworths (1983) vol 44 481–638, contributed by Peter Knowles and Stephen Law.
74. Sir W. Dale (Ed) *British and French Statutory Drafting* Institute of Advanced Legal Studies (n d).
75. "Bills are made to pass as razors are made to sell': practical constraints on the preparation of legislation' [1983] *Stat L R* 9. See also J. Bell and G. Engle (Eds) *Cross's Statutory Interpretation* (2nd ed) Butterworths (1987) esp at 195–200.

Officers, Members and Local Autonomy

C.M.G. Himsworth

A. Introduction

In the course of the parliamentary debates leading to the passing of the Local Government and Housing Act 1989 (the '1989 Act'), the Opposition claimed to have calculated that this was the Government's fiftieth local government Bill since 1979.[1] It was a measure to be understood against a background of an assumed much-reduced role for local authorities. Councils would cease to be substantial providers of services and become instead merely local enablers and regulators, for which purpose they might need to hold meetings only once a year.[2] Whilst Mr Ridley, then Secretary of State for the Environment, was lecturing local authorities on their abuse of the trust imposed by the unwritten constitution (in contrast, that is, with central government's recognition of its own need to abide by the spirit of that constitution), a substantially smaller place in the constitutional sun was the Government's ultimate aim for local government. In the decade to 1989, the local government debate was dominated by finance. Early acrimony over expenditure controls imposed through the rate support grant was supplemented by later, even fiercer, bitterness over the replacement of domestic rates by the poll tax. It was also, however, a period of conflict over structural change in local government including, above all, the abolition of the Greater London Council,[3] and over the substantial retrenchment of the powers of local authorities in deference to the higher demands of the market for deregulation, competition and the consumer's right to choose. On another front, new restrictions were imposed on the campaigning role of local authorities when their powers to engage in political publicity were trimmed.[4] Publicity had been the subject matter of the interim report published in 1985[5] of the Committee on *The Conduct of Local Authority Business* chaired by David Widdicombe QC, although the measures enacted in the Local Government Acts of 1986 and 1988 went beyond the recommendations of the Committee.

In the Widdicombe Committee's main report,[6] the emphasis was on other matters, to which the Government's response came first in the White Paper of 1988[7] and then in the Bill which became the Local Government and Housing Act 1989. Widdicombe included a substantial chapter called

'Public Challenge' containing a number of recommendations designed to strengthen existing patterns of external monitoring of and challenge to local authority activities. These met with only limited approval from the Government. Widdicombe joined the bandwagon already rolling towards judicial enforcement of the decisions of local ombudsmen, a bandwagon stopped abruptly in its tracks by the Government, which preferred the route of strengthened accountability through improved procedures for local authority deliberation on adverse reports. Widdicombe's proposals for the substantial extension of assisted judicial review of local authority decisions were never likely to amuse a Government for which the threat of an equivalent strengthening of review of the decisions of central departments would be an uncomfortably close parallel – and were dropped.[8] The Report's principal focus was, however, on the administrative heart of local government, the proper role of and relationships between officers and members, and the influence on both of party politics. These aspects of the Report attracted a fuller response from Government than that predicted by some commentators. It was not merely 'remaindered to use for Private Members' Bills',[9] and many of the Committee's recommendations have passed through the Government's filter on to the statute book. Even Parliament was permitted to contribute to the legislative process, in the shape of House of Lords intransigence over the fixing of the salary level at which the political restrictions on officers, including the bar on 'twin-tracking', would take effect.[10] The imposition of those restrictions, coupled with the rules designed to ordain political balance on committees,[11] have attracted most general attention. What I should like to probe in this essay is the extent to which some of the other changes effected by the 1989 Act have given renewed impetus to a general trend towards not only what Widdicombe called the 'need to accommodate politics in local government'[12] but also towards a quite deliberate shift of power within local authorities from members to officers. Measures taken to restructure the democratic element in local government and to equip it with 'an efficient, expert and politically impartial service'[13] may be interpreted not as the means of strengthening the existing structure of local authority decision-making but of its replacement by another.

This has not, of course, been the declared aim of the Government, which instead has claimed that no other system 'can be shown to be superior to the traditional British system'.[14] The Government was enthusiastic in joining Widdicombe in the rejection of such alien forms as the city manager model (perhaps for the reason that this might indeed create the environment for a genuinely strengthened local government even if not on 'traditional' lines[15]) but this would not preclude a hidden agenda on which the strengthening of the official grip on local government was a high priority.

The essay falls into four further parts. In part B, I look at the member-officer relationship as a defining characteristic of local government, its importance to any assessment of the constitutional status of local government, and its contribution to local autonomy. Part C is a sketch of the position prior to Widdicombe. Part D returns to the Widdicombe recommendations, the changes made by the 1989 Act, and other recent developments. The conclusions in Part E draw together some of the principal strands.

B. Local Self-Government

One of the consequences ascribed to the lack of a written constitution in the United Kingdom is the corresponding lack of any clear definition of the constitutional status of local government. Descriptions of how things are or were tend to be redeployed as prescriptions of how they ought to be. There is, therefore, an inevitable scepticism about the analytical strength of accounts of local autonomy and of measures designed to guarantee continuing significance for it.[16] This is due in part to the evident weakness of available sources of formal guarantee, whether of domestic or international origin, capable of withstanding the domination of a determined central government, but it is also a consequence of the suspicion of constitutional opportunism involved. Constitution-based arguments have followed the collapse of political arguments but have been used to try to defend the same political ground. It would, however, be grossly unfair to dismiss completely the efforts to develop theories establishing a place in the constitutional order for local government merely because they have been forced to yield to great political strength at the centre. W.J.M. Mackenzie wrote of 'an extremely vague notion of local self-government' but nevertheless adopted in his 'Theories of Local Government' the starting-point – and also, he said, the conclusion – 'that in some sense or other local self-government is now part of the English constitution, the English notion of what proper government ought to be'[17]

A full account of the underlying arguments for local government is, happily, well beyond the scope of this paper. It is sufficient to say that at least three inter-related groups of arguments have been involved. One takes as its primary focus the ultimate values of government and of local government in particular. Thus, for C.H. Wilson, the 'foundations of local government' were to be found in the need for local representative institutions to meet the 'fundamental requirements of participation, discussion and education':

> They do provide, on the largest scale, an opportunity for the citizen to share in public decision and administration, they do provide the machinery of discussion and vote to elicit his consent, they do provide, in the only possible way, for the political education of the people. It is their additional merit that they also serve the administrative purposes of central government as channels of local intelligence and agents of local executive action.[18]

In L.J. Sharpe's account, the two primary justifications of local government were participation and efficiency. Within 'participation' is a prominent role for local government as political educator. For such values to be sustained, such general roles to be performed, local government must have certain qualities, certain characteristics. These minimally required characteristics constitute a second way of building up the fundamentals of local government. Thus, for Sharpe, it was the fact that local authorities are elected and have independent sources of revenue that makes them different political animals from decentralized agents of a central department '. . . [A] local council is an independent agent and this independence means that it can if it wishes fight for what it wants, enlisting help politically where it will, through national associations of local authorities or professional associations; in Parliament or within one of the major parties . . . Local authorities, because they are independent, are very important pressure groups'.[19]

With the benefit of hindsight, one of the most interesting questions about these types of analysis concerns their continuing validity in the light of more recent developments. If a fundamental function of local government is as an independent pressure group in the political arena, how has this fared in the light of the restrictions on political publicity imposed by section 2 of the Local Government Act 1986? If that legislation has severely dented a 'fundamental' characteristic of local government, what remains?

Even more poignantly, it was Professor John Griffith who, in 1974, concluded a little booklet about relationships between local authorities and central government by saying, 'Once local authorities are deprived of their statutory power to increase their own revenue by determining their own rate levels, their slide into increasing subordination to the central departments will be fast and final.'[20] Thus it appeared to Griffith that, at the time of local government reorganisation in England and Wales, the last bastion of local autonomy (despite all the financial controls already imposed by the system of rate support grant) was the right of a local authority to set its own rate. If that went, subordination would be 'fast and final'. Since then, however, the bastion has crumbled. Secretaries of State both in England and Wales and in Scotland took (and used) not only new statutory powers to penalise individual authorities by limiting their rate levels but also the wider powers to cap rate levels of local authorities in general.[21] Equivalent powers have been retained to cap poll tax levels,[22] while, even more drastically, levels of non-domestic rates have become wholly a matter for regulation by central government.[23] Thus, Griffith's assertion in 1974 has the interest not only of being, in the first place, one commentator's suggestion of what constitutes the main criterion of local autonomy but also of requiring us to think about what has happened when we see the apparent abandonment of that criterion. Has local government – local self-government – in some sense died? Or can it be claimed that, in response to changing conditions, the concept of local autonomy has simply changed with them?

These are not simple questions and discussion of them is made the more difficult because of problems of distinguishing rhetoric from reality. On the 'localist' side of the argument there may sometimes be a tendency to cry wolf and to overstate the consequences of changes in rules and practice. On the part of central government, there is a different tendency. As D.N. Chester put it:

> Unfortunately for the clarity of the argument (about central–local relations) most of those who hold this kind of (centralist) view conceal it by loud protestations of their faith in local government. Phrases

emphasising the virtues of local government and of the democratic way of life trip readily from the tongue. If such people came forward and openly said that they wished to get rid of local government by transferring education, police and other major services to a central Department and for the rest turning Local Authorities into agents of Whitehall at least their intentions would be clear. But by proclaiming the virtues of local government whilst by this or that method quietly trying to reduce further and further the status of Local Authorities, the exponents of this second view can get a very long way without being discovered.[24]

There are also problems about defining what we mean by degrees of control or of autonomy or of interdependence when conditions and rules do indeed change over time. Detailed controls over minutiae may, for instance, disappear but when they are replaced by broader, more programmatic control, has the overall level of central control increased or has it been lessened? Nor, if an evaluation of central control is to be made, can attention be confined simply to relations between ministers and local authorities alone. There are other controlling or at least influential agencies to be viewed perhaps as 'surrogate controllers'. Courts, auditors and ombudsmen may be seen in this light.

Despite these problems of evaluation, illustrations drawn from the pressure-group role of local government and then from the freedom of authorities to determine their own levels of revenue expenditure may be considered as examples of attempts to identify characteristics claimed to encapsulate what, in some sense, are the fundamentals of local self-government, yardsticks against which may be measured the changes, whether explicitly acknowledged or not, made by subsequent developments.

The third angle from which the 'fundamentals' of local government may be viewed is in the very structure and organisation of local authorities. They must be distinguishable from other public bodies. 'In a nutshell', said Sharpe, 'the Birmingham Corporation is an entirely different body to the Birmingham Regional Hospital Board'[25] – a point compellingly elaborated by George Jones and John Stewart. The critical difference lies, they write, in the fact of election. This creates a relationship of accountability in local government which is lacking in a health authority with only appointed members.[26]

The Widdicombe Committee itself acknowledged that there were other means of providing local services but 'it needs to be considered', the Committee said, 'what distinguishes local government from other public sector local institutions – such as health authorities, water authorities, electricity boards, or indeed local offices of Government Departments'.[27] Local government had to be government *by* local communities rather than *of* local communities. Local government must allow a local view to be expressed through the taking of decisions. Mere delivery of services was not sufficient to constitute local government. Health authorities were not, therefore, local government but merely local administration.[28] Adopting the defining attributes of pluralism, participation and responsiveness, the Widdicombe Committee proceeded to address the central characteristics of local government democracy.[29] Although clearly pressing the theme of 'structuring' democracy further than in earlier treatments, their concern with maintaining the democratic core of local government is long-standing and inevitable. Nothing else more clearly identifies and justifies local government as a system of local administration than the quality of its democratic content. Both the formal characteristics of local democracy – especially the systems of election – and their operation in practice were major preoccupations prior to local government reorganisation in the 1970s but it is interesting to range back further, to the Final Report of the Royal Commission on Local Government in 1929,[30] to see the concern then expressed about the pollution of local democracy by the provision for ministerial appointment of members to statutory county agricultural committees.[31] 'Real' local government was elected local government.

But, accompanying concern about the quality of the democratic constitution of local authorities, there was also a concern about the quality of the professional local government service. The demands of democracy and of service delivery inevitably linked members and officers. Thus officers had to be of 'great ability and experience' but

> any proposals as to local government officers, to be of practical value, must have due regard to the fundamental principles on which local government has developed in this country, the conditions under which local authorities act, and the possibility, politically and administratively, of modifying those conditions . . . [T]he analogy which has been drawn between local government officers and the national Civil Service, and the suggestion that the chief executive official might be an officer analogous to the Town Manager as found in some States of America, are found to break down when they are applied to the structure of English local government. In particular, it is to be observed that the autonomy of local authorities with regard to the appointment of their own officers is a jealously guarded privilege; and, within proper limits, this is a valuable element in local government.[32]

The concern that local councils be served by high quality officers has been echoed many times in the period since 1929 and, both in the Widdicombe Report itself and in the Government's response, was again accompanied by a rejection of any substantial abandonment of the traditional basic structure. Widdicombe glanced briefly at 'alternative decision taking models' but only to reject them. 'Management boards' on the model proposed in the Maud Report[33] had never found favour, both because of their tendency to exclude many members of authorities from full participation in decision-making and also because of the ambiguous line of accountability for officers who could cease to be accountable to the full council but would instead be accountable, through a strengthened chief executive, to the board. Rejecting the management board, Widdicombe reminds us nevertheless of changes which *were* made in the years following the Maud Report. The legislation of 1972 and 1973 did increase the freedom of local authorities to determine their own internal organisation. There were fewer statutory requirements to establish particular committees or to appoint particular officers. The general power to delegate to officers was provided and, on an extra-statutory basis, the co-ordination of local authority activities through 'corporate' decision-making was encouraged.[34]

Widdicombe went on to reject the 'ministerial' system under which, by analogy to ministers in central government, senior executive councillors would have the formal responsibilities of the authority vested in them. Similarly rejected was any system based on the 'separation of powers', whether by establishing an elected 'strong mayor' executive or an executive appointed by the council and in whom would be vested all matters of detailed administration, subject to broad financial and policy guidelines established by the council. 'There would', says the report, 'be a substantial change in the character of local government, greatly reducing the position of its political leadership and enhancing the role of its administrative leadership'.[35] Acknowledging potential problems about appointments to the powerful post of chief executive, the report suggests that there would be a need, as in Ireland, for the intervention of an independent staff commission to approve or nominate appointees, thus further diminishing the power of councillors.[36]

The government lost even less time than the Committee in rejecting radical change. 'The traditional system has proved capable of responding to great changes in the work of local authorities, and of moulding itself to cope with them. Other systems may have equal flexibility and effectiveness. But none can be shown to be superior to the traditional British system, and certainly none offers sufficiently clear advantages to justify the upheaval that would be necessary to make such a change.'[37] Important changes can, however, be made as effectively by 'moulding' as by 'upheaval'. The Government accepted Widdicombe's conclusion that the existing system should continue, viz:

(a) the council is a corporate body;
(b) decisions are taken openly by, or on behalf of, the whole council, without any separate source of executive authority; and
(c) officers serve the council as a whole.[38]

Thus, the Government's acceptance of the main Widdicombe starting assumption and its consequential requirement for 'an efficient, expert and politically impartial service' appears to be a commitment to an 'essential' of local government.[39]

What should be the more detailed defining characteristics of management in local government (and other parts of the public sector) then becomes an important question, recently subjected to an interesting analysis by Stewart Ranson and John Stewart.[40] Management in the public domain is different from management in the private sector. Management processes have to be seen as set in a

> politico-management system . . . . The management process in government should therefore support that process of decision-making which enables political control and government in the common interest. The management challenge lies in managing the interaction between the elected representative and the officer structure. The problem of communication between a political structure and an officer structure

are peculiar to the public domain and can be resolved by increasing political awareness and political sensitivity; improving management understanding of political process; and by assisting communication across the political/management divide.[41]

A further characteristic is, however, omitted in this account but was one developed by D.N. Chester. In his *Central and Local Government*[42] he suggested the need to bear in mind three main points when considering the maintenance of a reasonable balance in central-local relations:

1. The need to distinguish between questions of broad national policy and the administration of everyday affairs of a local service.
2. The recognition that there are certain vital aspects of local government to which central control cannot properly be applied, if local government is to remain a reality.
3. The clear acceptance by Parliament of the right of locally elected bodies to its special attention and guardianship.[43]

Developing his idea of the vital aspects or elements of local government, he set these out as follows:

(i) The right of the local electors to elect whom they please to their local Councils.
(ii) The necessity for a local Council to be able to rely completely on the loyalty of its officials.
(iii) The freedom of a Local Authority, subject to the general doctrine of *ultra vires*, to spend the money it raises from local taxes any way which pleases the local electorate to which it is responsible.[44]

I shall not pursue Chester's first and third 'vital aspects' although they are interesting in themselves. The first concerns the essential democratic element in local government. The third is the familiar call for a degree of financial freedom. The second of the trilogy – and it is interesting to see it raised to this status – is my primary concern. Chester was not unique in identifying the loyalty of officials as important in any general consideration of central control over local authorities. Other prominent contemporaries were Sir Ivor Jennings and William Robson, whose main concern was over the powers of Ministers to control the appointment of local authority officials and also to influence the tenure of their appointments.[45] These controls were already viewed, sixty years ago, as something of an anachronistic hangover from the earlier assumptions of the need for a general tutelage exercised by central government over small and under-resourced councils. They were also a lingering reminder of the dead hand of Poor Law administration. As Jennings put it: 'It is evident that this is a most effective means of control. If the local authority has to act through paid officers, and if the paid officers in the last resort obey the orders of the Central Government (and poor law officers may be dismissed or fined if they do not) the local authority is not likely to follow for long a course of action opposed to the Minister's policy.'[46]

Chester explained that his own fears about interference with this 'vital aspect' were expressed more in the spirit of a warning than as an account of new developments already embarked upon. My suggestion is that central controls over officers and, through them, of authorities should be viewed in the same spirit. We may not, in this area, be witnessing, as yet, a substantial onslaught by central government but the government does have both the opportunity and, perhaps even more significantly, the motive for intervention. It must at some points have attractions. Ministers may invoke default procedures in respect of what are perceived to be recalcitrant local authorities but these powers are in many cases (and, once again, from the point of view of ministers) cumbersome and inefficient. In particular, whilst able to prevent action, they are less well fitted to requiring action of authorities. May there not be, therefore, a temptation to distance or 'hive-off' officials from their authority; to deal directly with them; and perhaps to impose specific statutory obligations directly upon them. Would it not be attractive to move away from a situation in which officers have an undivided loyalty to their own authority to require them to begin to owe allegiance to two different masters?

C. Complete Loyalty Reassessed

This idea of complete or undivided loyalty should be qualified. It is an idea, in the first place, not universally endorsed by officers themselves. There is no doubt that some officers have looked to central control over their operations – particularly in the more technical areas – as a protection from 'interference' or 'meddling' by councillors.[47] Operational relationships between authorities and central departments are conducted, for the most part, between officials and the opportunities have always been there for officials to impose their own mark upon their authorities' policies. During the 1980s a strain was imposed upon the loyalty of officials by the increasing party political pressures within local government. Viewed from the outside, it seems that some officers, whilst still regarding themselves as 'politically impartial' were enjoying the opportunities created by an increasingly politically polarised atmosphere, whether as 'twin-trackers' or not. Others found the situation much more uncomfortable.

The other qualification is that it has never been the legal position that officials are *merely* the servants of their authority's wishes. Some officials have indeed been granted a considerable distance from their authorities. The system of Poor Law administration condemned by Chester, Jennings and Robson has already been mentioned. This was a situation in which officials, nominally appointed and employed locally, were actually subject to the virtually total operational supervision and control of central government. Examples of forms of government necessitating the creation of a corps of officials freed from the direct control of councils still survive. The most prominent example must be in the field of police administration, where chief constables are in no sense the mere servants of their authorities. The standard outline of a form of local administration is retained but local police authorities do not enjoy complete freedom to hire and fire nor do they have vested in them the principal statutory (or indeed common law) responsibilities for policing. Chief constables necessarily, therefore, enjoy individual statutory responsibilities not shared by other chief officers in local government and their accountability to police authorities is much less direct.[48] Unlike Poor Law administrators, however, they do not fall under the direct control of central government.

The quality and extent of the accountability of chief constables have never been completely clear but the relationship between chief constables and police authorities has been a source of bitter controversy – on the one side, when chief constables have been forced or have elected to adopt a high profile locally or nationally and, on the other side, when measures, especially the Police Authorities (Powers) Bills of a decade ago, were proposed to curb their autonomy. More mundanely, difficulties in ordinary working relationships between chief constables and police authorities are well described by Chief Constable Ian Oliver in his account of the two versions of the Bains report[49] on the management of local government following reorganisation, an early draft of which treated the chief constable as simply another chief officer in charge of a local authority department – the police department – but subject to the corporate discipline of the authority's management team headed by the chief executive.[50] The temptation of Bains[51] to sweep chief constables into the new corporate plan and for chief executives to try to continue that process may be understandable but the resistance of chief constables based primarily on their claim to independence and freedom from any primary allegiance to the local authority is equally understandable and very nicely illustrates the institutional distance which may be achieved by an officer appointed by the authority but whose powers derive from a separate legal source. Although policing is quite different in this respect from any other locally provided service there are traces of similarity between the formal position of chief constables and some other local authority employees. For instance, weights and measures inspectors who are statutorily declared to be 'responsible to the local weights and measures authority'[52] nevertheless enjoy quite distinct statutory powers individually vested in them rather than in their employing authorities. This device represents a means (as with the police) for using existing patterns of local government to retain a form of local administration while still ensuring a very high measure of centralised control over the service operated. The alternative would presumably be to transfer the powers away from the local government sector altogether, but there are, no doubt, strong reasons of efficiency to retain the administration of the service in local authority hands. Much stronger forms of directly conferred statutory powers have operated in war-time and indeed the same possibilities are contemplated in existing guidance on emergency planning.[53]

Somewhat more routinely, the introduction of the poll tax has produced new circumstances where separately conferred official powers have been created. The community charges registration officer (CCRO) has been given responsibilities for determining individual liability to pay a community charge and for the maintenance of a register recording that liability, upon which the relevant local authorities rely at the stage of collection. Local authorities are statutorily restrained from direct involvement in the process of ascertaining liability and the self-interest they might have in maximising income is excluded. In Scotland, the statutory independence of CCROs was created by the device of instituting the existing assessors (officials responsible for maintaining the valuation roll for rating purposes) as CCROs.[54] They are also electoral registration officers. In England and Wales, because of the earlier capture of valuation for rating by the Inland Revenue under the Local Government Act 1948, the route to a degree of statutory independence for the finance officer as CCRO was different.[55]

These examples apart, however, the tendency in recent times has been away from the imposition of overt central regulation of local authorities in their employment and organisation of officials. The list of statutorily required officials was reduced upon local government reorganisation. Treasurers and clerks (or their modern replacement, chief executives) were not statutorily required and, if they were appointed, neither the process of appointment nor dismissal could be directly regulated by ministers. Authorities were, at the same time, given greater freedom in their deployment of officers with the extended powers to delegate functions.[56] It might be argued that these changes which permitted a stronger role for officers, viewed in conjunction with moves towards a more corporate style of decision-making, have enabled a less democratically accountable system to emerge;[57] however, it may then be argued in reply that any such developments have been, formally at least, controllable by the authorities themselves.[58]

Even without separately defined statutory powers, however, officers have never been wholly controllable by their employers. They have never been mere pawns in the hands of their councils and committees. There are points at which a statutory distance is maintained between officer and authority – for instance, where authorities are placed under the scrutiny of the auditor. Officers may themselves be made personally responsible for losses incurred but, equally, may be protected from responsibility for losses incurred by members in defiance of official advice.[59] Officers are obliged to provide documents and other information in aid of an investigation by auditor, ombudsman or court. They cannot shelter behind any general protection of anonymity, with the corresponding consequence for the authority itself that it cannot, if in difficulties, count upon the blind loyalty of officers. Most importantly, officers cannot be ordered to break the law and, presumably, the force of the old audit cases which imposed upon clerks and treasurers (and, by extension, presumably other chief officers) a responsibility to stand between their authority and the wider public, at least at the point where unlawful expenditure may be contemplated, is retained.[60] Such a duty arises not only from the possible exposure of officers themselves to audit procedures but also from a wider responsibility to protect the public interest. This claimed 'higher allegiance' to the public did not, however, come to the aid of the hapless Mr Smith, the town clerk of Bognor Regis, the correctness of whose dismissal was upheld in 1965 by Mr Ramsay Willis QC, who rejected Mr Smith's claims to a special relationship with local ratepayers.[61] This could lead to a clerk's claiming a duty to frustrate the will of his council and appeal over their heads to ratepayers. 'If a clerk is not answerable to his Council he is answerable to no-one. In my view he is the employee of his Council and it is to them that his primary loyalty and duty lie and it is to them that he is answerable for his actions.'[62] Only in exceptional circumstances such as where an offence is contemplated by the council would a different principle apply.

Even if some sort of an independent role can, on this basis, be defined, it does not necessarily lead to any greater control over local authorities by central government. We can, however, see how these two ideas may be related in circumstances where an officer's independence gives him or her the opportunity or indeed the duty to comply with a centrally imposed obligation with which the local authority is not itself inclined to comply. A side-effect of independence, whether intended or not, may be this greater susceptibility to the influence of central departments. One particular situation in which central government appears to have deliberately intervened to divide officer and member responsibilities is where ministers have taken powers to obtain information from authorities about the exercise by them of their duties under the right to buy provisions in the Housing Acts. The Secretary of State may request information from local authorities,[63] a power to be understood in parallel with powers he also enjoys to compel unwilling authorities to discharge their functions efficiently. There is nothing exceptional in a power to request information. Other such powers are available to ministers.[64] What *is* different is that, in this case, these Acts go on to provide that: 'Any officer of the landlord designated in the notice for that purpose or having custody or control of the document or in a position to give that information shall, without instructions from the landlord, take all reasonable steps to ensure that the notice is complied with.'[65] This is indeed exceptional in local government law. It is a provision calculated to drive a wedge between officers and their authority. From the point of view of central government, there was a foreseeable risk that a local authority would not itself comply with a request for information. Therefore, the strategy is to aim instead at the officers by imposing statutory obligations directly on them. When first introduced into housing law in 1980, this was presumably the first appearance of a provision of this type anywhere, because when challenged to produce a peacetime precedent, the junior minister could cite only section 158(1) of the Local Government Act 1972 which (although this was not admitted in debate) was the section which permitted *auditors* (rather than ministers) access to documents in the hands of officers.[66]

The enactment of these provisions did not go unchallenged in Parliament. There were, in the first place, doubts about how, exactly, the minister's powers might be interpreted and deployed. How would the Secretary of State know in whose hands lay the information he sought? How would communication between the central department and local authority be made? What does the phrase 'without instructions from the landlord' mean? In the absence of instructions? Or irrespective of any instructions issued by the landlord? Does not the duty to 'take all reasonable steps' require an officer to refuse to obey his or her authority? What sanctions would attached to a refusal to comply with a request from the Secretary of State?[67]

Secondly, objections were raised on the major point of principle involved:
It has always been strongly felt by local government officers and by
their trade unions that it is quite unacceptable for a Minister of the
Crown to be able to give them orders over the heads of their employers.
There is a particular problem here in that not only do they find this
objectionable because they are local government officers employed and
paid by their local authorities and not by the Secretary of State, but
also because they may find themselves doing actions that are against
their employers' wishes. That could put them into great difficulty.[68]
The point is whether the Government should take powers by statute
that fundamentally alter the relationship between central and local
government . . . . The central Government have powers legally to
enforce their will on the body corporate of the local authority. They
have no right and I think it quite wrong for them to take the power,
to try to pick out from within that local authority, going over the heads
of the elected councillors, local authority officers to be pressurised.[69]

Or, as Hugh Brown MP later put it when the Scottish version was proposed,
it was like the press secretary in the Department of Trade and Industry
being told to do something without even needing to consult the Minister![70]

The issue of access to and dissemination of information by and within
local authorities also arises in another context. In their consideration of a
number of matters relating to 'Access to Committee Meetings and
Documents', the Widdicombe Committee reviewed the legal rights of
councillors to inspect documents and proposed amendments of the law in
two 'relatively minor respects'.[71] The second need not concern us but the
first was the need for a 'simple neutral procedure' for deciding whether
councillors have a need to inspect a document. Leaving this to the council
and, therefore, to the majority party was unsatisfactory. In line with their
recommendations on related matters, their solution was to give to the chief
executive the right to decide. The Government, however, also in line with
similar rejections of Widdicombe proposals, dismissed it because it was
inappropriate to put an employee in the position of overriding elected
members.[72]

Even though their recommendation was not adopted for implementation,
the Widdicombe Committee's discussion of access by members to local
authority information is useful as a reminder of a very important strand
in a wider argument. In recent cases, well-established principles on
councillor access have been restated and refined.[73] Councillors do not
enjoy a roving commission to inspect all documents in possession of their
council. Rather the test is one based on a right of access to documents
'reasonably necessary to enable a councillor properly to perform his duties
as a member of the council'.[74] The councillor must have a 'need to know'
the information he or she seeks. Ultimately, it may be for a court in
appropriate proceedings for judicial review to establish whether a councillor
is being correctly denied, or indeed correctly permitted, access.[75] Two
further important principles have been established. The first is that it is
for the relevant committee or, in the last resort, the full council to decide
questions of access. Even though a preliminary power to decide may be

delegated to an officer (whether, for instance, the appropriate chief officer
or the authority's solicitor) the final decision lies with the council.[76]
Secondly, local authority officers do not hold information except on behalf
of the authority. In *ex parte O*[77], the social workers' 'confidential files'
were the authority's files and had to be available to councillors with a need
to know their contents. Lord Justice Donaldson spoke of the 'fundamental
fallacy' to regard a local authority social worker as being in the same position
as a general practitioner under the National Health Service. 'One is not
more professional than the other. It is just that they are different.' The
health service does not treat patients but employs doctors who do. A local
authority, on the other hand, *is* expected to care for children and does so
by employing social workers. Thus, in contrast with the position in the
health service, 'clients' of a social worker are equally the clients of the local
authority.[78] If this is true of social workers who, as in *ex parte O*, sought
to claim a professional 'distance' from their authority, it must be more
widely true of other officers. Their information is the authority's information
and is available to members (and indeed other officers) with a need to know.
The basis for this is important. It is the authority's statutory functions which
the officer is performing, something which is not true of those special
categories of officer, including the chief constable and the community
charges registration officer already discussed.

D. Recent Statutory Developments

The changes made by the Local Government and Housing Act 1989 may
be traced back to the written submission made by the Department of the
Environment, the Scottish Office and the Welsh Office to the Widdicombe
Committee on 'The Roles of Officers and Members in Local
Government'.[79] There it was argued that some practices affecting the
relationship between members and officers could 'jeopardise the proper
implementation of Parliamentary legislation and threaten the integrity of
local government as a public service'.[80] Officers had been subjected to
undue constraint or pressure by members and the Committee were invited
to consider whether it would not be 'appropriate to specify in statute the
responsibilities of chief officers for ensuring the proper management of their
authorities . . . [C]onsideration should be given to some specific statutory
role for the chief finance officer or other proper officer in relation to the
legality and propriety of Council spending'.[81] Then, in addition to
suggestions aimed at extracting senior officers from personal political
involvement, the Departments advised that attention be given to the
proposition that the local authority associations should set up a 'central
staffing organisation'.[82] It was acknowledged that, when this idea had last
been investigated by the Mallaby Committee (on the Staffing of Local
Government) in 1967, it was rejected because it would be expensive,
cumbersome and perhaps, in the light of the review of the local government
structure then underway, unnecessary.[83] The Widdicombe Committee
might, however, 'wish to consider whether current developments might
justify a fresh look at the proposal to create some kind of Local Government
Staff Commission to administer at least the selection and initial posting of

senior officers and to act as an ultimate safeguard of propriety and equity in this area'.

The Committee itself, however, took a different view. By the time they reported, they were aware of opposition from local authorities and rejected anything resembling a staff commission – even one with powers stopping short of direct involvement in making appointments to local authorities. Local government would not 'accept the need for a new national body regulating the making of appointments and they might well fear that once established its role would be widened'.[84] This did not rule out other means of regulating the appointment of senior officers which would leave final responsibility with the authorities themselves. Some of these (discussed below) reached the statute book in the 1989 Act. Meanwhile, however, the Widdicombe Committee, in addition to toning down the Government's centralising suggestions on staff appointments, failed to develop the Government's ideas on strengthening the statutory responsibilities of officers in the way which seemed to have been expected. It is true that the Committee devoted substantial attention to the role of senior officers and, attaching themselves single-mindedly to the enhancement of the role of chief executive, sought to pile upon that office a number of responsibilities which were either already scattered across the statute book or would be newly created.[85] Much of this the Government rejected. They were unpersuaded by the need to impose by statute the requirement to appoint a chief executive and were equally unimpressed by suggestions that the chief executive should assume politically contentious duties such as arbitrating on the rules about party balance on committees and, as we have seen, deciding whether a councillor needed to see a document or was entitled to attend a meeting. These proposed new tasks had been 'widely seen as undemocratic in that they would give an official who is appointed as a servant of the council an authority over elected members'.[86]

On the other hand, the Government had become firmer in its commitment to three major reforms, the first of which was to confer new obligations on officers to be designated by authorities in England and Wales as their chief finance officer. The Local Government Finance Act 1988 gives to these officers the power to report (with copies to the auditor and to all members of the authority) on any decisions or courses of action taken or proposed which appear to the officer to be unlawful (and, in the case of courses of action, likely to cause a loss or deficiency to the authority). The chief finance officer must also report where an authority's proposed expenditure appears likely to exceed resources available in the financial year. There is, then, provision for consideration of such reports by the authority.[87] Secondly, there was to be introduced the office of what the Government first called the 'propriety officer'[88] and then, in the Local Government and Housing Act 1989 itself, the 'monitoring officer'.[89] That officer may be the head of the authority's paid service or solicitor but, expressly, must not be the authority's chief finance officer.[90] The proposal for this office was made 'in the interests of improving internal accountability and reinforcing the observance of proper procedures'.[91] Thus, the monitoring officer must report in the event of contravention (or proposed contravention) of 'any enactment or rule of law or any code of practice' or of any 'maladministration or injustice'.[92] Once again, there is an obligation on the authority to suspend proposed action and to consider the report. By instituting the monitoring officer, the Government were going well beyond what Widdicombe was prepared to recommend. The Committee had doubted the wisdom of placing upon, in their version, the chief executive a direct duty to advise on legality since this might give the impression of exonerating councillors from any personal liability for their acts if official advice were not proffered. They preferred a 'reactive' role for the chief executive. He or she would advise on a matter only where such advice was explicitly sought by a councillor.[93] That risk of exoneration of councillors was not one directly addressed in the White Paper, although the Government did acknowledge the risk of conflicting opinion and advice tendered by, on the one hand, the chief finance officer and, on the other, the propriety or monitoring officer. In their view, however, this possible disadvantage was outweighed by the advantage of restoring the system of checks and balances ensured, prior to local government reorganisation in 1974 and 1975, by the two required offices of clerk and treasurer.[94]

The third change adopted by the Government was their insistence not on a person dubbed 'chief executive' for each authority but upon a person whose role nevertheless would be 'management co-ordination' and who would almost certainly be the chief executive if there were one.[95] Thus the 1989 Act now requires each local authority to designate one of its officers as head of its paid service.[96] As in the case of the chief finance officer and the monitoring officer, it is the function of that officer to report to the authority, with copies sent to each member and with an obligation upon the authority[97] to consider the report within three months. The matters for report by the officer include the manner in which the discharge of functions is co-ordinated and the organisation, appointment and proper management of staff; the report is to set out proposals in respect of these. Like the other designated officers, however, the head of the paid service has no powers to give direct executive effect to the contents of the report. They are for consideration only. It is important, on the other hand, to read these powers to report on staffing and management alongside other provisions in the 1989 Act which require that appointments be made on merit[98] and, more importantly, that local authorities incorporate into their standing orders regulations made by the Secretary of State relating to the appointment, discipline and dismissal of staff.[99] The Government's proposal is that these powers are to be used to ensure that councillors are excluded from participating in the appointment of officers outside the politically restricted categories. Appointments must be by an officer, within the politically restricted category.[100] Only the politically restricted may appoint the politically free. The Government rejected arguments from Widdicombe that special safeguards against dismissal should be created for the protection of chief executives or, by extension, the statutory officers now required and other chief officers. The Government were able to rely on the views of the Society of Local Authority Chief Executives who had 'stressed that there was a need for trust and confidence between a council (especially the leading members) and their chief executive: if this has broken down, then barrier [*sic*] to a change in the appointment will only create resentment'.[101]

E. Conclusions

How are we to assess the significance of the changes made by the 1988 and 1989 Acts? Retaining Chester's primary test of the need for councils to be able to rely completely on the loyalty of their officials, the question is how far this value has been retained. Two considerations make any immediate assessment no more than provisional. One is that informed speculation about the possible effect of statutory change on actual behaviour will need, of course, to be supplemented by the observation of actual future developments, including the use to be made by the Government of its delegated powers. The other is the problem, in any study of legislative impact, of interpreting the actual and discrete 'effect' of new rules. The surrounding framework of legal rules has been shifting in the implementation of other changes affecting local government and, furthermore, the new rules are not being applied to a monolithic or uniform system of local government. Impact must inevitably vary in different parts of the system. However, if we can distinguish and hive off for immediate purposes the pathological cases, the authorities where political 'abuse' was rife, are there general, if provisional, conclusions to be drawn in relation to the remainder? These are the authorities in respect of which, the Widdicombe Committee advised, the main changes reflect simply the structuring and extension of best practice, and its conversion into law.[102] But how far, on the other hand, has the Government, even in the absence of a clear vision at this stage of how much 'politics' should be retained in local administration, made the changes which will, in time, remove the important distinction between local authorities and other public authorities?

Although it will normally be prudent to interpret any group of changes affecting local government in the light of some understanding of an overall strategy, an 'ultimate aim' for the future role of local government as a whole,[103] this is made difficult where only unclear or conflicting signals are given. Furthermore, a 'reduced' role for local government or a view of local government as enabler rather than provider does not dictate any particular view of intra-authority relationships. A reduced role (with reduced funding) might demand an equivalently reduced political role. Alternatively, the conditions might be created in which the present or even an increased political role, for councillors rather than officers, would be more readily tolerated by a centralising government.

The provision of community care and of personal social services in general is a suitably confused example of possible future patterns of central control. On the one hand, the new proposals for community care[104] do concede a new role for local authorities which may have surprised some commentators. On the other hand it is a role on the enabling model and, even more significantly, it is a role made subject to considerably extended powers of central control, more reminiscent of the Secretary of State's powers to control local social security offices than local authorities. Authorities are to be required to exercise all their social services functions in accordance with such directions, in writing, as may be given to them by the Secretary of State![105] This represents a potentially huge invasion of remaining local autonomy. If such a level of central control were spread across the whole range of local authority functions, there might be little need for the government to trouble to extend the range of other controls of less direct effect.

In the meantime, however, the designation of new functions, under the Acts of 1988 and 1989, for the chief executive, chief finance officer and monitoring officer do alter relationships within authorities and do, thereby, tend to diminish the complete loyalty of officers of which Chester wrote. Three aspects of the changes may be picked out. Firstly, the formal statutory designation of officers with responsibilities separate from those of their employing authority creates an immediate dislocation in existing lines of responsibility. To the extent that the named officers are discharging their own statutory functions, they are not their authorities' men and women. They may not have acquired control of a whole function in the manner of the chief constable but neither are their functions merely equivalent to that of the accounting officer in a central department. That comparison, in respect of the monitoring officer, is one which was made by Mr Ridley.[106] He was correct in identifying the one textbook exception to ministerial responsibility for the actions of civil servants but the combined responsibilities of the newly defined offices in local government extend far beyond that of the accounting officer.

Secondly, and with a practical significance difficult to assess at this stage, the legislative practice has developed of giving the named officers themselves the right to decide the level of resources required to discharge their functions. Whilst, in the case of CCROs, local authorities are required simply to provide the officers 'with such staff, accommodation and other resources as are sufficient' to allow their functions to be exercised,[107] a chief executive, monitoring officer or chief finance officer must now be provided with resources which are sufficient 'in his opinion' to allow his duties to be performed.[108] This formula may be a necessary corollary to the achievement of the independence sought but it also serves to accentuate the changed relationship which has been created.

A related, and third, consideration is that of information supply. As already explained, information held by officers is normally the authority's information and is accessible to councillors. This access is guaranteed, however, only as long as officers are discharging the authority's own functions. The effect of hiving off to the chief executive responsibilities including the organisation of the authority's staff, even if confined to the stated purpose of reporting to the authority, is to establish management information that may legitimately be protected from councillor access. It is the chief executive's information and within his or her control. Similar considerations apply to the monitoring officer and this new position provides a model which might readily be built upon not only to disconnect officers from members within an authority but also to enable officers to deal with those outwith the authority, including central departments, in a manner which is quite independent of political control. Widdicombe may have shelved, for the time being, the Government's hopes of a local government staff commission. The Government may itself have rejected some of Widdicombe's more radical ambitions for the office of chief executive. They may both have discarded the strong mayor, but significant inroads have been made into the complete loyalty of officers to members. The institutional distance between the two has been widened and another vital aspect of local government eroded.

A present reluctance to write the obituary for local government may be justified.[109] Most obituaries are, however, drafted during the lifetime of the deceased and, even though death may not be imminent, it is prudent to keep the draft up to date and to add to the account of local government's surrender to the cancer of underfunding and the draining of its powers, the partial severance of its political heart from its managerial head.

Notes

1. See J. Cunningham MP 14 February 1989 HC Debs col 177.
2. Lord McIntosh 4 July 1989 HL Debs col 1070 (relying on claims made by Mr Ridley).
3. Local Government Act 1985.
4. Local Government Act 1986 s 2 as amended by the Local Government Act 1988.
5. A report enlivened by the spirited (dissenting) defence made by the late Sir Lawrence Boyle of the constitutional status of local government.
6. *The Conduct of Local Authority Business* Cmnd 9797 (1986).
7. *The Conduct of Local Authority Business: The Government Response to the Report of the Widdicombe Committee of Inquiry* Cm 433 (1988).
8. *Ibid* ch VI, in response to ch 9 of the Report. On the enforcement of reports of local ombudsmen, see the 1989 Act Part II.
9. Patrick McAuslan's prediction. See [1987] PL 154 at 162.
10. 1989 Act s 2(2). The salary limit for an unrestricted post was £13,500 in the original Bill but, as a result of Lords' amendments, became £19,500. For subsequent adjustments to the cut-off salary, see Local Government (Politically Restricted Posts) Regulations 1990, SI 1990/42.
11. *Ibid* ss 15–17 and Sched 1.
12. Cmnd 9797 para 4.17.
13. The title of ch V of Cm 433, note 7 *supra*.
14. Cm 433 para 1.4. There is further discussion of alternative management models below.
15. See Martin Loughlin (1987) 50 MLR 64 at 70.
16. See, in particular Malcolm Grant 'Central–Local Relations: The Balance of Power' ch 10 in J. Jowell and D. Oliver (Eds) *The Changing Constitution* (2nd ed) Oxford U P (1989).
17. W.J.M. Mackenzie 'Theories of Local Government', a paper published originally in 1961 but reprinted as ch 5 of the author's *Explorations in Government* Macmillan (1975). See 69–70.
18. C.H. Wilson 'The Foundations of Local Government' in Wilson (Ed) *Essays on Local Government* Blackwell (1948) 20–21.
19. 'Theories of Local Government' in L.D. Feldman and Michael D. Goldrick *Politics and Government of Urban Canada* (2nd ed) Methuen (1972) 404.
20. *Local Authorities and Central Control* George Allen and Unwin (1974).
21. Rates Act 1984; Rating and Valuation (Amendment) (Scotland) Act 1984.
22. Local Government Finance Act 1988 Pt VII; Abolition of Domestic Rates, Etc, (Scotland) Act 1987 s 22 and Sched 3.
23. *Ibid* Pt III; and ss 3A and 3B (as substituted by the Local Government and Housing Act 1989) respectively.

24. D.N. Chester *Central and Local Government* Macmillan (1951) 326.
25. *Op cit* note 19 *supra* 404.
26. *The Case for Local Government* George Allen and Unwin (1983) 125.
27. Cmnd 9797 para 3.34.
28. *Ibid* para 3.35.
29. *Ibid* paras 3.11–3.54.
30. Cmd 3436 (1929).
31. *Ibid* 111–114.
32. *Ibid* paras 379–380.
33. *Management of Local Government* HMSO (1967).
34. Cmnd 9797 paras 5.15–5.18.
35. *Ibid* para 5.29.
36. On staff commissions, see further below at note 83 and accompanying text.
37. Cm 433 para 1.4.
38. Cmnd 9797 para 5.36 and Cm 433 para 1.3 and Annex para 1. It should, in passing be observed that, in their quotation from Widdicombe at para 1.3, the word 'openly' (sub-para (b)) is discreetly omitted – perhaps simply in recognition of the fact that there are few requirements of openness where a decision is taken, on behalf of a council, by an officer rather than a committee or sub-committee.
39. Cm 433 ch V.
40. 'Citizenship and Government: The Challenge for Management in the Public Domain' (1989) XXXVII *Political Studies* 5.
41. *Ibid* 21.
42. *Op cit* note 24 *supra*.
43. *Ibid* 348.
44. *Ibid* 351.
45. W.I. Jennings *Principles of Local Government Law* (1st ed) University of London (1931) 165–170; W.A. Robson *The Development of Local Government* George Allen and Unwin (1931) 242–244.
46. W.I. Jennings *op cit* note 45 *supra* 168.
47. See, in particular, *Management of Local Government* (Maud Committee Report) HMSO (1967) vol 5 445–446.
48. For discussion of police accountability under the Police Act 1964 and the Police (Scotland) Act 1967 see E.C.S. Wade and A.W. Bradley *Constitutional and Administrative Law* (10th ed) Longman (1985) ch 20 and G. Marshall *Constitutional Conventions* Clarendon (1984) ch VIII.
49. *The New Local Authorities: Management and Structure* HMSO (1972).
50. *Police, Government and Accountability* Macmillan (1987) 50–55.
51. And, for Scotland, Paterson *The New Scottish Local Authorities: Organisation and Management Structures* HMSO (1973).
52. Weights and Measures Act 1985 s 72(3).
53. See e.g. *Emergency Planning Guidance to Local Authorities* Scottish Home and Health Department.
54. See Abolition of Domestic Rates, Etc. (Scotland) Act 1987 s 12.
55. See Local Government Finance Act 1988 s 26.
56. Local Government Act 1972 s 101, Local Government (Scotland) Act 1973 s 56.
57. For the most trenchant critique, see C. Cockburn *The Local State* Pluto (1977).
58. It is interesting to note at this point the rather different possibility canvassed before, but rejected by, the Committee of Inquiry (Stodart) into Local Government in Scotland Cmnd 8115 (1981), on which Professor Bradley served, that the planning functions of district councils might be discharged by officials employed by regional councils. See paras 47–48.
59. See Local Government Finance Act 1982 ss 11–25 and Local Government (Scotland) Act 1973 ss 100–106.
60. See eg *A–G v De Winton* (1906) 2 Ch 106.

61. *Report of the Bognor Regis Inquiry* HMSO (1965).
62. *Ibid* para 236.
63. Powers now consolidated in the Housing Act 1985 s 169 and Housing (Scotland) Act 1987 s 81.
64. See e.g. Local Government Act 1972 s 230 and Local Government (Scotland) Act 1973 s 199.
65. 1985 Act s 169(2); 1987 Act s 81(2).
66. 21 February 1980, Standing Committee F col 554 (Mr G. Finsbery MP).
67. *Ibid* cols 535–560.
68. 27 October 1983, Standing Committee B col 340 (Mr G. Kaufman MP).
69. 21 February 1980, Standing Committee F col 543 (Mr J. Tilley MP).
70. 23 January 1986 HC Debs col 314.
71. Cmnd 9797 para 5.69.
72. Cm 433 para 2.19.
73. In particular, *R v Clerk to Lancashire Police Committee, ex p Hook* [1980] 2 All ER 353; *R v City of Birmingham District Council ex p O* [1982] 2 All ER 356 (CA), [1983] 1 All ER 497 (HL).
74. *R v Barnes Borough Council, ex p Conlan* [1938] 3 All ER 226 at 230.
75. As in *ex p O op cit* note 73 *supra*.
76. [1982] 2 All ER 356 at 365–366.
77. *Ibid*.
78. *Ibid* 363–364.
79. Unpublished (1985).
80. *Ibid* para 5.
81. *Ibid* para 8.
82. *Ibid* para 17.
83. *Staffing of Local Government* HMSO (1967) ch X.
84. Cmnd 9797 para 6.194.
85. *Ibid* paras 6.143–6.152 and Annex K.
86. Cm 433 paras 5.5–5.8.
87. Local Government Finance Act 1988 ss 111–116 (as extended by the Local Government and Housing Act 1989 s 6). Note that (by s 115(4)) the duty to consider a report from the chief finance officer is not to be delegated to a committee or officer. In this respect, it joins resolutions to borrow and to determine levels of community charge. The same device has since been used in relation to the other reporting functions discussed below and in relation to reports from the local ombudsman.
88. Cm 433 paras 5.9–5.10, 5.14.
89. 1989 Act s 5.
90. In Scotland, to which the 1988 Act ss 111–116 do not extend, simply the officer having responsibility for the administration of the authority's financial affairs.
91. Cm 433 para 5.9.
92. The disjunctive reference here to 'maladministration' and 'injustice' is interesting. The monitoring officer's duties apparently extend to an authority's proposals which might cause 'injustice', even though they involve no 'maladministration'!
93. Cmnd 9797 para 6.155.
94. Cm 433 para 5.14.
95. *Ibid* paras 5.11–5.13.
96. 1989 Act s 4.
97. Again, without delegation. See note 87 *supra*.
98. 1989 Act s 7.
99. 1989 Act s 8.
100. Cm 433 paras 5.40–5.41.
101. *Ibid* para 5.46.
102. Cmnd 9797 paras 4.28–4.31.
103. See Lord Mackintosh *op cit* note 2 *supra*.

104.   *Caring for People* Cm 849 (1989).
105.   National Health Service and Community Care Act 1990 ss 50-51. The two
       sections introduce new sections 7A and 5(1A) into the Local Authority Social
       Services Act 1970 and the Social Work (Scotland) Act 1968 respectively.
       In the Scottish version there is no requirement that the directions be given
       in writing.
106.   14 February 1989 HC Debs col 165.
107.   Abolition of Domestic Rates, Etc (Scotland) Act 1987 s 12(5); Local
       Government Finance Act 1988 s 26(4).
108.   Local Government and Housing Act 1989 ss 4 – 5; Local Government Finance
       Act 988 s 114(7).
109.   See Malcolm Grant 'Central – Local Relations: The Balance of Power' in
       J. Jowell and D. Oliver (Eds) *The Changing Constitution* (2nd ed) Oxford
       U P (1989) 272.

'Scotland in Europe':
An Independent Scotland and the European Community

Robert Lane

A. Introduction

There has been much written since 1973 upon the constitutional implications of British accession to the European Community. This is not surprising, for adaptation to the requirements of Community membership probably marks the greatest challenge to British constitutional theory of the last two or three hundred years. Tony Bradley has contributed significantly to our understanding of the issues, both in encouraging debate through his editorship of *Public Law* and in his own writings.[1]

The issue of British membership of the Community, however, has taken a new twist of special importance to Scotland owing to the recent *volte-face* by the Scottish National Party. Long ambivalent, if not hostile, to Community membership as inconsistent with its aim of absolute sovereignty for Scotland, the SNP has now declared a commitment, under the slogan of 'independence in Europe', to independence from the rest of the United Kingdom coupled with continued Scottish membership of the European Community.

'Scotland in Europe' is a not entirely surprising product of the existence and increased pace of integration within the European Community. The political map of Europe and the Community consists of nation states as they happen to exist in the mid- to late-twentieth century, and they do not necessarily reflect the aspirations of a variety of nations within these states. Tension has always existed between the Basques, Catalans, Andalusians, South Tyroleans, Corsicans, Bretons and Bavarians, to name but a few, and the dominant, central authorities of the states of which they happen to form part. As a necessary corollary of European integration is a diminution of state sovereignty, a natural by-product is fresh heart to the nations and regions of the Community. Put simply, every transfer of competence to Brussels diminishes the relevance of Madrid and Paris to a Basque. The very success of European integration has produced, in the neat phrase of one German political scientist, an 'uprising in the provinces'.[2] In fact Scotland, and the SNP, have come rather late to perceive the advantages to nationalist aspirations which Community membership may bring.

On the SNP argument, Scotland is part of the territory of an existing member state, and so part of the Community; upon independence from the rest of the United Kingdom it will necessarily remain so and will therefore automatically accede to membership – i.e. it will become a member state – in its own right. It is this argument which seems to have allayed fears concerning what independence will mean and engendered a significant amount of public support.

The counter-argument is that Scottish independence would leave a legally intact, if geographically truncated, United Kingdom consisting of England and (presumably) Wales and Northern Ireland which would succeed to the United Kingdom's present membership of the Community. On this argument, Scotland would, upon independence, find itself outside the Community on a footing, so far as (re-)entry was concerned, equal to that of all other prospective applicant states.

Both arguments have been put with equal force and conviction, and usually little authority. For the debate ventures into untested waters – complex and interrelated issues of constitutional law, international law and European Community law not hitherto addressed in the Community. It also raises questions applicable to an issue now brought to the fore by events in Eastern Europe for which the Community has been equally unprepared but which it is required to resolve long before that of Scottish independence: German reunification.

The European Community now comprises, and recognises, twelve member states, one of which is the United Kingdom as presently constituted. It is of no relevance to Community law (although it may affect its administration) how a member state orders its own internal structure, be it federal (Germany), quasi-federal (Belgium), devolved (Spain) or unitary. The Community could therefore adapt without difficulty to the adoption of a scheme for legislative devolution, or even a form of federalism, within the United Kingdom of the types currently being debated in Scotland. It is not the intention of this essay to address these issues. The questions raised by 'independence in Europe' are quite different, and arise only upon the hypothesis that, by a process as yet undefined, the territory of the United Kingdom will be divided into two or more independent states, each of which will claim membership of the Community in its own right. The issue then, in essence, is the response of Community law to the mitosis of a member state: whether the United Kingdom or any other member state can for Community purposes unilaterally redefine itself, or extinguish itself, and the manner in which present rights of Community membership can be claimed by, or the concomitant obligations be devolved upon, what then emerges.

Even without imputing bad faith, it is fairly safe to say that there are those, both within and outwith the United Kingdom, who would oppose the result proposed by the SNP. The hostility of the present Conservative and Unionist government to devolution, let alone secession or dissolution, is well known. A number of other member states are potentially fissile, and any readiness to accord independent Community status to Scotland might be seen as encouraging similar demands in the Basque Country, Catalonia, Corsica, Flanders and Wallonia, to name but a few. Equally, some at least of the Community institutions, already faced with the problems of past and prospective enlargements, might feel inclined to resist any aggravation of those problems through division of the Community's existing component states. These concerns are genuine, not cosmetic; those in Scotland who view the issues as unique and the answer self-evident would do well to ask themselves how they might react to a proposal that, to choose an extreme example, the Federal Republic of Germany be dissolved into its eleven component *Länder*, each to be granted the rights and privileges of autonomous Community membership.[3]

The first step is to consider the issues of United Kingdom constitutional law. This does not imply that national law alone would be or could be decisive. A national law which dissolves a state may seek to designate one or more successor states which will inherit the rights and obligations of the predecessor state. But, as discussed below, the success of such a device in international law depends not upon the will of the predecessor state or its successors, but upon the willingness of other states to acquiesce in it. Nevertheless, constitutional law is relevant insofar as it assists in determining the manner in which the dissolution of the state might be viewed under international and Community law.

B. Constitutional Law

Unencumbered as the United Kingdom is by a comprehensive or complex theory of the state, the issues of British constitutional law are far more straightforward than they would be for most other member states. The United Kingdom was first established, as 'the United Kingdom of Great Britain', by the Treaty of Union of 1707 between the Kingdoms of England (including the Principality of Wales[4]) and Scotland, duly ratified by the Parliaments of both Kingdoms.[5] Notwithstanding the Personal Union of the Crowns in 1603, the conventional view is that the Treaty was a treaty *iure gentium* merging two sovereign independent states, equal in terms of international personality, into a new unitary state having a single and indivisible international personality.[6] By the Treaty and its implementing Acts, not only were the Parliaments of England and Scotland extinguished and replaced by a single new Parliament of Great Britain, but the Kingdoms of England and Scotland themselves ceased to exist as independent legal entities for purposes of international law.

In 1801 the United Kingdom of Great Britain merged with Ireland, so becoming 'the United Kingdom of Great Britain and Ireland'. The union was effected by the autonomous adoption of two Acts of the Parliaments of the United Kingdom of Great Britain and of Ireland,[7] by which, again, the two Parliaments were extinguished and a single new Parliament created in their place. However, it is a matter open to question whether Ireland immediately prior to the union could properly be regarded as a sovereign, independent state. There was no treaty of union as there had been in 1707; certainly through the regime of such legislation as Poynings' Law 1494 and the Declaratory Act 1719 Ireland had for some centuries been at least *de facto* an English, then British, colony. Even following the reforms of Grattan's Parliament shortly before the union, Ireland remained subject to dictation from London and effectively a colony.[8] So even if 'the Union Agreement of 1707 was secured by coercion and corruption and regretted soon after it took effect by Scots who had supported it',[9] there are at least elements by which the event of 1801 can be characterised as internal restructuring, of absorption of Ireland into an extant United Kingdom, and so fundamentally different from the union of 1707.

In 1921 Dáil Éireann, sitting as a constituent assembly, promulgated a constitution for the Irish Free State.[10] The constitution was formally adopted by the Parliament of Great Britain and Ireland in 1922,[11] creating as a matter of British (Imperial) Law in the 26 counties the Irish Free State, with the status of a dominion, and redefining itself as the United Kingdom of Great Britain and Northern Ireland. Whilst the Irish (Republican) view was that the Free State was created by the constitution enacted by Dáil Éireann – described by an Irish judge in 1925 as 'the one and all-sufficient root of title'[12] – the conventional ('Diceyan') British view is that the Free State acquired its status and legitimacy – and therefore separation from the United Kingdom – with the passing by Parliament of the 1922 Act. But whichever view is adopted, and whatever the train of events which led to the Free State becoming the Republic of Ireland (or Éire) in 1937, the United Kingdom of Great Britain and Northern Ireland on the one hand and the Republic of Ireland on the other came to be recognised, as a matter of international law, as independent sovereign states. It was the United Kingdom of Great Britain and Northern Ireland which was, and remains, the juridical person which acceded to the Community in 1973.

The United Kingdom of Great Britain and Northern Ireland deemed itself to be, and was recognised as being, the successor state in international law to the United Kingdom of Great Britain and Ireland.[13] So, it is argued, Scottish secession from the United Kingdom would produce much the same result. But there are fundamental differences between Irish and Scottish secession from the United Kingdom. Unlike Ireland, the Kingdom of Scotland was one of the basic building blocks of 'the United Kingdom of Great Britain'. It can therefore be argued that the separation of Scotland from England would, unlike the events of 1921/22, of necessity dissolve the entity which is 'Great Britain' and would, consequently, dissolve the 'United Kingdom' as such. No such thing as 'the United Kingdom of England and Northern Ireland' could survive since there has been no such thing as the 'Kingdom of England' since 1707. And so, it is submitted, Scottish independence would of necessity dissolve the existing state, leaving all parts of it in a position of equality as regards international and Community rights and obligations. Whatever the status of an independent Scotland in the Community, it would be identical to that of England and whatever else remained of the United Kingdom. Posturing by Mrs Thatcher that she would 'veto' Scottish accession to the Community, based as it is upon fundamentally misconceived assumptions, is therefore nonsense.

Leaving aside unilateral secession from the United Kingdom – a Scottish UDI – the mechanisms for bringing about Scottish independence rest with Parliament. There is no possibility of abrogation of the 1707 Treaty of Union because the parties to it have ceased to exist and could not, in any event, restore the *status quo ante*. The question then arises as to whether Parliament is competent to dismantle the 1707 Union which united the two Kingdoms 'for ever after . . . . into one Kingdom'.[14]

Whilst some member states face serious constitutional difficulties in addressing their own dissolution,[15] the United Kingdom encounters no real constraints. The only potential bar is Article I of the 1706/7 Treaty of Union, yet an identical provision in both of the 1800 Acts of Union did not prevent Parliament from jettisoning the major part of Ireland in 1922. Even accepting the view that Parliament is in some respects restricted in its competence by the 1707 Treaty – the 'Cooper-Smith' argument,[16] which Professor Bradley blessed as 'not at all far-fetched'[17] – the dissolution of the United Kingdom is a matter which would for Stair 'concern the state of the commonwealth',[18] that is, a matter of 'Public Right' outwith the entrenched safeguards of the Treaty of Union.[19] In the present context the Diceyan view of the omnipotence of Parliament would therefore prevail; the United Kingdom could be dissolved by simple Act of the Sovereign in Parliament.

The question is, then, whether the putative Act of dissolution may seek to nominate a successor state to the present United Kingdom. As discussed above, it would do injury to the basic underpinning of the British state to purport to do other than dissolve the state and define two or more new states in its place. Nevertheless, whilst objectionable, it would not be constitutionally impossible for the Act to provide expressly for a new state of 'Scotland' and another of 'the United Kingdom of England and Northern Ireland', and further purport to vest in this United Kingdom of England and Northern Ireland all international rights and obligations of the erstwhile United Kingdom, such that it, and it alone, constituted the successor state – that is, in the present context, such that it alone acceded to membership of the Community. This is by implication the clear understanding of those who argue that Scotland will be outside looking in. But even if the Act of dissolution were to purport to do all these things, the question then arises as to whether the claim would bind, or be accepted in, the international forum and/or the Community.

C. Public International Law

Customary rules of public international law of state succession in general, and to treaties in particular, are not conclusively established.[20] There are a number of precedents involving secession from, and dissolution (or more commonly in international law 'dismemberment') of, states.[21] In some cases (Belgium/Netherlands 1830; Panama/Columbia 1903; Norway/Sweden 1905; Irish Free State/United Kingdom 1921/22; Iceland/Denmark 1944; Pakistan/India 1947; Singapore/Malaysia 1963; Bangladesh/Pakistan 1971), a predecessor state continued to exist. In others (dissolution of the Holy Roman Empire of the German Nation 1806; Gran Columbia 1829-31; the Austro-Hungarian Empire 1918; the Ottoman Empire 1920-23; the United Arab Republic 1961) it did not. In some instances (Sweden and Norway; Hungary; Iceland and Denmark; Syria and Egypt) successor states have considered themselves to succeed automatically to treaties entered into by the predecessor states; this is of course especially true in cases where one (or more than one, e.g. People's Republic of China/Republic of China) successor state purports to continue to constitute the predecessor state, although it is also true for some seceding states and in some cases involving dissolution. In others (Belgium; Austria;[22] the Irish Free State; Pakistan; Singapore; Bangladesh) they have not, preferring what is now called the 'clean slate' rule.[23] Within the Commonwealth a number of dominions continued after the Statute of Westminster and continue still to be bound by some, but not all, 'Empire Treaties' entered into by the Imperial Crown. In the precedents involving membership of international organisations some successor states (the Irish Free State for the most part; Pakistan and Bangladesh in the United Nations) acceded independently to organisations of which the predecessor state had been a member, whilst in others (the Irish Free State as party to the Red Cross Convention of 1907; Egypt and Syria in the United Nations) they succeeded automatically to membership.[24]

These precedents provide no clear picture. But they do, upon closer analysis, indicate that it is not the intention of the successor state which is definitive but rather the recognition granted to that intention by third states. In most of the above cases the successor states indicated an intention to be bound or not to be bound by the obligations of their predecessors, and a concomitant wish to be deemed to constitute either a continuation of the original state or one or more completely new states. But what was crucial to the legal result was the acquiescence of other contracting parties in these intentions and wishes. This is consistent with customary rules of international law on recognition of states. In the present context, there is no reason to expect that the international community would accept an English claim, implausible in United Kingdom law, to succeed to all rights and obligations of the United Kingdom to the exclusion of a Scotland asserting a similar, if less exclusive and so more modest, claim.

Dissatisfaction amongst the newly independent states which emerged during the period of decolonisation with the ambiguity in the law of state succession led to the adoption in 1978 of the Vienna Convention on Succession of States in Respect of Treaties.[25] Generally, the Convention provides for the 'clean slate' rule, that is, an option but not an obligation to assume the treaty obligations of the predecessor state, for emerging newly independent states,[26] whilst prescribing continuity for all other cases of state succession. Article 34 of the Convention provides:

1. When a part or parts of a territory of a State separate to form one or more States, whether or not the predecessor State continues to exist:
    (a) any treaty in force at the date of succession of States in respect of the entire territory of the predecessor State continues in force in respect of each successor State so formed . . .
2. Paragraph 1 does not apply if:
    (a) the States concerned otherwise agree; or
    (b) it appears from the Treaty or is otherwise established that the application of the treaty in respect of the successor State would be

incompatible with the object and purpose of the treaty or would radically change the conditions for its operation.

Article 35 provides that where a predecessor state continues to exist following separation of parts of its territory, its treaty obligations continue in force in respect of its territory subject to exceptions (Article 35(c)) similar to those of Article 34(2).

Article 35 would therefore apply to bind only a continuing 'United Kingdom' (if it existed) to erstwhile treaty obligations, whilst Article 34 would apply to bind all successor states 'whether or not the predecessor State continues to exist'. The two articles have been criticised for unnecessary ambiguity and infelicity of drafting.[27] Nevertheless, it appears that the two articles taken together would, other things being equal, lead to the result that, irrespective of whether Scottish independence were to spring from secession from or from dissolution of the United Kingdom, treaty obligations would continue in force with respect to all successor states unless the 'escape clauses' of Articles 34(2)(b) or 35(c) apply.

However, the 1978 Convention is not yet in force. Since it constitutes for the most part a progressive development rather than codification of international law, it is difficult to predict the influence it may bring to bear prior to its entry into force. What is more important for present purposes, the Convention has not even been signed by a single member state of the Community. Since the European Court of Justice has traditionally taken no judicial notice of an international treaty unless it has been ratified by all member states,[28] the Convention clearly will not be applied by the Court. Moreover, as will be discussed below, it is unlikely that it could seriously be contended that dissolution of an existing member state into two or more new states, each claiming Community membership, would not involve a 'radical change' in the operation of the Community treaties, and so by virtue of Article 35(2)(b) or 35(c) fall outwith the application of the Convention.

In any event, even if the Convention were in force and ratified by all the member states, it is not clear that it would apply to the rights and obligations arising from membership of the Community. The Convention is intended to provide rules of international law for succession of states in respect of treaties the application of which are governed by rules of public international law. Such treaties include those constituting multilateral international organisations. But the Community is not simply an international organisation. Whilst it was created by international treaties, it has gone on to develop a semi-autonomous personality and authority independent of international law. The European Court of Justice has emphasised since its decision in *van Gend en Loos*[29] in 1963 that Community law constitutes a new, *sui generis* legal order, whose rules displace those of international law within its own legal structure. As the Community is essentially a creature governed by its own system of law, and as the member states have by the Treaty accepted the compulsory authority of the Court of Justice in Luxembourg, the status within the Community of an independent Scotland or of any other successor state is likely therefore to be determined neither by the wishes of the United Kingdom, of England or Scotland, nor, in accordance with the traditional rules of international law, by recognition of other member states, but by the rules of Community law as interpreted and applied by the Court of Justice.

D. European Community Law

But the issue is not addressed by Community law. The Treaties provide for the accession of new member states, which requires the consent of a unanimous Council of Ministers, of an absolute majority in the European Parliament and of the parliaments of each existing member state,[30] but not for the withdrawal or expulsion of a member state. *A fortiori*, the question of dissolution of a member state was neither envisaged nor addressed. How then will Community law resolve the issue which its rules must govern but for which it fails to provide?

There are two precedents, neither of them directly in point. The first is Algeria which, at the entry into force of the EEC Treaty in 1958, was in French constitutional law part of the territory of the Republic. It seceded from France in 1962, acquiring independent statehood. Following independence the relationship of Algeria with the Community was in limbo until the entry into force of a Cooperation Agreement in 1978.[31]

However, notwithstanding their status in French constitutional law, Algeria and the other overseas *départements* were never regarded by the EEC Treaty as an integral part of the Community. Article 227(2) recognised them (and continues to recognise them) but only in order to ensure that certain provisions of the Treaty should apply to them. So Algeria was never part of the territory of the Community. In any event, Algeria's relationship with France, notwithstanding French constitutional law, was in international law one of dependency. The process of Algerian independence is therefore best characterised as one of decolonisation, so that Algeria was entitled to adopt a 'clean slate' which allowed it unilaterally to opt out of obligations imposed upon it by the Treaty. In the same manner, Annex IV of the Treaty ceases to apply to overseas countries and territories listed therein upon their independence without need of formal treaty amendment.

The other precedent, Greenland, has been cited by the SNP in support of its case. Unlike Algeria, Greenland became an integral part of the Community as a constituent part of Denmark in 1973. With the grant of 'home rule' in 1979,[32] Greenland acquired the competence – like that enjoyed by the British dominions from the late 1890s – to opt out of Danish treaty obligations, and in a 1982 referendum Greenlanders elected (by a slim majority) to withdraw from the Community. But Greenland did *not* secede from the Kingdom of Denmark. It remained and remains subject to the Danish Crown and forms a part of the territory of Denmark,[33] but as a result of formal amendment to the Community Treaties in 1985[34] it no longer forms part of the territory of the Community. Thus the precedent is almost diametrically opposed to that claimed by some supporters of 'independence in Europe', who envisage a Scotland independent of the United Kingdom but a new member state of the Community.

Yet the precedent of Greenland is not *entirely* inapposite. It is authority for a principle that, so long as territory continues to form part of a member state, formal Treaty amendment (as onerous a process as admitting a new member state except that the European Parliament need only be consulted; its consent is not required[35]) is necessary in order to alter the territorial application of the Treaty. It was never suggested that the territory of Greenland could be withdrawn from Community competence by some form of unilateral act of the appropriate Greenland or Danish authorities. Rather it was universally accepted that Treaty amendment was necessary.

Opponents of the SNP view would argue that the Greenland precedent is a narrow one, indicating only that Treaty amendment is necessary in order to alter the territorial application of Community law *within existing member states*. As such, it does not squarely resolve the question of whether a member state may in accordance with its own constitutional rules unilaterally redefine itself and by doing so remove part of its erstwhile territory from, or bring acquired territory within, the jurisdiction of Community law.

The Treaty recognises but generally does not define the member states.[36] Customary rules of public international law, as codified in Article 15 of the 1978 Vienna Convention and implicit in Article 29 of the 1969 Vienna Convention on the Law of Treaties,[37] which *is* in force and is ratified by most Community member states, holds that generally a treaty is binding upon each party to it in respect of its entire territory at any given time. This 'moving treaty frontier rule' means that treaty obligations run with the territory. Thus, in international law, if by bilateral treaty the Orkney and Shetland Islands retroverted to the Kingdom of Norway they would automatically cease to be bound by the international treaty obligations of the United Kingdom and assume those of Norway.

This then raises the question of whether the moving treaty frontier rule would be recognised and applied by the European Court of Justice in the Community context. It is a question overtaken by events and at the forefront of the current Community agenda, in the guise of whether the reunified Germany has automatically assumed the erstwhile Federal Republic's membership of the Community. Clearly the accession of the German Democratic Republic in its own right would have required recourse to the formal accession procedure of Article 237. But in the event, German reunification was achieved on 3rd October 1990 with the entry into force of the 'Unification Treaty' (*Einigungsvertrag*)[38] which dissolved the Democratic Republic and reconstituted the five historic *Länder* which comprised its territory, which were then simply absorbed (in accordance with Article 23 of the Basic Law) into the Federal Republic which continues to be governed by the Basic Law. There remain questions in German constitutional law as to whether the Federal Republic now constitutes the 1937 German Reich, which according to the Federal Constitutional Court never ceased legally to exist[39]. But by adopting either of two views – (a) that the Federal Republic (provisionally) constituted the Reich and ratified the Community Treaties as such, so that (re)unification,[40] even minus the Eastern territories, represents not state succession but simply effective resumption of dormant German statehood; or (b) that both the Federal and Democratic Republics were autonomous states fully independent in international law (which is a construct not accepted in German constitutional law[41]) but nevertheless by bilateral agreement the Democratic Republic has been absorbed into the Federal Republic which ratified the Community Treaties – have either the German Reich or the New Federal Republic of 16 *Länder* assumed or acceded automatically to the rights and obligations of the erstwhile Federal Republic's membership of the Community? And if so, could the arguments be pressed further and to a more remote prospect, and taken to indicate that the moving treaty frontier rule would permit the reunification of Ireland by bilateral agreement between the United Kingdom and the Republic of Ireland, Great Britain succeeding to present United Kingdom membership and the reunified Ireland succeeding to that of the Republic?

The one precedent in Community law is the case of the Saar. After the war, the Saar was incorporated into French territory. Following a plebiscite within the territory, the Saar was returned to Germany by a bilateral treaty[42] and incorporated as a *Land* into the Federal Republic[43] with effect from 1 January 1957. The Saar (or Saarland) was therefore part of Germany prior to the entry into force and prior to signature of the Rome Treaties. However, it had been part of France at the entry into force of the European Coal and Steel Community (ECSC) Treaty. On the same day as the signature of the Franco-German treaty ceding the Saar to Germany, the ECSC member states signed another treaty[44] in order to amend the ECSC Treaty so as to recognise the cession. Owing to delay in Italian and Dutch ratification, however, the amending treaty did not enter into force until October 1958. Notwithstanding that the changes to the Treaty were minimal, for almost two years it remained unaltered, and the Coal and Steel Community therefore did not formally recognise the cession of the Saar.

It is therefore submitted that the moving treaty frontier rule does not apply in Community law. The reasoning of the Saar precedent – which is all the more persuasive now that the constitutional rules of Community law are more fully developed – and of the Greenland precedent properly construed indicate that the Treaty applies to the territory of a member state *as constituted at the point of ratification or accession* unless and until the Treaty is amended so as to produce a different result. The identity and constitution of each member state is therefore fixed for purposes of Community law and cannot be altered for those purposes save by the constitutional means provided in the Treaty: formal amendment.

It must be said that this is an opinion not shared, in the context of German reunification, by the governments of all the member states (expressed through a communiqué issued by the European Council), by the Council of Ministers, by the Commission or by the European Parliament. All of these authorities have expressed support for the view that the new Germany is either the same legal person as, or succeeds to the rights of, the Federal Republic which ratified the Treaties and so can be accommodated within the Community without need of Treaty amendment.[45] None of them has furnished much in the way of legal justification for this conclusion – and indeed it appears not to have been the intention of the German government at the time of ratification[46] – but all have stressed the special nature of the

German case, apparently accepting that the Treaty already recognised the provisional nature of the division of Germany.[47]

The one Community institution which has voiced no opinion on the matter is the Court of Justice, and it is submitted that the Court will have great difficulty in recognising the refurbished Germany as a member state in the absence of Treaty amendment. The reasons for this lie in the special nature of Community law. The 'new legal order' recognised by the Court of Justice in *van Gend en Loos*[48] is a product of the complex balance of rights and obligations shared amongst the member states *inter se* and collectively with the autonomous Community institutions. It would do injury to the bargain which led to this balance if a member state could move the goalposts by unilaterally redefining itself, just as a constituent state of a federation cannot do so except in accordance with the rules of the federal constitution. Thus the only way the Court of Justice could recognise the new Federal Republic is by adopting the German construct that it was the Reich which ratified the Treaty in 1957 – in effect, that the territory of the Democratic Republic has always been part of the Community. How this can be squared, should the Court seek to do so, with the fact that all the member states save the Federal Republic recognised the Democratic Republic as an independent sovereign state and with the precedent of the Saar remains to be seen. And if the Court were to support this position, would it then also do so in the event of unilateral Irish reunification in the light of the Republic's analagous 'constitutional imperative' of the reintegration of the 'national territory'?[49]

But even if the Court were to accept these fictions as an expedient adjustment to political fact, would it afford any assistance to the question of Scotland in Europe? The Court also said in *van Gend en Loos* that the subjects of the new legal order were not only the member states but also the people of the Community, upon whom the Treaty and its law, independently of the member states, confer patrimonial rights.[50] Since the subjects of Community law are not only the member states, and the rights created by it have their source in Community, not national, law, these rights cannot be abrogated either by a member state acting alone – or even by all the member states acting in concert; the people of the Community are entitled to protection of their rights, and are deemed to be so protected by the compulsory involvement of the European Parliament in treaty amendment, minimal though it may be. So it seems clear in Community law, and this is the majority legal opinion in the Community,[51] that a member state cannot withdraw unilaterally from the Community.

Of course, this is not consistent with the commonly asserted proposition springing from the doctrine of parliamentary supremacy that the United Kingdom could effectively disengage from the Community by simple repeal of the European Communities Act 1972. This, it is said, would disapply Community law within the territory of the United Kingdom and exclude the jurisdiction of the Community institutions. But it is clear that it would be inconsistent with the obligations of Community law for Parliament to do so. By Article 5 of the Treaty, the member states bind themselves to abstain from any act which would jeopardise the attainment of the objectives of the Treaty. Upon this basis, it follows that in the absence of Treaty amendment the territory of the United Kingdom as presently constituted will remain within the Community, *and also* that the United Kingdom is incompetent to provide unilaterally for its own dissolution into two or more states.

The reasoning is that Community law must confer upon all member states, in exchange for their loss of sovereignty, an acquired right as to the constitution of the other member states which comprise the Community. It also confers upon the people within the member states patrimonial rights which cannot be abrogated by a unilateral national act. So the SNP case is correct insofar as it holds that putative secession from or dissolution of the United Kingdom will not and cannot result in the ejection of Scotland from the Community.[52] But at the same time, it would necessarily defeat the objectives of the Treaty – and constitute a 'radical change' within the meaning of Articles 34(2)(b) and 35(c) of the 1978 Vienna Convention – if a situation could be brought about whereby part of the Community (say Scotland) necessarily remained within the territorial jurisdiction of Community law but the Community institutions were deprived of the means by which Community activities could proceed with respect to that territory or its inhabitants. As the precedents of the Saar and Greenland indicate, Community law will not and cannot respond to a *fait accompli* of this sort brought about by some unilateral, bilateral and even multilateral act outwith Treaty rules. And whilst it is submitted that this should, but accepted that it may not, apply both to bringing territory from outwith into the jurisdiction of the Community (German reunification) and altering the sovereignty of territories already within the Community (Irish reunification),[53] it applies in any event, manifestly to the mitosis of a member state. It is simply wrong to claim, as have some proponents of the SNP case (who seem to assume that England would succeed to United Kingdom membership), that Scottish independence, whether by unilateral declaration or by Act of Parliament, will somehow conjure from the ether a thirteenth chair in the Council, a Scottish Commissioner, a Scottish judge on the Court of Justice and seven or eight new Scottish MEPs. And the Community and its institutions simply could not function in and for Scotland (or in and for the remainder of the United Kingdom) if, to choose two of the most obvious examples, neither the budgetary nor the agricultural machinery of the Treaty formally recognised a Scottish member state and its institutions.

The answer in Community law to Scotland in Europe therefore seems to be that neither the United Kingdom nor Scotland (or any other successor state) can by unilateral action compel the Community and its law to recognise a member state or member states different from the United Kingdom as presently constituted. The proposition that Community membership could be 'claimed' by an independent Scotland or 'refused' by the remainder of the United Kingdom is based upon fundamentally misconceived assumptions. Independence in Europe for Scotland (and for England) can be brought about only if action at the national level proceeds concurrently with action at the Community level, thus producing, at the end of the day, an agreed result which necessarily includes the concurrence of the Community institutions and all member states. A Scotland bent upon independence grounded in the clear democratic support of the Scottish people would create a moral and, given the international law principle of self-determination, probably a legal obligation for all member states to negotiate in good faith in order to produce such a result, but this solution lies essentially within the domain of politics, not law. And that is a different matter.

Notes

1. See e.g. most recently 'The Sovereignty of Parliament: In Perpetuity?' in J. Jowell and D. Oliver (Eds) *The Changing Constitution* (2nd ed) Clarendon Press (1989) 25 – 52.
2. D. Gerdes (Ed) *Aufstand der Provinz: Regionalismus in Westeuropa* Campus – Verlag (1980).
3. But see note 15 *infra*.
4. With apologies to the Welsh, Wales will be viewed as having been annexed by England by, at latest, 1536 and, for present purposes, constituting part of the Kingdom of England.
5. Act Ratifying and Approving the Treaty of Union of the Two Kingdoms of Scotland and England 1707 c 7 (Scotland); Act for An Union of the two Kingdoms of England and Scotland 1706 c 11 (England).
6. See e.g. T.B. Smith 'Constitutional Law: Fundamental Law' in *Stair Memorial Encyclopaedia of the Laws of Scotland* vol 5 paras 338 – 360.
7. Act for the Union of Great Britain and Ireland 1800 c 67 (GB); Act for the Union of Great Britain and Ireland 1800 c 38 (Ireland).
8. See e.g. C. Munro, *Studies in Constitutional Law* Butterworths (1987) 16ff; for judicial recognition in England of this status see *Campbell v Hall* (1774) 1 Cowp 204 at 210.
9. T.B. Smith *op cit supra* note 6, para 344.
10. Constitution of the Irish Free State (Saorstát Éireann) Act 1922 (No. 1 of 1922).
11. Irish Free State Constitution Act 1922 (Sess 2) c 1.
12. *Cahill v A-G* 1 IR [1925] 70 at 76 *per* Meredith J. The irony in this is that whilst as matter of British (Imperial) law the Free State came to be empowered to amend its constitution in 1931 with the enactment of the Statute of Westminster, Irish fealty to the constitutional Act of the Dáil meant that it was unaffected by subsequent Imperial legislation, so that the Free State was incompetent to amend its own constitution in certain respects until the (revolutionary) creation of the Republic in 1937; see *The State (Ryan) v Lennon* [1935] IR 170.
13. It is here relevant that the Irish Free State did not contest this claim. The issues of the succession of the Free State (and the Republic) to the international rights and obligations of the erstwhile United Kingdom of Great Britain and Ireland are discussed below.
14. Treaty of Union Art I.
15. For example, Art 79(3) of the German Basic Law – the 'eternity clause' *(Ewigkeitsklausel)* – declares (subject to the termination of the Basic Law; Art 146) to be permanently inadmissible the abolition of the *Länder* and their role in the federal legislative process; amendment of Art 79(3) itself is viewed as equally inadmissible. There is therefore no constitutional means by which the Federal Republic could dissolve the federation.
16. See *MacCormick v LA* 1953 SC 396 *per* Lord President Cooper; T.B. Smith 'The Union of 1707 as Fundamental Law' [1957] PL 99; T.B. Smith 'Constitutional Law: Fundamental Law' *op cit* note 6 *supra*; Mitchell, *Constitutional Law* (2nd ed) W. Green & Son (1969) at 69 – 74; D.N.

MacCormick 'Does the United Kingdom have a Constitution?' (1978) 29 NILQ 1; M. Upton 'Marriage Vows of the Elephant: the Constitution of 1707' (1989) 105 LQR 79.

17. 'The Sovereignty of Parliament – In Perpetuity?' *loc cit* note 1 *supra* at 29.
18. *Institutes* I.1.23.
19. Treaty of Union Art. XVIII. For detailed consideration of Art. XVIII see *MacCormick v LA supra* note 16; *Gibson v LA* 1975 SC 136. For the most recent judical discussion of constitutional issues see the dicta of the Aberdeen and Stirling Sheriffs in *Stewart v Henry* 1989 SLT (Sh Ct) 34 at 37–8 and *Fraser v MacCorquodale* 1989 SLT (Sh Ct) 39 at 41.
20. See generally W. Fiedler 'State Succession', in R. Bernhardt (Ed) *Encyclopedia of Public International Law*, North Holland vol 10 (1987) 446–456.
21. For detailed discussion see the International Law Commission Commentary on the Draft Convention on Succession of States in Respect of Treaties (1974) YBILC vol II part 1 260–266.
22. It is worth noting that following the dissolution of the Austro-Hungarian monarchy Hungary considered itself to succeed to treaties entered into during the 'period of dualism' but Austria did not.
23. Discussed further *infra*.
24. In the case of the United Arab Republic it must be noted that both Syria and Egypt had acquired membership of the UN independently prior to the creation of the UAR in 1958, and so could be thought simply to have resumed their independent membership.
25. UN Doc A/Conf 80/31.
26. A newly independent state is defined by the Convention (art 2(1)(f)) as 'a successor State the territory of which immediately before that date of succession of States was a dependent territory for the international relations of which the predecessor State was responsible'. The term therefore applies to colonies, trusteeships, mandates and protectorates. Nationalist rhetoric aside, it is not seriously claimed that the status of Scotland within the United Kingdom is one of dependence in law.
27. See ILC Commentary *op cit* note 21 *supra* at 264–66. It seem apparent that article 35 was intended to apply to, and create a clean slate rule for, newly independent states within the meaning of the Convention.
28. The Court first took notice of the European Convention on Human Rights in Case 4/73 *Nold v Commission* [1974] ECR 491 only after France (the last member state to do so) had ratified it.
29. Case 26/62 [1963] ECR 1.
30. EEC Treaty art 237.
31. Agreement of 26 April 1976 OJ 1978 L263/2.
32. The home rule *(hjemmestyre)* granted to Greenland is not unlike that which was enjoyed by the dominions prior to the Statute of Westminster 1931; see the 'Home Rule Act' Law No 577 *Lovtidende* A 1978 at 1879. The Faeroe Islands already enjoyed a similar status prior to 1973, and so were competent to, and did, refuse to join the Community; see EEC Treaty art 227(5)(a).
33. In Danish law, part of the Kingdom of Denmark wtihin the 'national community' *(Rigsfealleskab)* – again, analagous to pre-1931 dominion status.
34. Treaty of 13 March 1984 amending, with regard to Greenland, the Treaties establishing the European Communities OJ 1985 L29/1; in force 1 February 1985.
35. EEC Treaty art 236.
36. Art 227. The exceptions are where certain territories of various member states (e.g., the Faeroe Islands, Greenland, the Canary Islands) are mentioned in order specifically to exclude them from the territorial jurisdiction of the Community.
37. Cmnd 7964 (1969).
38. Treaty of 31 August 1990 between the Federal Republic of Germany and

the Democratic Republic of Germany on the Creation of the Union of Germany, BGB1 1990 II 889.

39. Judgement of 31 July 1973 (the *Grundlagenvertrag* judgment) BVerfGE 36, 1. The legal issues of German reunification in both German and international law are extremely complex; for an overview in English see G. Ress, 'Germany, Legal Status after World War II', in R. Bernhardt (Ed) *op cit* note 20 *supra* vol 10 (1987) 191-206.

40. Note the Unification Treaty purports to implement *Einigung*, not *Wiedervereinigung*.

41. The *Grundlagenvertrag* judgment, note 39 *supra*.

42. Treaty of 27 Oct 1956 on the Resolution of the Saar Question, BGB1 1956 II 1589.

43. Law of 23 Dec 1956 on the Incorporation of the Saarland, BGB1 1956 I 1011.

44. Treaty of 27 Oct 1956 amending the Treaty establishing the ECSC consequent upon the Return of the Saar to Germany.

45. See COM(90) 400 final.

46. German ratification proceeded upon the clear understanding, although there is no mention of it in the Treaties, that reunification would lead necessarily to a 'revision' (*Überprüfung*) of the Treaties (E. Wohlfarth et al (Eds), *Die Europäische Wirtschaftsgemeinschaft: Kommentar zum Vertrag* Franz Vablen (1960) 616), and this view was supported by the French government of the day. But revision is not the same thing as automatic absorption or succession.

47. Protocol to the EEC Treaty on German Internal Trade and Connected Problems. This Protocol is sometimes cited as Treaty justification for regarding a reunified Germany as fully a member state, but this conclusion is a very creative reading of the Protocol.

48. Case 26/62 (1963) ECR 1.

49. See Arts 2 and 3 of the Irish Constitution and, most recently, *McGimpsey v Ireland* [1990] ILRM 441 (SC).

50. The French text (which is clearer than the English) reads at p 23 of the *Recueil*: 'le droit communautaire . . . . est . . . . destiné à engendrer des droits qui entrent dans leur patrimoine juridique'.

51. See e.g. J. Usher *European Community Law and National Law: The Irreversible Transfer?* Allen & Unwin (1981).

52. Were it to be otherwise, the sometimes turbulent issue of British membership of the Community could be resolved by the device of dissolving the United Kingdom and constituting Scotland to be the successor state to British membership, thus leaving England, whose attitude to the Community has long been ambivalent, outwith the Community. This proposition (however attractive it might be to, say, M Delors) is entirely untenable, but is consistent with the apparent views of those opposing the SNP position.

53. It follows that this should also apply to cession of territory. Thus it is submitted that retroversion of the Orkney and Shetland Islands to Norway without amendment to the Treaties would be an unlawful deprivation of both the acquired rights of other member states to view them as part of the Community and the patrimonial rights enjoyed by Shetlanders and Orcadians under Community law.

An Idea for a Scottish Constitution

Neil MacCormick

A. Introduction

This essay is offered with a certain hesitancy to the present volume of
scholarly essays in public law. The hesitancy has its origins in a distinction
I have always tried to maintain between academic writing and political
activism. There is of course no perfectly watertight boundary between the
legal and the political, nor between doctrinal legal theory and normative
political argument. Yet one may wish to try to maintain a distinction between
matters on which disinterested and objective commentary on the law or
on reform proposals is one's aim, and matters where one's role is that of
a party political advocate. It is just this distinction which I shall here
transgress.

My object in this essay is to give a general account of the document
appended to the essay. That document (reproduced with permission) is the
Scottish National Party's policy statement on a Scottish Constitution. I was
Vice-Convener to Dr Robert McIntyre as Convener of the policy committee
which drew up the text, as well as the principal draftsman of it in its present
form, and took a principal role in the advocacy of the proposals in the SNP's
National Assembly in 1976-7 and at its Party Conference in Dundee in 1977,
where the proposals were adopted as the party's policy defining what is
its most fundamental aim. (The policy has stood unaltered in essentials over
the intervening thirteen years.)

In itself, the policy document evidences a not uninteresting constitutional
experiment, one which operated internally to the constitution of the party,
and which owed its inspiration to Isobel Lindsay, then Executive Vice-
Chairman for Policy. The first part is a 'Statement of Principles', these
being the points to which the party fully and formally committed itself
through its supreme policy-making body, the National Conference. This
meets once a year over four days, under the glare of publicity which such
occasions are designed to attract. Inevitably, such a forum offers only
restricted opportunities for debate and for close and detailed deliberation
over a document so elaborate as the whole text of a draft national
constitution. But real debate, and real decision-making, is possible at the
level of general principle. This did indeed occur, and an amendment was

carried concerning the right to call an initiative referendum. A debate concerning the desirability of continuation of constitutional monarchy resulted in a decisive affirmation of the proposals upon this point.

The risk of such a way of proceeding is that people decide upon 'principles' without the remotest idea of how, if at all, these would or could be practically realised. This had, however, been foreseen and forestalled in the present case. The 'Principles' as adopted were not designed, proposed or adopted in pure abstraction, without due attention to the concrete form in which it was intended to make them effectual. On the contrary, an actual full text of a draft constitution had been carefully worked over in committee and then submitted to the appropriate deliberative forum, that provided by the party's policy-originating (but not finally authoritative) National Assembly, a body which meets in private, and can, over as many sessions as may be needed, hammer out points of relative detail. The principles and the constitutional text embodying them were hammered out alongside each other during this process, and the fact of this parallel process of development and the two documents it had produced were known to the delegates who voted upon the principles at the Dundee conference of 1977. The second part of the present Appendix, entitled 'The Scottish Constitution', is the constitutional text worked out in the manner explained. As an experiment in rational collective decision-making, combining as much openness as possible with real deliberative effectiveness under constraints of time, the process seemed to me to be a great success, for which all concerned were much indebted to Isobel Lindsay.

The constitutional text can be seen as a concretisation of more abstract principles. Its provisions thus constitute both an illustration of the practical sense of these principles and a test-case of their intelligible applicability in a workable set of constitutional norms. The two parts of the document, taken together, express a constitutional stance and propose a definite constitutional plan, both of which seem to deserve the attention equally of purely disinterested scholars and of political activists committed to rival aims and ends. The proposal states the terms on which the Scottish National Party would seek to implement its chief aim, viz., to re-establish the independence of Scotland (necessarily, within the framework of the European Community). Of course not everyone embraces this idea gladly. But quite apart from the question of whether Scottish independence is desirable or the reverse, the proposals put other questions in issue. For they also contain ideas concerning constitutional forms and reforms, most of which can be read as applicable in the United Kingdom context even by those who recoil in horror from the thought of Scotland's ceasing to be an incorporated part of the UK.

So the proposals should be seen as possessing a dual interest. Do they propose a viable and acceptable constitutional order for a Scottish state if ever again there is such a thing? And do they express attractive ideas for improved constitutional government, if read simply as advancing an improved form of parliamentary constitution within the forms of constitutional monarchy, where the executive emerges from and takes the leading role in Parliament, while the Courts implement law created in

Parliament as the democratic forum and yet also review legislative and executive acts to secure their conformity to the constitution and the guaranteed rights it entrenches? The second question is, of course, independent of the first.

However one looks at it, whether as advocate of these proposals and their underlying aim, or as opponent of both, or merely as a detached commentator concerned with public law, there does seem to be reason to open the proposals to the clear light of day and to the searchlight of scholarly discussion and criticism. This is something from which they have largely been exempted in the last decade (perhaps because they then seemed academic in the purely adversative sense). Despite the hesitancy to which I admitted in my opening paragraph, I take this as after all good reason to embark on what I hope will be only a first stage of public debate. That I am myself a far from unbiassed commentator will be the more forgivable if the effect of this essay is to bring into public currency proposals which could only be improved by being subjected to the ordinary rigours of scholarly criticism and public debate.

The spirit of such debate, it is fitting here to say, is very appropriate to the present volume, which *inter alia* commemorates A W Bradley's twenty-year tenure of the Chair of Constitutional Law at Edinburgh University. Few scholars have contributed more than Tony Bradley, or contributed in a more magnanimous spirit, to scholarly consideration of public law and to public debate upon its fundamental principles these twenty years. I know he will not agree with the fundamentals of what I say here, so far as this bears on the aim of Scottish independence; but I hope he will see in the style of presentation something of the kinds of concerns which animate all of his own work. At the level of constitutional reform proposals, I think he will find some points of positive agreement between us.

The rest of this essay comprises a commentary on 'The Scottish Constitution' in both its principles and its details. It has eight sections: the first of these reviews some general issues implicit in the proposals; the following seven deal in proper order with the six Articles of the draft constitution, and finally with the initiative referendum issue.

B. General Remarks

The general shape of this draft constitution is familiar, since it is a variation upon the present British Constitution. The variations are, however, important. First, it is made unequivocally clear that the constitution is fundamental law, and justiciable as such. (Some of the contradictions involved in the current leading English view of the Articles of Union of 1706/7 are therefore avoided.) Rights of citizenship and of residence are conferred in plainly non-racial (and non-racist) terms. The forms of constitutional monarchy are retained, for these have proved well-adapted to securing stable democratic government in Northern Europe generally and in the monarchies within the Commonwealth. Those who find it surprising that the Scottish National Party expresses allegiance to the present royal house ought perhaps to remind themselves that it is a house which enjoys a much more ancient and uninterrupted title in right of Scotland than in right of any other part of the UK. The choice for constitutional monarchy sits naturally with continuation of a Cabinet system of executive government under an elected Prime Minister; but a constitutional provision for election of the Prime Minister by Parliament, with recourse to the head of state's prerogative of appointment only in default of election, marks the firmly democratic intentions of the proposed governmental forms.

It is a widely held view that in the United Kingdom the Executive enjoys undue dominance over Parliament, and thus dangerously unfettered power. This view is heartily endorsed here. There is provision for a fixed-term four-year Parliament, subject to early dissolution only in a case where no government can command the confidence of Parliament. There is no provision for dissolution on the unilateral advice of a Prime Minister, and it is believed that this would somewhat adjust the present balance of power, as well as limiting a Prime Minister's power to play 'cat and mouse' over fixing the date of a general election. The Parliament itself is a single chamber Parliament, with a delaying power (akin to that of the present House of Lords) vested in a substantial minority, though overridable by referendum. Whether the absence of a revising chamber would prove a serious lack is unclear; New Zealand, with a similar size of population, seems to manage perfectly well with a single legislative chamber. A strengthened and expanded legislative committee procedure may be the answer, and is the one provided for here.

In any event, the key question is perhaps the issue of what (if any) constitutional limits there should be on either Executive or Legislature. This rekindles the great debate over entrenched rights. Some see an entrenched bill or charter of rights as involving the danger that the country which adopts such a thing will exchange possibly arbitrary but always reversible rule by democratic bodies for arbitrary and undemocratic rule by (usually rather conservative) judges. The strongest answers to this objection are: that democracy, with all its other virtues, contains no guarantee of justice to unpopular individuals or minorities, who can always be outvoted; that, anyway, the democratic control exercisable through elections can rarely if ever be so focused as to concentrate upon an issue of injustice or unfair discrimination affecting a minority; and that the style and discipline of legal argumentation as a public deliberation on fundamental issues in fact negates the possibility of judicial arbitrariness, though admittedly without guaranteeing a permanent and perfect sensitivity to all the values that constitutional rights ought to keep in play. Moreover, we live now in a Europe in which all members of the European Communities (hereinafter, EC) submit to one form of transnational judicial review of their legislation for conformity to Community Law and (most importantly here) to another form of transnational review for conformity to the European Convention on Human Rights (ECHR). It seems quite extraordinary to debar our own domestic judges from passing judgement on the very matters we have obliged ourselves to remit in the last resort to transnational tribunals. The SNP has found these arguments compelling, and thus the present proposals contain entrenched and justiciable rights modelled upon the ECHR.

This highlights the deep importance of the independence of the Judiciary, and the need to ensure that judicial appointments reflect more than the momentary preferences of the executive government in power. In this, existing UK arrangements seem less than fully satisfactory, especially when one considers the colossal proportion of nominations to the Scottish bench this century which happen to have occurred when the party in government in Westminster has been in the minority, even an almost derisory minority, in Scotland. (This remark is intended to reflect in no way adversely upon the character or quality of the judges so appointed, but only to highlight the undesirable features of a process of appointment which would become the more undesirable in case of an enhanced judicial power.) Under the proposals, the Judiciary will remain independent, but with what is hoped to be the better security that appointment would be by a commission rather than by pure executive decision.

Finally, attention should be drawn to the provision concerning proportional representation in parliamentary elections. This represents both a commitment to what has long been considered (both in the SNP and outside it) the elementary democratic justice of equal voting power and a further serious attempt to steer parliamentary government, with an executive rooted in Parliament, clear of the system of 'elective dictatorship' often held to be the most deeply undesirable feature of present British arrangements.

C. 'Constitution and People' (Article I)

One would expect a Constitution to pronounce itself supreme law, with entrenched status, that is, to be capable of amendment only by special procedure, and with provision for judicial review of regular legislation inconsistent with its provisions. The draft Constitution expresses itself to be supreme law in its opening article, providing for its amendment in Article VI. Judicial review is envisaged by implication throughout the text (in the sense that only legislation conformable to the Constitution is to be implemented). It is partly regulated by Article IV.2, where a special process of reference of constitutional questions to a seven-judge court of the Court of Session is provided for.

Also in Article I.1 is the declaration of the right of the people of Scotland to 'self-determination and to sovereignty over the territory and natural resources of Scotland'. These declarations came, more or less in these words, from earlier and very deep-seated policy statements and beliefs. Some purist international lawyers criticise the application of the concept of self-determination here, on the grounds that self-determination would be exhausted in the process of achieving political independence, and is an inept description of the condition of a free country enjoying democratic self-government. For myself, though I see the force of the argument about the specialist usages of international lawyers and the texts of relevant international conventions, I see no reason why a broader conception of the ideal of self-determination ought not to be adopted into domestic constitutional law. It is surely the case that the point of maintaining democratic institutions of internal self-government is precisely the same as the point of seeking self-government in the first place.

Article I also deals with territory and with citizenship. The significant point as to territory is that it is defined: first, in terms of the existing territorial jurisdiction of the Scottish Courts (thereby following the continuing legal definition of Scotland as a country which existed before, and has persisted throughout, the period of incorporation in Great Britain); and second, in terms of the relevant rules of international law governing the seaward extensions of such territory, both in the way of territorial waters and in the way of rights over the continental shelf, fisheries and the like. Since the question of national rights over the oilfields in the North Sea continental shelf has always enjoyed a certain liveliness and even controversy, it may be worth stressing the point that the SNP holds that Scotland's claim would be to neither more nor less than would accrue under international law, which seems a fair and practical view.

Scottish citizenship from the inception of the Scottish state would be based on either birth or residence, with guarantees against any possibility of legally removing citizenship from anyone who once possesses it. Conversely, though, there should obviously be a power of voluntary renunciation for those who would prefer to opt out and continue in, or acquire, some other citizenship. In this light, another crucial guarantee would be that entitling any permanent resident of Scotland at the time of independence to retain a right of residence for him/herself and his/her children, and a right to depart and return at will, even in the event of a renunciation of Scottish citizenship. Provision is made for each of these eventualities (all this has now to be read also in the light of the free movement of persons throughout the EC, which is a right incidental to membership thereof). Article I.3 also uses a device which appears throughout the proposals viz., of expressly empowering the Scottish Parliament to legislate upon the details of citizenship law, but only within constitutional parameters aimed at preventing unjust discrimination. This is intended to strike an appropriate balance between the continuing power of the democratic majority to determine the law in force, while retaining for special majorities and specifically defined referendums any change in the basic legal framework of the state, or in the fundamental rights its citizens and residents enjoy.

D. The Monarchy and the Executive: Article II

Much of what falls to be said here was anticipated in section B. The point of Article II is to settle upon retention of monarchical institutions, with an executive acting in the monarch's name but answerable primarily to Parliament, and chosen from within it, preferably by election, but in default of that, by the choice of the monarch as head of state, or, during her/his absence from Scotland, by one or more privy councillors chosen to act as head of state ('High Commissioner' was, of course, the former title for such an officer; and it is still in evidence in the title of the Lord High Commissioner who attends the General Assembly of the Kirk on the Queen's behalf and as her representative).

It can be, and has been, said that the defect of this proposal is that it reinstates an arrangement which was tried before, and which was a failure; namely, a Union of the Crowns without a union of Parliaments. It is true that a union of Crowns is envisaged (thus retaining a form of union which dates from 1603), but not true that previous attempts at what is envisaged here were failures. The seventeenth-century monarch was in truth, not in mere form, the chief executive as well as the head of state. The Queen's or King's Scottish Ministers were chosen to carry out the same policies as her/his English Ministers, and hence they could not be effectively answerable to or controllable by the Scottish Parliament. Constitutional monarchy in its present form evolved only after the Union of 1707. The idea that the Queen's Ministers for one of her realms should act as the people and Parliament of that realm determine, while in others of her realms quite different policies are pursued, is an idea wholly dependent on the separation of the monarchical head of state from the chief executive and the other ministers, all of whom are effectively chosen by and answerable to an elected Parliament. This separation dates at the earliest from the eighteenth century. The feasibility of a successful union of crowns subject to diversity of Parliaments and executives is demonstrated by the monarchies of the Commonwealth – and that is a matter of late nineteenth-century and early twentieth-century developments (in which, indeed, statesmen of Scottish origin played a considerable part). The writings and legislative proposals of Andrew Fletcher of Saltoun in the setting of the pre-Union debates of the early 1700s envisaged exactly such a possibility, and tried to procure it as an alternative to incorporating union. But his ideas, although they were realised in the end, were regarded as utopian in their own time. For all their prescience, one may doubt whether they were directly influential in what has finally turned out in this matter.

If the union of crowns did prove unworkable, it should be noted that the succession to the Scottish Crown is to be regulated by Scots law, and hence the Crown need not descend according to the same principles as that of England, if some otherwise insoluble tension were to arise. This again determines an issue much disputed in the pre-Union years. (The unilateral enactment of the English Act of Settlement gave profound offence in Scotland, provoking a series of Acts of the Scots Parliament which envisaged entire separation under possibly disunited crowns; this in turn led to the negotiations which finally brought about the Incorporating Union of 1707.)

Other points to note in Article II are those saving the existing royal prerogative as a residual legal category which prevents the risk of constitutional paralysis. This is, as now, capable of being overridden by ordinary legislation (II.5). In an attempt to restrict the influence of the 'payroll vote', the proportion of ministers in Parliament is not to exceed one fifth of the whole (II.7). And the usual financial controls on the executive are provided for in Article II.8 and 9, restricting the duration of any taxing statute to a maximum of eighteen months and requiring legislative authority for any expenditure of public money.

E. Parliament: Article III

Legislative power will vest exclusively in Parliament and those to whom it directly delegates power. Due publication of delegated legislation will be a constitutional requirement (III.1). Subject to any legislation passed by Parliament or its delegates, and save for any laws incompatible with the Constitution, all the existing law of Scotland will remain in force as at the date of independence (III.2). Parliament will be unicameral, but will be elected by proportional representation in accordance with detailed electoral law to be passed by Parliament (III.4). What system of proportional representation should be used is a question left to Parliament, subject to its securing 'the fair representation of all shades of opinion and all parts of Scotland'. This is a matter of great importance. A serious defect of the Scotland Act 1978, and one which considerably reduced support for it in the referendum of 1979, was the continuation of the present system of disproportional representation in a way calculated to over-represent the Labour Party and West Central Scotland. Both of these should of course receive their full share of representation in a reasonable constitution, but so should everyone else and everywhere else, and no party or place should be unfairly over-represented at any other's expense.

The choice of proportional representation systems would be for Parliament to determine from time to time. The SNP's currently favoured system would graft a German-style additional member system onto an Australian-style 'alternative vote' system in single member constituencies. Under this, the 'topping up' to secure fair representation would reflect first preferences among parties; but constituency representation would depend on majorities secured after elimination of weaker first-preference candidates (as happens also in France through the double ballot system).

Parliament would have a fixed four-year term (III.5) extendible in wartime (III.7), but only for a year. Dissolution of Parliament during its term would require not only that a sitting government lose the confidence of Parliament, but also that no alternative government could command confidence (III.6). As noted already, this is part of the package aimed at diminishing the overweening power of the Executive over Parliament. Legislative sanction would be required for effectual exercise of treaty-making power, and treaties inconsistent with the constitution would require authorisation by constitutional amendment (III.8). In 1977, this provision was regarded as leaving open the issue of continuing membership of the EC, the opinion then being that the first possible amendment of the Constitution would have been one reflecting a reconsideration of the desirability of membership. Matters have now clarified themselves in favour of the view that Scotland is now in the EC and should actively seek to remain within and achieve the position of a member state, rather than to stay a remote province of a member state. While this does not in itself require any alteration of the present text, it would be desirable, for clarity, that the point be made clear within it.

Finally, it should be noted that Parliament has appropriate privileges (III.12) and may regulate its own legislative procedures (III.10), but must allow for a four-stage legislative process akin to the present one – and with the significant variation of an expanded committee stage open to the taking of public evidence (III.10 (b)). The idea here is to compensate for the absence of an upper-house as revising chamber. To compensate for the loss of an upper-house delaying power, a two-fifths minority of Parliament is enabled (except in case of money bills, see III.10 (e)) by resolution to delay an Act's coming into force for up to eighteen months (III.10 (f), (g)). But this delay may in turn be overridden by a Referendum, to be called at Parliament's discretion (III.10 (h)).

The intriguing question overall is whether these proposals would succeed in redressing the balance of Legislature with Executive, while securing fair political proportionality, and yet leaving scope for effective government. The problems are acute and general, and these solutions are surely deserving of more than cursory consideration.

F. The Courts: Article IV

The supremacy of the Scots courts in Scotland is firmly declared, and therewith any question of appeal to the House of Lords or the Privy Council in London is closed. Since references to European courts are not by way of appeal, nothing in Article IV.1 excludes such references, but again it might be wise to make this explicit rather than leave it merely implicit. To secure that there should be a single supreme court on all constitutional questions, the appellate power over all such questions is vested in the Court of Session sitting as a court of at least seven judges, and freed from the fetters of binding precedent (IV.2). The Court of Session and High Court of Justiciary otherwise continue as now, with like procedural rule-making powers. So do Sheriff Courts and other jurisdictions, though subject to ordinary legislation.

The strong constitutional innovation, already mentioned in section B above, is the provision to shift the power of nominating judges to a 'Commission on Judicial Appointments' comprising of 'the Lord Advocate, the Presiding Officer of the Parliament of Scotland, a Senator of the College of Justice elected by the whole body of Senators, and two eminent and impartial persons elected to serve for a term of ten years by the Parliament' (IV.3). How this would work is a vital question. Surely some way of removing an unfettered executive power here, while leaving the Executive (through the Lord Advocate) with a substantial say in appointments, is an idea with real attractions.

G. The Charter of Rights: Article V

The fifth Article is in a way the most vital and innovative of all, for it writes into the Constitution entrenched and justiciable fundamental rights. This cuts against long-standing British practice, but not without reason. Further, the innovation is really quite unremarkable, for the Rights proposed substantially replicate those in the European Convention, by which Scotland will be (as the UK is) bound anyway. To repeat a point made earlier, Scottish legislative and executive action is subject to review by European tribunals. There, at present, judges have to decide about matters in Scotland or elsewhere in the UK without any Scottish or British input in the way of a human rights jurisprudence rooted in sensitivity to local conditions and political traditions. It is not that we do not have entrenched and justiciable rights; it is just that our own judges are prevented from adjudicating upon them. This seems unprincipled and undesirable.

The 'substantial replication' of the European Convention amounts to wholesale adoption of the Convention's provisions with some minor adjustments in wording for the Scottish legal context, and with adaptation for stronger requirements in cases where Scots law already achieves this, or ought to. The most spectacular strengthening comes in Article V.1 (d), where the Scottish 'hundred and ten day rule' is incorporated as a guarantee against unduly long detention before or during a criminal trial. This is a field in which Scotland outshines almost every other country at present, and ought to be jealously guarded. Regrettably, the Criminal Justice (Scotland) Act 1980 reduced the citizen's rights by reducing the requirement to one under which a trial must simply *start* within the hundred and ten days. The present proposal restores the stronger rule, requiring that trials start and finish in the prescribed time; but there is power to legislate enabling judges to grant extensions, and this would be a preferable way of achieving some of the substance of what the 1980 Act did, if anything of the sort is truly necessary. Article V.1 (e) regulates in outline the remedy for wrongful detention, the petition for liberation (our *habeas corpus*), a remedy which, when needed, takes priority over other court business.

Other points of special note are as follows: the provision for freedom of governmental information in Article V.10; the communitarian qualifications on property rights (V.14); the inclusion of traditional rights of access to open country and water in the standard European right to freedom of movement; and the Gaelic language right in Article V.19. So far as concerns the voting age of eighteen years (V.17), more recently policy now favours granting the franchise to persons of sixteen or above.

It may bear repeating that a civilised country nowadays ought to secure to its citizens by majority voting the right to determine public policy and legislation. But minorities have also rights, and experience does not suggest that pure majoritarianism ever adequately guards these. Judges do not have perfect wisdom either, but the judicial process is the best we have for guarding the interests of individuals and small groups of minorities. This is most fundamentally needed where interests are fundamental to personal security and well-being – that is, in cases of fundamental rights.

H. Amendments: Article VI

Not much need be said here. Constitutions need a degree of stability, but not so much that the dead hand of the past can stifle growth and development. The balance struck here is one whereby amendments should require a special Parliamentary majority, three-fifths of the whole membership being required in support of a constitutional amendment. Further, this falls to be confirmed by a National Referendum. In this case, however, a simple majority of those voting should suffice: that which Parliament passes by the special majority is in effect subject to a popular veto, but not to a second special majority requirement. The provisions for proportional representation in Parliament should be borne in mind as having significance in this case.

I. The 'Initiative Referendum'

As mentioned above, an amendment to the Principles was carried in 1977, allowing for resort to initiative referendum by a 'significant minority of electors'. This was never formally incorporated into the draft constitution itself, though I was asked to, and did, prepare some suggestions to work this out (or to work it in). The key points, it appears to me, would be to fix a high but not hopelessly unrealistic or uncheckable number of signatures required for any initiative referendum – say, thirty thousand, or perhaps one in ten electors. The task of managing and checking what is in effect a part of the legislative process should be entrusted primarily to Parliament and its permanent staff. There should not be more than one available 'referendum day' in every two years.

Apart from the problems of regulating and organising referendums, there is the issue of the relative standing of referendum-decided laws and laws passed by parliamentary enactment. The best course, I believe, would be to make any enacted referendum proposition be in effect co-ordinate with ordinary legislation by Parliament. Then consolidation of such propositions into later legislation, with amendments if desired, could be most simply achieved; and older propositions no longer enjoying much support could be quite straightforwardly repealed. This would not create a serious risk of high-handed legislative reversal of recent and popular propositions, because (a) they could be re-run in another referendum; and (b) politicians do not lightly take risks with their parliamentary seats. I do not pretend to be a great enthusiast for the initiative referendum as a political institution, but in the form suggested I believe it could be valuable and constructive in a mature democracy. In any event, a commitment to this device is a part of the constitutional principles presented for discussion here. I hope to have made out the case for my claim that the principles, taken as a whole, are well worthy of the serious attention of public lawyers.

APPENDIX

THE SCOTTISH CONSTITUTION

The following is a statement of principles followed by detailed proposals for a constitution for an independent Scottish State.

Statement of Principles

The Scottish National Party commits itself to the following principles:

Constitution and People

1. The right of the people of Scotland to self-determination and to sovereignty over the territory and national resources of Scotland is full and unqualified. Scotland's rights to territorial waters and national resources beyond territorial waters shall be determined according to international law.

2. The governance of Scotland shall be conducted in accordance with the provisions of a written constitution.

3. Citizenship shall be open to anyone who is permanently resident in Scotland at the date of independence, to anyone who was born in Scotland, and to such other persons as the Parliament of Scotland may prescribe. Everyone permanently resident in Scotland at the date of independence shall have the right to stay in Scotland as long as he or she wishes, even if he or she does not take up Scottish citizenship.

Head of State and Executive

4. The Monarchy will continue in the form of a limited constitutional Monarchy, with the Headship of State vested in Her Majesty Queen Elizabeth and her successors according to the law of Scotland.

5. Executive power shall be exercised on the advice of, and by a Cabinet of Ministers, led by a Prime Minister who shall be elected by the Parliament of Scotland or, in default of such elections, shall be appointed as being the person who, in the opinion of the Head of State, is best able to command the confidence of Parliament. A Government shall hold office only if and as long as it has the confidence of Parliament.

Legislature

6. Legislative power, and control of all forms of executive power, shall belong to the Parliament of Scotland, which shall be a single-chamber parliament, elected by a system of proportional representation to secure the full and fair representation of all shades of opinion and all parts of Scotland.

7. Every person over the age of eighteen years who is a citizen of Scotland and whose principal place of residence is in Scotland shall, subject to the electoral laws, have the right to vote in elections to the Parliament of Scotland; no person shall be permitted to cast more than one vote.

8. A substantial minority (two-fifths) of the Parliament of Scotland shall be able (except in the case of 'money bills') to delay the enactment of legislation for one year, but enactments delayed in that way may by a majority vote of parliament be referred to the people in a referendum and shall take effect at once if approved thereby.

9. The Parliament of Scotland shall elect its own presiding officer, shall control its own internal procedure, and shall normally sit for a fixed term of four years between general elections. Parliament shall be dissolved within the four year term only if it is unable to agree on a Government, in the sense that no person can be found who is able to command its confidence as Prime Minister.

10. With the exception of any rules of law inconsistent with the constitution, every rule of law in force in Scotland at the date of independence shall remain in force until such time, if any, as it is replaced or amended by an Act of the Parliament of Scotland.

Judiciary

11. The supreme judicial power shall be vested in the Court of Session and the High Court of Justiciary, which shall have the power to set aside any purported acts of legislation which contravene any provision of the Constitution, and which shall have supreme responsibility for upholding the law of Scotland.

12. The independence of the judiciary shall be guaranteed. All judicial appointments shall be made by the Head of State on the advice of a Commission on Judicial Appointments, comprising the Lord Advocate, the Presiding Officer of Parliament,

a Senator of the College of Justice, and two impartial persons elected to serve for ten years by Parliament. Judicial appointments shall be terminable only on achievement of the statutory retiring age, or on grounds of permanent incapacity by reason of ill health, or on the passing of a resolution by two-thirds majority of the whole membership of Parliament calling for dismissal of a judge on grounds of stated misconduct.

Fundamental Rights and Liberties

13. Fundamental rights and liberties of all citizens and all persons within the jurisdiction of the Scottish Courts shall be guaranteed without discrimination on any grounds such as sex, race, colour, religion, personal beliefs or status; the rights and liberties guaranteed shall be the same as those contained in the European Convention of Human Rights, except in so far as the legal and social traditions of Scotland justify a more extensive protection of rights – as in the case of the right to speedy trial under the '110 day rule' derived from the Scottish Parliament's Act 1701 cap. 6 'for preventing wrongous imprisonments and against undue delay in trials'.

14. The Courts shall be charged with securing a full, adequate and speedy remedy to any person for any infringement whatsoever of his or her guaranteed rights and liberties.

Amendment of the Constitution

15. The Constitution, as the supreme law of the land, shall override all other laws and shall be subject to amendment only by the following procedure:
by the enactment of amending legislation by a three-fifths majority (at 'third reading' stage) of the whole membership of the Parliament of Scotland, followed by a referendum in which a majority of those voting votes in favour of the proposed amendment.

Note: The following amendment was approved in principle. Detailed proposals will be produced after consideration by the Party's National Council.
'Provision shall be made for initiative referenda, whereby a significant minority of electors shall have the power to requisition a referendum on a proposition of their own formulation provided that it is within the Constitution, which if supported by a simple majority of the electorate shall be binding on the executive and the legislature.'

Article I – Constitution and People

1. The right of the people of Scotland to self-determination and to sovereignty over the territory and natural resources of Scotland is full and unqualified. That right shall be exercised in accordance with the provisions of this Constitution, which shall be the supreme law of the land, and which may be amended only in accordance with the provisions as to amendment hereinafter stated.

2. The Territory of Scotland comprises all those areas over which the Court of Session and High Court of Justiciary have exercised jurisdiction since the time of, and in virtue of, the ratification of the Articles of Union of 1707, and all the territorial waters ascertaining thereto under international law at the time at which this Constitution comes into force, and the sovereignty of the Scottish state extends over all such rights in relation to exploitation of the resources of the sea, the sea bed and the sub soil thereof beyond the limit of territorial waters as are enjoyed and exercised by states under international law at the time at which this Constitution comes into effect; and for the future, the extent of the territorial waters and of such

other rights shall be determined in accordance with the relevant provisions of the law of nations for the time being.

3. Citizenship

(a) Every person whose principal place of residence is in Scotland at the date at which this Constitution comes into force shall be a citizen of Scotland, and shall remain so until such time, if any, as he or she shall renounce such citizenship.

(b) Every person whose place of birth was in Scotland, being a person who is alive at the date at which this Constitution comes into force, shall be a citizen of Scotland, and shall remain so until such time, if any, as he or she shall renounce citizenship.

(c) As soon as is reasonably possible after the date at which this Constitution shall come into force, the Parliament of Scotland shall enact legislation making further provision as to citizenship, which shall *inter alia* prescribe:

  (i) What formal steps shall be required to constitute voluntary renunciation of citizenship

  (ii) What conditions and procedures shall be necessary to acquisition of Scottish citizenship by naturalisation, and

  (iii) What future provision shall be made as to acquisition of Scottish citizenship by birth or by marriage,

provided that no law may be passed whereby any person who is or at any time becomes a Scottish citizen may be deprived of that citizenship save by a voluntary act of renunciation, which may include, but only if and in so far as Parliament shall so prescribe by legislation, acquisition of or voluntary continuation in the exercise of, citizenship of any other state or states.

(d) Adopted children shall for purposes of citizenship be treated as though they had been borne to their adoptive parents.

(e) All persons whose principal place of residence is in Scotland at the date at which this constitution comes into force shall have the right to continue in residence in Scotland, and to return to residence in Scotland after any period or periods of absence, whether they exercise or renounce their rights to Scottish citizenship; and all children under the age of eighteen years whose parents' principal residence is in Scotland at the date at which the constitution comes into force shall have the same rights to residence and to citizenship as though they had been resident in Scotland at that date.

Article II – Head of State and Executive

1. The Head of State shall be Her Majesty Queen Elizabeth, and her successors as determined by the law of Scotland, acting in right of the Crown of Scotland.

2. Her Majesty may appoint citizens of Scotland who hold or have held high public office to serve as members of the Privy Council of Scotland.

3. Her Majesty shall appoint one or more of the Privy Councillors of Scotland to exercise the functions of Head of State during any period when she is absent from Scotland.

4. The Head of State shall be responsible for the exercise of all lawful governmental functions in Scotland, excepting functions expressly delegated to Ministers of the Crown or other public authorities. The Head of State shall exercise such functions only upon the advice of his or her Ministers who shall be chosen from among the

Members of, and who shall be directly answerable to, the Parliament of Scotland, and who shall be selected with a view to their ability to command and retain the confidence of Parliament.

5. The prerogatives of the Crown in Scotland at the date at which this Constitution comes into force shall be identical with those existing in the United Kingdom of Great Britain and Northern Ireland according to the law of Scotland immediately prior to that time, with the exception of any right, power or liberty or immunity belonging to the prerogative of the Crown which would be inconsistent with the provisions of this Constitution. Acts of the Parliament of Scotland shall override the prerogative of the Crown in any case of inconsistency.

6. The Head of State shall appoint as Prime Minister whichever person being a Member of the Parliament of Scotland is elected by Parliament to serve in that office, or in default of such election, whichever person being a Member of Parliament is in the opinion of the Head of State best able to command the confidence of Parliament.

7. The number of persons holding office as, or receiving payment as Ministers of the Crown in Scotland shall not at any time be greater than one fifth of the number of the whole membership of the Parliament of Scotland.

8. No Act passed by the Parliament of Scotland for the levying of any form of general taxation payable to the Crown in Scotland may remain in force for a period longer than eighteen months after the date upon which such Act came into force.

9. No public money shall be spent for any purpose save as authorised by or under Acts of the Parliament of Scotland.

Article III – Legislature

1. Subject to the provisions of this Constitution, legislative power shall be vested exclusively in the Parliament of Scotland, and in any person or body to whom Parliament shall expressly delegate the power to make subordinate legislation within some defined sphere of competence. Subject to detailed provisions to be made by Parliament concerning any matters of procedure in relation to subordinate legislation, no regulation made or order made by way of subordinate legislation may take effect as law until it has been laid before Parliament, approved by Parliament and published in such form as will reasonably bring it to the attention of the public in general or such section of the public as is directly affected by the provisions in question. Parliament shall elect its own Presiding Officer and shall under his direction regulate its own procedures in accordance with the provisions of this Constitution.

2. With the exception of any rules of law inconsistent with this Constitution, every rule of law which is in force in Scotland at the date at which this Constitution comes into force shall remain in force until such time, if any, as it is repealed or amended by Act of Parliament or other competent legislative act.

3. The Parliament of Scotland shall be a single chamber parliament and shall be composed of the persons elected to serve therein by the electors comprising the various constituencies into which Scotland shall be from time to time divided. Members shall be elected to Parliament by a system of proportional representation to secure the fair representation of all shades of opinion in all parts of Scotland.

4. The Parliament of Scotland shall enact laws making detailed provisions for all matters concerned with the conduct of elections.

5. The term of each Parliament shall be four years, save in the cases prescribed in Articles III.6 and III.7 below, and the date for each General Election shall be appointed by Proclamation of the Head of State to take place on a day not more than thirty days earlier nor more than thirty days later than the fourth anniversary of the preceding General Election. If any vacancy arises in the membership of Parliament at any time up to four months earlier than the end of the term of the Parliament, such a vacancy shall be filled by by-election for the remaining part of the term.

6. If at any time Parliament is unable to agree on a Government, in the sense that no person can be found who is able to command its confidence as Prime Minister, the Head of State may dissolve Parliament and by Proclamation appoint a date for the holding of a General Election to take place within one month of such a situation arising; and during the intervening period the Head of State may appoint an interim Prime Minister and Government. The Parliament of Scotland elected at such a General Election shall serve for the remainder of the unexpired term of the Parliament so dissolved.

7. Parliament shall in time of war have power by resolution to extend its term for a period not exceeding one year.
8. No treaty or binding international agreement of any kind shall be of any effect unless and until it is confirmed either by a resolution of Parliament, or by enabling legislation to the extent that it purports to affect any person's legal rights or duties. Every such treaty or agreement shall be valid and effective for all purposes and shall constitute valid law within Scotland, provided that no treaty which is inconsistent with the provisions of this Constitution shall take effect unless and until it is confirmed by the normal process of Constitutional amendment.

9. No declaration of war or conclusion of peace shall be made by the Head of State save in conformity with the terms of a resolution passed by Parliament.

10. The Parliament of Scotland shall from time to time by resolution make provisions as to the required procedures for the passing of Acts of Parliament and all such Acts as are passed in accordance with these procedures shall be submitted to the Head of State for signification of Assent, and upon signification of such Assent such Acts shall take effect as laws; but the following shall be required elements in any procedure adopted by Parliament:

(a) The first stage of legislation shall be publication of a Proposed Measure which shall be debated in principle by Parliament, and if approved by a majority of those voting, shall be carried forward to the second stage.

(b) The second stage shall be consideration of such a proposed measure by a Committee of Parliament; the Committee may during such period of time as is prescribed by resolution of the Parliament conduct hearings to which representations may be made by or on behalf of all persons or groups of persons interested in the subject-matter of the proposed measure. The Committee may recommend amendments to the proposed measure and shall report thereon to Parliament.

(c) The third stage shall be consideration by Parliament of the Report by the Committee, and Parliament shall adopt or reject amendments recommended by the Committee, or further amend the proposed measure as it sees fit.

(d) The fourth stage shall be a vote by Parliament to enact or not enact the proposed measure in the form adopted in conclusion of the third stage.

(e) In the case of any proposed measure which the Presiding Officer of the Parliament of Scotland certifies as concerning solely or mainly the raising or the spending of national revenues, the proposed measure may be submitted for Assent by the Head of State as soon as it shall have passed the fourth stage by the vote of a majority of members of Parliament present and voting.

(f) In the case of any proposed measure not so certified by the Presiding Officer the proposed measure may be submitted in like manner for Assent unless within ten days a resolution is supported by the vote of two fifths of the whole membership of Parliament requiring that adoption of the proposed measure be deferred; any such resolution moved within the prescribed period of ten days shall take precedence over other business in Parliament, and a vote on the resolution shall be taken within the prescribed period.

(g) In any case in which such a resolution is passed, the proposed measure may be reconsidered by Parliament in the manner appropriate to the fourth stage at any date not less than twelve months and not more than eighteen months after the date of such resolution, and if the proposed measure is then enacted by the votes of a majority of the members present and voting it may forthwith be submitted for Assent by the Head of State.

(h) If such a resolution as is mentioned in sub-section (f) above is passed, the Parliament shall have power by resolution of a majority of those present and voting to submit the proposed measure as a whole to a National Referendum, which shall concern only the question whether to adopt or not adopt the proposed measure as a whole. If a majority of the electors voting in such a referendum votes in favour of adoption of the proposed measure it shall forthwith be submitted to the Head of State for Assent.

11. All proceedings of the Parliament of Scotland or of any of its committees shall be held in public.

12. The Parliament of Scotland and its members shall enjoy all such privileges and immunities as are essential to the free unimpeded and democratic conduct of the affairs of the nation.

Article IV – Judiciary

1. The Supreme Courts in Scotland shall be the Court of Session and the High Court of Justiciary as constituted by law, and with the jurisdiction pertaining respectively thereto, at the time at which this constitution comes into force. There shall be no appeal to any other Tribunal from decisions of either Court on any matter which falls within its jurisdiction. All appeals to or within either Court on such matters shall be determined in accordance with the law in force at the time at which this constitution comes into force, which may for the future be amended according to the ordinary process of legislation.

2. Any question arising in any litigation whatsoever concerning the provisions of this Constitution shall, in the event of an appeal, be referred to the Court of Session sitting as a Court of not fewer than seven judges, and the decision of any such question by the Court shall be final and binding for all purposes. In interpreting the Constitution, the Court of Session shall not be bound to follow its own precedents.

3. The Senators of the College of Justice and the Lords Commissioners of Justiciary shall be independent of the executive and the legislature. The Head of State shall make appointments to the offices of Senator of the College of Justice, Lord Commissioner of Justiciary, Lord President of the Court of Session, Lord Justice

General and Lord Justice Cerk upon the advice of a Commission on Judicial Appointments comprising the Lord Advocate, the Presiding Officer of the Parliament of Scotland, a Senator of the College of Justice elected by the whole body of Senators, and two eminent and impartial persons elected to serve for a term of ten years by the Parliament. Judicial appointments shall be terminable only by resignation, or on the achievement of the statutory retiring age, or on grounds of permanent incapacity by reason of ill health, or by order of the Head of State upon receipt of a resolution passed by two thirds of the whole membership of the Parliament calling for the dismissal of a judge on grounds of stated misconduct.

4. So far as is consistent with the provisions of this Constitution:

(a) the Court of Session and High Court of Justiciary shall continue to have power to make Acts of Sederunt and Acts of Adjournal in the same manner and form and concerning the same subjects as they have power to do on the day on which this Constitution comes into force; and

(b) Parliament shall have power to legislate by ordinary process of legislation on all matters concerning the administration of justice in Scotland.

5. The Sheriff Court and all Courts or tribunals of inferior or local or otherwise limited jurisdiction shall continue in existence as provided for by laws in force on the day on which this Constitution comes into force; save that the power to advise on appointments to the office of Sheriff or Sheriff Principal shall be transferred to the Commission on Judicial Appointments, laws on any subjects concerning such Courts or tribunals may be passed by ordinary process of legislation.

Article V – Fundamental Rights and Liberties

1. (a) The following provisions shall have effect for the purpose of guaranteeing the fundamental rights and liberties of all Scottish Citizens and of all persons for the time being within the jurisdiction of any Scottish Court; the rights and liberties guaranteed shall be enjoyed by all persons without discrimination on any grounds such as sex, race, colour, religion, personal beliefs, or status; there shall be no limitation upon their exercise save such as is necessary to prevent or penalise actings by any person or group of persons calculated to infringe or destroy the rights and liberties of other persons or groups, or forcibly to subvert the constitutional order which establishes and guarantees those rights and liberties and, subject to the last mentioned qualification, no law may be passed which abrogates or derogates from the guaranteed rights and liberties, unless it shall be passed by way of a constitutional amendment in accordance with Article VI of this Constitution; every person shall be granted by a competent court a full and adequate and speedy remedy for any infringement whatsoever of his or her guaranteed rights and liberties.

(b) None of the rights guaranteed in this Article of the Constitution shall be subjected to any restriction or limitation other than as expressly provided, nor shall any such restriction or limitation be applied for any purpose other than that expressly prescribed.

2. (a) Every person has the right to life. No person shall be deprived of his or her life intentionally, save in the execution of a sentence of the High Court of Justiciary in respect of an offence of which he has been convicted and for which the penalty of death shall have been expressly provided by law at the date at which the offence was proven to have been committed.

(b) If any person's death occurs as a result of another person's acting in a manner which is permitted by law and which is no more than necessary:

(i) to defend a person or persons from unlawful violence;

(ii) to effect a lawful arrest or to prevent the escape of a person lawfully detained

the action so taken shall not be rendered unlawful by the fact that death has resulted from it.

3. No person shall be subjected to torture, or to inhuman or degrading treatment or punishment.

4. No person shall be held in slavery or servitude, nor shall any person be required to perform forced or compulsory labour; and for the purpose of this provision 'forced or compulsory labour' shall be interpreted in accordance with Article 4 of the European Convention on Human Rights.

5. (a) Every person has the right to personal liberty and security, and accordingly no person shall be deprived of liberty save in the following cases and in accordance with the procedures prescribed by the law of Scotland:

(i) in the case of his or her lawful detention in accordance with the sentence passed by a competent Court upon his or her conviction of an offence;

(ii) in the case of his or her lawful arrest or detention for non-compliance with the lawful order of a court;

(iii) in the case of his or her lawful arrest or detention upon reasonable suspicion of having committed, or being engaged in the commission of, or being about to commit, a criminal offence under the law of Scotland;

(iv) in the case of detention of a person under the age of sixteen years by lawful order for the purpose of his or her educational supervision or personal welfare;

(v) in case of the lawful detention of a person who is, or is reasonably believed to be, of unsound mind;

(vi) in case of the lawful detention of a person for the purpose of preventing the spread of an infectious disease;

(vii) in the case of the lawful arrest of a person to prevent his or her unlawfully entering Scotland, or of a person against whom lawful action is being taken with a view to deportation or extradition.

(b) Every person who is arrested or detained shall be informed, as soon as is possible in the circumstances of the case, in a language which he or she understands, of the reason for his or her arrest or detention and of any charge which is to be laid against him or her; he or she shall be entitled to inform a member of his or her family of his or her whereabouts and of the stated reason for his or her detention, and shall be entitled as soon as possible to consult a legal practitioner.

(c) Every person who is arrested or detained in accordance with paragraph 5(a)(iii) shall, wherever it is practicable to do so, be brought before a competent court not later than the first lawful day after being taken into custody, such day not being a public or local holiday: failing which, he or she shall be brought before a competent court as soon as is possible thereafter.

(d) Every person who has been arrested or detained in accordance with paragraph 5(a)(iii) shall be brought to trial as soon as is possible; no person who has been committed for trial of any offence shall be detained in custody for more than one hundred and ten days from the date of such committal, except in so far as the High Court of Justiciary shall have, and shall in any case have exercised power to grant extension of that period on any grounds which may be provided for in legislation for the time being in force; every person who has been committed for trial shall be set at liberty and declared forever free from all question or process for the crime for which he or she was committed, unless he or she has been brought to trial and the trial concluded within the aforesaid period of one hundred and ten days, subject to any lawful extension granted by the High Court of Justiciary.

(e) Every person who has been deprived of liberty by arrest or detention has the right to petition the Court of Session or High Court of Justiciary for liberation, and shall be liberated by order of the Court as soon as is practicable in the circumstances of the case unless such deprivation of liberty is proven to be lawful; if a person so deprived of liberty is for any reason unable to take proceedings on his or her own behalf any other person who can show good cause for so doing may petition the court in his or her name to test the lawfulness of any such detention.

6. (a) Every person has the right to fair and public judicial proceedings to determine any question raised by proper process of law concerning his or her legal rights or obligations, or any criminal charge against him or her. Every such question or charge shall be heard and determined by the competent court or tribunal established by law, and judgement shall be pronounced publicly, except if, or in so far as, the law permits a court or tribunal to exclude members of the public from part of such proceedings or to prohibit publication of reports concerning part of such proceedings on all or any of the following grounds:

(i) the protection of national security

(ii) the prevention of disorder in court

(iii) the protection of pupils and minors

(iv) the protection of the personal privacy of the parties

(v) the protection of the interests of justice in circumstances in which publicity would inevitably cause serious prejudice to the fair determination of an issue.

(b) Every person charged with a criminal offence shall be presumed innocent until proved guilty according to law.

(c) Every person charged with a criminal offence has the following rights:

(i) To be informed in detail, as soon as is possible in the circumstances of the case, and in a language which he or she understands, of the charge which is made against him or her;

(ii) to have adequate time and facilities for preparing a defence to the charge;

(iii) to defend himself or herself in person or through a legal practitioner of his or her own choosing;

(iv) to such financial assistance as is necessary in the light of his or her means to secure adequate legal assistance if desired;

(v) to examine or have examined witnesses against him or her and to obtain the attendance and examination of witnesses on his or her behalf in the same conditions as witnesses against him or her;

(vi) to have all proceedings in court connected with the charge against him or her translated by a competent interpreter into the language which he or she best understands, if that language is not the language of the Court;

(vii) to be informed in a language which he or she understands of the provisions of this paragraph of this Article of the Constitution, before the commencement of the trial.

7. No person shall be convicted of any criminal offence save in respect of an act or omission which, at the date of its commission, constituted a criminal offence under the law of Scotland or the law of nations, nor shall any penalty be imposed which is heavier than the maximum permitted under the law of Scotland at that date.

8. (a) Everyone has the right to respect for privacy in his or her personal affairs, family life, home, and correspondence.

(b) Every interference with personal privacy in these respects shall be unlawful unless it is proven to be in accordance with the provisions of the law which are necessary;

 (i) for the protection of national security;

 (ii) for public safety;

 (iii) for the prevention of crime or civil disorder;

 (iv) for the protection of public health; or

 (v) for the protection of the fundamental rights or freedoms of other persons

and every person who suffers unlawful interference with his or her personal privacy shall be entitled to an adequate civil remedy therefor.

9. (a) Every person has the right to freedom of thought and of conscience and to the free confession and practice of religion;

(b) A person's freedom in the practice of religion shall not be restricted by law save to such an extent, if any, as is necessary for the protection of public order or public health or for the protection of the rights and freedoms of others.

10. Every person shall have the right of access to governmental information save on a restricted range of matters in which secrecy or confidentiality is authorised or required by law and in the public interest.

11. (a) Every person has the right to freedom of opinion and of the expression of opinion, including the right to impart and receive information and ideas freely to and from any other person or persons whatsoever, except in so far as the law may restrict or penalise the expressing of opinion or the transmission of information so far as is necessary for any of the following purposes:

 (i) the protection of national security or public safety

 (ii) the prevention of crime

 (iii) the prevention of incitement to hatred on any grounds such as sex, race, colour, religion, personal beliefs or status

 (iv) for the protection of public health

 (v) for preventing the public display of obscene or indecent materials

 (vi) for the protection of individuals' rights and reputations

 (vii) for the protection of information given and received in confidence

 (viii) for protection of the Parliament and Courts of law from acts of contempt.

(b) The foregoing provision shall not be interpreted as invalidating laws regulating the licensing of broadcast transmissions or cinemas, theatres and other like places of public resort.

12. Every person has the right to freedom of peaceful assembly and to freedom of association with others for all lawful purposes including the right to form and to join trade unions for the protection of his or her interests: the right to freedom of assembly and of association shall be subject only to such restrictions as are prescribed by law and are necessary for any of the following purposes:

(i) the protection of national security or public safety

(ii) the prevention of crime and disorder

(iii) the protection of public health

(iv) the protection of the fundamental rights of individuals.

13. Men and women of marriageable age have the right to marry and to found a family, in accordance with the law of Scotland.

14. Every person has the right to hold private property, and to the peaceful enjoyment of his or her property; no laws may be passed which limit, restrict or abrogate the right to acquire or retain private property except in cases in which the Parliament determines that the needs of the community clearly require to be given precedence over the rights of individuals; and all laws which sanction measures of expropriation shall make provision for fair compensation.

15. (a) Every person has the right to work and to pursue freely any profession or vocation subject only to such requirements as to minimum qualifications as may be prescribed by or in accordance with the law;

(b) Every person who is unable to work by reason of age or physical or mental disability or infirmity, or by reason of family responsibilities, or because suitable employment is unavailable, has a right to be provided with reasonable alternative means of subsistence to be determined in accordance with law.

(c) Every person has the right to strike subject only to such restrictions as are prescribed by law and are necessary for any of the following purposes –

(i) the protection of national security or public safety

(ii) the prevention of crime or civil disorder

(iii) the protection of public health

(iv) the protection of fundamental rights of individuals.

16. Every person has the right to freedom of movement within Scotland, including the right of access to hills, mountains, waterways and open countryside, except in cases in which unrestricted access is likely to cause substantial interference with agriculture, forestry or fishing, and subject to any provisions of the law which are necessary;

(a) for the protection of national security or public safety

(b) for the protection of public health

(c) for the protection of the physical environment.

17. Every person who is over the age of eighteen years, who has not been detained in accordance with law as being a person of unsound mind, who is a citizen of

Scotland and whose principal place of residence is in Scotland, shall have the right to vote, and to present himself or herself as a candidate, in elections to membership of the Parliament of Scotland or (subject to such further requirements as to residence as may be prescribed by law) to any local authority. This right shall be exercised in accordance with the law for the time being in force concerning electoral procedures and regulating proper electoral practices; restrictions of the right to vote on grounds of citizenship may be established by ordinary process of legislation.

18. All forms of monopoly or of restrictive trade practice shall be unlawful except in so far as they are expressly permitted by or under laws in force at the time at which this Constitution comes into force, or subsequently enacted by the Parliament of Scotland.

19. For all public purposes, every person has the right to use the Gaelic language, which shall have equal status with English as an official language.

20. Nothing in paragraphs 10, 11, 13, 14 or 16 of this Article of the Constitution shall have the effect of invalidating legislation by the Parliament of Scotland, which imposes restrictions on the political activities of aliens.

21. The Parliament of Scotland may enact legislation providing for the restriction of the application of this Article of the Constitution during times of war or other grave public emergency, but such legislation must contain provision for approval by resolution passed with the support of not less than three fifths of the whole membership of Parliament of any declaration by the Government of a state of emergency within two weeks thereof, and for renewal of such approval not less frequently than three months from the date of any prior resolution approving of such a declaration; and such legislation may not authorise any derogation from paragraph 2 of this Article, except in respect of deaths arising from lawful acts of war, or from paragraphs 3, 4 and 7 of this Article of the Constitution.

Article VI – The Amendment of the Constitution

This Constitution, including this Article of this Constitution, may be amended only by the following procedure:

The passing of a proposed measure at its fourth stage by a majority of three fifths of the whole membership of the Parliament of Scotland followed, within a period of between two and six months, by reference of the proposed measure to a National Referendum in which a majority of those voting shall have voted for the proposed measure.

Rights

The United Kingdom before the Strasbourg Court 1975 – 1990†

A.W. Bradley

If our system is to remain essentially a system of government by 'law' then some form of control must be exercised over the agents of government. If we abandon the philosophy of law, how do we prevent mere expediency from degenerating into arbitrary government?[1]

A. Introduction

One of the most notable developments in the public law of the United Kingdom since 1960 has been a deepened awareness of the need for the country's systems of law to provide for controlling government and the authority of the state, and for protecting individuals and minorities against arbitrary or excessive actions by government. In the first edition of *Freedom, the Individual and the Law* (1963), the late Professor Harry Street wrote:

> Civil liberties in Britain have been shown to be a patchwork. Some of them rest on the chance that citizens have sued each other and given the Courts the opportunity to declare some isolated legal rule. Some rest on sporadic legislation, often passed to meet some specific emergency, real or imaginary. The extent of inroads on certain freedoms rest on the subtleties of ministerial responsibility and the muted insistence of Whitehall to be allowed to govern unhindered.[2]

Since then, we have seen developments in the judicial control of governmental action pinpointed by the creation of the procedure of application for judicial review; the introduction of the ombudsman model for redressing the individual's grievances in the face of bureaucracy; the creation of systems designed to outlaw discrimination on racial or sexual grounds and to promote equal opportunities for all sections of society. The movement for European integration in economic matters has led to the 'incoming tide' of a novel, supranational system of law that has in an important way promoted the equal treatment of the sexes and of nationals from Western Europe in economic and social affairs.

At the same time there has been formidable resistance to any express reordering of Britain's constitutional structure. The problems of Northern Ireland are far from being solved, nor have Scotland's claims been met. The powers of the state have been extended in response to the challenge

185

of terrorism and other threats to state security. Advocates of constitutional reform such as the Liberal Democratic party and the inter-party group Charter 88 entered the 1990s not appreciably nearer achieving their aims. By contrast, the national movement for greater protection of human rights has been immeasurably strengthened by the functioning of the European Convention on Human Rights (ECHR) and this is unlikely to diminish in the 1990s.

A short debate in the House of Commons took place in July 1989 soon after the decision of the European Court of Human Rights in *Soering v United Kingdom*.[3] Soering was a German citizen who was accused on strong *prima facie* evidence of a multiple murder in Virginia, and had been arrested in the United Kingdom in response to the US government's request for his extradition. The death penalty still being in force in Virginia, Soering had petitioned the European Commission of Human Rights against his extradition. The Strasbourg Court held that Soering, if extradited, would run a real risk of a death sentence and hence of exposure to the 'death row phenomenon', which as a source of inhuman and degrading treatment could constitute a breach of article 3 ECHR. Mr Teddy Taylor MP, a forthright supporter of the death penalty and opponent of European integration, argued that this decision by the Strasbourg Court was an astonishing extension of the powers of the Court, a major insult to the free democracy of the USA, and had dangerous implications for national security and the rights of the British Parliament. The British government had the power, he argued, to tell the Strasbourg Court 'to jump in the lake', since the court was not part of the EEC system. There was, he said, a rising tide of concern in Britain about the extent to which non-elected European bodies were seizing the rights of 'our elected Parliament, elected Government and respected courts of law'.[4]

In reply, the minister of state in the Home Office stated that it was the wish of the British government that the death penalty should not be imposed if Soering were extradited. While the government took seriously the constitutional issue, the Convention imposed binding international obligations upon the United Kingdom, and successive governments had been scrupulous in complying with the Court's judgments. If the US government could remove the potential threat of the death penalty, Soering would be extradited without any risk of the Convention being breached.[5]

In the light of this renewed government commitment to the Convention, it is piquant to consider some of the constitutional spectres that were evoked by members of the Labour government in 1950, faced with certain fundamental issues arising in the last stages of formulating the Convention.

> The Lord Chancellor (Jowett): 'The Cabinet all came to the conclusion – (the Attorney-General and Kenneth Younger dissenting) – that we were not prepared to encourage our European friends to *jeopardise our whole system of law*, which we have laboriously built up over the centuries, in favour of some half-baked scheme administered by some unknown court'.
>
> The Attorney-General, agreeing with the Lord Chancellor: '[W]e should

firmly set our faces against the right of individual petition which seems to me to be *wholly opposed to the theory of responsible Government'*.

The Lord Chancellor in Cabinet: 'Obviously the Government must continue to disclaim the jurisdiction of the proposed European Court of Human Rights, since this would *seriously compromise the sovereignty of Parliament.'* [6]

These extracts come from Anthony Lester's trenchant account of how the much-vexed Labour government in 1950 resolved to sign the European Convention on Human Rights after last-minute modifications had been made to it, notwithstanding these constitutional hobgoblins. Fifteen years later, in 1966, another Labour government decided to swallow its predecessor's objections and to accept the right of individual petition to Strasbourg and the jurisdiction of the Court. Remarkably, this later decision was taken by correspondence between ministers, and it was not considered sufficiently controversial to warrant *any* discussion in the Cabinet or in a Cabinet committee.[7]

The full effects of British acceptance in 1966 of the right of individual petition under article 25 of the Convention and the jurisdiction of the Court under article 46, an acceptance which has been renewed at intervals ever since, were not felt immediately. Only in 1975 was the first decision of the Strasbourg Court to which the United Kingdom was a party made, in *Golder v United Kingdom*[8], although by then many decisions on petitions from the United Kingdom had been made by the Commission at Strasbourg. By April 1990, some 30 substantive decisions involving the United Kingdom had been made by the Strasbourg Court. (This figure does not include related decisions made by the Court on such issues as whether an individual whose rights were held to have been infringed has received 'just satisfaction' under article 50 ECHR). The purpose of this article is to reflect upon this record of decisions by the Court in the years between 1975 and 1990, and to examine not only some implications to be drawn from it for our understanding of the relation between law and government in the United Kingdom today, but also the need to enhance respect in Britain for fundamental liberties.[9]

Since other published accounts exist,[10] I need not describe the contents of the Convention, its present legal status in the United Kingdom[11], or the procedure by which cases may reach the Court at Strasbourg, except to emphasise that while an individual alleging an infringement of rights is entitled to petition the *Commission* under article 25 ECHR[12], no petitioner can be assured that his or her case reaches the second tier, the *Court*. Only a small proportion of such petitions wend their laborious way to the Court. For a full study of how the Convention's effects have been felt in the United Kingdom, it would be necessary to include the innumerable decisions by the Commission that have been made on individual petitions from Britain, accepting or rejecting them as inadmissible, seeking a friendly settlement and so on. And some cases are disposed of by the Committee of Ministers in a hybrid legal-political manner.[13] But there is value in concentrating on decisions of the Court in cases brought against the United Kingdom, since in these decisions may be found the most authoritative application of the Convention rights to the law in the United Kingdom.

The Annex to this essay summarises the decisions under discussion. These decisions will be referred to hereafter by the name of the petitioner or complainant alone.

B. Observations on the record of British decisions

1. *The success rate*

Of these 30 decisions, one was an inter-state case *(Ireland v UK)* and the remainder were all the result of individual petitions. Between 1975 and 1985, when the first 14 of these decisions were made, in only two *(Handyside, Ashingdane)* was no breach found to have occurred. Of the 16 decisions made between 1986 and April 1990, in only 9 were breaches found. Thus, in the complete period 1975-1990, breaches of the Convention of greater or lesser seriousness were recorded in 21 of the decisions (that is, 70 per cent), but in 9 (30 per cent) no breach was found to have occurred. These 9 cases were *Handyside, Ashingdane, James, Lithgow, Rees, AGOSI, Monnell and Morris, Chappell,* and *Powell and Rayner.* This ratio (70:30) of the 'success rate' for cases against the United Kingdom is very nearly the same as for the Court's record as a whole between 1960 and 1987. During that period 108 principal decisions of the Court were made, and breaches were found to have occurred in 75 cases,[14] a 'success' ratio of 69:31.

2. *The volume of UK cases*

How does the number of British cases reaching the Court compare with the numbers of those against other countries? According to officially prepared statistics, between 1960 and the end of 1987 a total of 144 cases had come before the Court (not all of which had been decided by the end of 1987) from the following countries: United Kingdom (1966) 29, Belgium (1955) 21, West Germany (1955) 17, Austria (1958) 16, Italy (1973) 13, Sweden (1952) 12, Netherlands (1960) and Switzerland (1974) 10 each, Denmark (1953) 5, Ireland (1953) 4, Portugal (1978) and France (1981) 3 each, Spain (1981) 1.[15] The date shown after each country's name is the year in which the country accepted the right of individual petition under article 25; this is a reminder that the figures for different countries do not relate to the same periods of time, particularly as it takes several years from a state's acceptance of the right to petition for the first decision to reach the Court. Therefore, while more decisions have been made by the Court in cases coming from the United Kingdom than from any other country, it is not possible from the figures alone to conclude, for example, that the requirements of the Convention are (in relation to population) more liable to be infringed in the United Kingdom that in any other country.

While research into the origins of each case would help to explain the use of the Convention which is made in different countries, the most important proposition that can be based on this record of decisions is that in a significant number of cases the system of law and government in the United Kingdom has been found *not* to observe the minimum standards for the protection of human rights as these are now perceived by the Court to be required by the Convention. While the original position of the British government in 1950-51 was that it was not necessary to incorporate the Convention in national law because the Convention's minimum standards were already observed, this position is no longer tenable. The proclaimed position is now, as we have seen,[16] that the British government is scrupulous in ensuring compliance with the decisions of the Court once the Court has found breaches to exist.[17]

3. Subject-matter of the cases

With what subjects have the thirty cases been concerned? The cases could be grouped simply in relation to the Convention rights affected but, at the risk of adopting a somewhat arbitrary grouping by subject-matter, the largest group of cases (12) has concerned aspects of *criminal justice*, broadly understood as including police powers and the penal system. However, the emphasis has not been on the process of criminal trial: six of these cases were brought by prisoners or former prisoners claiming that aspects of the prison regime had infringed their Convention rights *(Golder, Silver, Campbell and Fell, Weeks, Monnell and Morris, Boyle and Rice)*. Of these six decisions, five were wholly or at least partly in favour of the complainant.[18]

These decisions asserting the rights of prisoners coincided with a period in which the British courts themselves showed an increased awareness of the need for judicial supervision of the prison regime.[19] Indeed, it is highly likely that the Strasbourg decisions informed and influenced Lord Wilberforce's dictum that 'a convicted prisoner, in spite of his imprisonment, retains all civil rights which are not taken away expressly or by necessary implication'.[20]

Although the main features of the criminal trial in the United Kingdom have not been challenged, the powers of the police to obtain evidence by telephone-tapping and telephone-metering were challenged in *Malone*; the possible extradition of an alleged murderer was considered in *Soering*; the corporal punishment of a juvenile male convicted of an offence in the Isle of Man was challenged in *Tyrer*; and the refusal of legal aid in a Scottish criminal case was challenged in *Granger*.

The special treatment of those suspected of terrorist offences in relation to Northern Ireland was considered in the *Republic of Ireland* case (when interrogation in depth was condemned as being degrading treatment contrary to article 3 ECHR) and in *Brogan*, where the power to detain suspected terrorists for up to seven days on the authority of the Secretary of State and without recourse to a court was held to infringe article 5.

Questions of *social welfare law* arose in six cases: the rights of mental patients were considered in two *(Ashingdane* and *X)*; aspects of child care were considered in three *(Gaskin, H* and *W,R,O,B)*; and parental rights in respect of education were considered in the context of corporal punishment in state schools in *Campbell and Cosans*.

Six cases involved various forms of alleged interference with *property rights: James, Lithgow, AGOSI, Gillow, Chappell* and *Powell and Rayner*. Except for the *Gillow* decision, which held that aspects of Guernsey's housing legislation as applied to Gillow involved a breach of his rights under article 8 ECHR, these challenges were all unsuccessful.[21]

In three cases there were allegations of *discrimination* on grounds of sex or sexual orientation: in *Abdulaziz*, Britain's immigration rules were held to be discriminatory on sexual grounds in breach of articles 8 and 14 taken together; in *Dudgeon*, the criminal law on homosexual offences in Northern Ireland was held to be in breach of the state's duty to respect an individual's private life (article 8 ECHR); and in *Rees*, official practice in relation to the giving of birth certificates for transsexuals was upheld.

Two cases concerned *freedom of expression (Handyside* and *The Sunday Times)*. The latter decision in particular has been frequently cited in British courts (for example, in the *Spycatcher* saga).[22]

Finally, *Young, James and Webster* concerned *freedom of association*, in particular the right of workers not to belong to a trade union where a post-entry closed shop had been introduced by public employers.

4. *Nature of impugned acts*

Another way of grouping the thirty cases is to consider whether the complaints that Convention rights had been infringed were directed against *legislative* provisions (whether contained in primary or delegated legislation), against *executive* actions, practices, policies or rules, or against *judicial* decisions.

Under the Convention, state responsibility applies to the acts of all public authorities within the state, including the legislature, government departments, the courts, police, local authorities and other agencies.[23] Proceedings under the Convention may bring under examination not merely the ill-treatment of an individual but a whole area of legislative, executive or judicial policy. Indeed, it would not seem worthwhile for an individual's case to be taken the whole lengthy course to a decision of the Court unless this may enable the Court to pronounce on issues of general significance. As the Court said in the *Republic of Ireland* case,

> The Court's judgments in fact serve not only to decide those cases brought before the Court but, more generally, to elucidate, safeguard and develop the rules instituted by the Convention, thereby contributing to the observance by the States of the engagements undertaken by them as Contracting Parties (art. 19).[24]

While a government determined to resist external control of all national policies may place little weight on the precise legal status of the decisions or measures being challenged, the consequences for the national legal system of an adverse decision at Strasbourg will vary according to the status of the decision challenged. Through the procedures of administrative law, we are already accustomed to judicial review of executive action. To read decisions of the Strasbourg Court is to become aware that many disputes reaching the Court are similar to those that come before national courts with jurisdiction in administrative law.[25] By contrast, judicial review of primary legislation raises issues of principle with which for historical reasons United Kingdom courts have seldom been concerned, given the constitutional 'sovereignty' of the Westminster Parliament.[26]

Some decisions of the Strasbourg Court have dealt with violations of human rights that arose directly from the provisions of primary legislation

(*Tyrer, Young, James and Webster, Dudgeon, James, Lithgow, Gillow, Monnell and Morris, Brogan* and *Powell and Rayner*). Others have concerned alleged violations caused by decisions and policies arising from the exercise of executive powers to a greater or lesser extent arising from legislation (*Golder, Republic of Ireland, X, Campbell and Cosans, Silver, Malone, Ashingdane, Abdulaziz, Cabales and Balkandali, Rees, AGOSI, Weeks, Boyle and Rice, H and W,R,O,B* and *Gaskin*). And some have concerned alleged violations arising directly from decisions of the courts (*Handyside, Sunday Times,* and *Chappell*). There have also been decisions in which both executive and judicial decisions have come under review. A good example is the *Soering* case, since the procedure of extradition from the United Kingdom requires decisions by both the Home Secretary and the courts.[27] Whatever the process required by national law before certain decisions are taken, the workings of a legal system are capable of producing a violation of rights for which no remedy is forthcoming if the body whose decision caused the violation enjoys a privileged constitutional status.[28]

5. Enforcement of the Convention

The legal status of the acts giving rise to an infringement of rights is important for another reason, since it directly affects the measures of compliance that may be sought if a breach of the Convention has occurred. The extent to which the Convention seeks to ensure compliance is difficult to ascertain,[29] but two issues need to be distinguished: first, the remedy that must be provided to the individual whose rights under the Convention have been infringed[30] and, secondly, the more general question of ensuring that similar infringements of rights do not recur. By contrast with Community law, which is both directly applicable within the United Kingdom as in all member states of the Community and may (depending on the measures in question) have 'direct effect' within national law,[31] the Convention leaves it in the first instance to member states to decide how to 'secure to everyone within their jurisdiction' (article 1 ECHR) the rights and freedoms defined in the Convention. In 1976 the Strasbourg Court held that the Convention does not lay down for member states 'any given manner for ensuring within their internal law the effective implementation of any of the provisions of the Convention'.[32] Thus, if the complaint is of a practice that is wholly unlawful under national law (as were the methods of interrogation in depth challenged in the *Republic of Ireland* case), it may be enough for the government to enable the victims to receive compensation for the illegal acts, to declare that it has abandoned the illegal practice and to take steps to ensure that it is not reintroduced. However, if the complaint is of action taken directly under an Act of Parliament, and without any illegality in national law, compliance may be impossible without amending legislation.

Thus in those twenty-one of the thirty decisions involving the United Kingdom where breaches were held to have occurred, further steps could well be needed beyond redress for the individual. In the *Republic of Ireland* case, no legislative measures were required. But in other cases the Strasbourg Court's decision has often led to amending legislation, and sometimes this legislation has been enacted even before the final decision at Strasbourg. In the closed shop case, *Young, James and Webster*, the offending (Labour) legislation had been altered by the incoming Conservative government before the Strasbourg Court made its decision, but further legislation was enacted to compensate others who had lost their jobs in a similar way.[33] The *Sunday Times* case, decided in 1979, was the catalyst for an overdue reform of the law, made by the Contempt of Court Act 1981. It is, however, debatable whether that Act has in every respect brought the law of the United Kingdom into line with the Convention.[34] As a result of the *Dudgeon* case, the criminal law on homosexual conduct in Northern Ireland was altered to place it on the same basis as in the rest of the United Kingdom. Other decisions at Strasbourg to which there was a direct legislative sequel include *X, Campbell and Cosans*, and *Malone*.[35]

The prisoners' rights cases did not so much involve challenge to primary legislation as to practices in the management of prisons that had grown up under the Prison Act 1952 and the Prison Rules 1964. The government's response has been to issue new Prison Rules and to change the relevant practices so as to comply with the Court's decisions. Such changes have not always gone far enough to avoid later challenge at Strasbourg.[36] Where a breach of Convention rights has occurred through a judicial decision (as in the *Sunday Times* case), the decision under review being that of the House of Lords, the government's response cannot be to direct the courts to act differently, because of the independence of the judiciary, which is itself protected by article 6(1) ECHR. Legislation may therefore be needed to amend the statutory or common law rules that were in issue. Such legislation may in turn, depending on how it is interpreted by the British courts, give rise to possible future breaches of the Convention.[37] In the absence of legislation expressly incorporating the Convention in national law,[38] what comes close to being a specific requirement to apply one provision of the Convention may be seen in the Police and Criminal Evidence Act 1984, section 76, whereby a trial court may not take into account any confession obtained by *inter alia* torture, inhuman or degrading treatment – language which derives directly from article 3 ECHR.[39]

6. *The unexpected results of Strasbourg decisions*

The response of the UK government to adverse decisions by the Court has not always been what proponents of human rights would wish to see. In *Abdulaziz, Cabales and Balkandali*, the Strasbourg Court had found that the British immigration rules discriminated against certain women permanently settled in the United Kingdom since their husbands and fiancés were not entitled to enter the United Kingdom, whereas the wives and fiancées of men settled in the United Kingdom *were* entitled to enter. The government's response was to amend the Immigration Rules so as to remove the entitlement to enter of the wives and fiancées, thus removing what the Court had seen as the source of discrimination.[40]

We have seen that the decision in *Tyrer* declared judicial birching of a juvenile in the Isle of Man to be in breach of article 3, but the law in the island was not altered.[41] And even before the case reached the Court, when the United Kingdom had renewed its acceptance of the right of individuals to petition under article 25 ECHR, this right was, at the wish of the Isle of Man government, declared not to extend to the Isle of Man.[42]

In *Brogan*, the Strasbourg Court had held that the Prevention of Terrorism (Temporary Provisions) Act 1984, by authorising detention without access to a court for up to seven days by decision of the police and the Secretary of State, infringed article 5 ECHR. The British government's response was to declare that the power in question was considered essential on security grounds and to deposit at Strasbourg a limited derogation from the Convention to the extent that the provisions of the legislation breached article 5.[43] The government's consideration of alternative machinery for review of detention by a court did not bear fruit and the derogation was subsequently renewed.[44]

7. *The government's awareness of Convention obligations*

We have seen that in 1950-51 the view of the British government was that UK law fully complied with the Convention. This view could no longer be sustained by the mid-1980s in the light of Britain's record before the Strasbourg Court. In 1987 the Cabinet Office issued a memorandum to all government departments considering how the risks of challenge to government action under the Convention might be reduced and stating:

> There is much case-law of the Commission and Court interpreting the Convention – often on the basis of its purpose rather than literally – and a consistently high level of applications and decisions concern the United Kingdom. The Convention has been held to apply in areas where it might not have been initially considered – e.g. school corporal punishment and aircraft noise. Questions on it can sometimes arise in most of the areas of law administered by Departments.[45]

In view of this, departments were advised that it should be standard practice for the effects of existing or expected Convention case-law on any proposed measures to be considered by departmental officials, in consultation with their legal advisers. If departments were in doubt about the implications of the Convention for any particular proposal, advice should be sought from the Foreign and Commonwealth Office.

Moreover, documents submitted to Cabinet committees should include an assessment of the impact of the Convention on the action proposed, 'much as Departments already do for European Community implications'. Where applications under the Convention had been made and there was a serious risk of a finding at Strasbourg adverse to the government, departments were advised to give early consideration to the possibility of a friendly settlement 'if this seems likely to offer a less damaging outcome'. Before a friendly settlement was offered, however, the responsible department was to ensure that other departments affected by the outcome of the case should have an opportunity to comment. Finally, the memorandum recommended departments to undertake a review of existing measures, where there was a serious risk of an adverse finding at Strasbourg which might affect them.

The origin of this advice to departments was prudential rather than principled. But the fact that its issue was considered necessary in 1987, at a time when the government was concerned about the vulnerability of its decisions to attack by judicial review in administrative law suggests that even without incorporation the Convention is capable of having potent effects in influencing the adoption of government policy and departmental practices.

In the following section, I consider some general aspects of the Strasbourg case-law that arise from the decisions made in the British cases. In view of the constitutional objections to the Convention taken by the Labour government in 1950-51,[46] we may ask ourselves whether any of those fears have proved to be justified and whether the British approach to 'the rule of law' has anything to learn from a court mainly composed of lawyers untrained in the common law tradition.[47]

C. Constitutional aspects of the Strasbourg case-law

1. *The Convention and the rule of law*

While human rights are often infringed by concentrations of private and corporate power, it is the interface between the individual and public (or state) power in its many forms with which the Convention is concerned. The preamble to the Convention refers to European governments as having 'a common heritage of political traditions, ideals, freedom and the rule of law'. In *Golder*, the Court refused to accept this as mere rhetoric and regarded the 'profound belief' of the member states in the rule of law as a basis for taking a broad view of article 6(1): '[In] civil matters one can scarcely conceive of the rule of law without there being a possibility of having access to the courts.'[48]

In 1978, in *Klass*, the German case on telephone-tapping, the Court said: 'The rule of law implies, *inter alia*, that an interference by the executive authorities with an individual's rights should be subject to an effective control which should normally be assured by the judiciary, at least in the last resort, judicial control offering the best guarantees of independence, impartiality, and a proper procedure'.[49]

2. *'Prescribed by law'*

This belief in the 'rule of law' as a system of checks on executive power in which the judiciary have a key role to play owes something to Dicey's view of the 'rule of law',[50] but it also owes much to cognate doctrines in other European legal systems and to the structure of the Convention. For example, the manner in which the Convention limits those protected rights which the Convention recognises cannot be absolute. Thus the right to respect for private and family life (article 8), the right to freedom of thought, conscience and religion (article 9), the right to freedom of expression (article 10) and the right to freedom of assembly and association (article 11) are each subject to such restrictions or limitations as are 'prescribed by law and are necessary in a democratic society' for (in each case) a list of specified purposes.[51] Thus the right to freedom of expression in article 10 is subject to such formalities, conditions, restrictions or penalties *as are prescribed by law* and are necessary in a democratic society, in the interests of national security, territorial integrity or public safety, for the prevention of disorder or crime, for the protection of health or morals, for the protection of the reputation or rights of others, for preventing the disclosure of information received in confidence, or for maintaining the authority and impartiality of the judiciary.

The meaning of the phrase 'prescribed by law' (in French, *prévu par la loi*) was considered by the Court in the *Sunday Times* case. In previous cases from the United Kingdom, the phrase raised no problems, since in *Golder* the interference with Golder's mail as a prisoner was authorised by the Prison Rules 1964 and in *Handyside* the prosecution had been conducted under the Obscene Publications Acts 1959 and 1964. But in the *Sunday Times* case, the decision of the House of Lords to uphold the ban on the thalidomide article was based on the common law of contempt of court, in particular on aspects of that law which the appeal in that case had shown to be in doubt.[52] Did this meet the requirement that the restriction must be 'prescribed by law', particularly since the five judges in the Lords gave separate judgments from which it was not easy to extract a single *ratio decidendi*? It was argued for the newspaper that the law on contempt, both before and after the decision of the Lords, was so vague and uncertain and the principles enunciated by that decision were so novel that the ban on publication could not be regarded as having been 'prescribed by law'. A contrary submission by the government was that, on the facts of the case, the restraint was at least 'roughly foreseeable'.

The Court held that, in the expression 'prescribed by law', the word 'law' covered not only statute but also unwritten law, i.e. the common law. To hold otherwise, said the Court, would be to deprive a common law state of the protection of article 10(2) and would 'strike at the very roots of that State's legal system'.[53] The further issue from the newspaper's submissions was whether on this matter the common law satisfied the principle of legal certainty. In the Court's view, for a limitation on a freedom to be 'prescribed by law', the legal rule in question must be (a) adequately accessible to the citizen, and (b) formulated with sufficient precision to enable the citizen to regulate his conduct: '(He) must be able – if need be with appropriate advice – to foresee, to a degree that is reasonable in the circumstances, the consequences which a given action may entail.'[54] Since the law must be able to keep pace with changing circumstances, 'many laws are inevitably couched in terms which, to a greater or lesser extent, are vague and whose interpretation and application are questions of practice'.[55]

Although different principles had been relied on by different judges in the Lords, the Court concentrated its attention on the 'prejudgment' principle. Looking in detail at the antecedents of the principle, the majority concluded that the newspaper had had an adequate indication of its existence. Despite doubts concerning the precision with which the principle had been formulated at the relevant time, the majority decided that the newspaper had been reasonably able to foresee a risk that publication of the article might fall foul of the prejudgment principle. It was nevertheless concluded that the restraint on publication, although prescribed by law, exceeded what was necessary in a democratic society for 'maintaining the authority and impartiality of the judiciary'.

Judges Zekia, O'Donoghue and Evrigenis disagreed with the majority on the 'prescribed by law' issue. Judge Zekia held that the common law on contempt of court was at the material date so uncertain and unsettled that it was not a law that was 'reasonably comprehensive' in describing the conditions for the imposition of restrictions under article 10(2).[56] Judge Evrigenis, while allowing for the special features of a case-law system, considered that the House of Lords in the *Sunday Times* case had applied a new principle which had not previously been the basis of any comparable decisions.[57]

The problem of foreseeability of the legal restrictions upon Convention rights also arose in *Silver*, in which the main issue was whether the censorship of prisoners' letters by the prison authorities satisfied the requirements of article 8 ('Everyone has the right to respect for his . . . . correspondence'). Seven applicants complained to Strasbourg of many different instances of censorship during the 1970s. At that time, the Prison Rules 1964 authorised the stopping of prisoners' letters in general terms, but the detailed rules applied by the prison authorities were contained in unpublished standing orders, circular instructions and internal rules and guidance. It was submitted by the applicants that to be 'prescribed by law', any restrictions upon the right to respect for one's correspondence must be contained in published rules. This was not, as in the *Sunday Times* case, a complaint at the vagueness of the common law, but a submission that the government could not justify its own acts by reference to rules that it had deliberately withheld from the prisoners affected.

In the Court's view, it followed from the *Sunday Times* case that for a restriction to be prescribed by law it must have some basis in domestic law. In the case of prison censorship, this basis was provided by the Prison Act and Prison Rules but not by the unpublished orders and instructions: these lacked the force of law and were not accessible to those affected. But it did not follow that the unpublished rules and instructions must be completely disregarded. The question was whether the rules in the Prison Act and Prison Rules were formulated with sufficient precision to enable the persons affected (the prisoners) to foresee the consequences of their actions. The Court considered that it would be impossible to formulate legal rules to cover every eventuality that might arise in the censorship of prisoners' letters, and discretion must be left to the authorities. Thus the prison directions and instructions, while lacking the force of law, could be taken into account if the criterion of foreseeability was satisfied – that is, to the extent to which their contents were known to, or could have been foreseen by, the prisoners. Accordingly, the Court proceeded to consider in detail all the disputed instances of censorship, deciding whether the reasons for stopping each letter were reasonably foreseeable by the prisoners.

A much more clearcut case than *Silver* was the telephone-tapping case, *Malone*. It had been known for many years in Britain that telephone-tapping as practised by the police and security services had an uncertain legal base. In the English High Court, Megarry V-C had held in *Malone v Metropolitan Police Commissioner*[58] that the practice involved no breach of the rights of the persons whose conversations were tapped; since there was no right of privacy in English law, no statutory or common law power was required to justify it. Nonetheless, in the judge's view the subject was one that cried out for legislation. Rejecting this plea for reform, the British government saw no reason to alter the position whereby telephone tapping rested essentially on administrative arrangements that provided no external safeguards against abuse.[59]

When Malone's case reached Strasbourg, the plenary Court agreed unanimously that the arrangements for telephone-tapping in the United Kingdom were not 'in accordance with the law' for the purposes of article 8(2). Applying the principles in the *Sunday Times* and *Silver* cases, the Court held that in the context of powers exercised in secret, such as telephone-tapping, there must be a measure of protection in domestic law against arbitrary interferences by public authorities with the Convention rights: '[T]he law must be sufficiently clear in its terms to give citizens an adequate indication as to the circumstances in which and the conditions on which public authorities are empowered to resort to this secret and potentially dangerous interference with the right to respect for private life and correspondence.'[60] It would in the Court's view be 'contrary to the rule of law' for the legal discretion granted to the executive in a matter like the secret surveillance of communications to be expressed in terms of an unfettered power.

It was as a direct consequence of this decision that the Interception of Communications Act 1985 was passed, providing a statutory basis for telephone-tapping and the interception of mail and introducing formal safeguards against the abuse of the powers conferred.[61] Executive discretion continues but must be exercised within a legal framework which, it must be hoped, will limit repetition of some security abuses of the 1970s.[62]

In the later case of *Gillow*, the Strasbourg Court considered whether the discretion conferred by a protectionist housing law in Guernsey exceeded the limits of certainty and foreseeability. The Court said: 'A law which confers a discretion is not in itself inconsistent with the requirement of foreseeability, provided that the scope of the discretion and the manner of its exercise are indicated with sufficient clarity, having regard to the legitimate aim of the measure in question, to give the individual adequate protection against arbitrary interference.'[63] In *Gillow*, the Court found that the scope of the discretion, coupled with the provision for judicial control of its exercise, was sufficient to satisfy the requirements of the Convention. And in *Chappell*, which concerned the scope of an Anton Piller order (i.e. an order obtained *ex parte* by one litigant authorising the search and seizure of another person's private property), the Court stressed that where (as in article 8 ECHR) action must have been taken 'in accordance with law', the test is not merely one of domestic law but also relates to the quality of the law; thus it must be compatible with the rule of law and there must be a measure of protection in domestic law against arbitrary interferences with the rights safeguarded by the Convention.[64]

3. *A constitutional minimum of judicial review?*

This stress on the values inherent in a broad view of 'law' presents a particular challenge to the constitutional position in the United Kingdom. On the orthodox view of the legislative sovereignty of Parliament, 'What the statute itself enacts cannot be unlawful, because what the statute says and provides is itself the law, and the highest form of law that is known to this country.'[65] One consequence of this is that it is often seen to be a matter for Parliament to decide what role should be played by the courts in respect of the statutory powers and duties conferred on executive and other bodies. It used to be remarked that there is no constitutional minimum of judicial review in English law.[66] This view still obtains in British government circles, it seems: provisions in both the Interception of Communications Act 1985 and the Security Service Act 1989 exclude actions taken or purporting to be taken under those Acts from any form of judicial review.[67] But this absolutist view is not held by all legal authorities; it has not always been shared by Britain's senior judges;[68] and on important areas of Community law it is certainly not held by the European Court of Justice at Luxembourg.[69]

So far as the Convention is concerned, we have already seen that the Strasbourg Court upholds the principle that there should be legal authority for the acts of government. The Court also holds that independent courts can provide essential safeguards against the abuse of official powers that affect rights protected by the Convention. So far as the right to one's physical liberty is concerned, the Convention itself refers to the role of a court in deciding whether an accused person shall be released pending trial (article 5(3)) and deciding whether a person in detention is lawfully detained (article 5(4)). In article 5(4), both the guarantee of a speedy decision by the court on the legality of a person's detention and the court's power to order release from unlawful detention are directly derived from the procedure of *habeas corpus* in English law.

The Court's clearest statement of the importance of judicial control through *habeas corpus* came in *Brogan*: 'Judicial control of interferences by the executive with the individual's right to liberty is an essential feature of the guarantee embodied in Article 5(3), which is intended to minimise the risk of arbitrariness. Judicial control is implied by the rule of law, "one of the fundamental principles of a democratic society . . . . , from which the whole Convention draws its inspiration"'.[70] *Brogan* concerned the powers of the police, with the approval of the Secretary of State, to detain those suspected of terrorist offences in relation to Northern Ireland for up to seven days without bringing them before a court. While the Court held that such detention involved certain breaches of article 5, no breach of article 5(4) was found to have occurred since the detainees could have resorted to the remedy of *habeas corpus*. The detainees thus had available to them a remedy allowing the High Court in Northern Ireland to examine not only compliance with the procedural requirements set out in the enabling legislation, but also the reasonableness of the suspicion on which the arrests were based and the legitimacy of the purpose pursued by the arrests and the ensuing detention.[71]

A very different view of *habeas corpus* was taken by the Strasbourg Court in the case of a mental patient X. After his conviction for a serious offence, X had been sent to a secure mental hospital and was later granted a conditional discharge from detention, but he was re-detained by the Secretary of State three years later. The High Court rejected an application by X for *habeas corpus*. In those proceedings, the Secretary of State relied on his formal power to re-detain X, and was not required to satisfy the court that he had reasonable grounds for so doing. The Strasbourg Court was unimpressed by this, finding that *habeas corpus* did not enable there to be a judicial determination of both the substantive and the formal legality of the detention.[72] The Court accepted that *habeas corpus* could on occasions constitute an effective check against arbitrariness in the context of mental health, but did not consider that judicial review 'as limited as that available in the *habeas corpus* procedure in the present case' was sufficient for a continuing detention of the kind undergone by X. The Court's decision in *X*, that *habeas corpus* was inadequate to meet the requirements of article 5(4) ECHR was not apparently cited to the Court in *Brogan*, and it is not easy to reconcile the two decisions.

The standards for judicial review of detention required to satisfy article 5(4) were also considered in *Weeks*, where a prisoner serving a life sentence had been released on licence but was subsequently recalled. The Court stated that article 5(4) does not guarantee a right to judicial control of such a broad scope as to empower the reviewing court, on all aspects of the case, including questions of expediency, to substitute its own discretion for that of the decision-making authority. 'The review should, however, be wide enough to bear on those conditions which, according to the Convention, are essential for the lawful detention of a person subject to the special kind of deprivation of liberty ordered against Mr Weeks.'[73] Considering the particular circumstances in the *Weeks* case, the Court found that the procedure followed by the Parole Board was not judicial in character, since it did not involve the full disclosure to the prisoner of adverse material that the Board had in its possession. Moreover, while there was scope for judicial review of the Parole Board's decisions, the grounds for review were not broad enough to include the crucial questions of whether the detention of Mr Weeks 'was consistent with and therefore justified by the objectives of the indeterminate sentence imposed on him'.[74]

The potential significance of judicial review has become evident in the Strasbourg case-law in respect of other kinds of official decision. Two examples, relating to other aspects of the Convention, suggest that the Court's view of the adequacy of review is not uniform and depends on the context of the decision under review.

The first concerned whether the confiscation by a government department of private property was consistent with the First Protocol, ECHR, article 1, which protects the right of property. In *AGOSI*, the Strasbourg Court was told of the far-reaching reforms made in English administrative law when the revised Order 53 procedure for applying for judicial review took effect in 1978. It suited the British government's lawyers at Strasbourg to stress the breadth of domestic procedures for judicial review (in a manner which they might not do when defending a decision against judicial review in the English High Court!). So they argued that the new Order 53 made it possible now for the High Court to obtain evidence on facts and other matters not appearing in the record of an official decision.[75] On the facts of the *AGOSI* case, which concerned a refusal by the Commissioners of Customs and Excise to restore smuggled gold coins to their owners, a German company, the Court held that the scope of judicial review in English law was sufficient to comply with the First Protocol to the Convention. Accordingly the company should have sought this remedy in the English High Court.[76]

The second illustration is from *Boyle and Rice*. Three prisoners and the spouse of one of them complained of a variety of interferences with their rights to correspondence and family life and they alleged discriminatory decisions. The applicants put in the forefront of their case article 13 ECHR, under which '[e]veryone whose rights and freedoms [under the Convention] are violated shall have an effective remedy before a national authority notwithstanding that the violation has been committed by persons acting in an official capacity'. However, in respect of one of the complaints which was considered well-founded the Court held that the prisoner could have sought judicial review of the Secretary of State's decision. (The complaints having arisen in respect of a Scottish prison, judicial review would have had to be sought in the Scottish courts, the grounds of judicial review being the same both in English and Scots law.)[77] Alternatively, he could have renewed his petition of complaint to the Secretary of State.[78] In short, the answer to the claim based on article 13 was that the applicants could have raised their complaint by means of an application for judicial review. However, apart from the implications that this may have for the rule in article 26 ECHR requiring exhaustion of local remedies before going to Strasbourg, a practical difficulty for a potential applicant is to know when judicial review in the national court will be held to have satisfied the Convention requirements; as we have seen, the Strasbourg Court's view of the adequacy of judicial review as a remedy appears to vary according to the official action in question and its effect on the individuals concerned.

Further insight into the Court's approach to judicial review may be gained from the case-law interpreting article 6(1) ECHR.

4. *The right to a judicial decision*

By article 6(1) the guarantee is given that '[i]n the determination of his civil rights and obligations or of any criminal charge against him, everyone is entitled to a fair and public hearing within a reasonable time by an independent and impartial tribunal established by law'. As we have seen, in *Golder* this guarantee was held to include a prisoner's right of access to a lawyer for advice on whether an action in defamation lay against a prison officer. Possibly the most complex body of case-law that has come before the Strasbourg Court concerns article 6(1), in part concerning the extent to which disciplinary and regulatory procedures in respect of certain professions fall within article 6(1)[79] and in part concerning the extent to which the guarantee of a fair hearing by an independent tribunal applies to decisions of administrative authorities.[80] It may be a tribute to the system of tribunals that now exists in the United Kingdom that relatively few decisions have gone to the Court from the United Kingdom raising fundamental issues about the status and procedure of such tribunals.[81]

One exception is *Campbell and Fell*, in which two prisoners challenged disciplinary decisions by the prison's board of visitors that had imposed substantial loss of remission after prison disturbances. The Strasbourg Court held that, because of the nature of the offences and of the penalties imposed, these disciplinary procedures were within the criminal sphere and were subject to the procedural guarantees of article 6. The Court held that the boards of visitors were sufficiently independent of the Home Secretary (although appointed by him), that the processes were conducted with due impartiality, and that the proceedings need not take place in public although the decisions should be published. However, article 6(3) had been breached as the applicants had been refused legal assistance and representation. A similar principle recognising that a prisoner may be entitled to legal representation in serious disciplinary proceedings has since been upheld by the House of Lords.[82]

In *Campbell and Fell* and other cases, the Strasbourg Court has taken the view that the word 'tribunal' in article 6(1) 'is not necessarily to be understood as signifying a court of law of the classic kind, integrated within the standard judicial machinery of the country'.[83] The Court has stated that both 'tribunal' in article 6(1) and 'court' in article 5(4) denote 'bodies which exhibit not only common fundamental features, of which the most important is independence of the executive and of the parties to the case, but also the guarantees . . . . of judicial procedures, the forms of which may vary from one domain to another'.[84] However, a power to *decide* the issues affecting the individual, rather than to take merely a consultative or advisory role, has been considered essential.

These not over-arduous criteria have been considered in relation to the following bodies in the United Kingdom:
(a) boards of prison visitors (*Campbell and Fell*)
(b) mental health review tribunals (*X*)
(c) the arbitration tribunal established for the purposes of assessing compensation under the Aircraft and Shipbuilding Industries Act 1977 (*Lithgow*)
(d) the adjudication procedures established by the Leasehold Reform Act 1977 (county court jurisdiction on specific issues, and the Leasehold Valuation Tribunal and Lands Tribunal) (*James*)
(e) the Parole Board (*Weeks*).
The independence and the impartiality of these bodies were accepted, but the procedures followed by the boards of prison visitors (as we have seen) and also by the Parole Board were not approved, in the latter case because of a failure to disclose to the prisoner adverse material that was held by the Board. The inability of the mental health review tribunals and the Parole Board to give binding decisions was also criticised.

At the heart of article 6(1) there is a problem of exceptional complexity which is being resolved with difficulty in the Strasbourg case-law.[85] In brief, the 'determination of [one's] civil rights and obligations' in respect of which one is entitled to a fair and public hearing before an independent tribunal is held to extend to many matters which as a result of social, regulatory or economic legislation are now decided (at least in the first instance) by executive bodies. How then may the requirements of article 6(1) be met? One way of doing this, although it would involve an immense upheaval in the decision-making process, would be to transfer first instance decisions from executive to judicial bodies. A second way would be to ensure that the individual affected by a first-instance executive decision has an adequate opportunity to seek judicial review. This second method of compliance with a broadened interpretation of article 6(1) throws into relief the adequacy and modalities of judicial review.[86]

Indeed, in a group of cases from Sweden, article 6(1) has been held to require that an individual affected by an executive decision concerning his property or his primary economic activity should have a right to seek judicial review of the decision.[87] However, where local authorities in Britain had taken decisions depriving parents of their parental rights and preventing them having access to their children, the right to apply for judicial review of those decisions on grounds confined to illegality, unreasonableness or improper procedure was held to be insufficient to comply with article 6(1). What was required, said the Strasbourg Court, was that a court or tribunal should have jurisdiction to examine the merits of the matters in dispute between the parents and the local authority.[88]

While the Strasbourg Court may require certain executive decisions to be subject to full judicial review, it held both in *James* (leasehold enfranchisement) and in *Lithgow* (nationalisation of shipbuilding industry) that article 6(1) does not require that a national court should have competence to invalidate or override national legislation directly authorising the expropriation of private rights of property.[89] The Court restated its view that the right of access to the courts secured by article 6(1) was not absolute but might be subject to limitations; these limitations were permitted by implication since the right of access 'by its very nature calls for regulation by the State, regulation which may vary in time and in place according to the needs and resources of the community and of individuals'.[90]

Since the potential scope of the whole Convention, and article 6(1) in particular, is so wide, statements of principle such as those made in *James* and *Lithgow* must be read in context. Nonetheless those decisions indicated a strong desire by the Court not to interfere with the aims of the legislation in question, to which the applicants in both cases were directly opposed on grounds of economic interest.

A final comment on one aspect of article 6(1) which has given rise to many decisions in cases coming from other countries[91] may be very brief. The right given by article 6(1) is to a hearing before a court or tribunal 'within a reasonable time'. There seem to have been few complaints at Strasbourg of unreasonable delay in the judicial system in the United Kingdom. Such a complaint was made in one of the child-care cases, where in *H* the court proceedings regarding a mother's access to her child were held to have been unreasonably delayed; in such a case, said the Court, the authorities must exercise exceptional diligence, since procedural delay could result in the *de facto* determination of the adoption issue before it even reached the court.[92]

In general, however, civil and criminal proceedings in the United Kingdom seem to operate more expeditiously than in many other countries and more so than in Strasbourg itself.

5. *Other issues*

Certain other aspects of the Convention case-law concerning the United Kingdom may be mentioned more briefly.

(a) **Devolution of legislative authority**

Most, but not all, cases against the United Kingdom have arisen from events governed by English law. Out of the thirty cases under discussion, there were three from Scotland (*Campbell and Cosans, Boyle and Rice, Granger*),[93] and three from Northern Ireland (*Republic of Ireland, Dudgeon* and *Brogan*). *Gillow* (Channel Islands) and *Tyrer* (Isle of Man) came from possessions of the Crown outside the United Kingdom: although the UK government is responsible for their international relations, by convention the United Kingdom does not legislate for the islands on domestic matters save at their request. To what extent does the Strasbourg Court pay heed to the argument that a small jurisdiction has distinct needs requiring different legal solutions? Or does it take the view that human rights are universal in their application?

The issue is in part an aspect of the 'margin of appreciation' discussed in the next section. In *Handyside*, where the publisher of the English language edition of *The Little Red Schoolbook* had been convicted in England of publishing an obscene work, the book in other languages was freely available in other European countries, and the English version was also circulating in parts of the United Kingdom without prosecution. Holding that the conviction had been for a purpose within article 10(2), namely the protection of morals, the Court ruled that there was no uniform conception across Europe of what was necessary for the protection of morals. While acts taken within the 'margin of appreciation' left to national authorities were subject to supervision by the Court, the Court did not see it necessary to interfere with the decision properly reached by the English court.

The *Dudgeon* case concerned the laws against adult male homosexual conduct which had remained on the statute-book in Northern Ireland although such conduct had ceased to be criminal elsewhere in the United Kingdom. The government submitted to the Court that the unreformed laws were necessary in a democratic society for the protection of morals and of the rights of others, within the meaning of article 8(2). Evidence was given of the strength of feeling in Northern Ireland against any change in the law, which (it was averred) would seriously damage the moral fabric of Northern Irish society. The Court held that, although the protection of morals was in issue, and although the fact that similar measures were not considered necessary elsewhere in the United Kingdom or in other states did not mean that they could not be necessary in Northern Ireland, the existing law interfered with 'an essentially private manifestation of the human personality' and went beyond what could be considered necessary for the protection of morals in a democratic society.

So, too, in *Tyrer* the Court was not impressed by the argument that public opinion in the Isle of Man was not outraged by judicial corporal punishment, preferring to take account of 'developments and commonly accepted standards' in the penal policy of the member states of the Council of Europe. The Court did, however, consider an argument advanced by the Attorney-General for the Isle of Man that under article 63(3) ECHR the Court had to apply the Convention 'with due regard . . . . to local requirements'. The Court did not regard a sincere local belief in the efficacy of corporal punishment as constituting a 'local requirement' for this purpose, nor indeed did the Court consider that article 63(3) applied to fully developed societies within Europe.

Campbell and Cosans concerned the conformity with the Convention of a traditional form of punishment used in Scottish schools (hitting the palm of the hand with a leather strap). The Court was told that its use was favoured by a large body of parents and teachers in Scotland. While the Court took this into account in deciding that the punishment was not degrading, it held that the parents' rights under the First Protocol, article 2, had been infringed since the functions assumed by the UK government extended to the supervision of Scottish education in general, including questions of discipline.

In *Gillow* it was argued that local circumstances in the island of Guernsey made necessary legislation that sought to restrict the occupation of houses to local people. The Court accepted as legitimate the reasons that had led the local legislature to adopt its restrictive housing policy, but found that the policy had been improperly applied in the applicants' own circumstances.

Except where, as in *Gillow*, an argument can be made that is wholly related to distinct local conditions, the Court is generally not inclined to make local exceptions from the standards that it believes justified in general. In particular, the fact that within the United Kingdom different laws or practices may apply makes it more difficult for the government's representatives to argue that one particular law or practice is 'necessary in a democratic society'.[94]

(b) The 'margin of appreciation'

The concept of the margin of appreciation that has been developed by the Commission and the Court at Strasbourg emphasises that these authorities must not as a matter of course substitute themselves for the national authorities whose decisions they have to review under the Convention.[95] Where a margin of appreciation is found to exist, and national authorities stay within it, there is no ground for the intervention of Strasbourg. The concept corresponds to the well-known approach of the courts in judicial review of administrative decisions when they insist that it is not for them to substitute their own decision for that taken by an executive body within the limits of its proper discretion.[96] The case-law under review brings out that the margin of national appreciation varies not only with the human right in issue but also, where interferences with a right are permitted by the Convention, with the particular purpose for which the interference is permitted. In *Handyside*, as we have seen, the conviction of the publisher of a book considered obscene was held to fall within the margin of appreciation of the national authorities. In the *Sunday Times* case, however, which also concerned freedom of expression under article 10, the Court held that the margin of appreciation was narrower in respect of the 'authority of the judiciary' (i.e. contempt of court) than in respect of the protection of morals. While the injunction against the newspaper was not 'unnecessary' simply because it would not have been issued in a different legal system, the Court by a majority did not consider that a 'pressing social need' existed for the ban sufficient to outweigh the public interest in publication of the article.

The margin of appreciation has proved to be a flexible instrument which is constantly invoked by the Court and is a not infrequent cause of dissent within it. In the *Republic of Ireland* case, the Court accepted that the UK government's margin of appreciation in its response to terrorism extended to authorising the use of internment and to securing the necessary derogation under article 15 ECHR from article 5, thus ensuring that the process of internment itself was not in breach of article 5.[97] But the margin of appreciation was not relevant to the methods of interrogation in depth that infringed article 3. In a very different context, the Court in *James* and *Lithgow* accepted that national authorities enjoyed a very broad margin of appreciation in determining their policies towards the enfranchisement of leasehold property and nationalisation of the shipbuilding industry.

(c) **Proportionality**

Like the margin of appreciation, the concept of proportionality features frequently in the reasoning of the Court. Its origins lie in German law and it is also found in the case-law of the European Court of Justice. Similar doctrines are found in the interpretation of provisions for fundamental rights in the US Constitution and the Canadian Charter of Rights and Freedoms.[98] In the *Sunday Times* case, where the English court's ban on publication was plainly an interference with the newspaper's freedom of expression, the Strasbourg Court held that the circumstances did not constitute a social need sufficiently pressing to outweigh the public interest in freedom of expression and that the ban was not proportionate to the legitimate aim pursued, namely maintaining the authority of the judiciary. In *Dudgeon*, the adverse effects on the privacy of homosexuals in Northern Ireland were held to be disproportionate to the aim of protecting health and morals and the rights and freedoms of others. By contrast, in *James* the Court held that legislation expropriating freehold owners of land for the benefit of the leaseholders was appropriate for achieving its aim and not disproportionate to it. Proportionality is likely to appear in any decision deciding the extent to which Convention rights may legitimately be encroached upon. Such cases from the United Kingdom included *Ashingdane, Abdulaziz, AGOSI, Lithgow, Gaskin* and *Chappell.* While there is some similarity between proportionality and unreasonableness as a ground for judicial review of executive action in English and Scots law,[99] the test of proportionality involves a process, which British courts would generally disavow, of balancing rights and interests against the effects of the action in question.[100] The Strasbourg Court's decisions have certainly done a great deal to bring the language of proportionality, with or without judicial blessing, into the vocabulary of national administrative law.

6. *The Convention as quasi-constitutional law*

It is time to consider whether with the help of these various elements of the Strasbourg jurisprudence (together with others that could have been mentioned), the nature of the edifice itself can yet be perceived.

The Convention retains its status as a multilateral treaty intended to protect minimum standards of human rights,[101] yet the organs it created (the Commission and the Court) have judicial powers which have been exercised so as to create out of the treaty something more comparable to a supranational constitutional text that provides a yardstick against which the legal systems of the party states may be judged. Compared with other classes of treaty, criteria of interpretation that look to the text of the Convention rather than to the intent of the parties are more appropriate.[102] Professor Schermers, the Dutch member of the Commission, has commented:

> When it was drafted, [the Convention] was intended to protect only those human rights which were generally accepted in all participating States. Its purpose was to add additional international protection to a limited number of existing fundamental human rights. Gradually, however, the Convention is developing into a far more dynamic instrument of European control over the way the participating governments treat their subjects. . . . . Thus the [Strasbourg] institutions . . . . are developing into a kind of constitutional court for Europe, protecting all individuals against unfair treatment by the governments . . . .[103]

And Drzemczewski has drawn an important implication from the same point: 'although still in embryonic form, there appears to be emerging a sort of European quasi-constitutional or common law, the maintenance of whose uniform minimum standards is considered the responsibility not only of the Convention's organs but also that of the domestic judiciary'.[104] As the majority of the Court said in *Tyrer,* considering whether judicial birching was degrading punishment contrary to article 3 ECHR, 'the Convention is a living instrument which . . . . must be interpreted in the light of present-day conditions. In the case before us, the Court cannot but be influenced by the developments and commonly accepted standards in the penal policy of the member States of the Council of Europe in this field'.[105]

It may have been a fundamental opposition to this transformation of the Convention that accounted for the number of occasions on which the British judge on the Court between 1974 and 1980, Sir Gerald Fitzmaurice, found

himself in dissent from the majority of the Court (in cases such as *Golder,*
Tyrer and the *Republic of Ireland*).[106] In the *Golder* case, for instance, he
could not find (as the majority had done) that a right of access to legal advice
as a preliminary to initiating litigation was implied within article 6(1) ECHR
'except by a process of interpretation that I do not regard as sound or as
being in the best interests of international treaty law'.[107]

In contrast, the British judge on the International Court of Justice, Sir
Robert Jennings, who has sat once at Strasbourg,[108] has recognised the
special purposes of a human rights treaty. Quoting in turn another
distinguished international lawyer, Sir Hersch Lauterpacht, Jennings has
written:

> [T]he assuring of human rights 'must be concerned not only with
> persistent and grave violations of its clauses but also with the normal
> supervision of its observance' [Lauterpacht]. In other words, a human
> rights regime that is indeed working . . . . will be normally and mainly
> concerned not so much with the outrageous, but with *highly technical*
> *questions*, e.g. concerning trade unions and their membership, the right
> to work, police powers, the minutiae of due process of law, and the
> like.[109]

Technical questions of this kind are indeed the regular diet of public lawyers
within national law. As the great constitutionalist, Justice Brennan of the
US Supreme Court, remarked in denying that the provisions of the US Bill
of Rights were technicalities, 'We are what we are *because* we have those
guarantees, and the Courts exist to see that those guarantees are faithfully
enforced. They are not technicalities!'[110] Some international lawyers may
find key terms in the text of the Convention and the subject-matter of the
Strasbourg cases unfamiliar. But this should not be the case with
constitutional and administrative lawyers, whose customary trade it is to
deal with disputes on such matters between the individual and organs of
the state in their own legal systems.

D. Conclusions

These reflections on the decisions of the Strasbourg Court in cases brought
against the United Kingdom have intentionally not dwelt on the issue about
which so much has been written, namely the present uncertain status of
the Convention in the municipal law of the United Kingdom.[111] It is
impossible to believe either that its present status is satisfactory or that it
will continue unchanged throughout the 1990s. Some measure of
incorporation, in a weaker or a stronger form,[112] seems inevitable, whether
this comes about as a result of a political initiative in Downing Street or
in Westminster, or because United Kingdom courts increasingly make use
of it, or because the Strasbourg Court departs from its earlier stance to adopt
a stronger interpretation of national obligations under articles 1 and 13.[113]
Again, it might come about because Anglo-Irish co-operation makes some
such step seem desirable in helping to resolve the future of Northern Ireland,
or because it is seen as an inevitable and appropriate accompaniment to
closer integration in economic and social matters within the European
Communities. This is not to say that the Convention is a comprehensive

solution to the problem of protecting rights and liberties within British society, or that the processes and institutions at Strasbourg cannot be improved.[114]

Nonetheless, forty years on from the signing of the Convention, the 'half-baked scheme administered by some unknown court', as the Lord Chancellor referred to it in 1950,[115] has a fair claim to rank as one of the finest achievements for closer integration in Western Europe. And after the historic developments in Eastern Europe that occurred in the second half of 1989, the movement for closer European integration may well extend its mantle to the protection and enhancement of human rights for many others beyond Western Europe.

Although the subject has proved to be distinctly more unruly than I had expected when I decided to write about it, I hope to have shown at least that there is a great deal in the procedures and decisions of the Strasbourg system that can enrich our understanding of constitutional and administrative law, provide a stimulus for reforms that may be needed in our national system of public law, and guard against these branches of legal study in the United Kingdom falling into insularity or a tired complacency.

Annex: European Court of Human Rights

Decisions in cases against the United Kingdom, 1975 – April 1990

In this list, the number in column 1 refers to the number allocated to the decision in Series A of the judgments of the Court. The year in column 2 is the year in which the Court's decision was made. The full name of the case is the name of the complainant (in column 3) followed by '*v United Kingdom*'. The entry in square brackets after the case summary indicates the reference to the European Human Rights Reports (EHRR), which is the most convenient collection in English of the Court's judgments. Thus the first case listed can be cited as *Golder v United Kingdom* (1975) 1 EHRR 524.

This list is confined to the principal judgments of the Court dealing with the substantive merits of the cases listed and it does not include prior proceedings before the European Commission on Human Rights, nor any subsequent proceedings that there may have been before the Court (e.g. in relation to the issue of 'just satisfaction' under article 50) or before the Committee of Ministers of the Council of Europe.

NUMBER YEAR NAME AND SUMMARY [AND EHRR REFERENCE]

18   1975 **Golder** – prisoner's right to sue a prison officer – access to
              legal advice – breaches of arts. 6, 8 [1:524]

24   1976 **Handyside** – conviction for obscene publication (Little Red
              Schoolbook) – within national discretion for protection of
              morals – no breach of arts. 10, 14, First Protocol (1) [1:737]

25   1978 **Republic of Ireland** – interrogation in depth of detainees –
              inhuman and degrading treatment, not torture – breaches of
              art. 3 – derogation from art. 5 upheld – no breach of art.
              14 [2:25]

26   1978 **Tyrer** – judicial corporal punishment of juvenile in Isle of
              Man – degrading treatment – breach of art. 3 [2:1]

30   1979 **Sunday Times** – court's ban on thalidomide article because
              contempt of court – breach of art. 10, not of art. 14 [2:245]

44   1981 **Young, James and Webster** – closed shop introduced by
              railways under industrial relations legislation – breach of art.
              11 [4:38]

45   1981 **Dudgeon** – criminal law against adult homosexuality in
              Northern Ireland – breach of art. 8 [4:149]

46   1981 **X** – mental patient with criminal conviction, re-detained
              after 'conditional' release – breach of art. 5(4), not of art.
              5(1) [4:188]

48   1982 **Campbell and Cosans** – corporal punishment in state
              schools – breach of First Protocol (2) – no breach of art. 3
              [4:293]

61   1983 **Silver** – prisoners' correspondence – breaches of arts. 6(1),
              8 [5:347]

80   1984 **Campbell and Fell** – prison disciplinary proceedings – loss
              of expected remission – denial of legal representation –
              breaches of arts. 6, 8, 13 [7:165]

82   1984 **Malone** – telephone tapping by police – breach of art. 8
              [7:14]

93   1985 **Ashingdane** – detention of mental patient – no breach of
              arts. 5, 6 [7:528]

94   1985 **Abdulaziz, Cabales and Balkandali** – sex discrimination in
              immigration rules – breach of arts. 8 and 14 read together,
              and art. 13, no breach of art. 3 [7:471]

98   1986 **James** – compulsory purchase by leaseholder of freehold title
              – no breach of Protocol 1(1), nor of arts. 6, 13, 14 [8:123]

102   1986 **Lithgow** – compensation for nationalisation of shipbuilding
              industry – no breach of Protocol 1(1), nor of arts. 6, 13, 14
              [8:329]

106   1986 **Rees** – change of sex – no right to altered birth certificate
              – no breach of arts. 8, 12 [9:56]

108   1986 **AGOSI** – smuggled krugerrands forfeited – no breach of
              Protocol 1(1) or art. 6 [9:1]

109   1986 **Gillow** – owner of house in Guernsey prosecuted for
              unlawful occupation of it – breach of art. 8 in application to
              G of Guernsey Housing Law, but no breach of arts. 6, 14
              [11:335]

114   1987 **Weeks** – life prisoner released on licence but subject to
              recall – no breach of art. 5(1), breach of art. 5(4) [10:293]

115	1987	**Monnell and Morris** – loss of time served in prison while appealing – no breach of arts. 5, 6, 14 [10:205]
120	1987	**H** – local authority taking child into care, undue delay in High Court proceedings regarding access and adoption – breaches of arts. 6(1), 8 [10:95]*
120/ 121	1987	**W,R,O,B** – local authorities taking children into care – removal of parental rights – unfair decision-making process – breaches of arts. 6(1), 8 [10:29 *et seq.*] *
131	1988	**Boyle and Rice** – prisoners' mail, family visits etc. – breach of art. 8, not of art. 13 [10:425]
145	1988	**Brogan** – detention on suspicion of terrorism – undue delay before brought to court – breaches of art. 5(3) and 5(5), but not of art. 5(1) and 5(4) [11:117]
152	1989	**Chappell** – execution of 'Anton Piller' order made *ex parte* by High Court authorising search of business premises and home, simultaneously with police search – no breach of art. 8 [12:1].
160	1989	**Gaskin** – G, in care of local authority until 18, denied access to documents on his file except with consent of person providing information – breach of art. 8, not of art. 10 [12:36].
161	1989	**Soering** – request for extradition of German citizen from UK to USA to stand trial for murder – extradition would breach art. 3 so long as risk of capital sentence [11:439]
172	1990	**Powell and Rayner** – interference with rights of property and with respect for privacy caused by aircraft noise – Civil Aviation Act 1982, s. 76(1) taking away right to sue for nuisance – no breach of arts. 6(1), 8, 13 [12:355].
174	1990	**Granger** – refusal of legal aid in difficult criminal appeal – breach of art. 6(3) (28 March 1990)

* The child care cases all raise broadly the same issues and could have been grouped together, except that H's case raises a separate issue of delay in court proceedings and it is therefore shown separately.

† An early version of this essay formed the basis of a lecture delivered to the Law Department, Staffordshire Polytechnic, on 6 December 1989. I am indebted to the staff and students of the Law Department for their hospitality on that and other occasions.

Notes

1. M.J.C. Vile *Constitutionalism and the Separation of Powers* Clarendon Press (1967) 238.
2. At 283. The passage was unaltered in Street's final edition (5th ed) Penguin (1982) 307.
3. (1989) 11 EHRR 439.
4. 20 July 1989 HC Debs col 638.
5. *Ibid* cols 639–642. Soering was later extradited to the USA after an undertaking had been given that he would not be subject to execution. His application for *habeas corpus* failed: *Re Soering* [1990] *Crown Office Digest* 162.
6. A. Lester 'Fundamental Rights: the United Kingdom Isolated?' [1984] PL 46 at 51–54 (emphases supplied).
7. *Ibid* at 59–61.
8. (1975) 1 EHRR 524.

9. See e.g. the report by Justice *Freedom of Expression and the Law* (1990) criticising both judges and the government for being too ready to accept or impose restrictions on the freedom of speech.

10. E.g. F. Jacobs *The European Convention on Human Rights* Clarendon Press (1975); R. Beddard *Human Rights and Europe* (2nd ed) Sweet & Maxwell (1980); P. van Dijk and G.J.H. van Hoof *Theory and Practice of the ECHR* Kluwer (1984).

11. For the most recent judicial discussion, see *R v Home Secretary ex p Brind* [1990] 1 All ER 469; and J. Jowell [1990] PL 149.

12. For an account of how applications are dealt with, see E. Fribergh 'The Commission Secretariat's handling of provisional files' in *Protecting Human Rights: the European Dimension* (Studies in honour of G.J. Wiarda) F. Matscher and H. Petzold (Eds) Heymanns Verlag (1988) 181.

13. See e.g. the Committee's decision in April 1990 regarding the abuse of telephone tapping in Britain in the 1970s: *Hewitt and Harman v UK, The Independent* 20 April 1990.

14. See the statistics contained in *Protecting Human Rights, op cit* note 12 *supra* at 717–721. I have treated the five related child care cases (*W,R,O,B and H v UK*) as two, as I do in the table of decisions in cases against the UK above.

15. *Protecting Human Rights, op cit* note 12 *supra* at 722.

16. Text at note 5 *supra*.

17. See the government's contribution to the abortive debate on the Human Rights Bill 1987: 6 Feb 1987 HC Debs col 1274 (Sir Patrick Mayhew, Solicitor-General).

18. No violation was found in *Monnell and Morris*. In *Boyle and Rice*, an isolated violation of article 8 was found, but on the main issues relating to article 13 no violation was found.

19. Possibly the turning point was *R v Board of Visitors of Hull Prison, ex p St Germain* [1978] QB 678. And see G. Douglas and S.Jones 'Prisoners and the ECHR ' in M.P. Furmston, R. Kerridge and B.E. Sufrin (Eds) *The Effect on English Domestic Law of Membership of the European Communities and of Ratification of the ECHR* Martinus Nijhoff (1983) 387.

20. *Raymond v Honey* [1983] 1 AC1 at 10.

21. See H.G. Schermers 'The International protection of the Right of Property' in *Protecting Human Rights op cit* note 12 *supra* 565.

22. See *A – G. v Guardian Newspapers Ltd* [1987] 3 All ER 316 and the same *(No. 2)* [1990] AC 109.

23. See A.W. Bradley, 'The ECHR and Administrative Law – First Impressions' (1983) 21 *Osgoode Hall LJ* 609 at 614–617.

24. (1978) 2 EHRR 25 at 78.

25. Bradley, *op cit* note 23 *supra* 617–621.

26. A.W. Bradley 'The Sovereignty of Parliament – in Perpetuity?' in J. Jowell and D. Oliver (Eds) *The Changing Constitution* (2nd ed) Oxford U P (1989) ch 2.

27. And see *X v UK* (1981) (recall of mental patient by Home Secretary, unsuccessful application for *habeas corpus*).

28. *Cf Maharaj v A – G for Trinidad and Tobago (No. 2)* [1979] AC 385 (state liable for breach by court of M's constitutional rights).

29. See e.g. H. – J. Bartsch 'The Supervisory Functions of the Committee of Ministers under Article 54 – a postcript to Luedicke – Belkacem – Koc' in *Protecting Human Rights, op cit* note 12 *supra* 47; A. Drzemczewski, 'Un Etat en violation de la [E.C.H.R.]: l'exécution interne des décisions des institutions de Strasbourg' *ibid* 149; and P. Mahoney 'Does Article 57 of the ECHR serve any useful purpose?' *ibid* 373.

30. Article 50 implies that an individual is entitled to 'full reparation' for the consequences of any breach and empowers the court to afford 'just satisfaction' to the injured party.

31. As recognised for the United Kingdom by the European Communities Act
     1972 s 2(1).
32. *Swedish Engine Drivers Union v Sweden* (1976) 1 EHRR 617 at 631.
33. Employment Act 1980 s 7 and Employment Act 1982 s 2 and Sched 1. See
     K.D. Ewing and W.M. Rees 'Closed Shop Dismissals 1974 – 80: A Study
     of the Retroactive Compensation Scheme' (1983) 12 Ind L J 148; and A.M.
     Dugdale and H.F. Rawlings 'The Closed Shop and the ECHR' in Furmston,
     Kerridge and Sufrin (Eds) *op cit* note 19 *supra* 283.
34. Despite the decision of the Committee of Ministers discharging its functions
     under Article 54: *Sunday Times v UK* (1981) 3 EHRR 615. And see N.V.
     Lowe 'The English Law of Contempt and article 10 ECHR' in Furmston,
     Kerridge and Sufrin (Eds) *op cit* note 19 *supra* 318; and *Times Newspapers
     v UK* (1985) 41 D & R 123.
35. See respectively the Homosexual Offences (Northern Ireland) Order 1982,
     S I 1982, 1536; Mental Health (Amendment) Act 1982 s 28(4) and Sched
     1; Education (No. 2) Act 1986, ss 47, 48; Interception of Communications
     Act 1985.
36. See the sequence of decisions *Golder, Silver* and *Boyle and Rice*.
37. See e.g. *X Ltd v Morgan Grampian Ltd* [1990] 2 WLR 1000 in which the
     House of Lords upheld an order to a journalist that he disclose his sources,
     deciding that he was not protected by the Contempt of Court Act 1981 s 10.
38. For the background to this, see A. Drzemczewski *European Human Rights
     Convention in Domestic Law: A Comparative Study* Clarendon Press (1983).
39. For similar legislation see the Northern Ireland (Emergency Provisions) Act
     1987 s 5 and see *R v McCormick* [1977] NILR 105 (interpreting earlier
     legislation in the light of the Convention).
40. For the amended Immigration Rules see (1984 – 85) HC 503 (1985) now
     replaced by (1988 – 89) HC 388 (1989).
41. In *Teare v O'Callaghan* (1981) 4 EHRR 232, the Isle of Man High Court
     stated that it would follow a sentencing policy which was as much in
     conformity with the island's treaty obligations as was consistent with domestic
     law, and set aside a sentence of birching in favour of a custodial sentence.
42. See 27 July 1976 HC Debs col 184 (WA) and 2 August 1976 HC Debs col
     535 (WA).
43. See 6 Dec 1988 HC Debs col 210; 30 Jan 1989 HC Debs cols 53 – 68; and
     The Times, 23 Dec 1988.
44. 14 Nov 1989 HC Debs col 209 (WA).
45. This and the next two paragraphs reproduce material from 'Protecting
     Government Decisions from Legal Challenge' [1988] PL 1 at 3 – 4.
46. See text at notes 5 to 7 *supra*.
47. Of the present court of 23 judges, 3 have a common law background: Sir
     Vincent Evans (UK), The Hon B. Walsh (Republic of Ireland) and Professor
     R. St J. Macdonald (nominated by Lichtenstein).
48. (1975) 1 EHRR 524 at 535.
49. (1978) 2 EHRR 214 at 235.
50. A.V. Dicey *The Law and the Constitution* (10th ed) Macmillan (1959) by
     E.C.S. Wade, 4. And see E. Barendt 'Dicey and Civil Liberties' [1985] PL
     596.
51. See also the requirement of legal authority, Article 5(1); the First Protocol,
     Article 1; and the Fourth Protocol, Article 2.
52. In *A-G v Times Newspapers Ltd* [1974] AC 273, the two central issues
     considered were (a) the risk of the article pre-judging the eventual trial of
     the action to establish liability, and (b) whether publication would have
     brought undue pressure to bear on the defendants in the action.
53. (1979) 2 EHRR 245 at 270.
54. (1979) 2 EHRR 245 at 271.
55. *Ibid*.
56. (1979) 2 EHRR 245 at 299.

57. (1979) 2 EHRR 245 at 304.
58. [1979] Ch 344.
59. Cmnd 7873 (1980). And see 1 April 1980 HC Debs cols 205–220.
60. (1984) 7 EHRR 14 at 40–41.
61. For comment, see I.J. Lloyd (1986) 49 MLR 86.
62. E.g. those which led to the Committee of Ministers' decision in 1990 confirming that breaches of the Convention had occurred through the tapping of telephones used by nuclear disarmers (*supra* note 13).
63. (1986) 11 EHRR 335 at 350.
64. *Chappell v UK* (1989) 12 EHRR 1 at 20, citing *Olsson v Sweden* (1988) 11 EHRR 259 at 283–4.
65. *Cheney v Conn* [1968] 1 All ER 779 at 782 (per Ungoed-Thomas J).
66. See S.A. de Smith *Judicial Review of Administrative Action* (2nd ed) Stevens & Sons (1968) 26. The passage was omitted from the 3rd ed (1973).
67. 1985 Act s 7(8); 1989 Act s 5(4).
68. Notably in *Anisminic Ltd v Foreign Compensation Commission* [1969] 2 AC 147; H.W.R. Wade *Constitutional Fundamentals* (1980) 68.
69. E.g. *Johnston v Chief Constable of the RUC* (Case 222/84) [1987] QB 129.
70. (1988) 11 EHRR 117 at 134 citing *Klass v Germany* (1978) 2 EHRR 214 at 235 and *Engel v Netherlands* (1976) 1 EHRR 647 at 672.
71. (1988) 11 EHRR 117 at 137 citing two Northern Ireland decisions *Ex p Lynch* [1980] NILR 126 and *Van Hout v Chief Constable RUC* (28 June 1984, unreported).
72. (1981) 4 EHRR 188 at 208.
73. (1987) 10 EHRR 293 at 315 and see *Ashingdane* (1985) 7 EHRR 528 at 545.
74. (1987) 10 EHRR 293 at 319.
75. (1986) 9 EHRR 1 at 9 citing the Law Commission's *Report on Remedies in Administrative Law*, Cmnd 6407 (1976). *Cf R v Lancashire CC ex p Huddleston* [1986] 2 All ER 941.
76. (1986) 9 EHRR 1 at 16 citing *R v Customs and Excise, ex p Haworth* (17 July 1985, unreported). See also *Allgemeine Gold (etc.) v Customs and Excise Commissioners* [1980] QB 390.
77. *Brown v Hamilton DC* 1983 SLT 397 at 414; and see *Stair Encyclopaedia of the Laws of Scotland*, Butterworths vol 1 (1989) 61.
78. (1988) 10 EHRR 425 at 447.
79. E.g. *Engel v Netherlands* (1976) 1 EHRR 647 (armed forces), *Le Comte v Belgium* (1981) 4 EHRR 1 (medical profession).
80. E.g. *Benthem v Netherlands* (1986) 8 EHRR 1; *Deumeland v Germany* (1986) 8 EHRR 448 (discussed in [1987] PL 3). And see A. Boyle 'Administrative Justice, Judicial Review and the Right to a Fair Hearing under the ECHR' [1984] PL 89.
81. But see *Kaplan v UK* (1982) 4 EHRR 64 (Commission), discussed by A. Boyle [1982] PL 218.
82. *R v Board of Visitors of Maze Prison, ex Hone* [1988] AC 379.
83. (1984) 7 EHRR 165 at 198.
84. *X v UK* (1981) 4 EHRR 188 at 207, citing *De Wilde, Ooms and Versyup v Belgium* (No. 1) (1979) 1 EHRR 373 at 407–408.
85. See P. van Dijk 'The interpretation of "civil rights and obligations" by the European Court of Human Rights – one more step to take' in *Protecting Human Rights op cit* note 12 *supra* 131.
86. As in *Benthem v Netherlands op cit* note 80 *supra* which has led to reforms in Dutch administrative law (see N Verheij [1990] PL 23).
87. *Sporrong and Lönnroth v Sweden* (1982) 5 EHRR 35, *Boden v Sweden* (1987) 10 EHRR 367 and *Pudas v Sweden* (1987) 10 EHRR 380. And see H. Danelius 'Judicial control of the administration – a Swedish proposal for legislative reform' in *Protecting Human Rights op cit* note 12 *supra* 113.
88. E.g. *W* (1987) 10 EHRR 29 at 58.
89. *Sporrong and Lönnroth v Sweden op cit* note 86 *supra* was distinguished, in

part because in that case there was an arguable case of non-compliance with Swedish law.

90. *Golder v UK* (1975) 1 EHRR 524 at 537.
91. E.g. *Buchholz v Germany* (1980) 3 EHRR 597; *Baggetta v Italy* (1987) 10 EHRR 325.
92. (1987) 10 EHRR 95 at 120.
93. In *Lithgow* the first applicant came from Scotland but the case applied equally to Scottish and English industries and there was no specifically Scottish dimension.
94. See the separate opinion of Judge Mosler in *Handyside* (1976) 1 EHRR 737 at 764–765.
95. J.G. Merrills *The Development of International Law by the European Court of Human Rights* Man U P (1988) ch 7.
96. Cf *A.P. Picture Houses Ltd v Wednesbury Corporation* [1948] 1 KB 223.
97. (1978) 2 EHRR 25 at 91–95.
98. The leading Canadian decisions are *R v Big M Drug Mart Ltd* [1985] 1 SCR 295 and *R v Oakes* [1986] 1 SCR 103.
99. See J.L. Jowell and A. Lester 'Proportionality: Neither Novel Nor Dangerous' in J.L. Jowell and D. Oliver (Eds) *New Directions in Judicial Review* Stevens & Sons (1988) 51.
100. As in *ex parte Brind op cit* note 11 *supra*.
101. See Merrills *op cit* note 95 *supra*.
102. R. Bernhardt 'Thoughts on the interpretation of human rights treaties' in *Protecting Human Rights op cit* note 12 *supra* 65 at 68–69.
103. Schermers *op cit* note 21 *supra* 566–567.
104. Drzemczewski *op cit* note 38 *supra* 326.
105. (1978) 2 EHRR 1 at 10. And see *Marckx v Belgium* (1979) 2 EHRR 330 at 346; and *Tyrer* (1982) 4 EHRR 149 at 167.
106. See also *Sunday Times* (1) (1979) 2 EHRR 245 at 285; *Sunday Times* (2) (1980) 3 EHRR 317 at 331; *Marckx v Belgium* (1979) 2 EHRR 330 at 364; *National Union of Belgian Police v Belgium* (1975) 1 EHRR 578 at 601 and *Guzzardi v Italy* (1980) 3 EHRR 333 at 376.
107. (1975) 1 EHRR 524 at 577.
108. As *ad hoc* judge in *X* (1981).
109. R. Jennings 'Human rights and domestic law and courts' in *Protecting Human Rights* (*op cit* note 12 *supra*) 295, 298 (emphasis supplied).
110. Profile of Justice Brennan, *New Yorker*, 12 March 1990 at 65.
111. See *ex p Brind op cit* note 11 *supra* and Drzemczewski *op cit* note 38 *supra passim*.
112. See Bradley *op cit* note 26 *supra* 43–50.
113. For a critique of the tortuous case-law on article 13, see van Dijk and van Hoof *op cit* note 10 *supra* 379–386.
114. See e.g. the Council of Europe *Report on European Human Rights Procedures* (1989) 11 EHRR 421.
115. Page 186 *supra*.

Political Strikes*

Douglas Brodie

A. Introduction

In this essay I wish to examine the position of strikes which might be regarded as political. The first problem is one of definition, since 'although the phrase "political strike" has from time to time been used in reported cases, it is . . . a phrase which should be used, at any rate in a court of law, with considerable caution, for it does not readily lend itself to precise or accurate definition'.[1] In a sense this does not matter, since both generally and in the particular context of political strikes, trade disputes law in the UK is not concerned with essential definition but rather provides a definition of an industrial dispute whose wider remit is to set 'the boundaries within which industrial conflict is legitimate'.[2] The aim of this essay is the critical assessment of the policy behind this definition with a view to reform of the law. However, even for policy purposes the distinction has to be drawn between political and economic or industrial aspects of industrial action. The economic or industrial aspect is that which bears upon the terms and conditions of employment, whilst the political aspect bears upon matters within government policy. Since the latter aspect includes matters which also bear upon terms and conditions of employment there is, inevitably, a conceptual overlap. If the policy and legal framework is drawn too narrowly then the capacity of trade unions to use industrial action in pursuit of their traditional industrial aims will be curtailed. If, on the other hand, it is drawn too widely it may be that the right to strike will be used to undermine the authority of democratically elected governments. The fundamental difficulty is that, given the modern state's role as economic manager, many disputes may be seen as challenging the government's authority. Against such a backdrop it is notoriously difficult to separate economic from political motives and economic action from political action.

There are different types of strike which might be conceived of as political in nature, each of which highlights this problem. One instance is the protest strike against government policy. In 1980 the Trades Union Congress (TUC) called for a one-day national strike in protest at the government's economic policies. The action was held to be unlawful since, as we will see, the trade dispute immunities do not protect action taken against the government *qua* government.[3] Similarly, in 1970 a proposed one-day strike called in protest against proposed industrial relations legislation was found to be unlawful.[4] A second type of political strike is one in which industrial action is taken in furtherance of a demand made against one's employer but where compliance with the demand will have implications for the fulfilment of government policy. One example would be a wage demand during the currency of an incomes policy which, if granted, would result in the policy being breached. Such a consequence would be an inevitable result of the strikers' demands being met and might, to a greater or lesser extent, motivate the union action. The Mercury dispute, discussed below, perhaps falls into this category.[5]

In the light of the boundary problems which arise in this area it is suggested that, if the right to strike is to be placed on a secure footing, strike law should be more firmly underpinned by principle, and assistance in this area is to be found from the writings of pluralists. This is not without its difficulties, because pluralism is by no means a narrow tradition of political theory. There are, nevertheless, certain common themes which can be extracted and applied,[6] in particular the need for a significant diffusion of power outwith the central institutions of government and an acceptance of the legitimate role of key consumer, producer and other interest groups in the policy-making process.

B. Recent Developments in the Law

It is perhaps true to say that the most commented-upon feature of the British law on strikes is the fact that the law takes the form of immunities against common law liabilities rather than a series of positive rights.[7] Immunity is granted to unions and union organisers with respect to certain actions in delict or tort, such as inducing breach of contract. In addition to this, with the exception of the period when the Industrial Relations Act 1971 was in force, the law traditionally did not seek to regulate the conduct of industrial action to any significant extent. The law intervened only at the margins. Thus, prior to 1984 and the introduction of strike ballots, statute did not impose any procedural restraints on the taking of industrial action.[8] The means by which industrial action was furthered were similarly unfettered.[9] Finally, until 1982 the range of purposes for which industrial action could lawfully be taken was very wide. The lack of legal regulation is arguably a more significant feature than the fact that the law was negative in form.

In the UK, statutory immunity is provided against certain common law liabilities so long as the action is taken 'in contemplation or furtherance of a trade dispute', the so-called 'golden formula'.[10] To gain the protection of the golden formula as a trade dispute industrial action must be taken for a proper purpose (i.e. for one of the purposes listed in s. 29(1) of the Trade Union and Labour Relations Act 1974 (henceforth TULRA)). These purposes include most of the matters likely to be the subject of a trade dispute.

Section 29(1) provides that 'trade dispute' means a dispute between workers and their employer which relates wholly or mainly to one or more of the following, that is to say:

(a) terms and conditions of employment or the physical conditions in which any workers are required to work;
(b) engagement or non-engagement or termination or suspension of employment or the duties of employment, of one or more workers;
(c) allocation of work or the duties of employment as between workers or groups of workers;
(d) matters of discipline;
(e) the membership or non-membership of a trade union on the part of a worker;
(f) facilities for officials of trade unions; and
(g) machinery for negotiation or consultation, and other procedures, relating to any of the foregoing matters, including the recognition by employers or employers' associations of the right of a trade union to represent workers in any such negotiation or consultation or in the carrying out of such procedures.

In so far as one is assessing the legal status of political strikes, two major questions arise. First, to what extent must industrial action be taken for a proper purpose? Prior to 1971 and in the period 1974-82 the dispute had only to be 'connected with' one of the matters listed in s. 29(1) TULRA. In the period 1971-74 and since 1982 the scope of the immunity was narrowed by substituting 'relates wholly or mainly to' for 'connected with'.[11] Secondly, the dispute must be between proper parties, i.e. between workers and their employer.[12] Disputes aimed against the government *qua* government have never enjoyed immunity.

1. *Linkage with proper subject-matter*

Of the cases arising under the 1971-74 statutory regime, two are particularly worthy of mention: *Sherard*[13] and *Gerard Aviation Services (GAS)*.[14] In both cases a strong political element existed: opposition to the government's income policy in *Sherard* and support for state ownership in *GAS*. Moreover, in both cases the union's industrial object was somewhat remote in the sense that in *Sherard* no wage claim had actually been made and in *GAS* redundancies had not been declared.

In *Sherard*, even though no wage claim had been made, or was about to be made, Phillips J (in a judgment upheld by the Court of Appeal) said that a strike against the government's incomes policy was arguably a trade dispute since '[i]t is quite likely that there were in the pipeline claims which the action taken was intended to, and would, support'.[15] Further, in *GAS* a dispute had arisen over fears about job losses which an independent report had declared to be 'groundless', yet the dispute was held to be 'mainly about' redundancies, since 'on the evidence there can be no doubt that the fears were genuinely and widely entertained'.[16] The Court of Appeal gave little weight to the evidence that the strikers also 'wished to see a State-owned agency running the service'.

It is important to note that both these cases were decided on the 'relates wholly or mainly to' formula which was used by the Industrial Relations Act 1971.[17] In 1974 the 'connected with' formula, which had been in place from 1906 until 1971, was restored.[18] This received an uncompromisingly restrictive interpretation by the English Court of Appeal until the decision of the House of Lords in *NWL v Woods*.[19] The Court of Appeal had treated the words 'connected with' almost as if they had read 'mainly about', which had the effect of narrowing the lawful objects of industrial action. Moreover, the permissive impact of the decision in *NWL v Woods* was short-lived, given the reintroduction of the 'relates wholly or mainly to' formula by the 1982 Act.

The first case on the reintroduced formula was *Mercury Communications v Scott-Garner*.[20] This dispute stemmed from the government's policy of privatisation and liberalisation within the telecommunications industry. Section 15 of the Telecommunications Act 1981 provided for the grant of licences for the running of telecommunications services. In furtherance of the policy of liberalisation, Mercury was granted such a licence (as agent for Cable and Wireless plc), and this effectively ended the monopoly previously enjoyed by the State-owned British Telecommunications (BT). In addition, the Telecommunications Bill 1983/84, which *inter alia* sought to alter the nationalised status of BT by converting it into a public company, had been introduced as a further step on the road to privatisation. The Post Office Engineering Union bitterly opposed these developments and launched a campaign to try to prevent both privatisation and liberalisation. This included a series of strikes and later a 'blacking' of BT services to Mercury. Mercury sought an interlocutory injunction in the High Court. This was refused, since it was held that the dispute related 'wholly or mainly to termination of employment'. However, this decision was overturned on appeal, where new evidence was produced as to the existence of a formal job security agreement between BT and the union. This sought to guarantee that there would be no compulsory redundancies, though it also contained a *force majeure* clause which provided that in the event of a major manpower problem arising from causes outside the control of BT and resulting in a manpower surplus, BT had the right to withdraw from the agreement. The main question before the Court of Appeal was whether the statutory immunities protected the union and its officers from common law liability. The answer turned on whether the 'industrial' action was wholly or mainly due to fear of job losses, or was mainly due to political objection to the breaking of the monopoly of a nationalised industry. An interlocutory injunction was granted, since it was held to be unlikely that the union would be able to establish at the trial that the dispute was mainly about possible job losses or redundancies.[21]

Thus the contention that the dispute was mainly about possible job losses or redundancies was rejected. This was despite the fact that 'there was a wrong and widespread belief among the members that the job security agreement would not protect their jobs'.[22] In the view of the Court 'if the dispute was mainly about jobs, the unions would have approached British Telecom asking for a strengthening of the Job Security Agreement',[23] the Court going on to hold that the action taken was 'mainly due to the political objection to the breaking of a monopoly'.[24] The contrast with the non-interventionist approach in *GAS* and *Sherard* is apparent. The courts can assert a large measure of control over the scope of legitimate industrial action simply by varing the degree of subjectivity/objectivity with which they view trade union demands. When a subjective test is applied, the reasonableness of the trade union views and aims is not at issue so long as they are genuinely held. On the other hand, when an objective approach is applied, concerns over job losses may be viewed as unfounded and immunity thereby forfeited. If one poses the question, 'Would a reasonable trade unionist strike over this issue?', one can obtain a high degree of control over the legitimacy of industrial action. The court must, of course, still identify the non-industrial purpose of the action. *Mercury* indicates that 'proof' of an extraneous purpose will often be easy to find, since, given the difficulty of disentangling industrial action from political action, it will be equally difficult to disentangle statements about the action. So union conference resolutions, press statements and so on may well prove to be fertile sources for a court inclined to find liability.

A further difficulty emerges from the importance which the Court placed on the wider dispute. As May LJ put it: 'all these matters have to be considered in the context that there is no doubt that the Union is, and has for some time been conducting a campaign against privatisation and liberalisation, in which the defence of its members' jobs and conditions of service has only been one of the issues'.[25] On reading the judgments, one detects something of an implicit assumption that if the wider dispute demonstrated that the union objected to the Government proposals on political grounds this would exclude the possibility of lawful industrial action having been taken mainly out of fear of job losses. The issue relevant to trade dispute proceedings concerns the predominant purpose of the industrial action and it is quite conceivable that, whatever other action a union might take for political purposes, it might take industrial action only for non-political purposes. The Court seemed disinclined to discriminate between the separate aspects of the campaign or, in consequence, between the different motives underpinning them. In those cases where industrial and political problems are closely interwoven, the impossibility of distinguishing the two elements can lead to the courts confusing the substantive merits of the case and the legal rights of the parties.

2. *Proper Parties*

Current concern over issues such as privatisation and associated techniques whereby the State, while divesting itself of formal legal ownership, retains significant control or influence over an industrial concern brings into sharper focus difficulties as to the parties to a trade dispute.[26] While disputes aimed against the government *qua* government (rather than *qua* employer) have never enjoyed immunity, the present-day role of the State in the running of the economy presents considerable problems. In *Sherard*,[27] government employees called a one-day national strike as a demonstration against the government's policy on industrial relations and incomes, and the Counter-Inflation (Temporary Provisions) Act 1972 in particular. In declining to interfere with the refusal of Phillips J to grant an interlocutory injunction, the Court of Appeal held it was arguably a trade dispute. Yet it is difficult to regard the action taken as anything less than a strike against the government *qua* government. The view of the plaintiffs that the case was on all fours with *Associated Newspapers Group (ANG) v Flynn*[28] (where a one-day strike in protest against the Industrial Relations Bill was held not to be a trade dispute) was attractive. After all, no wage claims had been made, the strike was part of a national one-day stoppage involving both government and non-government employees from various industries, and the strike was a protest about government policies in general.

It is submitted that *Sherard* undoubtedly reflects the social reality whereby the State is often the real moving force in trade disputes. Thus in *Duport Steels* the union called out its members in the private sector in furtherance of the dispute with the British Steel Corporation.[29] In the words of Lord Diplock, 'if the executive council honestly believed that a principal reason why BSC would not agree to raise wages to the level that the Iron and Steel Trades Confederation (ISTC) was demanding was that the government was adhering to a policy of refusing to provide BSC with the money to do so out of public funds what could be better calculated in its trade dispute with BSC than to take steps to create a nationwide shortage of steel which would induce the victims of the shortage to put pressure on the government to change its policy'.[30]

Section 29(2) TULRA, a provision of relatively unexplored ambit, is relevant here. It states:

> A dispute between a Minister of the Crown and any workers shall, notwithstanding that he is not the employer of those workers, be treated for the purposes of this Act as a dispute between those workers and their employer if the dispute relates –
> (a) to matters which have been referred for consideration by a joint body on which, by virtue of any provisions made by or under any enactment, that Minister is represented; or
> (b) to matters which cannot be settled without that Minister exercising a power conferred on him by or under an enactment.

As Lord Diplock said in *Duport Steels*, 'the existence of the provision disposes of the suggestion that Parliament intended that the mere fact that an act is done with the purpose of concerning the government is sufficient in itself to take the act outside the immunity'.[31] What is the ambit of the section, though? The paradigm situation under s. 29(2)(a) might appear to be where a Minister has statutory powers which directly involve him in the collective bargaining process (e.g. various ministerial powers under the Wages Councils Act 1979). Section 29(2)(b) is perhaps more wide-ranging. Might it extend to more general ministerial powers in relation to public corporations such as financial controls and powers concerning privatisation and the other techniques of deregulation referred to above? Thus if industrial action were aimed at the government to force them into allowing a public corporation to borrow to fund a pay claim, would s. 29(2)(b) apply? In *Duport* it was unnecessary to decide this point, but if a dispute relates to government financial assistance and 'cannot be settled without that Minister exercising a power conferred on him by or under an enactment' it would appear to come within s. 29(2).[32] Thus it might cover a dispute where it was intended to pressure the government into providing financial aid which was unavailable from other sources and which would enable a public corporation to make an offer acceptable to the union and so end the dispute. To gain the protection of the immunities a dispute would also, of course, have to have a sufficient connection with a proper purpose.

As for privatisation and deregulation, the statutory model for denationalisation has been to vest the assets of the public corporation in a successor company nominated by the Secretary of State.[33] Action by trade unions which is aimed at persuading the Minister not to exercise the power to nominate (e.g. British Aerospace Act 1980 s. 1(2)) might be considered to be a dispute between proper parties by virtue of s. 29(2)(b) despite the fact that the government is not the employer of the workers involved. Indeed, since in such cases the public corporation has no control at all over any 'sell-off', the dispute can be aimed only at the government.

Section 29(2) might conceivably have been relevant to the facts of the Mercury dispute. Even if it had been accepted that the dispute was wholly or mainly about potential redundancies and, therefore, satisfied the proper-purpose test, it was still arguably targeted against the government. Only the government had the power to decide not to proceed with either the privatisation or liberalisation. Thus, although the government was not the actual employer, s. 29(2)(b) might have served to convert the dispute to one between proper parties.

C. The Right to Strike and Representative Democracy

The exercise of the right to strike is, on occasion, viewed as illegitimate by defenders of the values of a narrow form of representative democracy based upon untrammelled majoritarianism. The difficulty with this is that a society would not be regarded as democratic merely because its citizens are entitled to vote. Associated rights such as the right to free speech and the right to associate should also exist. The right to strike would generally be regarded as such an associated right. At the same time, it would usually be accepted that there should be restrictions placed on the aims of industrial action.

Approaching the argument from another perspective, it may even be argued that the right to strike may be used to safeguard democracy. Thus McFarlane has pointed out that in 1920 in Germany 'a successful monarchist-military *Putsch*, . . . was defeated by the combination of the refusal of collaboration by higher civil servants and a highly successful general strike.'[34] It is submitted, however, that such exceptional situations cannot be legislated for, and that in such a crisis democracy could only be saved by the *ad hoc* intervention of a pro-democracy group or groups.[35] Alternatively, democracy and its associated rights are also at risk of being undermined by a process of gradual erosion. Since 1979 there have been a number of casualties in the realm of fundamental rights in the UK. In such circumstances resort to industrial action might be justified. Thus a strike in protest at a decision to restrict freedom of speech or freedom of association might be regarded as democratic. It is of course difficult to assess whether or to what extent there has been an erosion and opinion will obviously vary depending upon the values held. Rather than extending the ambit of the right to strike, a more sophisticated way of dealing with this problem, on the assumption that the greatest danger to civil liberties is elective dictatorship,[36] might be to enact a Bill of Rights which would spell out certain fundamental values, including the right to strike itself. For as Dahl observes:

> Why should the great bulk of the voters in the middle ranges of the income distribution co-operate with the poor in favour of further distribution rather than with the rich against further distribution? If civic orientations stimulate the pursuit of rational egoism rather than altruism or generalised benevolence, then a rationally self-interested majority coalition is likely to oppose further redistribution well before equality of incomes is approached.[37]

On the other hand, it has been stated that 'it would be a bold man who would argue that the Bill of Rights, applied or contemplated in democratic societies whose Common Law is comparable to ours, can succeed in preserving the fundamental rights of the citizens in those countries more effectively than does the ordinary law, as applied in the United Kingdom'.[38]

Another difficulty here is that Bills of Rights in the classical mode such as the European Convention on Human Rights, to which the UK is party, tend not to offer protection for social and economic rights. There is, of course, nothing to stop such protection being offered as a matter of form, although in practice significant problems would attend the reconciliation of these additional rights with classical liberal rights.

Whatever form the right to strike takes, the questions of substantive classification referred to in the Introduction remain. One possible way of distinguishing between political and economic strikes is based upon the assumption that economic strikes do not challenge the authority of elected government. The position is perhaps different where a general strike is concerned: 'In terms of democratic theory, as distinct from Marxist theory, the case for the 1926 general strike is at best a doubtful one. That example shows that a sympathetic strike by the whole trade union movement will necessarily assume for the government the form of challenge to its authority, irrespective of the limited purposes of the strike leaders themselves.'[39] However, a wide range of other disputes will be regarded by government as a challenge to its authority, such as a pay claim by a group of workers which, if granted, would breach government incomes policy. Accordingly, the coercion of government can hardly be the sole basis for distinction between general strikes and other industrial disputes, nor in turn between political and economic strikes.

The issues involved are best examined against a background of political principle. The recognition of the right to strike by the modern state is an acknowledgement of the legitimacy of group activity in society. The exercise of that right may curtail the freedom of government to act as it sees fit.

Once the right to strike is viewed as a fundamental right in a democratic society then democratic theory must incorporate or at least acknowledge pluralist claims. One of the resulting challenges is to set the boundaries to trade union actions in as principled a fashion as possible.

The principle of collective bargaining has long been viewed as the cornerstone of British industrial relations. For Donovan, collective bargaining was the best way of conducting industrial relations.[40] Moreover, 'properly conducted, collective bargaining is the most effective means of giving workers the right to representation in decisions affecting their working lives.'[41] While much has changed since then, collective bargaining remains an important method of rule-making in industry (creating, for example, the terms upon which employees work). It remains one of the principal activities carried out by trade unions and it is through this process that unions achieve their main aim of improving the terms and conditions of employment of their members. Indeed, the function of rule-making in industry has to a large extent been delegated to the process of collective bargaining. It is through the institution of collective bargaining that pluralism manifests itself in the workplace. The proper aims of collective bargaining may of course also be a cause of controversy. However, even from the perspective of a government committed to a labour law policy of restriction of trade union power, the list of 'proper purposes' contained in TULRA s.29 appears to be acceptable.[42]

Collective bargaining may be viewed as the core value of industrial relations and indeed there is a compelling connection between this core value and the pluralist belief in the desirability of the countervailing power of institutions located outwith the institutions of central government – both against the latter and against one another. However, if this value is to be effectively grounded it is essential that trade unions have sanctions at their disposal.

> If the workers could not, in the last resort, collectively refuse to work, they could not bargain collectively. The power of management to shut down the plant (which is inherent in the right of property) would not be matched by a corresponding power on the side of labour. These are ultimate sanctions without which the bargaining power of the two sides would lack 'credibility'. There can be no equilibrium in industrial relations without a freedom to strike. In protecting that freedom, the law protects the legitimate expectation of management that it can use the right of property for the same purpose on its side.[43]

Article 6 of the European Social Charter is also worthy of mention in this context: 'With a view to ensuring the effective exercise of the right to bargain collectively, the contracting parties undertake . . . to recognise . . . the right of workers and employers to collective action in cases of conflict of interests, including the right to strike, subject to obligations that might arise out of collective agreements previously entered into.'[44]

This is not to exclude the possibility of collective bargaining being made effective by other means, but merely to stress that traditionally in the UK the means used has been industrial action.

Viewed against the traditional framework, the government had earlier shown itself aware that reforms such as those introduced in 1982 would inevitably restrict 'many types of industrial action which are undoubtedly directed at improving terms and conditions of employment'.[45] One might therefore argue that these reforms breached a convention regarding the legitimate use of the strike weapon. As Kahn-Freund says, 'the strike is seen as the ultimate sanction available to the workers in labour relations and linked with collective bargaining and with grievances at the place of work. This seems to be the general doctrine underlying all our relevant legislation'.[46]

Alternatively, it has been argued that, within the political, and to some extent the legal, tradition of Italy and France

> the power to use and to withhold one's labour is a fundamental human freedom of the individual. It is available for all purposes not contrary to law, just as one can use one's property as one likes, except where the law forbids it. Hence workers are entitled to withdraw their labour by concerted action for any lawful object, even one having nothing to do with labour relations, e.g. to exercise political pressure, to demonstrate against measures taken by the government or by others, and also of course for any purpose connected with their relations with management.[47]

Thus, in such systems industrial purposes are a sufficient but not a necessary condition of the right to strike. On this wider view political purposes would be equally legitimate and one might avoid the vexed question of distinguishing industrial action from political action. However, legitimising all forms of political action would tilt the balance of power too far in favour of labour. While pluralist theory can be viewed as legitimating certain forms of industrial action it should not be invoked to provide *carte blanche* for the use of the strike weapon. It is submitted that the proper ambit of industrial action can be found by looking to the institution of collective bargaining.

D. Reform

If the underlying rationale of lawful industrial action is to be the vital importance of the strike weapon as part of the collective bargaining process then the current formulation of the golden formula must be critically appraised.

Most disputes in the workplace will be readily classifiable as trade disputes. It has been suggested that difficulties may arise in situations such as a pay claim during a period of statutory incomes policy or potential redundancies during privatisation. Then the question arises over the extent to which industrial action must be taken for a proper purpose. The majority view in *Mercury* was that, in applying the 'relates wholly or mainly to' test, the courts are compelled to look to the predominant purpose behind the action. Now, while the success or otherwise of an incomes policy will clearly be a major political issue, the pursuit of higher wages is a traditional industrial aim. The situation is essentially a hybrid. In such a situation it is difficult to see how one can classify the dispute as political or non-political. If it is perceived that the potential way to do this is to go beyond the apparent purpose and identify the motive behind the industrial action then one has to confront the possibility that workers may pursue industrial action with more than one motive in mind. And where there is evidence of the existence of a political or other ulterior motive it is not clear how the respective strengths of the two motives can be assessed.

An illustration of the potential difficulties is provided by a series of English Court of Appeal decisions in the late 1970s.[48] As previously suggested, during this period the Court felt that a literal interpretation of the statutory immunities gave too great a protection to unions.[49] One area of difficulty was identified by Brandon L J (as he then was):

> As regards the subject matter of the dispute, there are two possibilities. There may be a case where a dispute is ostensibly connected with a subject-matter which would make it a trade dispute but is in fact and in reality connected with some wholly different subject-matter. The other possibility is that the dispute is connected with both such subject-matters, but the predominant subject-matter with which the dispute is connected is the second rather than the first.[50]

The Court of Appeal felt that the reasonableness or otherwise of the strikers' demands could be used to infer the existence and extent of an ulterior motive. However, an objection to this line of reasoning is that 'there is no obvious correlation between the reasonableness of a demand and the existence of an ulterior motive',[51] and in disputes which involve incomes policy or privatisation there is clearly both an industrial and a political dimension. Such a dispute will almost inevitably be pursued for more than one motive. It is submitted that deciding which element is predominant is a virtually impossible task. If required to do so, the judiciary will find it difficult to avoid basing their judgment on fine distinctions which do little justice to the complexity of the issues involved.

In this respect, the advantages of the previous 'connected with' formulation are apparent. In the words of Lord Scarman:

> But predominance of subject-matter is an irrelevance, provided always there is a real connection between the dispute and one or other of the matters mentioned in the subsection. A dispute may be political or personal in character and yet be connected with – for example – the terms and conditions of employment of workers. [I]t is only if the alleged connection is a pretext or cover for another dispute which is in no way connected with any of the matters mentioned in the subsection, that it is possible to hold that the dispute is not a trade dispute.[52]

The use of the 'connected with' formula relieves the judiciary of the invidious task of attempting to separate industrial motives from political ones. Together, where appropriate, with a broad interpretation of s. 29(2) it prevents the ambit of lawful industrial action being restricted by virtue of more extensive economic intervention by modern government.

It may be objected that such an approach, which restores the 'connected with' formula, goes too far and revives Kahn-Freund's spectre of a right to strike entirely unrestricted as regards purpose. As Lord Diplock suggested: 'Even if the predominant object (of industrial action) were to bring down the fabric of the present economic system by raising wages to unrealistic levels . . . this would not . . . make it any less a dispute connected with terms and conditions of employment and thus a trade dispute, if the actual demand that is resisted by the employer is as to the terms and conditions on which his workers are to be employed.'[53] One may doubt whether such an extreme hypothesis would be a sensible basis upon which to legislate. However, some governments might regard it as desirable to remove the protection of the immunities where industrial action was pursued for certain specified reasons which impinged upon other significant rights and interests. For example, since the Employment Act 1988, industrial action which seeks to undermine the freedom to dissociate is rendered non-immune.[54] Arguably, courts also take cognisance of such protected values. For example, it has been suggested that the decision of the Court of Appeal in *BBC v Hearn* (see p 227 *infra*) was prompted by a desire to protect freedom of speech.[55] Vital concerns of social policy could also be protected in this way. Industrial action in furtherance of a pay claim which would breach a statutory incomes policy could be rendered non-immune. Earlier legislation on incomes policy has contained criminal sanctions.[56] The point is not to endorse the results arrived at in the examples given, but to cast light on the mechanism of protection.

It is thus suggested that the 'connected with' formula be restored but that the immunities be excluded where industrial action is taken over certain specified aims. It should be noted that where the excluded aim could not be specified with some degree of precision one would be faced with difficulties as a result of the ambiguity. However, since one is dealing with exceptions, at least the ambiguity would operate only at the margins of the formula and not be central to it. The point is not to set out definitively what the exceptions might be but simply to suggest the technique. The approach suggested reflects both the strengths and acknowledged limitations of pluralist theory. Pluralism cannot provide rigorous solutions as to where the precise balance between interests should be struck. However, it is consistent with pluralism both that the balance should be determined not by judicial attitudes but by Parliament, which itself provides a framework of debate which is pluralist in nature, and that the parties concerned should be informed of their legal rights and expectations with the greatest degree of precision possible. As has been suggested already and as is implicit in Cole's emphasis on the State's role as institutional co-ordinator, pluralist theory would accept the need for some limits on the powers of trade unions.

The state of today possesses increasingly important activities of co-ordination. It is largely concerned in adjusting the relations between association and association, or institution and institution, or institution and association, or between other associations or institutions and itself. In enacts laws regulating the form and scope of associative activity, friendly society law, law affecting banks, companies, partnerships, trade unions, clubs, associations of any and every sort. There is one theory of the state which regards it as primarily a co-ordinating body, devoted not to any specific functions of its own, but to the co-ordinating of the various functional associations within society.[57]

It follows from this that the State's co-ordinating function in relating to trade unions may be performed, in situations where it is demonstrated that it is necessary, by selective removal of the immunities.

Cole's analysis also alerts us to a fundamental difficulty inherent within the pluralist tradition. Thus he has written:

What then of activities of co-ordination? Here a far greater difficulty arises. To entrust the state with the function of co-ordination would be to entrust it, in many cases, with the task of arbitrating between itself and some other functional association, say, a church or a trade union. But just as no man ought to be the judge of his own case, so ought no association. Therefore, co-ordination cannot belong to the function of the state; but neither can it belong to that of any other functional association.[58]

There is an inevitable tension here between the need for co-ordination and the need to constrain the co-ordinator. The key to resolving this would appear to be the accountability of the co-ordinator, and in this respect, too, the demand for more precise statements of legislative intention seems desirable.

1. *Legal Implications*

It is argued that the law should be reformed so as to revert to the 'connected with' formula (but, where appropriate, excluding the immunities in specific instances) and that a broad interpretation be given to s. 29(2) (see below). Some further elaboration on these legal implications is necessary.

NWL v Woods contains dicta suggesting the outer limits of the immunity conferred by the 'connected with' formula. Thus Lord Scarman made clear that the connection must be a genuine one and went on to state that the facts in *BBC v Hearn* illustrate the sort of case in which there may be no connection – an objection by workers to apartheid leading to a decision to black out the transmission to South Africa of the television showing of the Cup Final.[59] However, the view has been expressed that this sort of situation could have been transformed into a trade dispute by a demand that 'the contracts of employment of employees of the BBC should be amended to incorporate a term that they should not be obliged to take any part in the transmission of sporting events to South Africa'.[60] Where such a demand is made, matters of conscience may become the subject-matter of a trade dispute.

In the subsequent case of *Universe Tankships*, a majority of the House of Lords appeared to sound a note of caution with regard to the scope of the 'connected with' formula.[61] Accordingly, it is necessary to refer to certain of the speeches in the case to assess whether they cast doubt on the value of the formula. Lord Diplock, for example, stated that where a demand was not connected with the terms and conditions of employment the necessary connection cannot 'be created merely by accompanying the demand with another demand that is connected with a trade dispute'.[62] This dictum would not seem to affect a demand which is pursued for mixed motives. However, it would affect industrial action which was taken in furtherance of a pay demand and, say, a demand 'that the employer should make a contribution to a particular political party favoured by the union'.[63] This approach should not impinge to any material extent on the protection offered by the 'connected with' formula. Denial of immunity is contingent on the union's making two demands, one of which is non-industrial. Lord Cross observed that '[a] trade union cannot turn a dispute which in reality has no connection with terms and conditions of employment into a dispute connected with terms and conditions of employment by insisting that the employer inserts appropriate terms into the contrcts of employment into which he enters.'[64] To a considerable extent this echoes Lord Scarman's qualification in *NWL v Woods* that the connection must be genuine. It perhaps should also be regarded as a warning of the unpredictability of judicial decision-making in this area.

What of proper parties? In the words of Kahn-Freund,

> Whatever the political colour of the government, it is involved in industry . . . . [I]s not every major industrial problem a problem of governmental economic policy? Is it not true that not only in publicly owned industries governmental decisions on wages policies – whether statutory or not – on credits and on subsidies . . . affect the terms and conditions of employment at least as much as decisions of individual firms? Where is the line between a strike to induce an employer to raise, or not to reduce wages, and a strike to press the government for measures which would enable the employer to do so?[65]

Even the government has acknowledged that 'particularly in the case of a public sector dispute, where the government is the direct employer or a main provider of finance . . . arguments about terms and conditions of employment can be inextricably tied up with attempts to persuade the government to change the policy.'[66] Section 29(2) is important because it recognises that irrespective of the identity of the employer under the employment contract the 'real' employer may be the State. Where matters cannot be settled without a Minister exercising a statutory power, a union cannot collectively bargain effectively unless it can with impunity bring pressure to bear on the Minister by industrial action. Where a framework of statutory powers impinges on an employer's autonomy (e.g. in the case of a public corporation) in settling trade disputes the government may be viewed as adopting the role of the employer. As a result, a dispute may well be targeted against the government or against both the employer and the government. Section 29(2) allows the requirement of proper parties to be satisfied and it is to be hoped that a liberal interpretation of this provision will take place; otherwise, the scope for industrial action in support of collective bargaining will be diminished.

E. Conclusions

The fact that the issue of strikes for political purposes is of such central relevance is due, to a large extent, to the modern State's role as economic manager. Tensions exist in a society which is a representative democracy but which also, and inevitably, recognises the right to strike. Those who would curtail that right must appreciate that it will be difficult to find a logical stopping-point, since almost any major dispute will have implications for the government's economic policy. I have sought to argue that the law should grant the right to strike to the extent necessary to further the aims of collective bargaining. It is important to remember that other bodies in the industrial and economic sphere also bring pressure to bear on the government. Perhaps one of the best examples is the ability of multinational companies to switch investment overseas. One may also note that the abolition of exchange controls facilitated the ease with which holders of capital could place economic pressure on the government.

One of the main aims of the 1982 reforms of the law of industrial action was to alter the balance of power between employers and the forces of labour. In so far as the reforms impinging upon political strikes are concerned, the main intention was probably simply to further this aim. Other concerns involved no doubt included union opposition to privatisation. Thus, although various aspects of the government's overall political strategy have influenced the reform process, it is doubtful whether it redrew the demarcation line between industrial and non-industrial strikes on the basis of any singular and coherent political theory. Should the law be underpinned by principle, it is likely to be more secure.

* Parts of this essay draw heavily upon an earlier article in 1984 SLT (*News*) 106. The co-operation of W. Green & Son is appreciated.

Notes

1. *Sherard v AUEW* [1973] ICR 421 at 435 (*Per* Roskill LJ).
2. See the Trade Unions and Labour Relations Act 1974 (TULRA) ss 13 and 29, as amended by the Employment Acts 1980–82 and R.C. Simpson 'A Not So Golden Formula' (1983) 46 MLR 463.
3. *Beaverbrook Newspapers Ltd v Keys* [1980] IRLR 247 I.
4. *Associated Newspapers Group Ltd v Flynn* (1971) 10 KIR 17.
5. *Mercury Communications Ltd v Scott-Garner* [1984] Ch 37.
6. See for example P.Q. Hirst (Ed) *The Pluralist Theory of the State* Routledge (1989); R.A. Dahl *Dilemmas of Pluralist Democracy* Yale U P (1982). These two works reveal some of the contrasts between British and American pluralism.
7. K.W. Wedderburn 'Industrial Relations and the Courts' (1980) 9 ILJ 65.
8. See now the Trade Union Act 1984, as amended.
9. See now Employment Act 1980 s 17.
10. TULRA 1974 s 13.
11. Amended by Employment Act 1982 s 18(2)(c) and TULRA 1974 s 29.
12. TULRA 1974 s 29 (1).
13. *Sherard v AUEW* [1973] ICR 421.
14. *GAS v TGWU* [1975] ICR 276.
15. [1973] ICR 421 at 427.
16. [1975] ICR 276 at 294.
17. Industrial Relations Act 1971 s 167 (1).
18. TULRA 1974 s 29.
19. *NWL v Woods* [1979] All ER 614 and on the approach of the Court of Appeal see K.D. Ewing 'The Golden Formula: Some Recent Developments' (1979) 8 ILJ 133.
20. [1984] Ch 37.
21. The case did not actually go to full trial.
22. [1984] Ch 37 at 77.
23. *Ibid* at 81.

230   *Douglas Brodie*

24. *Ibid* at 96.
25. *Ibid* at 92.
26. C. Graham and T. Prosser 'Privatising National Industries: Constitutional Issues and New Legal Techniques' (1987) 50 MLR 16.
27. [1973] ICR 421.
28. (1971) 10 KIR 17.
29. *Duport Steels v Sirs* [1980] ICR 161.
30. *Ibid* at 182.
31. *Ibid* at 183.
32. *Ibid* at 183.
33. H.W.R. Wade *Administrative Law* (6th ed) Clarendon Press (1988) 162.
34. McFarlane L.J. in W.E.J. McCarthy (Ed) *Trade Unions*, Pelican (1985) 455.
35. *Cf* K.W. Wedderburn in B. Aaron and K.W. Wedderburn (Eds) *Industrial Conflict* (1972) 330. The author cites the Bonn Basic Law, Art 20 Sec 4 (a right of resistance against anybody who attempts to overthrow the constitutionally established order if no other means are available).
36. Lord Hailsham *The Dilemma of Democracy* Collins (1978).
37. R.A. Dahl *op cit* note 6 *supra* 133.
38. Lord McCluskey *Law, Justice and Democracy* BBC Books (1987) 44.
39. McFarlane *op cit* note 34 *supra* at 451.
40. Royal Commission on Trade Unions and Employers Associations Cmnd 3623 (1968).
41. *Ibid* at para 212.
42. *Trade Union Immunities* Cmnd 8128 (1981) para 187.
43. P. Davies and M.R. Freedland (Eds), *Kahn-Freund's Labour and the Law* Stevens (1983) 292.
44. Art 6(4).
45. *Trade Unions Immunities* Cmnd 8128 (1981) para 200.
46. Davies & Freedland *op cit* note 43 *supra* at 309.
47. *Ibid* at 308.
48. K.D. Ewing 'The Golden Formula: Some Recent Develoments' (1979) 8 ILJ 133, and eg. *PBDS (National Carriers) Ltd v Filkins* [1979] IRLR 356.
49. See text of this essay at notes 20-21 *supra*.
50. *Star Sea Transport Corporation v Slater* [1978] IRLR 507 at 513.
51. K.D. Ewing *op cit* note 48 *supra* at 144.
52. *NWL v Woods* [1979] 3 All ER 614 at 632.
53. *Ibid* at 624.
54. Employment Act 1988 s 10.
55. [1978] 1 All ER 111. B. Doyle 'The Judicial Approach and the Betterment Test' (1978) 7 ILJ 126.
56. Prices and Incomes Act 1966 s 16.
57. Cole in Hirst *op cit* note 6 *supra* at 72.
58. *Ibid* at 80.
59. *NWL v Woods* [1979] 3 All ER 614 at 632.
60. *Ibid* at 623 (*per* Lord Diplock).
61. *Universe Tankships v ITWF* [1983] AC 366.
62. *Ibid* at 389.
63. *Ibid* at 387.
64. *Ibid* at 392.
65. Davies and Freedland (Eds), *op cit*, note 43 *supra* at 317.
66. *Trade Union Immunities* Cmnd 8128 (1981) para 198.

A Bill of Rights: Lessons from the Privy Council

K.D. Ewing*

A. Introduction

Little work has been done on the role of the Privy Council as the final constitutional court for many Commonwealth countries.[1] This is very surprising, particularly in view of the growing support for the introduction of a Bill of Rights in Britain. For the fact is that many of the (admittedly dwindling) Commonwealth jurisdictions which still recognise the Privy Council have constitutions which include Bills of Rights.[2] Many of these Bills of Rights are similar to the European Convention on Human Rights and Fundamental Freedoms (ECHR) which is known to have 'greatly influenced constitutional instruments drafted in the post-colonial period'.[3] Thus, the Privy Council deals with appeals from a number of different legal systems on matters as diverse as the right to a fair trial, freedom of expression, and the right to life, liberty and security of the person.[4] Hence, there is a superficial attraction in the simplistic assumption that with this experience the English courts must be well-equipped to deal with a Bill of Rights which would flourish under the guidance of English judges.[5] But no-one has examined their work in any detail to discover just how they have been responding. The purpose of this essay is to begin to fill this large gap in the literature. The essay continues by examining, first, the underlying policy approach of the Privy Council to constitutional adjudication; second, the principles of constitutional interpretation to put this policy into effect; and third, the practical consequences in terms of constitutional content of the application of these principles.

B. The Policy of Deference

Perhaps the most significant feature of the cases decided by the Privy Council is the remarkable deference shown by the Board to the executive and legislative branches of government. The tone is set nicely by the decision in *Runyowa v The Queen*,[6] a challenge to the death penalty, where it was said that 'once laws are validly enacted it is not for the courts to adjudicate upon their wisdom, their appropriateness or the necessity for their existence'.[7] Given that *Runyowa* appears to be one of the first human rights cases decided by the Privy Council, its lack of sophistication is not surprising. But since then, of course, their Lordships have become much more experienced in this field and also have had their attention drawn to the jurisprudence of other jurisdictions such as the United States, Canada and India.[8] The fact remains, nevertheless, that despite the occasional flourish of rhetoric, and despite the occasional strongly worded dissent, the policy of deference not only survives but thrives. A good example of this recently is *Ong Ah Chuan v Public Prosecutor*[9], concerning the death penalty for the possession of drugs, where Lord Diplock said that punishment was a question of 'social policy', which 'it is a function of the legislature to decide, not the judiciary'.

1. *The problem of ignorance*

One possible explanation for this policy of deference is that the Privy Council is far removed geographically from the cases which come before it.[10] As a result there is often a degree of cultural ignorance which must surely encourage a rather low-key approach. The point is well made by two cases, the first of which is *Grant v Director of Public Prosecutions (DPP)*,[11] where an inquest on five deaths in Jamaica resulted in a verdict of murder. The jury was unable to name the persons whom it thought were involved, as a result of which it was criticised by newspapers having an island-wide circulation and which then openly accused the applicants of murder. This led to charges being brought against the accused, following which the newspaper campaign continued and hostile crowds gathered and shouted abuse at the accused. Thereupon the applicants sought relief on the grounds that their right under section 20 of the Constitution to 'a fair hearing within a reasonable time by an independent and impartial court' was being undermined by 'the massive prejudicial publicity'. The court in Jamaica had dismissed the challenge, on the ground that the prejudice was not so widespread and so indelibly impressed on the minds of potential jurors that a jury unaffected by the publicity could not be obtained. The Privy Council also dismissed the challenge, principally on the following ground: 'The judiciary in Jamaica have wide and up-to-date experience of juries in criminal cases. In face of (*sic*) their opinion that despite the prejudicial pre-trial publicity that had taken place it had not been shown that it would be impossible to impanel an impartial jury, their Lordships, lacking that experience, would hesitate long and anxiously before being persuaded to the contrary.' This finding – as well as a concession by counsel that it would not be 'impossible to find a Jamaican jury capable of ridding their minds of any former prejudice that might have been engendered by the pre-trial publicity' – made quite unarguable the applicants' case that their rights under section 20 of the Constitution had been contravened.

Also instructive in this respect is *Bell v DPP*,[12] again concerning section 20 of the Constitution of Jamaica, but on this occasion the right to be tried within a reasonable time. Mr Bell had been convicted in October 1977 by the Gun Court for the illegal possession of a firearm, robbing with aggravation and wounding with intent. The conviction was, however, quashed by the Court of Appeal, which ordered a retrial. Thereafter,

> On 12 March 1979 the registrar of the Court of Appeal sent written notice to the registrar of the Gun Court and to the Director of Public

Prosecutions that the applicant's appeal had been allowed and a retrial ordered. That notice was not received by the Gun Court until 19 December 1979. Before a retrial could take place, original statements of witnesses were required to be served on the applicant but the investigating officer was not available and the statements were not traced. The case was mentioned in the Gun Court on 28 January 1980, 8 February 1980 and 15 February 1980. On 21 March 1980, when the case was again mentioned, bail was granted to the applicant. On some of the appearances of the applicant before the Gun Court he was represented by counsel. Thereafter there were more adjournments by the Gun Court until finally on 10 November 1981 the Crown offered no evidence stating that the witnesses were not available and the applicant was discharged. On 12 February 1982 the applicant was rearrested. Despite the objections of the applicant's attorney, the applicant was ordered to be retried on 11 May 1982.[13]

The local courts held that these facts did not give rise to any violation, despite the fact that the delay was 'presumptively prejudicial'[14] and that the delay was due to the factors for which 'the ultimate responsibility . . . must rest with the government rather than with the defendant'.[15] Rather complacently – in the light of the clear constitutional guarantee – the Privy Council thought that '[d]elays are inevitable', before proceeding to hold that:

The solution is not necessarily to be found in an increase in the supply of legal services by the appointment of additional judges, the creation of new courts and the qualification of additional lawyers. Expansion of legal services necessarily depends on the financial resources available for that purpose. Moreover an injudicious attempt to expand an existing system of courts, judges and practitioners, could lead to deterioration in the quality of the justice administered and to the conviction of the innocent and the acquittal of the guilty. The task of considering these problems falls on the legislature of Jamaica, mindful of the provisions of the Constitution and mindful of the advice tendered from time to time by the judiciary, the prosecution service and the legal profession of Jamaica. The task of deciding whether and what periods of delay explicable by the burdens imposed on the courts by the weight of criminal causes suffice to contravene the rights of a particular accused to a fair hearing within a reasonable time falls upon the courts of Jamaica and in particular on the members of the Court of Appeal who have extensive knowledge and experience of conditions in Jamaica.[16]

And, to eliminate any doubt, Lord Templeman insisted that 'the courts of Jamaica are best equipped to decide whether in any particular case delay from whatever cause contravenes the fundamental right granted by the Constitution of Jamaica'. The only reason why the Privy Council allowed the appeal in this case was that a delay of thirty two months was too long for a retrial, though it would not have been in the case of the original trial.

2. *The question of propriety*

Ignorance of local conditions does not provide the whole answer to the policy of deference. If it did, it would of course be difficult to draw any meaningful

conclusions from the activities of the Privy Council. A second explanation
lies in what appear to be perceptions about the proper role of the judiciary
in a constitution under the 'Westminster system of government', a phrase
to which frequent reference is made in the decisions of the Board. It is this
which is reflected in Lord Diplock's remarks in *Ong Ah Chuan* above,[17]
and in his earlier remarks in *Hinds v The Queen*.[18] This was a wide-ranging
assault on the Gun Court Act 1974 of Jamaica which had provided for the
creation of a court to deal particularly with firearms offences and for
purposes incidental thereto. One of the controversial features of the Act
was section 13, which started with the introductory statement that '[i]n the
interest of public safety, public order or the protection of the private lives
of persons concerned' all proceedings of the Court were to be heard *in
camera*. This, it was argued, was inconsistent with the Constitution, which
provided that all proceedings of every court shall be held in public save
that a court could be empowered or required by law to sit *in camera* in the
interests of, *inter alia*, public safety and public order. In holding that section
13 was consistent with these provisions of the Constitution, Lord Diplock
said first:

> By section 48(1) of the Constitution the power to make laws for the
> peace, order and good government of Jamaica is vested in Parliament;
> and prima facie it is for Parliament to decide what is or not reasonably
> required in the interests of public safety or public order. Such a decision
> involves considerations of public policy which lie outside the field of
> the judicial power and may have to be made in the light of information
> available to a government of a kind that cannot effectively be adduced
> in evidence by means of the judicial process.[19]

Lord Diplock then observed:

> In considering the constitutionality of the provisions of section 13(1)
> of the 1974 Act, a court should start with the presumption that the
> circumstances existing in Jamaica are such that hearings in camera are
> reasonably required in the interests of 'public safety, public order or
> the protection of the private lives of persons concerned in the
> proceedings'. The presumption is rebuttable. Parliament cannot evade
> a constitutional restriction by a colourable device. . . . But in order
> to rebut the presumption, their Lordships would have to be satisfied
> that no reasonable member of Parliament who understood correctly the
> meaning of the relevant provisions of the Constitution could have
> supposed that hearings in camera were reasonably required for the
> protection of any of the interests referred to; or, in other words, that
> Parliament in so declaring was either acting in bad faith or had
> misinterpreted the provisions of section 20(4) of the Constitution under
> which it purported to act.[20]

In this case the challenge failed because no evidence had been adduced to
rebut the presumption in respect of the interests of public safety and public
order.

The presumption of legality is one device used by the Privy Council to
support its perception of the proper role of the judicial branch. A second
is the 'notwithstanding' clauses often found in constitutional documents.

Thus, section 10(1) of the then Constitution of Saint Christopher, Nevis and Anguilla guarantees freedom of expression, but section 10(2) provided that notwithstanding this guarantee, nothing would be inconsistent with it to the extent that (a) it is reasonably required in the interests of defence, public safety, public order, public morality or public health; or (b) that it is reasonably necessary to protect the reputations, rights and freedoms of others. This is similar in principle to the structure of the ECHR, and it will be recalled how in the *Spycatcher* case the notwithstanding clause in article 10(2) was used by the House of Lords, and by Lord Templeman in particular, not to liberate the press but to justify maintaining (and indeed tightening) the injunctions on the *Guardian* and the *Observer*. Privy Council adjudication suggests that this was perfectly predictable, with such clauses providing a valuable crutch to non-intervention. So in *Francis v Chief of Police*[21] the Board was confronted by a statute from Saint Christopher, Nevis and Anguilla which gave 'to the Chief of Police an absolute, unfettered discretion to grant or refuse permission for the use of a loudspeaker' at a public meeting. Although the US Supreme Court had earlier condemned a similar provision on the ground that 'a more effective previous restraint is difficult to imagine',[22] the Privy Council found no constitutional violation, with the legislation being covered by section 10(2). This, advised Lord Pearson, and in particular the phrase 'public order', must be given a meaning 'wide enough to cover action taken for the avoidance of excessive noise seriously interfering with the comfort or convenience of a substantial number of persons'.[23] But what about the fact that the decision was left to the unfettered discretion of the police chief? Again, no trouble:

> As some regulation of 'noisy instruments' is required, and a system of licensing is the natural method, there must be some licensing authority to grant or refuse the permission. The legislature of the state concerned has decided that the Chief of Police is the suitable officer to be given this power and duty. There is convenience in that choice, as he is concerned with the preservation of public order and knows the prevailing conditions affecting it and therefore is able to give a quick decision. There is no evidence, and no reason to infer, that he has abused the power or would be likely to abuse it in any way. It is reasonable to assume that the legislature, knowing the local conditions, made a suitable choice of licensing authority.[24]

An even more vivid example of the importance of the notwithstanding clause to the Privy Council in its policy of deference is *A-G v Antigua Times Ltd*.[25] This quite remarkable case concerned two statutes of Antigua passed in 1971, the first requiring newly formed newspapers to obtain a licence from the secretary to the Cabinet on payment of a fee of $600, and the second enacting that it was unlawful to print or publish a newspaper without first depositing $10,000 with the Accountant General as a surety against libel. Both were challenged as violating the constitutional protection for freedom of expression which, however, was qualified by a notwithstanding clause similar in terms to the one discussed above. Yet although it might have been thought that there was a compelling and irresistible case, the Privy Council thought otherwise. In a quite remarkable judgment, their Lordships held that in determining whether or not something was 'reasonably required' for the purposes of section 10(2) of the Antigua Constitution, the Court should 'presume, until the contrary appears or is shown, that all Acts passed by the Parliament of Antigua were reasonably required',[26] though again the presumption was to be rebuttable.

In this case, the first restriction – the licence fee – was regarded as a tax, and, although taxation was not referred to in section 10(2) as a basis for limitation, '[r]evenue requires to be raised in the interests of defence and for securing public safety, public order, public morality and public health and if this tax was reasonably required to raise revenue for these purposes or for any of them, then [the relevant provision] is not to be treated as contravening the Constitution'.[27] In a frankly unbelievable passage, Lord Fraser concluded:

> Was the revenue to be raised by the licence fees required in the interests of defence or for securing public safety, public order, public morality or public health? Though there may be some taxing statutes which state the purposes for which the revenue raised will be applied ordinarily they do not. The purposes stated cover a very wide field of government expenditure and in the absence of any indication to the contrary, their Lordships think it right to presume that the revenue derived from the licence fees was to be applied to these purposes. That being so, in their opinion section 1B, in so far as it requires the payment of a licence fee, is a provision which comes within section 10(2) of the Constitution and which cannot therefore be treated as contravening it, even though it requires the payment of the licence fee in the first place before publication of a newspaper.[28]

Notably, there was no response to the other concern that the right to publish was subjected to the grant of a licence, at the discretion of the Cabinet! The surety against libel was also upheld, there being no valid reason to rebut the presumption that this particular enactment was not reasonably required.

C. The Principles of Interpretation

So, perhaps for a combination of reasons, the adjudication of the Privy Council in this field is characterised by caution and deference to political authority. Surprising and disappointing though this may be, it remains now to consider how this policy has been implemented by the development of appropriate principles of constitutional interpretation. What the cases reveal here is that the Privy Council has been pulled between, on the one hand, what has been described as 'the austerity of tabulated legalism' and, on the other, the need to develop new principles of interpretation appropriate for the process of constitutional adjudication. Yet although their Lordships have recently expressed an awareness of the need to adopt a new generous and liberal approach, despite the rhetoric the case-law remains characterised by its austere legalism masquerading in slightly different garb. Such formalism is, however, perfectly consistent with the policy perspective which underpins the work of the Privy Council in this area. Apart from providing the means for implementing the policy, the principles of interpretation applied by the Board provide further evidence of it.

1. *The austerity of tabulated legalism*

In the early cases in particular, there was a tendency to approach the question of interpretation as if the document in question were an ordinary statute and therefore subject to the same literal construction. The point is perhaps best illustrated by *Runyowa v The Queen*,[29] strongly criticised by Pannick not only for its 'unsophisticated philosophy of constitutional adjudication', but also for the 'unjustifiably passive principles of constitutional adjudication' adopted by the Board.[30] The appellant had been convicted of murder and sentenced to death under the Law and Order (Maintenance) Act 1960 of Southern Rhodesia. The murder had been committed by another person throwing a 'petrol bomb' into a house, and although the appellant had bought the paraffin, he was not present when the murder was committed. One of the arguments on his behalf was that the mandatory death penalty in a case such as this was contrary to section 60 of the Constitution which provided that '[n]o person shall be subjected to torture or to inhuman or degrading punishment or other treatment'. The argument continued on the basis that 'the word punishment conveys the notion of the infliction of some penalty which is deserved or warranted by reason of the commission of some offence. Hence . . . a punishment which is out of relation to that which, in particular circumstances or in reference to an offence of a particular nature, is deserved, may be an "inhuman" punishment.'[31] But after reviewing a number of US authorities, the Board rejected this argument on a very narrow reading of the Constitution:

> The problem before their lordships is that of construing the particular words of section 60 of the 1961 Constitution. No person is to be subjected (a) to torture (b) to inhuman or degrading punishment or (c) to inhuman or degrading treatment. As a matter of construction their Lordships . . . consider that the ban that is imposed is on any such type or mode or description of punishment as is inhuman or degrading. Since it is not suggested that the death penalty is of such type or mode or description, it follows that the argument advanced on behalf of the appellant must fail.[32]

The austerely legal approach was a dominant feature of Privy Council adjudication in this field even as late as 1978. *Government of Malaysia v Selangor Pilot Association*[33] concerned the rather different question of compulsory acquisition of property. Before the introduction of legislation in 1972 the Association provided pilotage services within Port Swettenham. The effect of the legislation was to impose a duty on the port authorities to provide these services, and to employ people for this purpose, the Act also providing that it was an offence for anyone else to provide the service. The challenge to the legislation was based partly on article 13(2) of the Constitution of Malaysia which provided that '[n]o law shall provide for the compulsory acquisition or use of property without adequate compensation'. In a quite remarkably restrictive decision a majority of the

Board held

> In the opinion of their Lordships . . . the restriction placed on the activities of individual licensed pilots did not deprive them of property and if this be the case, it is hard to see that it can be said to have deprived the licensed pilots who were partners in the association of property. All they lost was the right to act as pilots unless employed by the authority and the right to employ others on pilotage, neither right being property. The result was that the association could no longer carry on its business and employ licensed pilots but unless it was deprived of property otherwise than in accordance with law or its property was compulsorily acquired or used by the port authority, there was no breach of article 13.[34]

This contrasts sharply with the minority judgment delivered by Lord Salmon, who observed that 'when the amending legislation of 1972 came into force all the shipping companies and charterers and the like who had formerly been customers of the respondents for pilotage services would have no choice other than to transfer their custom to the authority'. 'In other words', he claimed, 'it was obvious that the respondent's business would be taken over by the authority without compensation as a result of the Act of 1972 – as indeed it was'.[35] And unlike the majority, only he seemed sensitive to the fact that the appeal raised 'constitutional issues of vital importance' and was concerned that the decision of the majority would 'encourage and facilitate nationalisation without compensation throughout the Commonwealth'.[36]

2. *The principle of generous interpretation*

The austerity of tabulated legalism which both *Runyowa*[37] and *Selangor Pilot Association*[38] demonstrate is not the only principle of interpretation to emerge from the Privy Council. A rejection of this approach by the Board appears in the important decision in *Minister of Home Affairs v Fisher*,[39] where an attempt was made to develop new principles suitable for the interpretation of constitutional documents. The case was an appeal from Bermuda concerning the status of four illegitimate children who had been born in Jamaica. In 1972 the mother, who had also been born in Jamaica, married a man who had Bermudan status and who accepted the children as his own, following which they all took up residence in Bermuda. In 1976, however, the immigration authorities ordered the mother and the four children to leave because under the relevant immigration laws they did not have the requisite status. Section 11 of the Constitution provided a right to enter and reside in Bermuda, save that restrictions could be imposed on people who did not belong to Bermuda, it being further provided that a person would be deemed to belong to Bermuda if she were the wife of someone with Bermudan status or if he or she were the child, stepchild or adopted child of such a person. The issue here was whether the reference to child in the constitution was restricted to a 'legitimate' child, as the authorities contended. In approaching this question, Lord Wilberforce thought it appropriate to point out that the Privy Council was 'concerned with a Constitution' which had 'certain special characteristics' which included the fact that it was 'drafted in a broad and ample style' and was 'greatly influenced by' the European Convention on Human Rights. These considerations called for 'a generous interpretation' – avoiding the 'austerity of tabulated legalism'.[40]

In an important passage which was to be referred to by the Board in subsequent cases, Lord Wilberforce continued:

> When therefore it becomes necessary to interpret 'the subsequent provisions of' Chapter I – in this case section 11 – the question must inevitably be asked whether the appellants' premise, fundamental to their argument, that these provisions are to be construed in the manner and according to the rules which apply to Acts of Parliament, is sound. In their Lordships' view there are two possible answers to this. The first would be to say that, recognising the status of the Constitution as, in effect, an Act of Parliament, there is room for interpreting it with less rigidity, and greater generosity, than other Acts, such as those which are concerned with property, or succession, or citizenship. On the particular question this would require the court to accept as a starting point the general presumption that 'child' means 'legitimate child' but to recognise that this presumption may be more easily displaced. The second would be more radical: it would be to treat a constitutional instrument such as this as sui generis, calling for principles of interpretation of its own, suitable to its character as already described, without necessary acceptance of all the presumptions that are relevant to legislation of private law.
>
> It is possible that, as regards the question now for decision, either method would lead to the same result. But their Lordships prefer the second. This is in no way to say that there are no rules of law which should apply to the interpretation of a Constitution. A Constitution is a legal instrument giving rise, amongst other things, to individual rights capable of enforcement in a court of law. Respect must be paid to the language which as been used and to the traditions and usages which have given meaning to that language. It is quite consistent with this, and with the recognition that rules of interpretation may apply, to take as a point of departure for the process of interpretation a recognition of the character and origin of the instrument, and to be guided by the principle of giving full recognition and effect to those fundamental rights and freedoms with a statement of which the Constitution commences'.[41]

Applying these principles to this case, Lord Wilberforce said that they must approach the question of what is meant by 'child' with 'an open mind'. Having regard to the ECHR and to the United Nations Declaration of the Rights of the Child, the Board felt compelled to conclude that the word 'child' in the constitution was to have an unrestricted meaning. These documents tended to emphasise 'the unity of the family as a group and acceptance of the principle that young children should not be separated from a group which as a whole belongs to Bermuda'.[42] Although neither of these (or any related) international documents had legal force in Bermuda, 'they can certainly not be disregarded as influences upon legislative policy'.

3. *The rhetoric and the reality of the new approach*

The principles of interpretation developed in the *Fisher* case have proved, at least rhetorically, to be important and influential. So in *A-G of St Christopher, Nevis and Anguilla v Reynolds*,[43] the Board commented that 'a Constitution should be construed with less rigidity and more generosity than other Acts'. *Fisher* was also referred to as a benchmark in *Ong Ah Chuan v Public Prosecutor*[44] while in *A-G v Momodou Jobe*,[45] its legacy no doubt inspired Lord Diplock's claim that '[a] constitution, and in particular that part of it which protects and entrenches fundamental rights and freedoms to which all persons in the State are to be entitled, is to be given a generous and purposive interpretation'. The rhetoric is not met by the reality of adjudication since *Fisher*, with several extraordinarily formal majority decisions drawing strong criticism in dissent. Perhaps the best example of this is *Riley v A-G of Jamaica*,[46] where the five applicants had all been convicted of murder in 1975 and 1976 but warrants for their execution were not issued until 1979. This was partly due to the delay caused by the applicants' exhausting appeals procedures, but also to political factors in Jamaica which led to executions being held in abeyance for a period of almost three years during a period of acute controversy over capital punishment. The question which this delay raised was whether the execution of the applicants would violate section 17(1) of the Jamaican Constitution, which offers protection against inhuman or degrading punishment, but which also provides by section 17(2) that '[n]*othing* contained in or done under one authority of any law *shall be held to be inconsistent with or in contravention of this section* to the extent that the law in question authorises the infliction of any description of punishment which was lawful in Jamaica immediately before the appointed day'.

The majority did not need to decide whether the delayed execution of a sentence of death could be described as inhuman or degrading punishment. This is because even if it was, it would still not be unconstitutional because of the unambiguous terms of section 17(2). After reminding us that '[i]n the last analysis this question must depend on the language of section 17', Lord Bridge advised that an act would be protected by section 17(2) if it satisfied three related conditions:

(a) it must be an act done under the authority of law;
(b) it must be an act involving the infliction of punishment of a description authorised by the law in question, being a description of punishment which was lawful in Jamaica immediately before the appointed day;
(c) it must not exceed in extent the description of punishment so authorised.[47]

He continued by claiming that:

There can be no doubt whatever that a delayed execution would satisfy conditions (a) and (b). The only words in section 17(2) that are even arguably ambiguous are the words 'to the extent that'. It seems to their Lordships that in their context these words pose the question: to what extent did the law in Jamaica before independence authorise the description of punishment which is under challenge? This question can only be answered by asking in turn the further question: if the like description of punishment had been inflicted in the like circumstances before independence, would this have been authorised by law? An obvious instance of a description of punishment exceeding in extent that authorised by law would be the execution of a death sentence by burning at the stake. But since the legality of a delayed execution by hanging of a sentence of death lawfully imposed under section 3(1) of the Offences against the Person Act could never have been questioned before independence, their Lordships entertain no doubt that it satisfies condition (c). Accordingly, whatever the reasons for or length of delay in executing a sentence of death lawfully imposed, the delay can afford no ground for holding the execution to be a contravention of section 17(1).[48]

Little wonder that the majority drew a strong dissent from Lords Scarman and Brightman, who contended that 'the majority judgment is in error because it has adopted in its construction of the Constitution an approach more appropriate to a specific enactment concerned with private law than to a constitutional instrument declaring and protecting fundamental rights. An austere legalism has been preferred to the generous interpretation which in *Fisher's* case was held to be appropriate'. In a powerful judgment, it was held clearly and unequivocally that a delayed execution did amount to cruel and unusual treatment and that section 17(2) 'is concerned only to legalise certain descriptions of punishment, not to legalise a "treatment", otherwise inhuman, of which the lawful punishment forms only one ingredient'.[49]

D. The Practical Content of Human Rights

So, despite this rhetoric of liberalism, for the most part the Privy Council has developed the principles of constitutional interpretation in such a way as to implement its policy of deference. The practical result of all this, of course, is that the constitutional rights themselves are often puny and insubstantial, offering the bare minimum of protection, if even that, from oppressive governmental action. Given the choice between a narrow and a wide reading of constitutional guarantees, the Privy Council, it seems, will almost always choose the former. Indeed, as the large number of cases on the death penalty show, this is a process which can be carried to quite remarkable lengths. It is, however, not only the protection from 'inhuman or degrading punishment or other treatment' or from 'cruel or unusual punishment' which has been restrictively interpreted and applied. The wide variety of so-called 'legal rights' have also been very narrowly construed, as indeed have the classical civil liberties such as freedom of association, assembly and expression. What is perhaps most significant is that the Privy Council has made no positive contribution to the jurisprudence of human rights, there being not a single example of a new sophisticated approach to rights.[50] Indeed, the case-law of the Privy Council has had a negative impact on developments elsewhere.[51] For some inexplicable reason, courts in other jurisdictions still look to the Privy Council for guidance even though it has little to offer. Trade unionists in Canada in particular have little cause to respect the Privy Council,[52] which still has a small influence there even though the last appeal was in 1949.[53]

1. *Death penalty*

One of the most distressing features of the Privy Council's record is its approach to death penalty appeals. In many Commonwealth countries the death penalty is still provided for by law despite constitutional guarantees of life, liberty and security of the person, and against cruel or unusual punishment. Attempts have been made in a number of cases now to challenge the legality of capital punishment either head-on or because of some defect in the trial procedure. All have been unsuccessful. *Runyowa v The Queen* is a good example.[54] The Privy Council rejected the argument that the penalty was disproportionate to the offence, for while the relevant constitutional provision enabled 'the court to adjudicate whether some form of or type or description of punishment . . . is inhuman or degrading, . . . it does not enable the court to declare an enactment imposing a punishment to be ultra vires on the ground that the court considers that the punishment laid down by the enactment is inappropriate or excessive for the particular offence.'[55] Similarly, in *Ong Ah Chuan v Public Prosecutor*[56] the mandatory death penalty for drug traffickers was upheld against a constitutional challenge that people were being deprived of life, but not 'in accordance with law'. The essence of the argument was that the mandatory nature of the sentence rendered the legislation arbitrary 'since it debarred the court in punishing offenders from discriminating between them according to their individual blameworthiness'.[57] But, as with the similar argument in *Runyowa*, this fell on deaf ears, with the Privy Council holding that '[t]here is nothing unusual in a capital sentence being mandatory' and that 'its efficacy as a deterrent may be to some extent diminished if it is not'.[58]

Perhaps the most disturbing manifestation of the cautious and restrictive approach of the Privy Council in this area is *Baker v The Queen*,[59] a case which concerned section 29(1) of the Juveniles Law of Jamaica, providing that '[s]entence of death shall not be pronounced on or recorded against a person under the age of 18 years'. The question which arose was whether someone who was 18 years old could be sentenced to death for a crime which he or she committed while under the age of 18. Lord Salmon held that the words of the legislation were capable of meaning that the accused had to be 18 at the time the offence was committed or 18 at the time of sentence. But because the latter position would lead to 'shocking and indeed barbarous results',[60] he preferred the former, claiming also that to hold otherwise would inevitably produce arbitrary, unreasonable and unjust results:

> Suppose two boys of say about 16 years of age jointly commit a murder; one is apprehended before the other. He is tried expeditiously, convicted and sentenced before reaching the age of 18. He of course cannot be sentenced to death. The other is caught later at a time when there is a good deal of congestion in the courts; he is not sentenced until one week after his 18th birthday. He has to be sentenced to death. Suppose a boy of 17 is tried with a number of other defendants for murder. The

trial starts three months before his 18th birthday. Perhaps through the prolixity of counsel, perhaps unavoidably, at any rate through no fault of the boy, the trial lasts just over three months. He is found guilty and has to be sentenced to death. If there had not been so many defendants, if the trial had been conducted more expeditiously (all matters for which the boy was in no way responsible), he would have been convicted some weeks before his 18th birthday and could not have been sentenced to death.[61]

These views are all the more forceful in view of the rather cavalier treatment – subsequently – of the right to a speedy trial in *Bell v Director of Public Prosecutions*.[62] Yet Lord Salmon's judgment was delivered in dissent. Despite the barbarity and the arbitrariness, the majority held in favour of the narrow interpretation favoured by the Crown. According to Lord Diplock, 'if the words are to be given their ordinary grammatical meaning they are free from any ambiguity'.[63] In so holding, their Lordships effectively reversed an earlier decision of the Privy Council on the same statute in which it was held that, by virtue of section 20(7) of the Jamaican Constitution, there was 'no jurisdiction in the court to pass sentence of death upon the accused if he was under 18 at the time of the commission of the offence'.[64]

2. *Legal rights*

The same narrow perspective has been brought to the adjudication of what are sometimes referred to as legal rights. These include freedom from arbitrary arrest, detention and search and seizure of property. They also include the right to a fair trial, embracing the right to a public hearing with legal representation within a reasonable time. Yet again constitutional guarantees have been read down in many cases to the point of extinction. So far as police powers and pre-trial procedure are concerned, a good example of this is *King v The Queen*,[65] where the appellant had been charged with the possession of dangerous drugs which allegedly had been found in his possession following a personal search which was held by their Lordships to be unlawful. A search warrant had been issued for the search of premises but had not given authority to search anyone who might be on these premises. In these circumstances, said their Lordships, the personal search was not justified by the warrant. There was thus no legal justification for the search, so the question for the court was whether the evidence illegally obtained should be admitted. The case for exclusion was strengthened here by the provisions of the Jamaica constitution which gave protection against search of persons or property without consent. In the view of their Lordships, however, this constitutional guarantee did not affect the law as laid down in cases such as *Kuruma v The Queen*,[66] which conferred a common law discretion on the courts to admit or exclude illegally obtained evidence: 'This constitutional right may or may not be enshrined in a written constitution, but it seems to their Lordships that it matters not whether it depends on such enshrinement or simply upon the common law as it would do in this country. In either event the discretion of the court must be exercised and has not been taken away by the declaration of the right in written form'.[67] On the facts, the Privy Council accepted that the lower courts had properly accepted the evidence.

If we turn to the fairness of the trial itself, we have already seen how the Privy Council has played fast and loose with questions of prejudicial pre-trial publicity;[68] with the principle of open justice;[69] and with the right to a speedy trial;[70] to say nothing of the right to silence.[71] But any concerns which decisions in these areas might present are eclipsed by the treatment of the presumption of innocence,[72] the right to trial by jury,[73] and the right to legal representation.[74] In *Robinson v The Queen* the appellant was convicted of murder and sentenced to death. An appeal to the Court of Appeal was dismissed, without reasons, and the appellant proceeded further to the Privy Council. The essence of his case was that his conviction without legal representation violated section 20(6) of the Jamaica Constitution, which provided that every person who is charged with a criminal offence 'shall be permitted to defend himself in person or by a legal representative of his own choice'. Apparently Robinson's counsel had withdrawn because of 'the impecuniousness of the defendant and his family'[75] and the trial judge refused the request for an adjournment for fear that a prosecution witness might disappear, even though 'a short adjournment would [not] have imperilled the trial' and though 'the actual witness was already being accommodated under police arrangements at a secret address'.[76] Yet despite the clear and unequivocal provisions of the Constitution, a majority in the Privy Council were unable to 'construe the relevant provisions of the Constitution in such a way as to give rise to an absolute right to legal representation'.[77] The crucial word was 'permitted', which meant that the accused 'must not be prevented by the state in any of its manifestations, whether judicial or executive, from exercising the right accorded by the subsection'.[78] In another strong dissent, however, the minority contended that the word 'permit' in this context imposes an 'obligation not to prevent the accused from choosing to be defended by a legal representative'.[79] The minority were guided by the fact that the word 'permit' is an ordinary English word of wide range and scope which should be construed generously and purposively to protect the accused's rights.

3. *Civil liberties*

Turning finally to the 'civil liberties' (such as freedom of association, assembly and expression, and the protection of private property), an important case from Trinidad and Tobago is *Collymore v A-G*,[80] which related to legislation restricting collective bargaining and the freedom to take industrial action. So far as the former was concerned, collective agreements had to be submitted to a Minister for examination and then registered by the Industrial Court, which was empowered to amend the agreements following representations from the Minister. So far as industrial action was concerned, the legislation constructed a system of compulsory arbitration for the settlement of disputes and provided that no employers should call a lock-out and no trade union a strike in breach of these provisions – obligations underwritten by fines, imprisonment and the dissolution of trade unions. This legislation was challenged on the ground that it violated the constitutional guarantees of freedom of association:

> The argument runs thus: 'Freedom of association' must be construed in such a way that it confers rights of substance and is not merely an empty phrase. So far as trade unions are concerned, the freedom means more than the mere right of individuals to form them; it embraces the right to pursue that object which is the main raison d'être of trade unions, namely collective bargaining on behalf of their members over wages and conditions of employment. Collective bargaining in its turn is ineffective unless backed by the right to strike in the last resort. It is this which gives reality to collective bargaining. Accordingly to take away or curtail the right to strike is in effect to abrogate or abridge that freedom of association which the Constitution confers.[81]

But as we have now come to expect, any opportunity to give constitutional guarantees any substantial content was rejected, the Privy Council endorsing the now well-known observations of Sir Hugh Wooding CJ in the court below:

> In my judgment, then, freedom of association means no more than freedom to enter into consensual arrangements to promote the common interest objects of the association group. The objects may be any of many. They may be religious or social, political or philosophical, economic or professional, educational or cultural, sporting or charitable. But the freedom to associate confers neither right nor licence for a course of conduct or for the commission of acts which in the view of Parliament are inimical to the peace, order and good government of the country.[82]

As we have already seen, it is not only freedom of association which has been read down. The same was true of freedom of assembly in *Francis v Chief of Police*[83] and of freedom of expression in the *Antigua Times*[84] case. This is not to deny that in one case, *Olivier v Buttigieg*,[85] a freedom of expression challenge did succeed. But that was a rather blatant attempt at censorship, from the unconstitutional consequences of which not even a forensic Houdini could escape. But it is not only association, assembly and expression rights which have been curtailed. The same degree of uncreative restraint has been brought to the analysis of property rights.[86] So in *Harrikissoon v A-G of Trinidad and Tobago*[87] the appellant was a teacher who claimed that he had been unlawfully transferred from one post to another. It was suggested on his behalf that the public office which he held constituted 'property' which he had been deprived of in breach of the constitutional guarantee of the right of the individual to life, liberty, security of the person and enjoyment of property, and the right not to be deprived thereof except by due process of law. But rather than take the suggestion seriously, Lord Diplock said that it 'needs only to be stated to be rejected'.[88] It may be, however, that at least in the area of property rights, this caution is a mixed blessing.[89] We have already encountered the *Selangor Pilot Association* case where the decision of the majority authorised the effective nationalisation of the Association's business.[90] The point here, however, was not whether the property should be nationalised, but whether it should be nationalised without compensation. Hence Lord

Salmon's fear that the narrow and literal approach of the majority would encourage and facilitate nationalisation without compensation throughout the Commonwealth.[91]

E. Conclusion

The evidence provided by the case-law hardly demonstrates 'a strong concern for fundamental rights and a willingness to defy legislative or Government authority in the name of higher principles of constitutionality'.[92] By the judgment of their peers, the members of the Privy Council have been arbitrary, shocking and barbarous. Having regard to cases such as *Baker*[93] and *Robinson*[94], even that assessment seems remarkably restrained. It is of course true that not all of the decisions have been negative. Apart from the freedom of expression case dealt with above,[95] there is a case where an arbitrary arrest was successfully challenged on constitutional grounds[96] and another where an arrested person was held entitled to legal representation following arrest.[97] And apart from *Fisher*[98] there are two other cases where citizenship and immigration laws were successfully challenged.[99] But these cases are few and far between and it is, quite frankly, not much of a record to put it generously, even allowing for the successful freedom of expression challenge from Antigua in 1990.[100] It might still be argued, of course, that even a single successful challenge is enough to vindicate a jurisdiction such as this and Bills of Rights in general. For on that occasion, if on no other, a government has been restrained from acting in an authoritarian and unconstitutional manner, and the government will be aware that the unpleasant experience may be repeated. But, on the other hand, with a record of adjudication as dismal as this, a Bill of Rights or an incorporated European Convention may serve to undermine rather than promote the cause of civil liberties and human rights. What the Privy Council has been doing has been to give constitutional authority and legitimacy to deeply disturbing and illiberal conduct. This is the danger of a Bill of Rights in the hands of a judiciary with no liberal vision. The condition of liberty is too serious for it to be protected in this way by people with such a record.

*   I am happy to acknowledge my very considerable debt to Jennifer Anne Thornton, who as a (successful) candidate for the degree of LLM in the University of Cambridge in 1986-87 wrote a particularly valuable thesis, entitled 'A Review of Privy Council Decisions (1966-86) on Individual Rights and Fundamental Freedoms Entrenched in Commonwealth Constitutions'. I am happy also to record that Ms Thornton was rather more positive and optimistic about the work of the Privy Council than I am.

Notes

1. For background on the Privy Council, see Sir G. Barwick 'Some Observations on the Privy Council' (1985) 2 MLJ CXIX, and L.P. Beth 'The Judicial Committee: Its Development, Organisation and Procedure' [1975] PL 219.
2. For a critique, see K.R. Evans and M. Fordham 'Singapore Appeals to the Judicial Committee of the Privy Council – An Endangered Species?' (1985) 27 *Mal L R* 284. See also 'Abolition of Appeals to the Privy Council. A Symposium' (1947) 25 *Can Bar Rev*. 557. The number of countries which recognise the Privy Council has gradually declined and is presently seventeen. On this, see D.B. Swinten *Imperial Appeal* Manchester UP (1987), Ch 6 and H.H. Marshall 'The Judicial Committee of the Privy Council: A Waning Jurisdiction' (1964) 13 ICLQ 697.
3. *Minister of Home Affairs v Fisher* [1980] AC 319 at 328. See also *A-G v Antigua Times Ltd* [1976] AC 16 at 24.
4. See L. Barnett 'The Present Position Regarding the Enforcement of Human Rights in the Commonwealth' (1980) WILJ 97: and F. Alexis 'Two Decades of Human Rights Adjudication in the Commonwealth Caribbean, (1981) WILJ 5. See also L. Barnett *The Constitutional Law of Jamaica* O.U.P. (1977) ch 14; A.R. Carnegie 'Judicial Review of Legislation in the West Indian Constitutions' [1971] PL 276; R.W. James 'The State of Human Rights Enforcement in the Co-operative Republic of Guyana' (1983) WILJ 14.
5. See M. Zander *A Bill of Rights*? (3rd ed) Sweet & Maxwell (1985) at 62–64.
6. [1967] 1 AC 26.
7. *Ibid* at 49.
8. These cases are usually dismissed as not being relevant. This contrasts, for example, with the approach taken by the Supreme Court of Canada, which has freely resorted to the jurisprudence of other systems to guide it in the interpretation of the Charter of Rights and Freedoms. The best examples of the approach of the Privy Council are: *Ong Ah Chuan v Public Prosecutor* [1981] AC 648 at 669; *Runyowa v The Queen* [1967] AC 26 at 47; *Government of Malaysia v Selangor Pilot Association* [1978] AC 337 at 347–8. But Cf *Olivier v Buttigieg* [1967] 1 AC 113; *Francis v Chief of Police* [1973] AC 761; *A-G v Antigua Times Ltd* [1976] AC 16; *Mootoo v A-G* [1979] 1 WLR 1334.
9. [1981] AC 648.
10. See further on this, Evans and Fordham *op cit* note 2 *supra*.
11. [1982] AC 190.
12. [1985] AC 937.
13. *Ibid* at 947.
14. *Ibid* at 951, following the classic decision of the US Supreme Court in *Barker v Wingo* 407 US 514 (1972).
15. *Barker v Wingo* 407 US 514 (1972). It was accepted that '[i]n the present case part of the delay after arrest was due to overcrowded courts, part to negligence by the authorities, and part to the unavailability of witnesses' [1985] 1 AC 937 at 951.
16. *Ibid* at 953.
17. *Ong Ah Chuan v Public Prosecutor* [1981] AC 648.
18. [1977] AC 195.
19. *Ibid* at 223–4.
20. *Ibid* at 224.
21. [1973] AC 761.
22. *Saia v New York* 334 US 558 (1948). *Cf Kovacs v Cooper* 336 US 77 (1949).
23. [1973] AC 761 at 772.
24. *Ibid* at 773.
25. [1976] AC 16.
26. *Ibid* at 32.
27. *Ibid* at 32.
28. *Ibid* at 32–3.
29. [1967] 1 AC 26.

30. *Judicial Review of the Death Penalty* Duckworth (1982) at 54, 148.
31. [1967] 1 AC 26, at 46.
32. *Ibid* at 47–48.
33. [1978] AC 337.
34. *Ibid* at 346.
35. *Ibid* at 353.
36. *Ibid* at 355.
37. [1967] 1 AC 26.
38. [1978] AC 337.
39. [1980] AC 319.
40. *Ibid* at 328.
41. *Ibid* at 329.
42. *Ibid* at 330.
43. [1980] AC 637 at 655.
44. [1981] AC 648. For the positive aspects of this case, see T.K. Iyer 'Article 9(1) and "Fundamental Principles of Natural Justice" in the Constitution of Singapore' (1981) 23 *Mal L R* 213. See also A.J.H. Harding 'Natural Justice and the Constitution' (1981) 23 *Mal L R* 226.
45. [1984] AC 689 at 700. See also Lord Templeman in *Société United Docks v Government of Mauritius* [1985] 1 AC 585: 'A Constitution concerned to protect the fundamental rights and freedoms of the individual should not be narrowly construed in a manner which produces anomalies and inexplicable inconsequences' (at 599).
46. [1983] 1 AC 719. See H.A. Fraser 'Commentary: *Noel Riley and Others v A–G of Jamaica*' (1983) WILJ 1.
47. [1983] 1 AC 719 at 726.
48. *Ibid*.
49. *Ibid* at 730. On the question of delay, see also *de Freitas v Benny* [1976] AC 239; and *Abbott v A–G of Trinidad and Tobago* [1979] 1 WLR 1342.
50. Witness also the caution in the use of an equal protection clause: *Howe Yoon Chong v Chief Assessor, Property Tax, Singapore* (1981) MLJ 51.
51. See especially *Reference re Public Service Employee Relations Act, Labour Relations Act and Police Officers Collective Bargaining Act* (1987) 38 DLR (4th) 161.
52. See T.J. Christian and K.D. Ewing, 'Labouring under the Canadian Constitution' (1988) 17 ILJ 73.
53. See W.S. Livingston, 'Abolition of Appeals from Canadian Courts to the Privy Council' (1950) 64 *Harv LR* 104.
54. [1967] 1 AC 26.
55. *Ibid* at 49.
56. |1981| AC 648.
57. *Ibid* at 672.
58. *Ibid* at 673. See also *de Freitas v Benny* [1976] AC 239.
59. [1975] AC 774.
60. *Ibid* at 790. Lord Salmon has used equally colourful language in other cases, including *A–G of St Christopher, Nevis and Anguilla v Reynolds* [1980] AC 637, at 656.
61. *Ibid* at 791.
62. [1985] 1 AC 937.
63. [1975] AC 774, at 780.
64. *Maloney Gordon v The Queen* (1969) 15 WIR 359.
65. [1969] 1 AC 304. See also *A–G v Momodou Jobe* [1984] 1 AC 689.
66. [1955] AC 197.
67. [1969] 1 AC 304 at 319.
68. *Grant v Director of Public Prosecutions* [1982] AC 190.
69. *Hinds v The Queen* [1977] AC 195; *McBean v The Queen* [1977] AC 537.
70. *Bell v Director of Public Prosecutions* [1985] 1 AC 937.
71. *Haw Tua Tau v Public Prosecutor* [1982] AC 136.

72. *Ong Ah Chuan v Public Prosecutor* [1198] AC 648.
73. *Stone v The Queen* [1980] 1 WLR 880.
74. *Robinson v The Queen* [1985] 1 AC 956.
75. *Ibid* at 972.
76. *Ibid* at 973.
77. *Ibid* at 966.
78. *Ibid* at 966.
79. *Ibid* at 973.
80. [1970] AC 538. For subsequent developments, see C. Okpaluba, 'The Implications of the Constitutional Guarantee of Freedom of Association in the West Indies: The Case of the Moruga Cane-Farmer' [1977] PL 217.
81. *Ibid* at 546.
82. *Ibid* at 547.
83. [1973] AC 761.
84. [1976] AC 16.
85. [1967] 1 AC 115.
86. In addition to the cases which follow, property rights were read down in *Howe Yoon Chong v Chief Assessor, Property Tax, Singapore* (1981) MLJ 51 and *Blomquist v A–G (Dominica)* (1989) 35 WIR 162.
87. [1980] AC 265.
88. *Ibid* at 268.
89. See especially *Mootoo v Attorney General of Trinidad and Tobago* [1979] 1 WLR 1334.
90. For evidence that this was no aberration, see *Société United Docks v Government of Mauritius* [1985] 1 AC 585.
91. [1978] AC 337 at 355.
92. M. Zander, *A Bill of Rights?* (3rd ed) Sweet & Maxwell (1985) 64.
93. [1975] AC 774.
94. [1985] 1 AC 956.
95. *Olivier v Buttigieg* (1967) 1 AC 115.
96. *A-G of St Christopher, Nevis and Anguilla v Reynolds* [1980] AC 637.
97. *Thornhill v A–G of Trinidad and Tobago* [1981] AC 61.
98. *Minister of Home Affairs v Fisher* [1980] AC 319.
99. *Akar v Attorney General of Sierra Leone* [1969] 3 All ER 384; *A-G v Ryan* [1980] AC 718.
100. *Hector v A-G of Antigua and Barbuda* [1990] 2 WLR 607.

Public Order Law in Scotland and England 1980–1990

Wilson Finnie

A. Introduction

No excuse is needed for contributing an essay comparing substantive Scots and English law to a collection of essays in honour of Professor A.W. Bradley. Like his immediate predecessor, the late Professor J.D.B. Mitchell, Bradley began his career and established his reputation with the study of English law. Both, on appointment to the Chair of Constitutional Law in Edinburgh threw themselves wholeheartedly into the study of Scots public law; both celebrated retirement (or in Mitchell's case, translation) from the Chair by the publication of a major, indeed unprecedented, contribution to Scots legal literature;[1] and in both cases the work in question is self-evidently enriched by the profound knowledge of other legal systems which underpins the exposition of the rules of Scots law. Moreover, and largely by their example, the former situation in which statements in the major textbooks of UK constitutional law were presumptively false, in that they habitually stated rules which often were of English law, as if they were statements of UK law (if such a thing exists), has largely been reversed, so that most textbooks now carefully differentiate by jurisdiction. Nonetheless, at a level of detail beyond that of the introductory textbook, there is still a dearth of systematic comparison of Scots and English law (still less of Northern Irish law). This essay attempts to fill that gap with respect to Scots and English law in one area of civil liberties. Thus, at one level, all that is attempted is an outline of Scots and English law on public order/freedom of assembly. Comparison, however, is only the first stage in comparative law as a discipline;[2] some conclusions inevitably suggest themselves from, or are illustrated by, the materials presented; these appear in Part F below. Finally, some more abstract reflections arising from the coexistence under one Parliament of different substantive rules of law and the ways in which these have evolved over the past ten years are offered.

For purposes of exposition Scots law in 1980 is considered first, followed by English law in 1980, then by a consideration of the major changes in the period 1980-90 in each of the systems, although the date 1980 in particular is a marker rather than a cut-off point as some examples of the law as it stood in 1980 are taken from later in the decade. Within those

251

sections the law is divided into: (a) direct prior controls over freedom of assembly; (b) offences against public order; (c) the hybrid category of police powers based on apprehended breach of the peace.

B. Scots Law in 1980

1. *Direct prior controls over freedom of assembly*

(a) Although the distinction between the two is not hard and fast[3] there is a difference between the law on meetings and assemblies on the one hand and processions on the other, and a further difference according to where the meeting or assembly is being held. On private land the consent of the owner is required and, contrary to popular belief, 'lodging or encamping' on any land or buildings without such consent can constitute criminal trespass;[4] though a procession would not fall within this definition, a meeting or a 'sit-in' protest would. On publicly-owned open space it could conceivably be argued that there was a tenuous right or presumptive right to assemble, and the frustration of this right could be used to strike down as unreasonable bye-laws unduly restricting it.[5] The need to provide by statute[6] for access to public halls during election campaigns suggests that such a 'right' did not extend beyond public open space to publicly owned meeting halls. As to streets, it was emphasised in *McAra v Magistrates of Edinburgh* that 'the primary and overruling object for which streets exist is passage';[7] citizens who stay for a chat with acquaintances do not necessarily do wrong; it is a question of degree for the magistrates (presumably by 1980 this responsibility would have shifted to the police) to decide, but there is no right to hold or participate in a public meeting in the ordinary sense of the word. Finally, there had at one time existed a statute of the Scots Parliament[8] which required prior notice to town councils of intended meetings, but in *McAra* this was declared to be in desuetude.

(b) Processions were considerably more regulated, under two layers of powers. First under an exotic system involving the Burgh Police (Scotland) Act 1892 and equivalent local Acts and secondly, under the Public Order Act 1936.

The Burgh Police Act system was highly complicated.[9] 'Police' was used in the older sense of government and the Acts were in effect a code of the local government powers applying in towns and villages before the granting of vast new powers to local government in the twentieth century. For historical reasons the Acts did not apply in Aberdeen, Dundee, Edinburgh, Glasgow or Greenock, which had their own Acts governing roughly the same areas but not granting identical powers. Under the Edinburgh local Act the organiser of a street procession was obliged to give seven days notice to the town clerk;[10] in Aberdeen forty-eight hours notice was required;[11] whilst no requirement of notice was imposed elsewhere, either under this system of Acts or by the Public Order Act 1936.

However, irrespective of any requirement of notice, all district councils or local magistrates had powers of regulation of processions which by other means they came to know about. Thus in Aberdeen[12] the magistrates could alter the route of procession or even forbid it if it would be likely to cause or result in any disorderly behaviour or breach of the peace or nuisance or annoyance or obstruction of traffic. This was understood to permit the banning of a march because the magistrates disliked the politics of its organisers.[13] The Edinburgh Act[14] gave similar powers based on 'the interests of public safety or order' whilst the Greenock local Act[15] gave a power with no limiting criteria for its exercise. Outside these three areas no specific powers based on public order considerations or control specifically over processions were granted. A way round this, however, was found just before the demise of the Burgh Police Act system and its replacement by the Civic Government (Scotland) Act 1982. Under the heading 'Regulation of Street Traffic', s. 385 of the Burgh Police Act 1892 as amended gave the local authority powers temporarility to divert traffic 'and the islands or district council may from time to time make bye-laws . . . prohibiting or regulating public processions'. Where a local authority purported to forbid a procession on public order grounds under s. 385 it was argued that this was *ultra vires* since s. 385 was limited to traffic considerations.[16] This argument was rejected, however, and a remarkably wide power of control over processions was thus granted to all islands and district councils.

Over and above this system there were the powers granted by s. 3 of the Public Order Act 1936 to chief constables and regional and islands councils (although until 1975[17] these powers did not, in Scotland, involve chief constables, but only the burgh magistrates in that overwhelming majority of cases where the procession took place in an urban area).

Section 3 conferred powers to regulate and to ban processions. In the case of regulation the initiative lay entirely with the chief constable after 1975. He was to have regard to the time, place, circumstances and route of the procession or proposed procession. If, having done so, he reasonably believed[18] that the procession would occasion 'serious public disorder' he could impose such conditions as appeared to him necessary to preserve public order, including conditions as to route and conditions forbidding entry to any specified public place. Conditions were usually only imposed after negotiation between police and organiser, so there was little authority as to limits on their scope.[19] Lord Scarman suggested – speaking of English law, but there is little reason to suppose any difference in Scotland – that conditions could not be imposed in such a way as to deprive a march of its symbolic function,[20] and thus, in effect, ban it.

As to bans on processions, these could be achieved only by agreement of the Chief Constable, the regional or islands council and the Secretary of State.[21] Again the initiative lay with the Chief Constable; if he felt the power of regulation conferred on him to prevent serious public disorder would be insufficient to enable him to avert the threat of serious public disorder, by reason of 'particular circumstances existing in any region or part thereof', then he could apply to the appropriate regional or islands council for a ban. The council, with the consent of the Secretary of State, could make a ban in the terms requested by the Chief Constable or with any modifications approved by the Secretary of State. The effect of such a ban was to prohibit the holding of all public processions, or public processions of a class or classes specified, in all or part of the region, for a period not exceeding three months. These provisions were not free from ambivalence, not least as to what degree of generality (or, put another way, injury to innocents) was required of a ban before it could be said to apply to a 'class' of processions.[22] There was no Scottish case-law.[23]

2. *Public order offences*

(a) **Common law offences**

At common law only two public order offences are known to Scots law. Or rather, strictly speaking, there are three, but sedition has not been charged since 1922, and before that, not since 1848[24] and looks, therefore, to be obsolete. Those actively used are mobbing and rioting, and breach of the peace.

Mobbing and rioting occurs when a number of people come together to effect a common illegal purpose by intimidation or by violence. There is no fixed minimum number to constitute a mob. In *HMA v McAndrew*[25] the jury was directed that seven would suffice and in *Sloan v McMillan*[26] it was observed, without ruling on a defence submission that five was too few people to constitute the offence, that it was not a question solely of numbers but also of the actions of the people in question and the degree of threat and violence used. The illegal purpose is the *immediate* purpose of the crowd; that is, if a crowd attempts to use violence in pursuit of an aim which is itself lawful, then the crowd's immediate purpose is the (illegal) use of violence. In modern conditions the offence is most often used to deal with fights between youths of different gangs or where one group inflicts violence on passers-by at random.[27] In such cases it may be difficult to specify with precision the common illegal purpose of the mob and some concern is raised by the fact that the indictment need not specify the purpose, thus in theory leaving a jury free to convict without necessarily agreeing what common illegal purpose was present.[28] As to the mob's conduct, violence, particularly in the most common modern cases, is normally present but is not of the essence of the offence which is, rather, 'effecting, or attempting to effect their purpose, either by violence or by demonstration of force of numbers, or by any species of intimidation, impediment or obstruction, calculated to effect their object and to impede, obstruct and defeat others employed in discharge of duty'.[29] Thus, in *Sloan*,[30] during a pit strike striking miners were able to prevent maintenance work in the pit in part by terrifying those doing the work by representing that Sloan was backed by 'hundreds of desperate men' and this was held sufficient to constitute mobbing.

Breach of the peace is by far the commonest offence in Scotland. Unlike in England, breach of the peace is far from being restricted to its core meaning of actual or apprehended violence to persons or property.[31] Indeed, so loosely defined is it that it is almost impossible to state concisely or precisely what types of conduct producing what kind of reaction are penalised. In one appellate decision[32] the accused was at a football match in an area reserved for one side's supporters and separated by a twelve-foot gangway, patrolled by police, from the supporters of the other side. He was shouting insults at the other side, making a noise and waving his scarf. The sheriff acquitted him on the grounds that exchange of insults and making noise were inevitably attendant on football matches, that the police presence prevented any mischief and that there was no evidence of anyone's having been alarmed, upset or annoyed, or tempted to make reprisal. On appeal the sheriff was held to have misdirected himself. Lord Dunpark, giving the opinion of the Court stated that it 'is well settled that a test which may be applied in charges of breach of the peace is whether the proved conduct may reasonably be expected to cause any person to be alarmed, upset or annoyed, or to provoke a disturbance of the peace. Positive evidence of actual alarm, upset, annoyance or disturbance created by reprisal is not a prerequisite of conviction'. As if this were not broad and vague enough, over the years other results produced by the accused's conduct have been held or suggested to satisfy the requirements for breach of the peace. Thus, in his recent book on the subject, Christie has considered as possibly sufficient results of the accused's conduct 'concern', 'danger', 'distress', 'disturbance', 'embarrassment', 'fear', 'obstruction', 'outrage', 'shock' and 'terror'![33]

Thus far, the implicit assumption is that, whichever reaction is alleged, it is the reaction to the accused's conduct of the *reasonable* observer. So far as a conviction proceeds on the basis of likely, not actual, reaction, this is necessarily the case, but what if an unusually sensitive observer did in fact manifest one of the required reactions? This issue was raised in *Deakin v Milne*.[34] Members of the Salvation Army were accused of breach of the peace on the ground that on successive Sundays their harmless parades had led to public disorder on being broken up by the Skeleton Army (the latter were an organisation funded by the big brewers to oppose the Rechabite principles of the Salvation Army). The Salvation Army members' convictions were upheld on the grounds that, whether or not they desired it, they foresaw the result and it was irrelevant that the reaction of the Skeleton Army was unreasonable. Although Mitchell argued[35] that the Salvation Army's conduct was itself in breach of the peace, *Deakin* appears to accord with Hume's views.[36] As to the *conduct* which can constitute the offence, a similar latitude has been recognised by the courts. Of course the core conduct is fighting, bawling and shouting and so on. Much else, however, is also caught, e.g. playing marbles in the street on a Sunday, taking part as a professional boxer in a boxing match, transvestitism, voyeurism, doodling under a bank's video-camera what looks like plans for a robbery, glue-sniffing in public, making a V-sign to a passing police car, displaying in his constituency a placard referring to Sir Nicholas Fairbairn MP as 'the perjuror's pal', disrupting church services and threatening suicide.[37] It is quite clear then that the offence is ineptly named, as it can be, and frequently is, used as a means of maintaining nothing more important than public decorum.

As if all this did not widen sufficiently the scope of the offence, it was held in *Young v Heatly* that it can be committed entirely in *private*, though the basis of this is unclear.[38] Thus, according to an anonymous commentator on that case,[39] 'a breach of the peace can be committed anywhere, even in a locked, sound-proof windowless room on a desert island, provided the court is prepared to say that had it taken place in public it would have been likely to lead to an actual breach of the peace'.

One final point worth noting about breach of the peace is the extent to which *de facto* the police define it. Fact and law merge imperceptibly in its definition. What exactly the football supporter in *Wilson v Brown*[40] was doing could reasonably have been placed anywhere on a spectrum from exulting in his team's performance *via* encouraging them coarsely to 'get stuck in' or 'crowing it' over the opposition, to threatening them with violence. Of that, and even more so of the reaction produced in bystanders, the police are well-placed to judge and a trial court would reasonably be unwilling to substitute its own evaluation for that of those on the spot. Furthermore, given that matters of fact are not appealable, the low level of fines in most breach of the peace cases and the expense of appeal, it is not surprising that Scots policemen view the offence as being the most useful weapon in their arsenal.

(b) Statutory offences

It is obviously a question of judgement which statutory offences are so bound up with public order as to be worthy of mention here and no claim is made that the following list is exhaustive. In general, offences are included because they may be committed *only* at a meeting or march, or were contained in the Public Order Act 1936.

(i) Trespass. Mention has already been made of the Trespass (Scotland) Act 1865.[41]

(ii) Obstruction. In 1980 the Burgh Police Act, the Glasgow local Act and the Aberdeen local Act[42] contained a provision penalising obstruction of the street. By contrast with the equivalent English provisions,[43] there was no requirement of obstruction wilfully and without lawful excuse or authority. Perhaps more important was the *meaning* of 'obstruction' as established in the leading case of *Aldred v Miller*,[44] decided under an earlier incarnation of the Glasgow local Act. There, Aldred had addressed a meeting on a pavement beside a broad street. The crowd had spilled off the edge of the pavement onto the street and there was thus necessitated a slight detour by passing cars and pedestrians, though there was no suggestion that the road was blocked in the sense of being rendered impassable. His appeal against conviction was rejected *inter alia* on the grounds that there was sufficient evidence of obstruction.

(iii) Public Meeting Act 1908. This penalises anyone who at a public meeting acts in a disorderly manner so as to prevent the transaction of the business for which the meeting was called. Under s. 1(3) (added by the Public Order Act 1936) a constable, if so requested by the chairman of the meeting and if he suspects a person of committing an offence under the Act, can require that person to give his name and address, and if he refuses to do so or gives a false name and address, the constable may arrest him. Since, in Scotland, the deliberate disruption of a meeting even without disorderly conduct is a breach of the peace[45] and since suspicion and apprehension of a breach of the peace respectively give powers to constables to require the suspect's name and address[46] and to enter a private meeting[47] the Act was and is redundant in Scotland.

(iv) Prohibition on political uniforms. The Public Order Act 1936 s. 1 made it an offence to wear in a public place or at a public meeting a uniform specifying association with a political organisation or the promotion of any political offence. Designed to deal with Moseley's Fascists and similar organisations this provision appeared to be virtually in desuetude, until it was revived for use against displays of support for the IRA.[48] The latter conduct was and is caught now by the Prevention of Terrorism Act and subject to much more severe penalty.

(v) Statutory breach of the peace. Under s. 5 of the Public Order Act 1936 as amended by the Race Relations Act 1965 it was an offence at any public meeting or in any public place either to use threatening, abusive or insulting language or to distribute or display any sign, writing or visible representation which was threatening, abusive or insulting with intent to provoke a breach of the peace or whereby a breach of the peace was likely to be occasioned. In its application in Scotland it was never decided whether the narrow, English concept of breach of the peace would apply here or whether upset, alarm or annoyance etc. would suffice. What *is* clear is that if the terms 'threatening', 'abusive' or 'insulting' were to be given the same interpretation in Scotland as the House of Lords gave them in England the offence would be considerably narrower than common law breach of the peace in Scotland.

This clearly appears from the words of Lord Reid in *Cozens v Brutus*[49] where he said that '[i]t would have been going much too far to prohibit all speech or conduct likely to occasion a breach of the peace because determined opponents may not shrink from organising or at least threatening a breach of the peace in order to silence a speaker whose views they detest. Therefore vigorous and it may be distasteful or unmannerly speech or behaviour is permitted as long as it does not go beyond any one of the three limits'. Probably for this reason, prosecutors preferred to charge common law breach of the peace in Scotland. The same would apply to the local Act and Burgh Police Act offences of breach of the peace, which echoed the language of s. 5.[50]

Nonetheless, if this first hurdle were cleared and the quality of the speech established, then the speaker had to take his audience as he found them (even if unusually sensitive). However, in England, this cut both ways, so that if the sole observer or hearer was a police constable, who presumptively would not create a breach of the peace, the accused benefitted equally from the unusual *insensitivity* of the audience.[51]

(vi) Incitement to racial hatred. Section 5A of the Public Order Act 1936 (as inserted by s. 70 of the Race Relations Act 1976) made it an offence to publish or distribute written matter which was threatening, abusive or insulting or to use in a public place or at a public meeting any threatening, abusive or insulting words where in all the circumstances hatred was likely to be stirred up against a racial group in Great Britain by the matter or the words in question. Again, of course, on the hypothesis of a member of the racial group in question hearing the words or seeing the literature, such behaviour would also constitute breach of the peace at common law.

3. *Police controls based on the power to prevent a breach of the peace*

This development, giving very wide powers to the police, is entirely based on English law, although there is every reason to believe that the Scots courts would take a similar line (a view shared by the Solicitor-General for Scotland in a statement to the House of Commons concerning police powers on 14 May 1984[52] during the miners' strike). This being the case, the exposition of the law is deferred to the section on English law. Note, however, that such a power is even wider in Scotland than in England by virtue of the breadth of the concept of breach of the peace.

C. English Law in 1980

1. *Prior controls*

In 1980 the position in England was roughly the same as in Scotland. In the case of assemblies there was in principle no need either to give prior notice or to obtain permission. As in Scotland, the major practical prerequisite was the consent of the owner of the premises of the meeting. So far as private premises were concerned there was no direct equivalent to the criminal responsibility under the Trespass (Scotland) Act 1865. In 1974 the House of Lords had held that *conspiracy* to trespass could constitute a criminal offence[53] but this decision was negatived by Part I of the Criminal Law Act 1977 which, generally speaking, requires an agreement to commit an offence as opposed to an unlawful act as an ingredient of conspiracy. However, the Act creates new offences related to trespass, one of which, failure to vacate residential premises and adjunct land which have been occupied as a trespasser when required to do so by a person entitled to occupy the premises, was not likely to restrict freedom of assembly much, although the other, occupation of the premises of a foreign diplomatic or consular mission, might. As in Scotland, local authorities were under no special duty to make public land or premises available for meetings either at all or on a non-discriminatory basis, although bye-laws governing the use of public open space could be attacked as *ultra vires*.[54] The use of highways for meetings was also subject to much the same restrictions as in Scotland. The primary purpose of, and right over, a highway was that of passage, and since the soil of the highway was usually vested in the owner of the adjoining property, to abuse the highway by doing other than using it for passage could constitute a trespass against the adjoining landowner.[55]

With regard to processions the same principles applied, except in the case of processions along the highway which are in essence no more than a collective exercise of the individual's right of passage. There was no general requirement of advance notification and English law did not reflect the same patchwork system of control over these important areas of law as was found in Scotland, although there were deviations from the general law found in the areas of particular local authorities. In the West Midlands, for example, there was a requirement of 72 hours' notice of a procession.[56]

Where a procession or intended procession did come to the notice of the authorities, however, the provisions of the Public Order Act 1936 s. 3 applied in England outside London as in Scotland. In London the Commissioner of Metropolitan Police had the power himself to impose bans on a class of processions, with the consent of the Secretary of State. The Commissioner also had a power under the Metropolitan Police Act 1839 s. 52 to make regulations prescribing routes and avoiding obstruction of the streets 'in all times of public processions'.

2. *Public order offences*

The statutory offences under the Public Meetings Act 1908 and the Public Order Act 1936 described above applied in relation to England as they applied in relation to Scotland. There was also an offence of obstructing the highway[57] although, as has already been pointed out, the offence in England required 'wilful' obstruction 'without lawful excuse or authority', qualifications missing from the Scottish versions. The English common law offences, however, differed significantly from the Scottish ones. Strictly speaking, they were four in number: rout, affray, unlawful assembly and riot. Rout was identical to riot except that the common enterprise required to commit riot was not put into effect or embarked upon. Rout had long since fallen into desuetude.

Until *R v Sharp and Johnson*[58] the offence of affray had also been unused for over 100 years and had been generally thought to be obsolete.[59] Following that decision there had been a steady increase in its use to around 1000 cases a year and the House of Lords had restated the elements of the offence in *Button v DPP*[60] and *Taylor v DPP*.[61] As etymology suggests (*cf.* modern French *effrayer*), the essence of the offence was the causing of fear. More particularly, the *actus reus* consisted of *either* unlawful fighting (i.e. where both sides were acting unlawfully) or unlawful violence used by one or more persons against another (not unlawful fighting since the person to whom the violence was offered might lawfully use violence in self-defence[62]) *or* of an unlawful display of force by one or more persons without actual violence. The latter was understood to include threats backed up by, for example, the brandishing of a weapon, but not mere verbal aggression.[63] In the period 1820-1966 it was held that the offence could be committed only in a public place but in *Button v DPP*[64] the older view, that it could be committed on private premises as well, was reinstated. The fighting or violence had to be such that a bystander of reasonable firmness of character might reasonably be expected to be terrified. If the fighting or violence occurred in a public place there was no need to prove that any bystander had actually *been* terrified, but, though the point was not wholly clear in 1980, if the fighting or violence occurred on private premises it probably was required to show actual terror produced on a bystander.[65] Since, as the Law Commission pointed out,[66] the *actus reus* involved unlawful fighting, and it is difficult to conceive of a person fighting unlawfully and involuntarily, the *mens rea* of the offence had not raised any particular controversy.

The other two public order offences at common law were unlawful assembly and riot. The more serious offence, riot, had not often been prosecuted in modern times, and had not been considered by the House of Lords. Indeed, the most widely-accepted definition, that by Phillimore J in *Field v Receiver of Metropolitan Police*[67] was given, not in the course of criminal proceedings but on a claim for compensation by property owners under the Riot (Damages) Act 1886 for damage caused 'riotously'. In accordance with that definition, the offence was committed when at least three persons who share a common purpose and who intend to help each other to attain that purpose, if necessary to the extent of using force against those who oppose them, execute or begin to execute the purpose using force or violence displayed in such a manner as to alarm at least one person of reasonable firmness and courage. Although this definition covered the everyday understanding of riot, it was also much wider; Lord Goddard C J gave the example of three men who enter a shop and forcibly or by threats steal goods; they would be committing riot.[68]

Surprisingly, given its venerable status and the important consequences and powers on the part of the police which flow from it, the definition of an unlawful assembly had never been universally agreed upon.[69] That it could be committed only by an assembly of three or more persons and that it would be committed if those persons had a common purpose to achieve some object, whether or not lawful, in such a way as to cause persons of reasonable firmness to apprehend a breach of the peace was not in dispute. However, a second possibility was of an assembly of three or more persons gathered together for purposes forbidden by the law. The area of disagreement here was whether the forbidden purpose had to be violent or tumultuous.[70] Much could hinge upon it, as the case of *R v Chief Constable of Cornwall and Devon ex p CEGB*[71] shows. There, peaceful protesters prevented a survey of a possible site for a nuclear reactor. By doing so they committed a non-violent criminal offence under the Town and Country Planning Act 1971. Nor was it clear that they would violently resist expulsion using reasonable force. The CEGB (Central Electricity Generating Board) appealed to the local chief constable for assistance but he declined, saying it was not clear that the assembly was unlawful. Lord Denning M R and Templeman L J thought it was, but Lawton L J insisted that in modern law violence or tumult were an essential part of the definition of the offence.

Further difficulty, or at least complexity, is introduced in the offence by the *mens rea* required. The difficulty is shown by the facts in two cases. The first, *Beatty v Gillbanks*,[72] had facts almost identical to those of *Deakin v Miln*[73] discussed above. The English court, however, took a robustly liberal approach and held that since the Salvation Army members had not *intended*, even if they foresaw, the reaction of the Skeleton Army, they could not be bound over to keep the peace. Where, however, a Protestant zealot relied upon and actively fomented a hostile reaction from the inhabitants of a Catholic area in Liverpool he could be bound over.[74]

3. *Powers based on apprehended breach of the peace*

In English law, breach of the peace is not a substantive offence but apprehension of its occurrence gives powers to magistrates and police to restrict the liberty of those who appear likely to cause it. However, the concept of breach of the peace even for these purposes is much narrower than in Scots law. A breach of the peace is an act 'done or threatened to be done which either actually harms a person or in his presence his property, or is likely to cause such harm, or which puts someone in fear of such harm being done'.[75] Aside from the importance of breach of the peace in public order *offences*, fear of it also grounds three powers, or groups of powers.

(a) **Binding over**

Under this procedure of ancient but uncertain origin, magistrates in England and Wales can order any person to enter into a recognisance to keep the peace or to be of good behaviour, either in general, or particularly in their attitude towards another named person. This may be accompanied by a requirement of surety. The person so 'bound over' need not have been convicted of an offence, or indeed have been shown to have done anything from which an intention to offer personal violence to anyone else in particular can be inferred.[76] Refusal to enter into a recognisance can be punished by up to six months' imprisonment.[77] An appeal against a binding-over order lies to the Crown Court.[78]

(b) **Entry powers**

Where an assembly takes place on public land or on public premises, the police have the same rights of attendance as any other member of the public. Likewise, if a meeting on private premises is open to the public generally, the police may attend, at least unless and until the organisers request them to withdraw. But what is their position after withdrawal of such permission or in the case of a private meeting? In *Thomas v Sawkins*[79] it was held that they could remain at a public meeting even after being asked to withdraw, if they reasonably anticipated that an offence was likely to be committed, and indeed that they could enter to prevent commission of an offence. In the period 1935-84 there was uncertainty as to the scope of the power in *Thomas v Sawkins*. Did it give power of entry to a private meeting and did it give powers of entry to forestall commission of *any* offence?[80] The Police and Criminal Evidence Act 1984 s. 17 abolished all common law entry powers except to prevent or suppress a breach of the peace.

(c) **Police powers to give directions**

These powers find their origin in the general duty of the constable to prevent breaches of the peace[81] and in two nineteenth-century Irish cases. In *Humphries v Connor*[82] a woman wearing an orange lily (the symbol of the

Protestant Ascendancy) was walking through a hostile crowd. A constable, fearing a breach of the peace, asked her to remove it, and, when she refused, did so himself. The woman then sued him for assault. The court, however, accepted the defence that what he had done was necessary to preserve the peace, provided the jury accepted this necessity as a matter of fact. Similarly, in *O'Kelly v Harvey*[83] the Justices of the Peace for an area where a meeting was being held decided that dispersal of the meeting was the only way to prevent a breach of the peace. When the participants refused to disperse the Justices laid hands upon one of them who, in consequence, sued for assault. It was not alleged in defence that the meeting was an unlawful assembly; instead it was argued that the only means open to the defendant to fulfil his duty and maintain the peace was to disperse the meeting, and the court accepted this. Both these cases, it should be noted, offered a shield to the defenders of the peace, not a sword.

That step was taken in 1936 by the marrying of the thinking in the nineteenth-century cases to the criminal offence of obstructing a constable in the execution of his duties.[84] In *Duncan v Jones*[85] the appellant spoke to a crowd outside an employment training centre and a disturbance occurred because of her speech, or so at least the superintendant of the centre believed. When another meeting was announced a police officer whose presence had been requested by the centre's superintendant told Mrs Jones that she could not address the crowd outside the centre, although she might do so some distance away. From her point of view this would have deprived the meeting of its full effect and she refused to desist and was charged and convicted of obstructing the constable. Her appeal was dismissed, Humphrey J saying that 'it is the duty of a police officer to prevent apprehended breaches of the peace. Here it is found as a fact that the respondent reasonably apprehended a breach of the peace. It then . . . became his duty to prevent anything which in his view would cause that breach of the peace. While he was taking steps to do so he was wilfully obstructed by the appellant. I can conceive no clearer case within the statutes than that'. In similar vein, in *Piddington v Bates*[86] there was a trade dispute in the course of which pickets were stationed at both entrances to the employers' premises. A constable who arrived on the scene reasonably (as found by the magistrate) feared a breach of the peace unless the number of pickets at each entrance was restricted to two, and gave instructions accordingly. The defendant refused to obey and was arrested and charged with obstruction. He was convicted and his appeal dismissed on the same reasoning as *Duncan v Jones*.

These cases, then, establish the existence of an important common law police power to impose conditions on assemblies. Indeed, until 1986 they were the only powers to impose conditions on assemblies as opposed to processions. Moreover, it was and is a broader power than the statutory power to do so, particularly in Scotland where the offence of breach of the peace is so much wider, but also in England since, as *Piddington v Bates* shows, the trigger number of twenty participants under the statute is not required (on which see further part D2, below). Perhaps paradoxically, then, although reported cases reveal instances of the police giving such directions,[87] the existence of the power does not appear to have been directly discussed in Scotland, perhaps because breach of the peace, as in *Alexander* itself, is a preferred charge, or perhaps because of the more restricted interpretation given in Scotland to obstruction.[88]

Two questions remain after the discussion thus far. Does the power apply to processions also, and is there a power to ban an assembly? Both these powers would seem to be only a short logical step from what has already been established and it is not surprising that the police have claimed such powers, despite the fact that, outside London, the police cannot themselves ban processions under the Public Order Act or the Civic Government (Scotland) Act 1982. Thus, in 1981 the death of IRA hunger-striker Francis Hughes provoked the most violent rioting in Belfast for years. The police knew that funeral arrangements had been taken over by the IRA and feared that violent disorder would result. In consequence the decision was taken by the Chief Constable of the RUC to prevent the *cortège* from entering the city, a decision purportedly made at common law.[89] In January 1984 the police used common law powers to turn back a National Front march outside Wakefield.[90]

The greatest use made of the powers, however, was during the miners' strike of 1984 – 85. To defeat the phenomenon of 'flying pickets' the police set up road blocks to intercept and turn away huge numbers of suspected miners, particularly at the Dartford Tunnel (to prevent miners leaving Kent) and on the county boundaries of Nottinghamshire, where the Chief Constable estimated that in the first 27 weeks of the strike 164,508 'presumed pickets' were denied entry to the county. By any standards this was prevention of assemblies on a grand scale. The legality of the police actions in Nottinghamshire was tested in *Moss v McLachlan*,[91] which was an appeal against convictions for obstruction by refusing to desist in accordance with police instructions from entering the county. The police were held to have acted within their powers. Skinner J gave it as the opinion of the court that '[t]he situation has to be assessed by the senior police officers present. Provided they honestly and reasonably form the opinion that there is a real risk of a breach of the peace in the sense that it is in close proximity both in place and time, then the conditions exist for reasonable preventative action including, if necessary, the measures taken in this case'. This appeared to recognise as lawful the massive and systematic use of police powers to forbid assemblies and processions to which the police had resorted during the strike.

D. Scots Law in 1990

1. *Introduction*

Without meaning to suggest that there has ever been a long time when major problems with public order did not exist, the late 1970s and the 1980s seem to have produced more than their fair share of violent disorder. At any rate, the combination of violence provoked by the clash of National Front supporters and their rivals, inner-city riots across the UK, protracted industrial disputes involving large-scale picketing, and recent poll tax riots in central London has served to produce a public perception that such is the case and has led to an increase in controls over freedom of assembly.

In Scotland the first stage of reassessment of the law had a more accidental beginning in the need, following local government reform, to replace the ramshackle system of the Burgh Police Acts and local equivalents. A Working Party set up in 1972 to consider this vast corpus of legislation reported in 1976,[92] and in its 156-page Report it devoted just over a page to the regulation of processions. In the late 1970s the Scottish Office and the Home Office jointly reviewed the Public Order Act and related legislation[93] and because of this the reference to processions, which had been included in the White Paper and Draft Civic Government Bill produced in 1980 to give effect to the recommendations of the Working Party, were dropped from the Bill as introduced.[94] Only when it transpired that the review of English public order law was to be protracted were provisions on control of procession introduced in the Lords as a series of government amendments to the Civic Government Bill.

2. *Prior controls over processions and assemblies*

These are now found in Part IV of the Civic Government (Scotland) Act 1982 as slightly amended and supplemented by the Public Order Act 1986. In effect, they divide processions into five classes.[95] Those 'customarily or commonly' held do not require to be notified in advance. In the second class are processions which fall into the first category but in relation to which the regional or islands council has disapplied the exemption, thus requiring notification of them. Thirdly, there are processions which, by reason of their nature as a response to events or otherwise, *cannot* be notified seven days in advance. The councils may in such cases waive the full seven days' notice but not the matters to be notified themselves. Fourthly, there are processions falling into a class which the council has exempted from notice requirements. The use made of this power varies enormously from council to council, from no exemptions to (in Strathclyde) processions organised by 238 different bodies and constant additions to that list.[96] Finally, there is the major class of processions falling into none of the other four categories. In respect of these, seven days' notice in writing must be given to the regional or islands council and the local chief constable, specifying date, time, route, estimated numbers, arrangements for control (if any) and the organiser's name and address.[97]

In consultation with the chief constable, the council may then prohibit the procession or impose conditions on it, including conditions as to route, time, date or duration, or forbidding entry to particular public places.[98] There are no explicit limits on the council's discretion to ban or impose conditions, carrying the obvious danger of councils forbidding marches because they do not like the politics of the organisers (and there is indeed evidence that this has been done).[99] The only safeguard takes the form of a right of appeal to the Sheriff, who may overturn a decision only on the grounds of error in law; the decision's having been based on any incorrect material fact; that the decision was unreasonable; or that in some other way the council has exceeded its legal powers.[100] It would appear that there has only been one such (unsuccessful) appeal.[101] To organise a march without giving due notice or to fail to honour the conditions imposed is an offence.[102] It is also an offence to take part in such a march and to refuse to desist when required to do so by a constable.

These provisions give no power to the police alone to impose conditions – a potentially significant omission, particularly in the case of unforeseeable developments at the time of the march. Arguably, such a power is unnecessary since common law powers exist, and until 1986 the powers under the Public Order Act 1936 continued to exist in tandem. The repeal of that Act would have left a statutory *lacuna* in Scotland, so s. 12 of the Public Order Act 1986 extends to Scotland. However, it gives powers only when a procession is under way, or when people are assembling with a view to taking part in a procession.[103] It gives powers to give directions only to the senior police officer present at the scene.[104] His powers may be exercised only if, having regard to the time or place at which, and the circumstances in which, any public procession is being held, and its route, he reasonably believes that it may result in serious public disorder, serious damage to property or serious disruption to the life of the community, or that the purpose of the organisers is to intimidate others into doing or refraining from doing something they are legally entitled to do or not do. If those preconditions are met he may impose such conditions as to the route or prohibiting entry to specified public places as appear to him necessary to prevent the envisaged mischief.[105] Any conditions imposed under this power override conditions previously imposed by the regional council.[106]

Finally, controls have been imposed over static assemblies by the Public Order Act 1986. For this purpose 'public assembly' is defined to mean an assembly of twenty or more people in a public place wholly or partly open to the air.[107] The power of regulation is (somewhat illogically in Scotland, in view of the Civic Government Act controls over processions, which are primarily vested in elected authorities) given to the chief constable or his delegate with regard to a future assembly and to the senior officer present with regard to an assembly taking place.[108] Again, the prerequisites for the exercise of the power are a reasonable belief, having regard to the (intended) time or place at which and circumstances in which the assembly is taking place, that the assembly will result in serious public disorder, serious damage to property or serious disruption to the life of the community or that the organiser's purpose is intimidation.[109] The conditions imposed may concern the place of the assembly, its maximum duration or the maximum number of persons who may take part. It is an offence knowingly to organise or take part in an assembly and fail to comply with an imposed condition.

3. *Offences*

The common law offences have seen no significant change in the 1980s. The Scottish Law Commission undertook a review of the law of mobbing and rioting in 1984.[110] It floated, rather than discussed, the idea of the replacement of the common law by a statutory offence, but focused on two problems within the present law. First, as noted in Part B2 above, there is no requirement to spell out the mob's common purpose in the indictment, thus leaving it open to a jury to convict without any common view as to what the mob's purpose was, and making it unnecessary for the Crown to lead any evidence of common purpose. The Commission's understanding, following the decision in *Hancock v HMA*,[111] had been that the Crown would in practice specify the common purpose in future, but it had not uniformly done so. Should this be a statutory requirement? Secondly, the indictment may specify that the mob committed particular offences. It is not clear in such a case whether individual members of the mob are each guilty of each of those offences and to be sentenced as such, or whether the specified offences only aggravate the mobbing offence. In the case of offences carrying a fixed penalty (i.e. murder) this is a crucial distinction,[112] but it is important anyway in applying the sentencing tariff. Should the law be clarified? Astonishingly, in a view of the importance of the issues, but perhaps less so in view of the general lack of concern with civil liberties issues among the Scottish clerisy, public response to the Memorandum favoured the status quo and the Commission dropped the issue.[113]

Statutory offences were somewhat changed by the Public Order Act 1986. Section 5 of the 1936 Act was repealed without replacement, being in any case narrower than common-law breach of the peace. Section 5A was repealed and replaced by Part III of the 1986 Act, which creates a whole series of offences centring around the using of threatening, abusive or insulting words or behaviour. Thus, to use such words or behaviour with intent to stir up racial hatred, or where, having regard to all the circumstances racial hatred is likely to be stirred up is an offence.[114] To publish or distribute written material possessing those qualities with similar intent or likely effect is also an offence.[115] The director of a play using such words or behaviour with the same intent or likely effect thereby commits an offence[116] as does a person who shows, plays or distributes a visual or auditory recording[117] or broadcasts or produces or directs a broadcast of similar quality and intent or likely effect.[118]

E. English Law in 1990

1. *Introduction*

The process of recasting English public order law was much more drawn out than that in Scotland. The earliest contribution was Lord Scarman's *Report on the Red Lion Square Disorders of 15 June 1974*.[119] Continuing sporadic disorder led to an investigation into the whole area by the House of Commons' Home Affairs Committee[120] and a general *Review of the Public Order Act 1936 and Related Legislation*[121] by the Home Office and the Scottish Office. Shortly afterwards, as part of its programme of consolidation of criminal law in England and Wales the Law Commission published a Working Paper on *Offences Against Public Order*[122] followed in due course by its *Report* on the subject.[123] Knitting together these strands was the White Paper *Review of Public Order Law*[124] which led, eventually to the Public Order Act 1986 which, in its application to England, virtually codifies the law of public order.

2. Prior controls

In England, the 1986 Act is very much an update of the 1936 Act with new, enlarged versions of the same powers being distributed in the same way among the police, district councils and the Secretary of State. One novelty, however, was the introduction of a general requirement to give notice of a proposal to hold a public procession. The exclusion of traditional or ceremonial processions by harmless organisations is achieved by the specific restriction of notifiable processions so as to include only those to mark or commemorate an event, to publicise a cause or campaign and to demonstrate support for or opposition to the views or actions of any person or body of persons[125] and the explicit exclusion of processions 'customarily held' in the area and funeral processions 'organised by a funeral director in the normal course of his business'.[126] The required notification must give the intended date, time and route of the procession and the name and address of the organiser. It must be delivered six clear days before the procession or, if that is not 'reasonably practicable', as soon as it is reasonably practicable[127] to a police station within the police area where the procession will be held. It is an offence to hold a procession without notice being given, or not in accordance with the provisions of the notice.[128]

Once notice is given there are powers to impose conditions or bans in the same way as under the 1936 Act, except that the power to impose conditions has been widened. Thus, whereas under the 1936 Act this could be done only where the chief constable, having regard to the time and place at which and the circumstances in which a procession was taking or was to take place, reasonably anticipated serious public disorder, the prerequisite of serious public disorder is now joined by serious damage to property, serious disruption to the life of the community, or belief that the purpose of the organisers is the intimidation of others to compel them to do or refrain from doing acts which they are legally entitled to do or refrain from doing.[129] In addition, under the 1936 Act the chief constable was required to give his personal attention to the matter, but may now delegate his functions under the Act[130] and where a procession is under way, the power to impose conditions lies with the senior police officer present.[131] The conditions which may be imposed are such as appear necessary to prevent the envisaged harm and include conditions as to the route and preventing entry to any public place.

The power to ban processions is identical to that under the 1936 Act. Thus, only fear of serious public disorder which cannot be avoided by use of the power to impose conditions justifies the police in seeking, and the district council in imposing, a ban.[132] The only novelty in this section of the Act is the recognition of a power to act by himself, with the consent of the Home Secretary, in the Commissioner of Police for the City of London, in the same way as does the Commissioner of Police for the Metropolis.[133]

The other major novelty in the area of prior controls is the introduction of powers over static assemblies. This applies in the same way in England as in Scotland, in relation to which it has already been discussed.

3. *Offences*

The common law offences discussed above were, as the Law Commission had recommended, abolished, together with ss. 5 and 5A of the Public Order Act 1936.[134] They were, however, replaced by a series of new offences which bear more than a passing similarity to, and in the case of riot and affray even the name of, the common law offences.

(a) Riot

As reformulated by s. 1 of the 1986 Act, riot differs from the common law version in a number of ways. First, the minimum number of participants is increased from 3 to 12. Second, the *mens rea* is reformulated. A person is guilty of riot only if he intends to use violence or is aware that his conduct is violent[135] and there is no longer any requirement of intent on the part of the rioters to assist each other by force. Third, the accused must himself have actually used unlawful violence. Fourth, the maximum penalty is reduced from life to ten years' imprisonment. Thus 'where 12 or more persons who are present together use or threaten unlawful violence for a common purpose and the conduct of them (taken together) is such as would cause a person of reasonable firmness present at the scene to fear for his personal safety, each of the persons using unlawful violence for the common purpose is guilty of riot'.[136]

(b) Violent disorder

The Law Commission[137] proposed to replace the common law of unlawful assembly by two offences, one of violent disorder and one of conduct intended or likely to cause fear or provoke violence. The Act reflects this division although the Law Commission's second proposed offence and the logic behind it were not adopted. Violent disorder thus corresponds to the more serious end of the spectrum of offences previously caught by unlawful assembly. To commit the offence, the accused must have been one of a group of at least three persons, who use or threaten violence (not necessarily at the same time) and their conduct (viewed collectively) must be such that a person of reasonable firmness present at the scene would fear for his personal safety (though such a person need not actually be present). The accused must have intended to use or threaten violence or be aware that his conduct might be violent or threatening. The maximum penalty is five years' imprisonment.[138]

(c) Affray

This is not greatly changed from the common law offence. A person commits affray by the use or threat of unlawful violence to another if his conduct would cause a person of reasonable firmness present at the scene to fear for his own safety.[139] In the case of affray, violence does not include violence to property[140] and 'threats', as at common law, cannot be constituted by mere words.[141] The accused must have intended to use or threaten violence or be aware that his conduct may be violent or threaten violence.[142]

(d) Fear or provocation of violence

As already mentioned (text at note 137 above) the Law Commission proposed two replacement offences for common law unlawful assembly. The Government, however, chose a different path, preferring to build on the precedent of s. 5 of the Public Order Act 1936, extending its reach far into the realm of conduct previously not punishable at all and dividing the extended offence into two, which are now ss. 4 and 5. Section 4, headed 'fear or provocation of violence' in effect creates eight different offences by the specification of two modes of acting, each of which may interact with one of two mental states or two possible outcomes. The two modes of action are the use towards another person of threatening, abusive or insulting words or behaviour and the distribution, or display to another person, of any writing, sign or other visible representation which is threatening, abusive or insulting. The offence is completed if the speaker, distributor or displayer *intends* to cause the person towards whom his behaviour is directed to believe that unlawful violence will be used against him or a third party by the speaker etc., or *intends* to provoke the person addressed or a third party to the immediate use of unlawful violence. Alternatively, the offence is completed if, as a result of ('whereby') the speaker's, distributor's or displayer's actions, it is *likely* that the person towards whom his words or conduct are directed will believe that unlawful violence will be used[143] or it is *likely* that unlawful violence will be provoked.[144] As with all the new offences, it may be committed either in public or in private, but in the case of this offence not if the speech, distribution or display took place inside a dwelling and the recipient is also inside that dwelling. The maximum penalty is six months' imprisonment.

(e) Harrassment, alarm or distress

The new offence of causing these results by disorderly conduct was the most controversial aspect of the Bill which became the 1986 Act. It was not recommended by the Law Commission, or floated in the Green Paper of 1980. Even in the White Paper the offence was only tentatively proposed, and was considerably more restrictive than the version in the Bill and now the 1986 Act. The offence is committed either by using threatening, abusive or insulting behaviour or words; or by using disorderly behaviour; or by displaying threatening, abusive or insulting writings, signs or representations, in each case within the sight or hearing of a person likely to be caused harassment, alarm or distress by such conduct. The major extension here is the penalisation of disorderly conduct, particularly as that concept is not defined. It has been suggested that it requires more than an offence against good taste or the canons of decorum[145] but nonetheless moves English criminal law considerably in the direction of the Scots concept of 'breach of the peace'. Likewise, causing harassment, alarm or distress is a low-level reaction threshold to involve someone in criminal liability, especially as there is no requirement to show that a person actually *was* harassed etc. but only the likelihood of this occurring. This is slightly mitigated by the three defences specifically provided for,[146] namely that the accused had no reason to believe that there was any person within sight or hearing who was likely to be caused harassment, alarm or distress, or that he was within a dwelling and had no reason to suppose his conduct or its result would be seen or heard by anyone outside the dwelling or that his conduct was reasonable.

(f) Other statutory offences

The 1986 Act also altered the previously surveyed statutory offences in the same way as described above in relation to Scotland. In relation to England, however, it also significantly extended the law of criminal trespass. As already outlined, the Criminal Law Act 1977 created offences of trespass in English law but principally only in respect of residential property. During 1984-86 there was much press coverage of the phenomenon of the 'hippy convoy', large groups of people driving around in old vans and buses in which they lived, and often descending *en masse* and without the owner's permission on private land, allegedly to its despoliation. Private law remedies were perceived as inadequate and accordingly s. 39 of the 1986 Act creates new offences and gives new powers to the police to deal with this phenomenon. Thus the senior police officer present can direct persons to leave land if he reasonably believes that two or more of them have entered as trespassers with the common purpose of residing there for a time, that the owner has taken reasonable steps to remove them and that either between them they have brought twelve or more vehicles onto the land, or that any of them has caused damage to the land or has used threatening, abusive or insulting language to the occupier, his family, employees or agents. It then becomes an offence for a person directed to leave to refuse to do so, or to return within three months.

F. Conclusion

Having looked in some detail at the substance and evolution of the provisions of Scots and English law we are now in a position of being able to offer some observations which emerge from the juxtaposition of these two *corpora* of law.

The first point which emerges is that over the decade both systems have become relatively less liberal, relatively less willing to recognise the rights of protest or freedom of assembly of individuals. This is most evident in the restructuring of the powers of prior restraint over processions, and the extension of such controls for the first time to static assemblies (although, in truth, this may only represent statutory recognition of police powers at common law). It is evident also, however, in England in the extension of criminal trespass and in the way the opportunity for codification suggested by the Law Commission was used drastically to extend the area of distasteful behaviour subject to the reach of public order law. However, the relatively greater steps taken in England to restrict freedom of assembly must not be allowed to distort the overall picture. The snapshot of the Scottish system as it stood in 1980 can be contrasted with that of the English system in

1990 and the overwhelming impression is still that of the relative illiberality of Scots law. The most *important* area here is the Scottish offence of breach of the peace, which must surely be in the running for any prize for the most repressive criminal offence in any European legal system (including Eastern Europe), and which certainly goes far beyond even the provisions of the Public Order Act 1986 s. 5. However, the relative liberalism of the English law of offences against public order is a feature of the whole field of public order law. Although an argument can be made in favour of allowing elected councillors to decide whether and on what conditions a march can go ahead, it is difficult to see why in Scotland this should be in the form of an entirely unstructured discretion, potentially allowing overt political censorship and discrimination, whilst in England only a few specific, public-order-related criteria justify such restrictions. Again, in England, the tradition that bans on particular marches, as opposed to bans on classes of marches (public authority thus standing neutrally between the twin viewpoints which only when brought together constitute a threat of public disorder) are unacceptable was maintained in the 1986 Act, whilst in Scotland the authorities are free to take sides between disputants and ban the public manifestation of only one of two opposed viewpoints. In Scotland, but not England, it is an offence to take part in an unnotified march, or one in breach of conditions imposed on it. Conviction of a public order offence in England is conviction only of that offence and the maximum punishment at common law was reduced for each offence in the 1986 Act. In Scotland, mobbing and rioting, carrying inculpation far beyond the normal rules of art and part guilt or conspiracy, may involve indirect conviction of, and commensurate punishment for, any offence committed by any member of the mob whilst the maximum punishment in theory is life imprisonment. The 'may' in that last sentence betrays another difference of degree between the two systems, and one which is essential to the traditional understanding of the rule of law, particularly in its application to criminal law, namely that a citizen should be able to plan his conduct in the knowledge of what he is entitled or forbidden to do. Both in form and in content the English citizen is aided by his law in this aim to a degree unimaginable to his Scottish counterpart. Leaving aside offences not wholly within the field of public order and carping over antiquities such as 'going armed to the terror of Her Majesty's subjects',[147] the 1986 Act provides a self-contained public order code for England. The Scottish citizen must look to common law (some of it so old that it can scarcely be presumed directly applicable in modern conditions), to the Civic Government (Scotland) Act 1982, to the very messy application to Scotland of the Public Order Act 1986 and the 1982 Act's regulation of the relationship between the two (inserted by the 1986 Act in the 1982 Act) and to the Trespass (Scotland) Act 1865. As to content, the 1986 Act fails in some contexts[148] adequately to define key concepts within the definition of criminal offences; but, for the most part, it makes the effort, and the redesigned riot, affray and violent disorder provisions reflect the lengthy consideration given to their elements by the Law Commission and respondents to its Working Paper. There are structuring principles for the exercise of controls over processions and assemblies. Scots law is remarkable for the absence of these guides to certainty.

These differences in the substantive law of the two jurisdictions raise another issue, that of the convergence or divergence of the two systems. Part of nationalist objections to closer European unity lies in the fear that an over-mighty central legislature might extinguish justifiable differences between the legal systems of the member-states. Certainly in the case of Scotland and England, after almost three hundred years of sharing a legislature and in view of the provisions of art. XVIII of the Treaty of Union between England and Scotland, which presumptively permit unification of *public* law (whilst permitting unification of private law only 'for the evident utility' of the subjects of Scotland[149]), we would expect this process of convergence to be far advanced.

Of course, the *meaning* of 'convergence' or of 'divergence' is not free from ambiguity. At the one extreme would be the position of two legal systems with nothing in common save by accident; no means of enforcing each other's decisions and no commonly-arrived-at policies underlying specific rules. At the other would be a system of unified courts subject to a common final appellate authority and a common legislature, applying the same legislative texts and with all courts applying each other's interpretation of the rules embodied in those texts or derived elsewhere, e.g. from common law. The relationship between Scots and English law necessarily falls between these extremes. In deciding whether they are advancing towards or receding from the converged state, however, it is suggested that the following tests are relevant: is the balance between common law and statutory law within each system on a given subject the same, becoming the same, or becoming more different; whether embodied in statute or common law, are the *policies* underlying the rules of law tending to become more alike or more different; and even if the underlying statutory *policies* are the same, are they tending increasingly or decreasingly to be embodied in identical textual form? From the foregoing analysis of substantive public order law, the somewhat surprising conclusion is that the law not only shows few signs of converging, but even shows signs of *diverging*. Thus, the textually common regulation of prior controls over processions in the Public Order Act 1936 has been succeeded by a textually separate series of controls under the Civic Government Act 1982 and the Public Order Act 1986. Even more surprising is that the common *policy* under the 1936 Act has been succeeded by a radically different policy in the controlling English and Scottish Acts. Likewise, in the case of offences against public order, where previously there had been a common core of statutory offences and a series of (probably more important) separate common law offences, now English law is almost entirely statutory, whereas the most common *and* the most important Scots law offences remain common law; moreover, there is no question of the new statutory English offences being similar in policy to the Scottish ones. Although it goes beyond the scope of this essay to produce evidence to that effect, this trend towards divergence is surprisingly common across the field of public law (although there are also large areas where the reverse is the case; for example James Wolffe in the present volume).

This leads to the final observation offered on the basis of ten years' evolution (the word eschews the concept of *improvement* over time) of public order law in the two systems. Why are they becoming more different? Is it that Parliament can hold in its collective head two separate notions of 'the public good', one for Scotland and one for England, based on the differing needs and social problems of the two nations? In theory the continued existence of two separate legal systems with different policies underlying legislation requires that it should. In practice it is not suggested that such feats of liberal intellectualism are the real explanation. Rather, Parliament cares little about the rules under which Scots live. There are well-rehearsed explanations as to why Scots business takes so little of the time of Parliament, and why Scots MPs, who want to make their name in the larger UK pond, are unwilling to spend much time on purely Scottish affairs. And certainly it is true that the complexity of any legal system reflects the number of varieties of any social problem which it has to regulate, and indirectly thereby the relative populations so that we should not be surprised in principle that English law makes greater demands on Parliamentary time. The relationship between population and legal complexity is far from direct, however, and while Scots law retains its formal independence across the whole of private law and much of public law, it is ludicrous to suppose that it can be dealt with in 10 per cent of the time spent by Parliament on legislation which would be its "fair share" on a population basis. The Public Order Bill merited (or took) 34 sessions and 1042 columns of discussion in Committee stage in the Commons and 246 columns even in Committee in the Lords, and, of the total time, about half was devoted to Part II (controls over processions and assemblies). Part IV of the Civic Government Bill (the Scottish equivalent to Part II of the 1986 Act) was introduced as a series of amendments in the Lords, receiving 25 columns of discussion[150] and, as one part of a massive Bill concerned more with local government than with civil liberties, a similarly restricted proportion of the already short debates on an elephantine Bill.

Nor could it be argued, in this case, that what was being done was merely an extension to Scotland of a principle already established in English law, since the reformulation of the 1936 Act for England was still four years distant. By the same token it is difficult to see how the pitched battle fought over what became s. 5 of the 1986 Act could occur in the knowledge that an even less liberal regime had applied since time immemorial in Scotland. The answer, of course, is that on the part of most participants in the Parliamentary struggle there was no such knowledge. English law is made on the basis of (comparatively) principled debate. In the UK legislature, Scots law is made on the nod by a tiny clique of the great and good (and also politicians) and rubber-stamped by Parliament.[151]

Notes

1. In Mitchell's case the 2nd edition of his *Constitutional Law* W. Green & Son Ltd (1968); in Bradley's his book-length contribution *'Administrative Law'* to the *Stair Memorial Encyclopaedia of the Laws of Scotland* (1988) Butterworths vol 1.

2. Or perhaps the second in that some criteria of choice and ordering of material for further study is involved after a preliminary survey of the area of study.

3. E.g. those assembling with a view to processing presumably constitute an assembly (although the Public Order Act 1986 s. 12(11) appears to proceed on the assumption that the assembly forms part and parcel of the procession).

4. Trespass (Scotland) Act 1865.

5. *Rothesay Town Council, Petnrs* (1898) 14 Sh Ct Rep 189, *Burgh of Dunblane, Petnrs* 1947 SLT (Sh Ct) 27; but *cf contra Aldred v Langmuir* 1932 JC 22.

6. Representation of The People Act 1949 s. 82.

7. *McAra v Mags of Edinburgh* 1913 SC 1059 *per* the Lord President (Dunedin).

8. Act of 1606 c 16.

9. For a full explanation of where and how the system worked see W. Finnie 'The Burgh Police Acts: A Summary' (1981) 26 JLSS 447.

10. Edinburgh Corporation Order Confirmation Act 1967 s. 184.

11. Aberdeen Corporation (General Powers) Order Confirmation Act 1938 s. 182.

12. *Ibid* s. 182(3).

13. *The Scotsman* 8 September 1981 (Orange march).

14. S. 184.

15. Greenock Corporation Act 1909 s. 424.

16. *Loyal Orange Lodge No. 493 Hawick First Purple v Roxburgh DC* 1981 SLT 33.

17. Public Order Act 1936 s. 8(5), repealed by District Courts (Scotland) Act 1975 Schedule 3.

18. The objective requirement of reasonable belief was deliberately introduced as an amendment to the original Bill to ensure judicial reviewability.

19. *The Law Relating to Public Order* Fifth Report from the Home Affairs Committee (1979–80) HC 756–1 para 24.

20. *Report on the Brixton Disorders 10–12 April 1981* Cmnd 8427 (1981) para 7.42.

21. Public Order Act 1936 s. 3(2).

22. See *op cit* note 19 *supra* paras 52–55; *op cit* note 20 *supra* paras 7.47–7.49.

23. On Scottish practice see K.D. Ewing and W. Finnie: *Civil Liberties in Scotland* (1st ed) W. Green & Son (1982) 155–157.

24. *James Cumming, John Grant and Others* (1848) J. Shaw 17; G. Gordon: Criminal Law (2nd ed) W. Green & Son (1978) 967.

25. Unreported but see Scottish Law Commission Memorandum No. 44 *Mobbing and Rioting* (1984) para 2.8.

26. 1922 JC 1.

27. See *Hancock v HMA* 1981 SCCR 32.

28. See Scottish Law Commission *op cit* note 25 *supra passim*.

29. *John Robertson et al* (1842) 1 Brown 152.

30. See note 26 *supra*.

31. *R v Howell* [1982] QB 416; *Albert v Lavin* [1982] AC 546; Thornton: *Public Order Law* Financial Training (1987) 73–74.

32. *Wilson v Brown* 1982 SCCR 49.

33. M. Christie *Breach of the Peace* Butterworths (1990) 85–95.

34. (1882) 10 R(J) 22.

35. J.D.B. Mitchell *Constitutional Law* W. Green & Sons (2nd ed 1968) at 333.

36. Christie *op cit* note 33 *supra* at 6, citing Hume "Commentaries on the Law of Scotland respecting Crimes" (4th Ed, 1844) vol 1 p 25.

37. For further information on these cases see Christie *op cit* note 33 *supra* at 102–104 and Ewing and Finnie *op cit* note 23 *supra* (2nd ed 1988) 412–14.

38. *Young v Heatley* 1959 JC 66; for the more obvious case of conduct in private producing an effect on the public in general see *Ferguson v Carnochan* (1889) 16 R(J) 93.
39. 'Breach of The Peace' 1959 SLT (News) 229.
40. See note 32 *supra*.
41. In Section B1 above.
42. Burgh Police Act 1892 s. 380(14) and (53); Glasgow Corporation Consolidation (General Powers) Provisional Order Confirmation Act 1960 s. 160(32); Aberdeen Corporation (General Powers) Order Confirmation Act 1938 s. 188(33).
43. Now Highways Act 1980 s. 137.
44. 1924 JC 117.
45. *Dougall v Dykes* (1861) 4 Irv 101.
46. Criminal Justice (Scotland) Act 1980 s. 1.
47. *Thomas v Sawkins* [1935] 2 KB 249.
48. *O'Moran v DPP* [1975] 1 All ER 473.
49. [1973] AC 854. See also P. Wallington 'Insulting Behaviour and Public Protest' 1973 SLT (News) 31.
50. Burgh Police Act 1892 s. 380(9), (10) and (12); Greenock Corporation Act 1909 s. 368; Dundee Corporation (Consolidated Powers) Order Confirmation Act 1957 s. 467(5), (6)(b) and (7); Aberdeen Corporation (General Powers) Order Confirmation Act 1938 s. 186(b)(ii); Glasgow Corporation Consolidation (General Powers) Order Confirmation Act 1960 s. 152(1) and (8); Edinburgh Corporation Order Confirmation Act 1967 s. 450.
51. *Jordan v Burgoyne* [1963] 2 QB 744; *Parkin v Norman* [1983] QB 92.
52. 14 May 1984 HC Debs cols 358–9.
53. *R v Kamara* [1974] AC 104.
54. *De Morgan v Metropolitan Board of Works* (1880) 5 QBD 155; as in Scotland there was an exception for political meetings during a General Election (Representation of the People Act 1949 ss. 82 and 83).
55. *Harrison v Duke of Rutland* [1893] 1 QB 142.
56. Home Affairs Committee *op cit* note 19 *supra*; a complete list of local Act provisions requiring notice is given in vol II at 230–231 of the Report.
57. Highways Act 1959 s. 2.
58. [1957] 1 QB 552.
59. Law Commission *Offences Relating to Public Order* (Law Commission No. 123) (1983–84) HC 85 at 12.
60. [1966] AC 591.
61. [1973] AC 964.
62. *Ibid*.
63. *Ibid* at 987.
64. See note 60 *supra*.
65. Law Commission *op cit* note 56 *supra* para 3.28; in fact the eventual decision was that it was *not* necessary to show the actual effect; *A-G's Reference (No. 3 of 1983)* [1983] 1 All ER 501.
66. *Ibid* para 3.41.
67. [1907] 2 KB 853 at 860.
68. *R v Sharp and Johnson* [1957] 1 QB 552.
69. See Law Commission Working Paper No. 82 *Offences Against Public Order* para 2.43 quoting the perplexity of Lambard 400 years ago.
70. *Ibid* at 38–43 discusses the division of opinion among influential writers.
71. [1982] QB 458.
72. (1883) 9 QBD 308.
73. (1882) 10 R(J) 22.
74. *Wise v Dunning* [1902] 1 KB 167.
75. *R v Howell* [1982] QB 416 at 426.
76. *Lansbury v Riley* [1914] 3 KB 229; *R v Sandbach ex p Williams* [1935] 2 KB 192.

77. Magistrates Courts Act 1952 s. 91 (now Magistrates Courts Act 1980 s. 115); Justices of The Peace Act 1968 s. 1(7).
78. Magistrates' Courts (Appeals From Binding Over Orders) Act 1956.
79. [1935] 2 KB 249.
80. As to other offences see *Swales v Cox* [1981] 1 All ER 1115.
81. In Scotland this is laid down in the Police (Scotland) Act 1967 s. 17 which has no direct English counterpart, though it is quite clearly true at common law (*R v Brown* (1841) Car. & M 314).
82. (1864) 17 1rCLR 1.
83. (1883) 14 LR 1r 105.
84. Now Police Act 1964 s. 51(3).
85. [1936] 1 KB 218.
86. [1961] 1 WLR 162.
87. E.g. *Alexander v Smith* 1984 SLT 176.
88. *Curlett v McKechnie* 1938 JC 176.
89. *The Scotsman* 14 May 1981.
90. Home Office *Review of Public Order Law* Cmnd 9510 (1985) 5.
91. [1985] IRLR 76.
92. Scottish Office *Report of the Working Party on Civic Government* (1986).
93. Cmnd 7891 (1980).
94. *Proposals For a Code of Civic Government in Scotland* Cmnd 7958 (1980).
95. Civic Government (Scotland) Act 1982 s. 62.
96. See J.L. Murdoch 'The Civic Government Act and Public Processions' (1984) SCOLAG 144 and J.L. Murdoch 'Protest and Public Order' 1988 SLT (News) 165.
97. Civic Government (Scotland) Act 1982 s. 62(3).
98. S. 63.
99. See e.g. *The Scotsman* 21 August 1987 (Aberdeen ban on Orange march, and only on legal advice not extended to a blanket ban on such processions) and J.L. Murdoch 'Protest and Public Order' 1988 SLT (News) 165.
100. Civic Government (Scotland) Act 1982 s. 64.
101. Based on returns to a questionnaire sent by the present writer to local authority officers.
102. Civic Government (Scotland) Act 1982 s. 65(1).
103. Public Order Act 1986 s. 12(11).
104. *Ibid* s. 12(2).
105. *Ibid* s. 12(1).
106. Civic Government (Scotland) Act 1982 s. 66.
107. Public Order Act 1986 s. 16.
108. *Ibid* ss. 14(2) and 15.
109. *Ibid* s. 14(1).
110. Scottish Law Commission Memorandum No. 44 *Mobbing and Rioting* (1984).
111. 1981 SCCR 32.
112. And incidentally would produce the same result as the universally-execrated South African case of the Sharpeville Six who were condemned to death for a murder by members of a mob of which they formed part, but in which they personally took no part.
113. *21st Annual Report* paras 2.8–2.9.
114. Public Order Act 1986 s. 18.
115. *Ibid* s. 19.
116. *Ibid* s. 20.
117. *Ibid* s. 21.
118. *Ibid* s. 22.
119. Cmnd 5919 (1975).
120. *Fifth Report of the Home Affairs Committee: The Law Relating to Public Order* (1979–80) HC 756.
121. Cmnd 7891 (1980).
122. Working Paper No. 82 (1982).

123. *Criminal Law: Offences Relating to Public Order* (Law Commission No. 123) (1983–84) HC 85.
124. Cmnd 9510 (1985).
125. Public Order Act 1036 s. 11.
126. *Ibid* s. 11(2).
127. *Ibid* s. 12(5) and (6).
128. *Ibid* s. 12(7).
129. *Ibid* s. 12(1).
130. *Ibid* s. 15.
131. *Ibid* s. 12(2).
132. *Ibid* s. 13.
133. *Ibid* s. 13(4).
134. *Ibid* s. 9. Law Commission *op cit* note 118 *supra* paras 1.5–1.6 and 2.1.
135. Public Order Act 1986 s. 6(1).
136. *Ibid* s. 1(1).
137. *Op cit* note 123 *supra* para 5.23.
138. Public Order Act 1986 ss. 2 and 6(2).
139. *Ibid* s. 3(1).
140. *Ibid* s. 8.
141. *Ibid* s. 3(3).
142. *Ibid* s. 6(2).
143. This overrides the rule under the 1936 Act s. 5 that a threatener etc. benefits from the unusual stolidity of an audience such as a policeman (*Parkin v Norman* [1983] QB 92).
144. Public Order Act 1936 s. 4(1).
145. P. Thornton *Public Order Law* Financial Training (1987) at 42, quoting the New Zealand case of *Melser v Police* [1967] NZLR 437.
146. Public Order Act 1986 s. 5(3).
147. See A.T.H. Smith 'The Public Order Act 1986' [1987] *Crim L R* 156 at 158.
148. Particularly in s. 5.
149. This proceeds on the assumption that unification would not be achieved by England adopting Scots law rules.
150. 9 March 1982 HL Debs cols 122–147.
151. For a particulary egregious recent example see W. Finnie 'International Co-operation Against Crime and Scots Legislation' 1990 SLT (News) 205.

Administrative Law

The Nature of the Supervisory Jurisdiction and the Public/Private Distinction in Scots Administrative Law

The Hon. Lord Clyde

There are few better starting-points for a consideration of judicial review than the writings of Lord Kames. In his work on *Equity*[1] he writes: 'It belongs to a court of police to regulate commerce and other public matters. The Court of Session is not a court of police: but it is a court of review, to take under consideration the proceedings of courts of police, and to rectify such as are against the public interest. This jurisdiction is inherent in the Court of Session as the supreme court in civil matters, founded on the great principle. That every wrong must have a remedy.' In his *Historical Law Tracts*[2] the matter is explored at greater length and with more reserve. He criticises the narrow approach adopted by the Court and observes:

> No defect in the constitution of a state deserves greater reproach than the giving licence to wrong without affording redress. Upon this account it is the province, one should imagine, of the sovereign, and supreme court, to redress wrongs of every kind, when a peculiar remedy is not provided. Under the cognisance of the privy council in Scotland came many injuries, which, by the abolition of that court, are left without any peculiar remedy: and the Court of Session have with reluctance been obliged to listen to complaints of various kinds that belonged properly to the privy council while it had a being. A new branch of jurisdiction has thus sprung up in the Court of Session, which daily increasing by new matter will probably in time produce a new maxim. That it is the province of this court, to redress all wrongs for which no other remedy is provided. We are, however, as yet far from being ripe for adopting this maxim. The utility of it is indeed perceived, but perceived too obscurely to have any steady influence on the practice of the court, and for that reason their proceedings in such matters are far from uniform.

Examples of the varied complaints which came before the former Scottish Privy Council can be found in the records. One can find in the early years of the sixteenth century a variety of matters of public administration considered, such as the disputed audit of the accounts of the burgh of Aberdeen[3] as well as complaints by private individuals based on the unorderly proceedings of magistrates and inferior authorities.[4] To take an example from the end of the century, in 1593 the Council by a suspension enabled a vacant professorship in the University of St Andrews to be filled by election in accordance with statute rather than by the following of an order of seniority among the teaching staff.[5] Further to that the Privy Council exercised ministerial powers which, as Erskine states,[6] 'if they were not now transferred to the Court of Session there would be a defect in that part of our constitution, and many wrongs would be without a remedy. For which reason the author of *Historical Law Tracts* reasonably conjectures that it will soon be considered as part of the province of the Court of Session to redress all wrongs for which a peculiar remedy is not otherwise provided'. But it is not to be supposed that Lord Kames was concerned only with what may be described as ministerial matters. In the chapter in *Equity* from which the first quotation was taken he instances not only the regulation by the Court of Session of the hours for the holding of a market in Stirling but the control of monopolies in relation both to commercial affairs and to rights of audience before the bailie-court at Leith. Examples of what Lord Kames may have had in mind in his reference to matters of police may be found in *Morison's Dictionary* under the title 'Public Police'. That title encompasses not only questions of public nuisance, such as iron manufacturing, glass works, blacksmiths and fencing schools, but also review of the decisions of magistrates in matters of building, of Justices of the Peace in the matter of their orders for mending roads, and of statutory trustees. Indeed, one of the cases recognises the principle to which Lord Kames refers. In *Proprietors of Carrubber's Close v William Reoch*[7] an advocation was taken in a matter relating to the building of a wright's shop in a crowded town where it was thought that the building might constitute a fire hazard. The extent of the Court's power to intervene was discussed, but it appears to have been recognised that 'the Court of Session indeed may correct unsuitable regulations made by the Dean of Guild upon the principle that every wrong must have a remedy'.

Lord Kames had no doubt where the basis for the Court's power of review lay. 'This extraordinary process of redressing wrongs, far from a novelty, has a name appropriated to it in the language of our law. For what else is meant by the *nobile officium* of the Court of Session, so much talked of and so little understood?'[8] As the law has developed, the term has undergone a significant change. In the hands of Stair the distinction was drawn between an *officium nobile* and an *officium ordinarium*, the former being an extraordinary equitable power and the latter involving a strict adherence to the ordinary forms of process.[9] But once the Sheriff Court had come to develop its own equitable jurisdiction a simple equation between the *nobile officium* and equity was no longer apt. The term *nobile officium* came to be used at least in the context of civil cases to describe what is seen as a distinct branch of judicial activity confined to a somewhat restricted series of situations where resort has to be made to an exceptional remedy to meet an extraordinary or unforeseen problem. Thus More in his notes to Stair deals distinctly with cases falling under the *nobile officium* and cases of review.[10] Lord Wark, writing both in the first volume of the Stair Society's publications[11] and in *Green's Encyclopaedia*,[12] while he lists judicial review as one of the classes of exercise of the *nobile officium*, adds that it is not strictly speaking an equitable jurisdiction but that it introduces equitable considerations into all matters dealt with in the inferior courts. In *Forbes v Underwood*[13] Lord President Inglis observed of the Court's power of review that 'it is not of very much consequence to determine whether it is in the exercise of its high equitable jurisdiction, or in the performance of what is sometimes called its *nobile officium*.' But whether or not the term *nobile officium* is appropriate nowadays in relation to the source of the jurisdiction for judicial review, if the basis is to be found in the equitable power of the Court of Session as a Supreme Court and the principle is that every wrong must have a remedy then the power to redress wrongs ought to be absolute in its width. The only prerequisite for its use is that there should be no other remedy provided. By definition the jurisdiction is the prerogative of a supreme court.

The distinction between the power to provide remedies in extraordinary and unforeseen circumstances, to which the term *nobile officium* is sometimes restricted, and the power to review decisions of inferior courts, which has already been noticed in Erskine, is also adopted by Alison in his *Practice of the Criminal Law of Scotland*.[14] He there recognises the existence in the Justiciary Court of a power akin to the *nobile officium* of the Court of Session for providing a remedy for any unforeseen occurrence in the course of criminal business in any part of the country. The passage was quoted with approval in *Wylie v LA*,[15] where a quotation was also made from Moncrieff on *Review in Criminal Cases*: 'In addition to its power of reviewing, the High Court of Justiciary as the Supreme Court in criminal matters has in respect of its *nobile officium* the power of interfering in extraordinary circumstances for the purpose of preventing injustice or oppression although there may not be any judgement, conviction or warrant brought under review.' In practice the High Court appears to recognise that both in cases of extraordinary remedies and in cases of review where no alternative remedy exists the Court is exercising its *nobile officium*. In *Wylie* what was sought was review of a sentence and it was under the *nobile officium* that the Court recognised its jurisdiction.

The narrow meaning of the term *nobile officium* is reflected in the forms of action that have been employed to invoke it. In civil matters, when the remedy sought was against the determination of some inferior body, various forms of action were available, of which declarator, suspension, reduction, and advocation, were the most obvious examples. On the other hand, where a remedy was sought for an exceptional eventuality the application came to be one by petition to the *nobile officium* in the Inner House. Something of a parallel situation can be seen in relation to the High Court of Justiciary, although the definitions may there not be so clearly cut. Hume[16] states that the forms of process for review of the decrees of inferior courts are advocation, suspension and appeal. Reduction was not suitable for a court which has no permanent or stated time for sitting. Advocation was formerly used in both the Court of Session and the High Court but was abolished in the former case by s. 64 of the Court of Session Act 1868. Advocation in the High Court has come to be regarded as the form of review available to the prosecutor, although it is not technically so restricted.[17] Suspension remains as a means of review in both the Court of Session and the High Court, albeit by distinct forms of application. In practice the distinction is recognised by the High Court in so far as what might generally be described as matters of judicial review are raised by way of a Bill of Suspension and matters arising out of extraordinary and unforeseen circumstances are raised by way of petition to the *nobile officium*. Thus, questions of fundamental nullity in the proceedings or oppression or breach of the rules of natural justice are raised by a Bill of Suspension.[18] A possible partiality of the judge[19] and the necessity for justice to be seen to be done[20] are matters canvassed in a Bill of Suspension. On the other hand, recourse to the *nobile officium* may extend to all kinds of relief in extraordinary and unforeseen circumstances.[21] In *Muirhead*[22] a petition for production of shorthand notes was made under the *nobile officium*. But the procedural distinction is not a precise one. In *Rae*[23] the Court held that a trial judge had acted oppressively in refusing to certify a case as having been of 'exceptional length' for purposes of the legal aid provisions. The application was in effect for review of the decision. The Court had 'no difficulty in accepting that the High Court of Justiciary as the supreme court in criminal matters has, in respect of its nobile officium, the power of interfering in extraordinary circumstances for the purpose of preventing injustice or oppression'. In *Gerrard*[24] a petition was brought under the *nobile officium* seeking to suspend an order made by the Sheriff for detention of a witness prior to a trial. That appears to reflect the basic position that whatever may be the form of procedure and the proper terminology the Supreme Court has the power to give redress in case of wrong where no other remedy exists. In some cases the term *nobile officium* has been restricted to unforeseen and exceptional circumstances.[25] In *Berry*[26] it was held to be incompetent to invoke the *nobile officium* on the same grounds as those which would have been open under the form of redress provided by statute. In *Gibbon*[27] what might be seen as an *ultra vires* decision of the Sheriff was in effect quashed in an application to the *nobile officium* without any express reference to any extraordinary circumstances unless the absence of any statutory right of appeal is to be seen as providing that factor.

It may be observed in passing that the diversion of jurisdiction between civil and criminal matters in this context has not always been recognised. At one time, it seems that the Lords of Session would review sentences of lower courts in certain criminal cases and indeed there was a view formerly expressed that they could review proceedings of the Court of Justiciary.[28] But the latter view appeared to have been put to rest in 1684[29] and there are several examples in the notes to Hume's text[30] to show that the former practice was recognised as incompetent at least by the nineteenth century. In *McCaul v Millar*,[31] review of a matter arising in the police court being of a criminal nature was held to be incompetent in the Court of Session. It was observed that it was the proper duty of the Court of Justiciary to review such matters, whether by advocation or suspension. What was and what was not a criminal matter was however still open to debate. In *Phillips v Steel*[32] the Court of Session held that it had jurisdiction to review a conviction arising from a breach of the terms of a liquor licence by allowing tippling during the hours of divine service. It was considered that this was a breach of regulations and not a criminal matter. Following that and like cases, the High Court of Justiciary held in *Park v Earl of Stair*[33] that a Bill of Suspension against a conviction and fine under a local fishery statute where proceedings were instituted by a party and not by the procurator-fiscal and where the offence was merely the contravention of a statute was incompetent. In *Bruce v Linton*,[34] suspension of a statutory offence was brought in the civil court. On the other hand, in *Scott v Muir and Annan*[35] a reduction of a summary conviction of an alleged breach of the Act of 1621, c. 23 anent card-playing was held to be, as a criminal procedure, outwith the jurisdiction of the Court of Session. A distinction between statutory offences and common law crimes might not hold today, when statutory offences have become even more common, although a recognition of matters of breach of regulation not involving criminality is something which should perhaps not be lost. It cannot, however, be affirmed that all matters relating to criminal proceedings require to be taken to the High Court rather than the Court of Session for review. In the matter of review of a decision to refuse a grant of criminal legal aid it was held in *Reynolds v Christie*,[36] where the refusal was by a magistrate of the District Court, that review in the Court of Session was incompetent. But, after the granting of legal aid in criminal cases was taken over by an independent Board regulated by the Secretary of State, it was held in *K v Scottish Legal Aid Board*[37] that a decision of that Board in a matter of criminal legal aid was open to review in the Court of Session.

The wide scope of the jurisdiction of the Court in matters of judicial review may also be seen in the matter of *locus standi*. In this context further quotation may be made from Lord Kames's *Historical Law Tracts*:

> The only difficulty is, How far this extraordinary jurisdiction of nobile officium is or ought to be extended. The jurisdiction of the Court of Session, as a court of common law, is confined to matters of pecuniary interest; and it possibly may be thought that its extraordinary jurisdiction ought to be confined within the same bounds . . . . But the power to redress wrongs of all kinds must subsist somewhere in every state: and in Scotland subsists normally in the Court of Session. And with respect to the wrongs in particular that came under the jurisdiction of the privy council, our legislature, when they annihilated that court, must have intended that its powers should so far devolve upon the Court of Session; for the legislature could not intend to leave without a remedy, the many wrongs that belonged to the jurisdiction of the privy council.'

The Court has, however, now moved away from an insistence in every case on the presence of a pecuniary interest. A recognition of the wider approach can be seen in the line of cases relating to the Court's intervention in the affairs of churches and voluntary associations. In *Forbes v Eden*[38] it was affirmed that without averments of the violation of a civil right the Court will not interfere in the affairs of a non-established church. The point was further developed in *McDonald v Burns*, where Lord Justice-Clerk

Aitchison[39] identified in general terms two situations where the Court would intervene in the judgments of ecclesiastical bodies. One was where the body had acted *ultra vires* 'and in a manner calculated to affect the civil rights and patrimonial interests' of any of its members. The second was where the procedure of the tribunal had been marked by gross irregularity. In *St Johnstone Football Club Ltd v Scottish Football Association Ltd*[40] it was held that in cases falling into that second category, that is cases of gross irregularity, the Court had jurisdiction whether or not there was interference with the civil rights and patrimonial interests of the members. The point is now seen as one of interest to sue. In *Gunstone v Scottish Women's Amateur Athletic Association*[41] the sufficiency of the interest required is said to be a matter of circumstances in which considerations of patrimonial or pecuniary or proprietary interest are not regarded necessarily as definitive tests. In relation to voluntary associations this development of the law appears to be realising Lord Kames's principle that every wrong should have a remedy, although the development has found expression not in terms of the competency of the action or the scope of the jurisdiction but in terms of the *locus standi* of the applicant. The development, moreover, has occurred similarly in cases not concerned with private voluntary associations. The case of *Wilson v Independent Broadcasting Authority*[42] may serve as an example. While differences can be drawn between the situation of a voluntary association from which a member can withdraw if dissatisfied with its administration and a body from the control of which withdrawal is practically impossible, the same approach in principle so far as *locus standi* is concerned now seems to be recognised. If the application of the principle depends essentially upon the circumstances of the case, the basic criteria for *locus standi* may be the same in all situations where the Court is exercising its extraordinary power to redress wrong.

The foregoing consideration of *locus standi* demonstrates the width of the subject-matter with which the supervisory jurisdiction is concerned. It extends not only to the actings of central government and of local authorities but to voluntary associations and private bodies. Indeed, the jurisdiction of the Court of Session to reduce the awards of private arbitrations, albeit restricted by the Articles of Regulation 1695, is to be traced to the same root as that identified by Lord Kames. In *Forbes v Underwood*[43] it was held that the power to compel an arbiter to proceed was indistinguishable from the exclusive power which the Supreme Court possesses to review the actings of inferior judges as well as statutory trustees and commissioners. The obligation to keep within his jurisdiction and to follow all the rules for securing the proper administration of justice are based on the common law[44] and it is at common law that redress is open.

Given the variety of the bodies over which the Court's powers may extend it is difficult and probably undesirable to attempt an exhaustive catalogue of them, far less to identify any single characteristic which would encompass the whole. Such a classification is, however, sought to be made in England in the distinction between what is called 'public law' and 'private law'. An authoritative definition was formulated by Lord Justice Woolf[45] to the effect that public law enforces the proper performance by public bodies of the duties which they have to the public while private law protects the private rights either of private individuals or public individuals. The public are the beneficiaries of what is protected by public law and the individuals or bodies who enjoy private rights are the beneficiaries of the protection provided by private law.[46] While the distinction may be useful in England, where judicial review has grown from the specialised forms of action used in what might be seen as the public sphere, there seems to be no obvious reason why the classification should necessarily be seen as directly and completely applicable in Scotland. As Sir John Donaldson MR noted in *R v East Berkshire Health Authority, ex parte Walsh*,[47] the Scottish procedure of reduction is 'akin to *certiorari*, but it is available whether or not the claim involves "public" or "administrative" law'. The decision in that case was, however, applied in the recent Scottish case of *Tehrani v Argyll and Clyde Health Board (No. 2)*.[48]

The distinction developed in England has been described as necessary because of the role which the Court is required to perform, a role different from that which it traditionally has performed in private law disputes.[49] In private law the Courts decide the facts and apply the law to them, deciding what is reasonable and applying their own standards, bearing in mind considerations of public policy. On the other hand, in public law the Courts do not usually find the facts and do not specify what is reasonable; moreover, their views on policy are not relevant because the statute places the responsibility for the decision on the public body responsible for making the decision. The principle that the Court may not usurp the function of the particular authority has long been recognised as applicable in Scotland. As Lord Shaw put it, 'it is not within the power or function of the Court of Session itself to do work set by the Legislature to be performed by those administrative bodies or inferior judicatories themselves'.[50] But in Scotland the different role which the Court plays in matters of judicial review as distinct from an ordinary action does not appear to relate to any difference between the nature of the rights or duties which are under consideration, whether 'public' or 'private', or of the bodies who are the parties to the case, whether 'public' or 'private'. The difference in role appears rather to be nothing more than a difference of function. In an ordinary action the Court is exercising an original jurisdiction. In that context it is required to find facts, apply the law, decide what is reasonable and apply its standards. Its jurisdiction encompasses the whole merits and substance of the issue before it and it has the competence to determine the whole matter both in respect of the fact and of the law.

On the other hand, in matters of judicial review the Court is not exercising an original jurisdiction but a supervisory one. The whole subject-matter is not within its competence. The Court steps in after the body in question has acted or failed to act. Usually the Court is concerned with a decision or resolution or determination or some kind made by some individual or corporate body. It is not for the Court to reassess the facts or to impose its own decision on the issue. It is concerned with procedure, to secure that the decision has been made fairly and properly. To an extent it is concerned with the merits. If the decision is utterly unreasonable the Court may intervene. It may intervene if the decision has proceeded with no factual basis. But it does not explore the facts of the matter resolved upon, not because the case is one of public law but because the Court's function is one of review. Similarly, the Court's view on the policy aspect of the decision which is challenged is not of relevance, not because that is a matter of public law but because the Court is exercising a function of review as opposed to an original jurisdiction. The supervisory character of the jurisdiction presupposes the existence of some individual or body whose behaviour is subject to supervision; however, it is not easy to see why any distinction should be drawn between the kinds of individual or body concerned or why it should make a difference if the functions which are exercised by the individual or body are based on statute as opposed to contract.

The same difference in respect of function can be identified if the matter is considered from a point of view of remedies. This distinction has already been recognised by Professor Bradley in his valuable article on administrative law in the *Stair Encyclopaedia*.[51] When what is sought is implement of a contract no speciality arises if the defender is a public body rather than a private individual. When the remedy sought is one of reparation, then the action to be raised is an ordinary action for damages. That will apply whether the wrong in question was a delict, a quasi-delict or a breach of contract and whether the defender is a governmental body, a local authority, a commercial organisation or a private individual. Interdict has been sought in an ordinary action against an Electricity Board based on a departure from an alleged contract for the supply of fuel.[52] No difference arises between public and private law in this context. Where the claim for damages is based on actings alleged to be *ultra vires* or contrary to natural justice, as for example on the part of a disciplinary committee, an ordinary action is appropriate.[53] Where reparation is sought from a public body on the grounds of a negligent exercise of a statutory power, an ordinary action will lie.[54] In such a case it is not evident that the character of the defenders as public or private is of any significance. Where the remedy sought is one of payment of a sum due under a statutory provision, the action may competently be brought in the Sheriff Court, where the jurisdiction sought to be invoked is not a jurisdiction of review. It was on that ground that Lord Fraser distinguished the case of *McTavish v Commissioners of Caledonian Canal*[55] in *Brown v Hamilton DC*.[56] On the other hand, where what is sought is a declarator of invalidity or a reduction, then the action is competent only in the Court of Session because it is then that the supervisory jurisdiction is being invoked and the action is in that respect in a distinct class. It is not any element of the public or private nature of the dispute which makes the difference but the nature of the jurisdiction which is being invoked and the kind of remedy which may be required. The fact that in applications for judicial review a wide variety of remedies is open does not affect the basic position. It is, obviously, convenient that in the same process wherein the supervisory jurisdiction is invoked a whole range of remedies should be available. It may be noted that a question might still be raised about the competency of suspension and interdict in the Sheriff Court in matters open to judicial review. In *McGowan v City of Glasgow*

Friendly Society,[57] as Lord Dunpark observed in the Court of Session in *Brown v Hamilton DC*,[58] the crave for declarator was dropped, the only remedy sought was interdict and the issue of competency did not arise. On the other hand, in *Bell v The Trustees*,[59] which also involved a motion for interdict, the Sheriff expressed grave doubt about the competency of the proceedings.

The making of categories to identify various types of case undoubtedly has its uses but the practice may also tend to restrain the free exercise of an equitable jurisdiction. The classification of tribunals as ministerial or judicial, or as judicial or quasi-judicial has long been recognised as not of much importance.[60] Indeed, the view has been expressed that there is no reason to retain the word 'quasi-judicial' within the vocabulary of administrative law.[61] The classification of the grounds of review as illegality, irrationality, procedural impropriety and perhaps proportionality should never be regarded as definitive or exhaustive. Accordingly, one approaches the introduction of a classification of public and private matters with some caution.

But the recognition of a distinction between 'public' and 'private' law in the field of judicial review has featured in certain recent applications to the Scottish Courts. It is raised, however, not as an issue of the jurisdiction or power of the Court of Session. It would indeed be difficult to argue that the power of review was restricted by consideration of the public or private nature of the issue. The case of *Forbes v Underwood*[62] related to a dispute between the ingoing and outgoing tenants of a farm and it is not easy to see an arbiter in that matter as performing a public function. What has prompted the use of the distinction in Scotland is the introduction of the new procedure for judicial review contained in Rule of Court 260B. But it has to be remembered that this rule is purely a procedural measure. It does not in any way affect the jurisdiction of the Court of Session as it, in fact, states. The question has been raised purely as a matter of the competency of adopting the expeditious procedure for an application under Rule of Court 260B instead of that of an ordinary action.

Credit for the initiative for the new procedure is attributed to Lord Fraser. In *Brown v Hamilton District Council*[63] he recommended a special procedure 'for dealing with questions in the public law area, comparable to the English prerogative orders'. In *Stevenson v Midlothian District Council*[64] he spoke of the 'developing or reviving [of a] special procedure in Scotland, comparable to the procedure under Rule 53 of the Rules of the Supreme Court in England, for obtaining judicial review of decisions by public bodies'. But the Rule which emerged in Scotland was quite general in its terms. The Rule introduced a procedure for application 'to the supervisory jurisdiction of the Court'. No restriction is specified as to matters of public or administrative law. It has been used for a variety of different kinds of case. Indeed it was used in *Ross v Lord Advocate*[65] to test the question whether the Trustee Savings Bank was an unincorporated association whose assets were the property of its members. But more recently the tendency has been towards a view that a restriction involving ideas of public and private law has to be read in to the phraseology which has been used. In *Tehrani v Argyll and Clyde Health Board (No. 2)* the point did not require to be determined because, as the Lord Justice-Clerk narrated,[66] counsel for the petitioner accepted that he had to be able to focus upon a matter of public law, which was regarded as synonymous with administrative law. But the Court seemed inclined to prefer a restricted interpretation of the phrase in the Rules of Court.

It might be thought that if the matter merely concerns the availability of the particular procedure it is not of immense consequence. If it is only a matter of the forms of procedure in the Court of Session then there may be something to be said for avoiding barren disputes on technical classifications in relation to a procedural issue, whether a particular question is one of 'public' or of 'private' law. This is particularly so if there is room for dispute about the precise scope of the terminology involved. Further, the procedure under Rule 260B has a flexibility and expedition which are wholly in line with the current trend towards faster and simpler forms of action. It would perhaps be regrettable if these advantages were to be unavailable to matters of 'private' concern where a speedy determination may be as important as in matters of public concern. But the choice may have deeper implications than the mere choice of procedure in the Court of Session. If a narrow construction of the phrase 'supervisory jurisdiction' in the Rule is to be adopted and if the intention is that the phrase should be defined so as to coincide with the scope of what is comprised in judicial review in England there should be a full awareness of what is being implied and what developments may follow.

As Lord Wilberforce explained in *Davy v Spelthorne BC*,[67] the terms 'private law' and 'public law' have only recently been imported into England from countries which, unlike our own, have separate systems concerning public law and private law. The adoption of such a classification may be seen as a step towards a greater uniformity but the question should also be asked whether the structural division which prevails in those other countries is desirable here. Even although the distinction has been adopted in England it may be questioned whether the historical development of judicial review in each country is sufficiently similar to warrant the adoption of the classification in Scotland. In some respects, assistance may be obtained from English case law in matters of judicial review in Scotland, but where the issue is one of the competency of the application it may be dangerous to look for guidance in English law. Yet the distinctions both in the history and in the substance of the law have been on occasion unnoticed and a decision reached on a concession that English law may appropriately be considered.[68]

Furthermore, what has followed on the development of the process of judicial review in England is not only the identification of particular judges to hear and determine such cases but also a wholly distinct system for the processing of cases through the Crown Office. One feature of judicial review in Scotland which is immediately noticed by the continental lawyer is the fact that, while there are judges nominated for cases of judicial review, not only may other judges hear such cases but the nominated judges may engage in other judicial work. The continental commentator with experience of a quite distinct system of administrative law may well see it as a point of curiosity or even criticism that a judge in matters of administrative law should be involved in any other kind of case. If a structural separation is developing in England and the Rule is intended to follow English and continental ideas then the narrow definition of its scope may pave the way towards a development of a distinct administrative jurisdiction which might gradually accord with the system of continental Europe in matters of administrative law.

But it is not easy in Scotland to see such a distinct jurisdiction as growing naturally from the present root on which the supervisory jurisdiction is based. The question of whether Scotland should develop its administrative law as a system separate and distinct from the ordinary Court's is still an open one. It is not impossible that the idea of entrusting judicial review to the independent judiciary of the Supreme Court, exercising the general power of that court to secure that no wrong is without redress, may be seen by some as a secure constitutional system for regulating matters of public law. The view that such matters are of a technical nature or require a particular expertise is not one which readily commends itself to a Scottish lawyer, whose practice tends to greater variety and to call for greater versatility than is experienced in larger jurisdictions. In the same passage in his *Historical Law Tracts* from which quotation has already been drawn, Lord Kames recognised the degree of versatility required in dealing with matters which would nowadays fall under the broad umbrella of 'administrative law'. But he also recognised the ability of the court to meet the challenge:[69]

> This is peculiarly the case of the subject under consideration: for beside its novelty, it is resolvable into a matter of public police; which, admitting many views not less various than intricate, occasions much difficulty in the law questions that depend on it. Such difficulties, however, are not insuperable. Matters of law are ripened in the best manner, by warmth of debate at the bar, and coolness of judgement upon the bench; and after many successful experiments of a bold interposition for the public good, the Court of Session will clearly perceive the utility of extending their jurisdiction to every sort of wrong, where the person injured have no other means of obtaining redress.

Notes

1.   (5th ed) (1825) book 2 ch 3 341.
2.   (4th ed) (1817) 228–229.
3.   *Acta Dominorum Concilii* 1501–1503, published by the Stair Society (1943), vol 8 123.
4.   *Ibid* at xlv.
5.   D. Masson (Ed) *Register of the Privy Council of Scotland* vol VI 58.
6.   *Institutes* 1, 3, 23.
7.   (1762) M 13175.
8.- *Historical Law Tracts* 231.
9.   *Institutes* 4, 3, 1.
10. *Ibid* ccclxviii *et seq.*

11. Vol 1 255.
12. Vol 6, Equity, para 582.
13. (1886) 13 R 465 at 468.
14. Vol II paras 13, 14.
15. 1986 SLT 149.
16. *Commentaries on the law of Scotland respecting crimes* II 509.
17. Renton and Brown's *Criminal Procedure According to the Law of Scotland* (5th ed by G. Gordon) (1983) 16 – 169.
18. *Ibid*.
19. *Harper of Oban (Engineering) Ltd v Henderson* 1989 SLT 21.
20. *Bradford v McLeod* 1986 SLT 244.
21. *Anderson v LA* 1974 SLT 239.
22. 1983 SLT 208.
23. 1982 SLT 233.
24. 1984 SLT 108.
25. E.g. *Anderson* 1974 SLT 239; also *Mathieson* 1980 SLT (Notes) 74.
26. 1985 SCCR 106.
27. 1988 SLT 657.
28. Hume *op cit* note 16 *supra* II 72, 508.
29. *Ibid* at 508.
30. *Ibid* at 72.
31. (1838) 16 S 617.
32. (1847) 9 D 318.
33. (1852) J Shaw 532.
34. (1860) 23 D 85 and (1861) 24 D 184.
35. (1868) 7 M 270.
36. 1988 SLT 68.
37. 1989 SLT 617.
38. (1867) 5 M (HL) 36.
39. 1940 SC 376 at 383.
40. 1965 SLT 171.
41. 1987 SLT 611.
42. 1970 SC 611.
43. (1886) 13 R 465.
44. *Adams v Great North of Scotland Railway Co* (1890) 18 R (HL) 1 at 8; *Holmes Oil Co Ltd v Pumpherston Oil Co Ltd* (1891) 18 R (HL) 52, 55.
45. [1976] PL 220.
46. *Ibid* 221.
47. [1985] QB 152 at 162.
48. 1990 SLT 118.
49. See the Lord Justice Woolf [1986] PL 225 at 225.
50. *Moss' Empires v Assessor for Glasgow* 1917 SC (HL) 1 at 11.
51. Vol 1 in para 400 at 195.
52. *British Coal Corporation v South of Scotland Electricity Board* 1988 SLT 446.
53. *Tait v Central Radio Taxis (Tollcross) Ltd* 1989 SLT 217.
54. For example, *Bonthrone v Secretary of State for Scotland* 1987 SLT 34.
55. (1876) 3 R 412.
56. 1983 SC (HL) 1 at 45.
57. 1913 SC 991.
58. 1983 SC (HL) 1 at 28.
59. 1975 SLT (Sh Ct) 60.
60. See the late Professor J.D.B. Mitchell 'Reflections on Law and Orders' 1958 *Jur Rev* 19.
61. A.W. Bradley *Stair Memorial Encyclopaedia* vol 1 para 212.
62. (1886) 13 R 465.
63. 1983 SC (HL) 1 at 49.
64. 1983 SC (HL) 50 at 59.
65. 1986 SLT 391 (1st Div); 60 R (HL).

66. 1990 SLT 118 at 131.
67. [1984] AC 62 at 262.
68. E.g. *Connor v Strathclyde RC* 1988 SLT 531.
69. *Op cit* note 2 *supra* 230–1.

Local Administration in Scotland: the Role of the Sheriff

Gavin Little

A. Problems for Sheriffs?

The purpose of this paper is to categorise the statutory powers of the sheriff in Scottish local administration. It is hoped that this classification may be of use in any future allocation or interpretation of shrieval functions. The unusually diverse and unstructured nature of the jurisdiction was noted by Professor Bradley in Volume One of *The Stair Memorial Encyclopaedia*:

> The ordinary courts of law may, in addition to their general jurisdiction, exercise specialised functions involving the confirmation of, or hearing of appeals from, the decisions of public authorities. Thus the Sheriff has a wide variety of statutory tasks in matters concerning local government. Some of these have been held to be administrative, even although they are exercised in a judicial forum, partly because a Sheriff may by legislation be expected to exercise a broader discretion than would normally be appropriate to a court reviewing the decisions of local authorities. Other statutory functions have been held to be judicial, for the reason that a true *lis inter partes* is before the Sheriff. However, the reasoning in these cases has seldom been clear cut.[1]

In Scottish Law Commission Memorandum No. 14, 'Remedies in Administrative Law', Professor Bradley also pointed out that 'a fully satisfactory means of answering the uncertainty relating to the Sheriff's powers on administrative appeals would be the application of general principles on which the Sheriff's powers should be exercised'.[2] Given the lack of certainty surrounding much of Scottish, indeed British, public law, it is fair to ask why the confusion surrounding sheriffs should be singled out for particular attention. The answer lies in the nature of the powers themselves, and the issues that they raise. The sheriff's extant powers within local administration are acute examples of the peculiarly British tradition of law and government, which is frequently characterised as pragmatic, *ad hoc* and lacking in theoretical direction. If the sheriff's powers are viewed as a microcosm of the overall system of law and administration, an examination of them raises issues which are of wider interest. As will become clear, under some statutes the sheriff holds an unfettered (and usually final) discretion to review public authority decisions. In others, powers are

295

interpreted as providing for a 'true *lis*' between the parties; or a statutory
style of common law judicial review limits shrieval discretion. In the first
category the sheriff is carrying out his historical role as a local crown official,
and in the last two categories the sheriff is serving in his usual role of local
judge. The first category raises questions of how judges perceive their ideal
role when reviewing the decisions of democratically accountable public
bodies: even where statutes have granted an apparently unfettered power
to substitute a judicial opinion for the decision of a public body, a self-
limiting process has been developed. This in turn raises questions of
statutory interpretation in the public law arena, and also the unquantifiable
significance of inchoate concepts of discretionary power and justiciability
within the judicial mind. The latter categories raise respectively the spectres
of differentiating a 'public' law dispute from a 'private' law dispute, and
the ability of the legislature to make statutory provision for a judicial review
which has as its object the removal of matters of 'fact and policy' from the
court's ambit.

Looming large over the discussion is the legislature's lack of interest in
providing anything which approaches a coherent system of statutory review,
and the court's inability to produce one in the face of this. The sheriff's
powers to review public body decisions are confined to statute, with the
Court of Session exercising the power of common law judicial review as
part of its exclusive jurisdiction. However, as indicated above, some of the
sheriff's powers are essentially judicial review under statute, whereas others
are more akin to the powers held by a senior public official, or a tribunal.
Like tribunals, the sheriff's powers have, like Topsy, 'just growed'.

This situation raises in turn the more general point that attention should
be given to the sheriff's powers in local administration, in order that the
emerging system of administrative justice in Scotland has coherent
foundations. It is not in the interests of good government, however defined,
that the public should have to rely on an anachronistic and confused system
of administrative justice. This was the general premiss upon which the new
procedures for common law judicial review under Rule of Court 260B were
based. However, the sheriff's functions and status provide ample
opportunity for both anachronism and confusion; accordingly, the sheriff's
powers require examination and categorisation. Categorisation will provide
a firmer base from which 'general principles on which the sheriff's powers
should be exercised' can be developed. The nature of ideal development,
as in most public law issues, is ultimately subjective, and depends on the
viewpoint of the commentator. With this in mind, 'general principles' will
be suggested briefly at the conclusion. For reasons of space, this paper is
concerned primarily with a discussion of the existing jurisdiction of the
sheriff in local administration, and with categorising its constituent powers
within the context of an analytical framework. However, devising a
framework of even limited utility is not an easy task, for five interrelated
reasons.

First, there is a lack of comprehensive official data regarding the frequency
with which the individual statutory powers which make up the sheriff's
jurisdiction in local administration are exercised. The Civil Judicial Statistics,

as compiled by the Scottish Courts Administration, merely categorise 'miscellaneous and administrative' business into general headings, which can raise more questions than they answer.[3] Such evidence as there is suggests that administrative business takes up little of the court's time.[4] However, this does not necessarily mean that the sheriff's powers are insignificant. Many are of considerable importance to the parties involved. In addition, it should be noted that a single decision by a sheriff may have profound effects on a public authority's policy.[5]

Secondly, the amorphous nature of the sheriff's jurisdiction within local administration causes a degree of difficulty. Indeed, to use the term 'jurisdiction' is in itself potentially misleading, as it implies a homogeneous character to a large and seemingly disparate body of statute law. The most recent textbook on Sheriff Court Practice provides a list (which is not exhaustive) of approximately 200 statutes, which empower sheriffs to act in local administration.[6] For example, sheriffs may be called upon to decide cases dealing with licensing, mental health, social work, education, public health, housing and the environment.[7] Many of these powers are not inconsiderable, and may involve controversial issues: under s. 18 of the Mental Health (Scotland) Act 1984, sheriffs are responsible for the compulsory hospitalisation of the mentally ill; under s. 16 of the Social Work (Scotland) Act 1968, they decide what constitutes the 'best interests' of a child in actions concerning the assumption of parental rights by a local authority; and under s. 28 of the Education (Scotland) Act 1980, sheriffs effectively decide on the merits of a local authority's policy on school admissions.[8] It is important to note at the outset Professor Bradley's observation that the role of the sheriff varies from statute to statute, with the sheriff appearing at different levels of the decision-taking process (i.e. first instance and appellate), and frequently with little or no regard for the traditional supervisory role in judicial review.

Sheriffs, in common with all judges, are by necessity no strangers to controversy. However, Scottish judges are traditionally wary of overt interference in public policy areas, as is exemplified by the fitful development of judicial review in the Court of Session.[9] Consequently, the problems faced by sheriffs in interpreting a statutory power which *prima facie* requires overt policy-based decision-taking are not easy to resolve, as will be made plain. How did Parliament intend them to exercise their discretion when reviewing a public body's decision? How can a sheriff evaluate the democratic dimension of a public body's policy decision? Lord President Cooper made the nub of the sheriff's dilemma clear: 'In every case the answer must be found in the provisions of the statute in question.'[10] Unfortunately, the opaque nature of much of the legislation in this area has merely compounded the sheriffs' difficulties.

With these problems in mind, Professor Bradley has suggested loose grounds-based groupings for the sheriff's powers.[11] The first (and largest) group consists of powers where 'the legislation not precisely defining the sheriff's powers, the sheriff may review the decision not only on grounds relating to *vires*, jurisdiction and error of law, but also on broader policy considerations concerning the expediency of the decision'. The second group imposes a duty on the sheriff to 'find certain states of fact to exist' before upholding the decision under challenge. In the third group, the sheriffs are given rather more Parliamentary guidance: their powers are confined 'to considering specified grounds of *vires*, jurisdiction, fair procedure and error of law'. My intention is to build on these basic distinctions in the course of this paper.

It should be noted that although the nature of the sheriff's powers may vary considerably, the basic process by which the final decision is reached does not. Not surprisingly, the adversarial system of adjudication is used, usually within the loose limitations of the civil summary application procedure. It should also be appreciated that there is a wide variation in the degree of procedural formality felt to be appropriate. This variation goes beyond that which one would expect between sheriffs, but shifts generally from power to power. Accordingly, compulsory hospitalisation of the mentally ill tends to be conducted in an informal style, with considerable judicial intervention, whereas procedural formalities would be more closely followed in cases concerning the assumption of parental rights under s. 16 of the Social Work (Scotland) Act 1968.[12]

The third connected problem which hinders classification of the sheriff's powers is the convoluted development of the office of sheriff itself. It would appear that many of the confusions and difficulties which face sheriffs when interpreting their role under statute have been caused by an incremental and institutionally conservative development. An important factor in this development has been a lack of Parliamentary interest in defining 'basic principles', or in revising obsolete provisions and practices. Accordingly, a historical excursus is appropriate.

The sheriff is thought to have been a Norman, twelfth-century importation by King David I (1124–1153). The medieval sheriff (sometimes referred to as High Sheriff or Sheriff Principal) was both judge and chief royal executive officer of his sheriffdom, with important military, financial and administrative roles. The title was normally granted 'in fee and heritage', and became part of the feudal powers of the influential Scottish nobility.[13] Throughout the middle ages and early modern period it was beyond the *de facto* power of the Scottish Crown and Parliament to interfere with the heritable jurisdictions of the magnates, but following the Union Agreement with England in 1707 change was, in retrospect, inevitable. Although the Acts of Union guaranteed the continuance of the heritable jurisdictions, they provided a potential power base for Jacobite or patriotic nobles,[14] and were thus politically unsustainable. However, the traditional medieval system remained in operation until the aftermath of the 1745 rebellion, when Westminster's attention was focused on Scottish government and administration. Political considerations required the abolition of the heritable jurisdictions, and this was effected by the Heritable Jurisdictions (Scotland) Act 1747. The Act provided that the office of sheriff-depute was to be held by a member of the Faculty of Advocates.[15] The Faculty was viewed as a 'stable' from which ambitious, legally qualified and politically reliable administrators could be selected for government service.[16] The sheriffs-depute came to perform not only the judicial functions of the (largely defunct) office of High Sheriff, but also their military and administrative duties.[17] In time, the sheriff-deputes came to be referred to informally as Sheriffs Principal.[18]

From 1747 until the late nineteenth century, the sheriff was an important, indeed crucial, official in Scottish county government. In that period, the Edinburgh-based sheriffs-depute (assisted locally by legally qualified sheriffs-substitute) served as quasi-colonial administrators, with extensive executive and judicial powers.

Scottish county administration was, until the advent of what are recognisable as modern, democratically accountable local authorities in 1889, institutionally primitive.[20] The office of sheriff was the local embodiment of an essentially Lockean *laissez-faire* tradition of government, which had evolved incrementally with the 'enabling' social improvement legislation of the nineteenth-century: the separation of powers was never a powerful concept in Scotland.[21] However, Parliament did not alter, or define, the sheriff's role in local administration following the significant changes brought about by the Local Government (Scotland) Act 1889, and his duties as royal executive officer, as well as local judge were continued. The 1927 Commission on the Court of Session and Office of Sheriff Principal gives some indication of the wide nature of the sheriff's powers within local administration. As suggested above, the powers held were not dissimilar to the powers of a colonial District Officer: sheriffs were entrusted with overall control over the preservation of public order, and important functions with regard to local registration, electoral administration, prisons, lunatic asylums, tax collection, poor law administration, roads and bridges, housing, planning, public health and the confirmation of bye-laws.[22] Nor were sheriffs-depute uncertain as to their role as the local agents of central government, as Lord Dunedin, who had served as a sheriff-depute, made clear: 'From the point of view of Dover House he (the Sheriff Depute) is the one man you have to depend upon.'[23]

By the 1967 Grant Report on the Sheriff Court, the statutory duties of the sheriffs (depute and substitute) within local administration had been much reduced, although a large number of important powers still remained.[24] Interestingly, despite the many profound changes in central and local government and public administration generally, the attitude of sheriffs-depute towards their role as 'local ministers of the crown' echoed Lord Dunedin's views of forty years before. Parliament had, it may be argued, left sheriffs in an increasingly anomalous constitutional 'bubble'. Nor has the bubble been burst. In *Carvana v Glasgow Corporation*,[25] Sheriff Macphail gave wide-ranging consideration to the sheriff's historical, but still *extant*, statutory position as the monarch's local 'representative and executive officer for civil affairs' when he commented on 'the fallacy of the suggestion so earnestly pressed upon us that a remit to a sheriff is a remit to a judicial officer, who is "only a lawyer", and on that account assumedly incapable of dealing with anything but purely legal issues'.[26]

It is difficult to refute the view that these contentions, and the 'uncertainty' noted by Professor Bradley which arises from them, stem from a lack of active parliamentary consideration of the sheriff's position, rather than from any shrieval eccentricity. Historically, legislation for Scottish local administration has frequently tended to be an afterthought to equivalent English reform; consequently, peculiarly Scottish institutions, such as the office of sheriff, have often been given insufficient detailed consideration.[27] This point, and the problem faced by sheriffs when attempting to interpret a modern 'administrative' role, are exemplified by the fate of the recommendations of the Grant Report concerning the future allocation of shrieval functions:

> The scope of administrative appeal would vary according to the nature of the original decision, and should therefore be defined in the Act . . . We particularly commend this for the attention of anyone responsible for the drafting of such an Act, because it is not always clearly covered in existing legislation . . . We recommend that in the creation of new administrative appeals to the sheriff, or in the revision of existing legislation which provides for such appeals, the enabling legislation should clearly define the extent of the appeal and the powers of the sheriff to interfere with the original decision.[28]

Although Parliament has introduced limitations in some statutes since 1967, there was no revision of existing legislation, and, as mentioned above, most provisions empowering sheriffs to act in local administration are still unclear as to the extent of the appeal and the ability of sheriffs to reverse local authority decisions.[29] It may be that this reflects Parliamentary intention, but it is difficult to avoid the impression that enactments concerning the sheriff and public authorities are simply of an *ad hoc*, arbitrary nature, with little thought being given to 'basic principles' for the allocation of powers.

Professor Bradley has noted that '[i]n conferring such [administrative] power on the sheriff Parliament must be taken to be aware of the general nature of the sheriff's office.'[30] This is certainly the assumption that sheriffs must labour under in court, but speaking extra-judicially a number of sheriffs have indicated otherwise. The Grant Report's recommendation noted above also suggests that there is room for a closer consideration of the possibility of loose Parliamentary drafting.[31]

A possible example of semantic disjunction between Parliamentary intent and practical effect may be found in the recent case of *T.F. v Management Committee of Ravenscraig Hospital*,[32] which concerned an appeal under ss. 29(4) and 113(1) of the Mental Health (Scotland) Act 1984. One of the questions before the court was whether the sheriff, in dealing with mental health matters, was exercising his 'administrative' jurisdiction (i.e. further appeal on the merits was incompetent) or acting in a judicial capacity. Sheriff Principal (now Lord) Caplan made the following comments:

> [The relevant statutory provisions] may well have been introduced as a result of certain pressures created when the European Court of Human Rights decided that . . . those detained in hospital should have recourse to judicial review. However, . . . there was nothing to suggest what degree of judicial review would have been required. I was referred to Hansard, but clearly it is not appropriate to construe a statute by reference to Parliamentary proceedings.[33]

Leaving aside the unresolved question of what 'judicial review' meant in this context, it should be noted that even if Lord Caplan had been able to follow the passage of the Bill through Parliament, he would have been unable to discern whether an administrative or judicial role was intended. The possible distinctions in the sheriff's authority were not considered overtly. Was Parliament even aware that the sheriff possessed an 'administrative' jurisdiction, to which it was adding another power? Judgement must be reserved, and it is within this rather unsatisfactory historical context that court-based attempts to define shrieval functions should be considered.

The fourth problem which has stood in the way of the construction of a conceptual framework has arisen from the self-limiting and time-consuming process of judicial decision-taking. As Professor Bradley has noted, attempts by sheriffs (subject to Court of Session supervision) to analyse the nature of their powers have not always been conclusive.[34] The reasons for this are as follows.

As indicated above, sheriffs are bound to follow the rules of statutory interpretation in each case. Naturally, problems arise when sheriffs interpreting their statutory administrative powers are uncertain as to the extent of their discretion – that is, the extent of their legitimate discretion, in the absence of express statutory guidance, to interfere with public authority decisions. Different sheriffs, in different cases, dealing with different facts and provisions, in different periods, and subject to review by different judges, naturally feel themselves to have different degrees of discretion. However, the range of shrieval discretion may be viewed within Professor MacCormick's description of judicial discretion:

> In all cases, judicial discretion exists only within the framework of some predetermined standards. Where these standards are legal rules, the discretion extends only within rather a restricted field, though rarely eliminated completely. Where the rules give no guidance, recourse may be had to other standards of judgement. But since these standards are all less precise than rules, the discretion involved in interpreting and extrapolating from them is greater.[35]

It is important to note that the traditional 'standards of judgement' (legal and otherwise) which sheriffs are likely to rely on in cases where statutes impute less guidance – and therefore a potentially wider discretion – are themselves inherently restrictive. The general ethos and law of statutory interpretation (and the extent of judicial power) was set out by Lord Hailsham:

> A judge in Britain is hedged about by a far more restrictive view of precedent than are [foreign judges], and since most decisions nowadays consist in the interpretation and application of Acts of Parliament, it is even more important that the rules of construing Acts of Parliament followed by English and Scottish judges are far more rigid and limiting than any country in the world not operating the British system . . . [O]ur traditional method of Parliamentary draftsmanship is so much more detailed than in any European country as to fetter judicial independence to an extent quite unparalleled elsewhere. Even on

matters in which we are wont to leave a question to a judge's discretion, his use of it is subject to scrutiny by the pyramidal system of appeal.[36] The 'standards of judgement' are therefore based on the ideal of autonomous law, underpinned by concepts of parliamentary supremacy, weak judicial discretion (or perhaps none at all), and the principle of *stare decisis*.

Accordingly, it may be argued that the judicial tradition of non-activist interpretation, coupled with the necessarily *ad hoc* and lengthy process of developing concepts via case-by-case adjudication, has meant that the court's attempts to provide an analytical framework of basic principles for shrieval involvement in local administration are bound to be conservative in nature. Indeed, as indicated by Professor Bradley, given the differing lines of arguments presented to the courts, and the vagaries of different cases and sheriffs, it has taken the courts most of this century to conclude that shrieval duties may be classed loosely as administrative or judicial. Judicial reasoning has also had to contend with rapidly developing, increasingly politicised and professional public authorities, and shifting concepts of public law. It is therefore unsurprising that modern commentators were questioning the general 'appropriateness' of unelected sheriffs exercising administrative powers in public authority decision-taking by the time that judicial precedent had finally developed.[37] The weakness of the court process in this area serves to reinforce the argument made above: the legislature must accept primary responsibility for the creation of basic principles of shrieval involvement in local administration. Incremental case-by-case development, in an area involving local democracy and public policy, is not suited to the task.

The fifth interrelated factor hampering the classification of the sheriff's powers is the failure of 'public law' theory and terminology to provide the answer to the question of what the ideal limitation of shrieval involvement in public authority decision-taking should be in cases where a statute implies a wide discretion. This point was inferred by Professor Bradley, when he commented on the difficulties encountered by sheriffs defining their statutory role in terms redolent of the Report of the Donoughmore Committee on Ministers' Powers:

> Although the courts may adopt conceptual language in classifying functions for specific purposes, they rarely undertake a full analysis of the nature of administrative, judicial and legislative functions . . . While the term 'administrative' has often been used where a sheriff has a wide discretion enabling him to reach his own decision on the merits of a local government matter, the term 'ministerial' has sometimes been used in the same sense as 'administrative'. But usage is not constant.[38]

As has been clear since Jennings' critique at the time of the Donoughmore Report,[39] the use of such terms is fraught with semantic and conceptual difficulties: perhaps as a result, it would appear that sheriffs have sought to avoid discussion of underlying concepts of constitutional propriety. Not surprisingly, particular problems have arisen when 'administrative' powers were under consideration. Most cases in this category concern private individuals appealing against a public authority decision. Attempts to use Donoughmore-style classifications must therefore be reconciled with

Jennings' contention that 'there is no essential distinction between an administrative decision in an instant case and a judicial decision'.[40] Looming large over the question of terminology and the extent of powers conferred by statute (although rarely considered directly) is a conundrum which obviously causes some difficulty: the inherent 'justiciability' of certain issues, notwithstanding what the instant statute may provide for. In this context, 'justiciability' may be seen as an ideal of what 'judges' work' should be, and as such it is perhaps best viewed as a conceptual 'will-o'-the-wisp'.[41]

As indicated above, the orthodox positivist position is that sheriffs ideally should not take policy (i.e. 'administrative') decisions directly: it is far more acceptable to avoid overt policy consideration via the judicialised technique of common law judicial review. This approach cannot be sustained untarnished in the majority of statutory appeals to the sheriff. Judicial practice has led accordingly to the present position in which sheriffs have limited their powers to some degree, even when *prima facie* they have unfettered and final powers under statute. However, as Sheriff Macphail has made clear, the limitation is not as structured as common law judicial review: 'Although there is . . . an unrestricted right of appeal to the sheriff, the sheriff should not . . . vary or reverse the decision of the magistrates' committee unless he is satisfied that their decision is wrong, and he should pay due regard to the competence of magistrates in arriving at their decision.'[42]

Various themes may be detected in this and similar comments,[43] which are of obvious relevance to the many academic theories which have been constructed to allocate functions according to generic concepts of what 'judges' work' should be. In general, these devices have been concerned with improving procedural efficiency and wide concepts of democratic accountability. It is instructive to note that few of them would enlighten sheriffs attempting to decide whether a public authority's decision is 'wrong', or evaluating the 'competence' of the authority.

The logical inconsistencies of the Donoughmore Committee's attempts to tackle the problem of the ideal limitation of powers have already been noted. Academic writers such as Fuller saw the problem in conceptual terms, concentrating on efficiency in the decision-taking process: adjudication by courts was unsuitable when the degree of polycentric effect became procedurally inefficient. Fuller himself was aware that the recognition of this point was ultimately subjective. 'It is not a question of distinguishing black from white. It is a question of knowing when the polycentric elements have become so significant and predominant that the proper limits of adjudication have been reached.'[44] Fuller's appreciation of the lack of objective standards involved in determining the appropriate limit of judicial intervention in public body decision-taking is mirrored by Hartley and Griffith, who argue that the ideal limit is reached via a symbiosis of natural justice and interests: 'The interests of the individual concerned must be balanced against the public interest and the extent to which natural justice will apply (if it applies at all) will depend on the way the balance is struck.'[45]

The notion that the applicability of the procedural restraints embodying adjudication is dependent on circumstances in individual cases was also endorsed by Mullan when he stated: 'The nearer one is to the type of function requring straight law/fact determinations and resulting in serious consequences to individuals, the greater is the demand for procedural protection.'[46]

The democratic legitimacy of involvement in the decision-taking process as 'administrators' has also troubled sheriffs. For example, in *Rothesay Town Council – Petitioners*, the sheriff was unwilling to interfere with the local authority's bye-laws despite his statutory discretion to refuse assent. He stated that the authority's deliberations were to receive the 'utmost respect', and that bye-laws should be approached, 'with the conviction that they represent the mind of the community expressed through their representatives'.[47] Accordingly, notwithstanding the potential for unfettered discretion, sheriffs have usually succumbed to a natural judicial reflex, and felt themselves to be under a variant of the pressure more commonly associated with common law judicial review.[48]

As noted by Galligan, 'The fact that [courts] are outside the lines of direct accountability to the political process makes the position of the courts problematical in imposing constraints on discretionary authorities, which are themselves politically accountable.'[49] Galligan goes on to argue that review by courts is generally desirable, provided that the judiciary's conduct is in accordance with, and indeed promotes, justifiable political and constitutional principles. This would involve sheriffs working out their own theory of democracy, which must 'accommodate the positive constitutional values that are to be derived from political and legal practice'.[50] The sheriff's theory must also operate within a generic conception of 'his role in the constitutional order . . . parliamentary sovereignty, and the extent to which administrative authorities are authorised and accountable, either to Parliament or to a wider sense of democratic process'.[51]

Without being unduly negative, it can be argued that these and similar attempts to define the ideal limits of adjudication and the judicial role are no more helpful in practical terms than Sheriff MacPhail's uncomplicated test of wrongness and competence. Unfortunately for sheriffs, most academic theories in this area are either the conceptual equivalent of asking the length of a piece of string, or merely a rephrasing of the original question. Notice should be taken of the point made by de Bono when he asked: 'Can one escape from the circular self-satisfaction of elaborate philosophical description?'[52] Given the restraints on judicial time, *stare decisis* and an attendant desire to avoid an overturned judgment, it is hardly surprising that sheriffs should seek to do so.

As a consequence of this, and of the factors mentioned earlier, discussion of functions in the sheriff court has tended to focus on narrow statutory interpretation as opposed to abstract theory. For example, it has been held that various statutory appeals to the sheriffs are judicial because further appeal is available to the Court of Session; similarly, if statutes refer to an appeal to 'the sheriff' (as opposed to 'the Sheriff Court'), then the function is seen as administrative, and a final jurisdiction 'on the merits' of the public authority's policy is thereby implied.[53]

Clearly, any attempt at classification of shrieval functions within administration which is based on mechanical, statutory interpretation is bound to have its limitations. As indicated at the outset, and with the above problems in mind, it is possible to devise broad conceptual categories, to which the sheriff's powers may be allocated. These categories build on the distinctions in grounds of review noted by Professor Bradley, but are based primarily on an appreciation of the sheriff's historic role. It is hoped that this exercise will enable those interested in revising and interpreting extant powers, or in allocating new functions, to do so on firmer foundations than have existed to date.

B. A classification of powers

The analytical framework of the sheriff's jurisdiction within administration consists of four categories. It should be noted that these classifications are not exhaustive: for example, the sheriff's duties in arbitration have been excluded from the study, as have *ex officio* ceremonial duties. The common factors linking statutory provisions in the four categories are as follows: (i) the sheriff is empowered under statute to resolve a dispute, and (ii) the parties to the dispute are a private citizen and a public authority (usually a democratically accountable local authority). What does vary is the extent and nature of the sheriff's powers. The categories are not intended to be rigid classifications, and it should be recognised that in some cases allocation may be a matter for conjecture.

The four categories are the sheriff as

1. a 'first instance governmental authority'
2. a 'higher governmental authority'
3. an 'administrative judge'
4. a 'civil judge'.

The term 'governmental' authority may be alternated with 'administrative' or 'ministerial' authority. It is submitted, however, that the first term is preferable. The main features of the four groupings are set out below.

1. *The sheriff as a first instance governmental authority*

This is an unusual area of shrieval activity, and may be seen as the derivative of the sheriff's eighteenth- and nineteenth-century role as local 'minister of the crown' acting on behalf of central government in the absence of effective, or democratically accountable, public authorities.

In effect, the sheriff's role is that of a first instance government official. Their statutory duties empower them to make decisions on the same 'on the merits' criteria as are used by public officials in broadly similar types of cases, although they are not democratically accountable. Usually, the decisions are final. The *ad hoc* nature of the legislation can place sheriffs in an unusual position. For example, sheriffs are responsible for granting licences to private clubs (and for maintaining the register of such licences in the summary application register), whilst local licensing boards register public houses.[55] The purpose of this distinction is doubtless to maintain a differentiation between private and public premises. However, given the appeal procedures from licensing boards and the administrative desirability of standardising environmental health and fire safety standards, the continued relevance of such powers should be questioned. In a similar (and now defunct) governmental role the Grant Committee Report of 1967 noted that in 1965 sheriffs granted 19,146 dog licences, presumably because the dogs were the private property of individual citizens.[56] It is worth remembering that this power was extant long after the advent of more obviously appropriate local authority public health departments.

The suitability of shrieval involvement in such matters was questioned in the oral evidence presented to the Grant Committee by members of the Faculty of Law at Edinburgh University:

> Have you given thought to the question of whether some of the sheriff's administrative duties . . . should be taken away, divorced from the judicial system altogether? Take the case like (*sic*) the local authority that wishes to have a burial ground . . . in a certain place. It can take the same land for housing or sewage works . . . without interference from the judiciary, and if it wants to have a burial ground in the same place it has to go to the sheriff. Does it seem sensible in this day and age that these smaller matters should be retained . . .?[57]

The sheriffs-depute themselves had rather mixed views on such arguments. They accepted that some major administrative functions, such as hearing planning appeals, should be allocated to the Secretary of State for Scotland, but sought to retain other equally weighty, but less contentious, administrative functions (e.g. that of Returning Officer at elections). In general terms, the sheriffs took the view that minor powers could be allocated to local authorities, which existed 'to interpret the wishes of the citizen, whereas the sheriff [did] not'.[58] Where weighty matters were involved, a Diceyan view was adopted: the sheriff operated as 'a valuable safeguard of the rights of the individual against the powers of the executive'.[59]

Even today, not all of the statutory powers in this category are minor. As mentioned above, a frequently exercised power is that of compulsory hospitalisation of patients under the Mental Health (Scotland) Act 1984, where sheriffs may be put in the potentially difficult position of taking 'on the merits' decisions on psychiatric evidence.[60] As was made clear in *T.F. v Management Committee of Ravenscraig Hospital*, '[the decisions] were all administrative acts. In every case the sheriff was acting as an integral part of the administrative process . . . [H]e was not being invited to deliver judgement on a question of law.'[61]

It is worth noting that the sheriffs' powers developed from their long-standing 'governmental' role in mental health provision, as well as from the intention of the legislature to provide for the protection of patients' rights. Indeed, the sheriff's powers concerning compulsory hospitalisation are little more than an updated and restricted version of his duties under the Madhouses (Scotland) Act 1815, which stipulated that 'no Person or Persons shall be received into any House kept for the Reception and the

Care or Confinement of furious or fatuous Persons or Lunatics . . . without an order made by the Sheriff or Stewart Depute or Substitute.'[62] The sheriff's more obviously governmental powers in mental health, such as licensing asylums, appointing medical inspectors, ensuring the security of asylums, making internal orders and regulations, and inspecting asylums have since been allocated to other bodies.[63] However, such provisions are clearly of relevance in establishing the 'governmental' pedigree of extant powers from an historical context.

2. *The sheriff as a 'higher governmental authority'*

This category of powers is also derivative of the sheriff's historical role as local representative of the crown. Once more, the statutory powers held by the sheriff cover a wide range of subject-matter.

As in category 1, the conceptual position of the sheriff does not correspond with the recognisably judicial function of Court of Session judges conducting a judicial review. The sheriff's statutory role in this area is that of an appellate body, retaking decisions (usually *de novo*) made by a public authority, following an appeal by a member of the public. The decision is usually final. In general terms, sheriffs are free to exercise a wide 'on the merits of the case' discretion (i.e. one similar to that of the original decision-taking body), although it should be noted that 'it is likely that a sheriff will be particularly alert to legal points relevant to jurisdiction and competence.'[64] Accordingly, unelected and unaccountable sheriffs are performing the 'governmental' role of taking decisions which may be direct and final rulings on the merits of a local-authority policy-based decision, as opposed to a more recognisably judicial role, which may lead to an indirect, 'polycentric' ruling on a policy under the guise of a decision based on law or *Wednesbury* unreasonableness.[65]

A recent example of a case involving a higher governmental power may be found in *Roddie v Strathclyde RC*, which concerned an appeal from a decision of Strathclyde Regional Council under s. 6(4) of the Nurseries and Childminders Act 1948.[66] The question before the court was the competence of an appeal 'on the merits' to the sheriff following a refusal by the council to register the appellant as a fit person to run a private nursery. The sheriff noted with approval the argument advanced for the appellant that 'the effect of [s. 6(4)] was to give the sheriff unfettered discretion in the conduct and determination of the appeal'.[67] In his judgment, the sheriff concurred with Sheriff MacPhail's decision in *Carvana v Glasgow Corporation*: 'In sum, therefore, I have formed the view that the sheriff is entitled, in his administrative capacity, to substitute his own opinion for that of the local authority, if he is satisfied that their decision is quite demonstrably wrong.'[68]

It should further be noted that a sheriff may also be acting as a higher governmental authority in cases where he is required to 'find certain states of fact to exist before a local authority decision may be upheld'.[69] It may be impossible to interpret 'states of fact' without reference to policy. The Education (Scotland) Act 1980 (as amended) provides a clear example. The 1981 Act introduced parental choice of school, and allows parents to put the case that their children should be educated at a particular school to the education authority, and then to an Education Appeal Committee. A further right of appeal lies to the sheriff. The sheriff effectively hears the appeal *de novo*, and can confirm the refusal of the request only if satisfied that certain states of fact exist, and that it is appropriate 'in all the circumstances'.[70] The 'states of fact' may, however, be policy issues: will placing a child in a school necessitate the employment of an extra teacher, or require alterations to school facilities? Is the answer to be found in policy or an evaluation of circumstances in individual cases? The approach taken by sheriffs to these questions has varied, and is clearly of significance to the local authority concerned. An adverse decision may result in a reversal of policy, and a requirement to review all like decisions. The policy implications of decisions have proved to be a contentious area for sheriffs.[71] Some have opted for a 'single child' approach, and have been unwilling to consider overtly the polycentric implications of reversing a decision.[72] For example, Sheriff Maguire in *Duggan v Strathclyde RC* noted that the education authorities had 'suggested that I look at the overall picture in the school. While one more [pupil] or two more or three more might not make a great difference to the overcrowding, a line had to be drawn'. Rejecting this view, Sheriff Maguire cited with approval a previous decision of the Sheriff Principal, which stated: 'The local authority has to consider each case individually and cannot make a blanket decision'.[73]

However, a contrary approach has been taken by sheriffs in Lothian Region, where a 'school-level'[74] approach has been taken: consideration being given to the policy-based arguments advanced by the Regional Council. In *Forbes v Lothian RC* the sheriff commented that it 'is in the interests of sound management of a school that that situation [i.e. overcrowding and its attendant difficulties] should be prevented from arising, and that cannot be achieved if the number of pupils is allowed to creep up little by little until an acceptable total is reached. But if . . . each placing request is to be considered in isolation, it is virtually impossible in any one case to say that pupil's admission will raise a detrimental level of overcrowding to one that is seriously detrimental.'[75]

3. *The sheriff as an 'administrative judge'*

This is an interesting and potentially very significant category. Sheriffs are empowered to review the decisions of local licensing boards, but their jurisdiction is limited to what may be categorised as the provision of common law judicial review under statute (albeit with some differences). The main statutory provision in this section is s. 39 of the Licensing (Scotland) Act 1976, which stipulates that a sheriff may uphold an appeal only if he considers that the licensing board in arriving at its decision: (i) erred in law; (ii) based its decision on an incorrect material fact; (iii) acted contrary to natural justice; or (iv) exercised its discretion in an unreasonable manner.[76]

As in common law judicial review, there has been an attempt to exclude from the judicial process issues which may (however hazily) be discerned as 'non-justiciable'. The framers of the legislation considered the thorny question of whether adjudication in areas involving democratically accountable public authorities was suitable, which, as Fuller has pointed out, is a difficult question of degree.[77] It should, however, be recognised that the Second Report of the Guest Committee on Scottish Licensing Law did not appear to give deep consideration to conceptual issues, and contented itself by stating that 'on matters of fact and policy, the decision of the licensing board would in effect be final'.[78]

It would be an over-simplification to imagine that cases concerning questions of law or discretion allegedly exercised in an unreasonable manner cannot have a profound effect on policy. Notwithstanding this point, it is important to note that this category is broadly in line with the orthodox judicial view of what should constitute the court's role *vis-à-vis* public authorities.

4. *The sheriff as a 'civil judge'*

This category is potentially problematic, as it may be difficult to separate its constituents from other provisions in categories 1 and 2. It is recognised that opinions may differ on whether or not a provision should be included. As before, the applications involve individuals appealing against a public body, and the sheriff may possess a wide discretion. Significantly, however, appeal to the Court of Session is competent. The distinction between provisions in this category and 'governmental' appeals turns on whether the nature of the case is what Lord President Clyde termed 'a true *lis* between the parties'.[79]

It is clearly the case that making such a distinction is potentially very difficult in terms of both statutory interpretation and public law theory. This is not to say that courts are unable to differentiate a 'true *lis*' from a governmental decision: however, it is inevitable that the reasoning behind any classification of functions will be subjective, and based on general and inchoate 'feelings' of propriety and suitability as well as a close consideration of precedent. Circular theoretical arguments are unlikely to be considered.

Accordingly, some of the sheriff's statutory powers are seen as unexceptional civil hearings, in which one of the parties happens to be a local authority: the 'public law' content is negligible. Deciding what is negligible and what is not is a question of degree in difficult cases and perhaps incapable of resolution to the satisfaction of all. The courts have sought the answer in narrow statutory interpretation, their unarticulated statements as to what the court's role should be serving as a powerful motivating force.

An example of this type of power is s. 16 of the Social Work (Scotland) Act 1968, which provides for an appeal to the sheriff by a parent against the assumption of parental rights by a local authority. Although the sheriff is on one level reviewing the authority's compulsory care resolution (and potentially a child care policy), the paramount concern of the court is to secure the best interests of the child. In general terms, the nature of the case is that of a family law dispute, concerning the well-being of children and powerful individual rights which have their foundation in private law.[80] The special provisions of the Act are essentially to provide safeguards against the *de facto* lack of parity in resources and expertise between parents and the local authority. This view is supported by recent developments. The Child Care Law Review has recommended that s. 16 should be repealed, and that local authorities should instead seek custody of children under the Law Reform (Parent and Child) (Scotland) Act 1986.[81] The 1986 Act was originally intended as a traditional 'family law' measure to enable relatives to obtain custody of a child. If the proposal is implemented, it would mean that local authorities would utilise their corporate legal personality to qualify *de jure* as a person showing 'sufficient interest in a child' to apply to the court. Leaving aside the desirability of this in practice, it should be noted that the nature of s. 16 appeals is highlighted as that of a traditional 'private law' court dispute between parties: it is within this context that s. 16, and similar powers in this category, should be viewed.

C. Conclusion

It is hoped that much of the confusion surrounding the sheriff's statutory powers within local administration has been brought into perspective. It is also hoped that the suggested analytical framework will be of use in any attempt to revise or interpret existing powers, or in any future allocation of functions. Detailed consideration of how and by whom these tasks would be undertaken is beyond the scope of this paper, but it is submitted that more weight should be given to the recommendation of the Grant Committee as quoted above: there should be a general recasting of the sheriff's powers, and the responsibility for this lies with the legislature. Professor Bradley's suggestion that 'general principles' should be adopted in the revision of extant powers and in the allocation of new functions is clearly a challenge for Parliament; the nature of the existing jurisdiction suggests that party political considerations would inevitably assume some significance. For example, the insertion of the sheriff as an 'on the merits' decision-taker into the Conservative Government's procedure for parental choice of school was almost certainly viewed as a means of negating the discretion of the local authority to refuse a parental request.[82] Equally, the lack of any judicial intervention in parental choice of school prior to the legislation of the early eighties was itself a reflection of an opposing political philosophy. The former position is very much in the character of Harlow and Rawlings' 'red light' typology, whereas the latter exemplifies the distrust of judicial interference prevalent in 'green light' theory.[83] Parliamentarians at both ends of the political spectrum are, however, likely to agree on one point: 'general principles', whatever they may be, would not count for much if they hampered the policy implementation of any government. Notwithstanding the inherent dislike of British politicians for 'general principles', however loose, some basic proposals should be put forward for consideration, which may be seen as occupying the 'middle ground of public law'.[84]

A revised role for the sheriff in Scottish local administration should correspond with Yardley's interpretation of the ideal function of a court as being 'the control of power, and the maintenance of a fair balance between the competing interests of the administration . . . and the citizen'.[85] This would not hamper Parliament's ability to make statutory provision for the involvement of the sheriff in specific appeals from public authority decisions: it may be felt that recourse to a full-scale judicial review in the Court of Session is not appropriate in all cases. The local and relatively inexpensive access to sheriffs for citizens is clearly a relevant consideration for Parliament, as are the procedural safeguards and impartiality offered by shrieval review. These features may be seen as the 'positive values' of a statutory appeal to the sheriff. Yardley's guiding principle would, however, have profound implications for the distinctions within the sheriff's extant jurisdiction. The sheriff's role as 'governmental authority' (both first instance and appellate) should be recognised as a historical anomaly: sheriffs are members of the judiciary, and their lack of democratic accountability requires that the obscure theoretical confusions as well as the political tensions which inevitably attend such an obsolete role should be brought to an end. There is no real justification for sheriffs registering private clubs or regulating burial grounds.[86] Even if these and similar duties take up little court time, they obscure the potential that the sheriff has as a statutory complement to common law judicial review in the Court of Session. An important jurisdiction such as the powers held under the Mental Health (Scotland) Act 1984 should no longer be confused with the venerable but anomalous 'governmental' jurisdiction; it should simply be recognised as an attempt by Parliament to make special provision for mental health, which is geared towards a sensitive but effective protection of patients' civil liberties. Appellate 'governmental' powers, which effectively insist that an unrepresentative sheriff should sit in judgment over the merits of a democratically accountable public authority's policy should be recognised as inappropriate as a matter of principle; the sheriff's inclusion in an appeal process and the extent of his powers of review should not be used by governments as a means of politically 'weighting' a procedure in favour of the appellant or the authority. The sheriff's powers under statute should be made consistent with the common law powers of the Court of Session in a judicial review.[87] Accordingly, in an appeal over school admissions, the sheriff would be limited to a statutory formula similar to that in s. 39 of the Licensing (Scotland) Act 1976 (i.e. an appeal could only be upheld if the sheriff considered that the authority had erred in law; based its decision on an incorrect material fact; acted contrary to natural justice; or exercised its discretion in an unreasonable manner). Clearly, not all appeals involving public body decisions should be challengeable on these grounds. The legislature should decide whether an appeal should be limited to a s. 39-type formula, or should be viewed as a 'true *lis inter partes*'. The latter category may be more appropriate when the principal aim of the legislation is to protect the rights of the vulnerable (e.g. children or the mentally ill), rather than the review of a decision-taking process. Allocating functions may give rise to debate, but it is submitted that Parliament is a more suitable forum than the court. Finally, to avoid unnecessary confusion, legislation should always make it clear whether an appeal from the sheriff to the Court of Session is competent.

In conclusion, the 'general principles' suggested above do not seek to avoid the point that a review of law, facts, jurisdiction or unreasonably exercised discretion by a court may inevitably involve some consideration of a public authority's policy. However, it is argued that these or similar principles would accentuate the 'positive values' of an appeal to the sheriff, retain flexibility and shield sheriffs from the damaging allegation that they lack the requisite democratic accountability.[88] Perhaps most importantly, the proposals would bolster recent attempts by the Court of Session to create a coherent and procedurally efficient system of administrative justice in Scotland.[89]

Notes

1. *The Laws of Scotland, Stair Memorial Encyclopaedia*, Vol 1 para 210.
2. SLC Memorandum No 14 *Remedies in Administrative Law* para 10.2.
3. See e.g. *Civil Judicial Statistics Scotland 1984* Scottish Courts Administration (1985) para 3.14.
4. See The Grant Report on the Sheriff Court Cmnd 3248 (1967) Part IV of Appendix VIII and note 2.
5. See generally Fuller 'The Forms and Limits of Adjudication' (1978) 92 *Harv L R* 353.
6. E.R. Colwell Wilson in I.D. Macphail *Sheriff Court Practice* W. Green & Son (1988), 893–95: *NB* Many of the statutes create more than one power for the sheriff.
7. E.g. Mental Health (Scotland) Act 1984, s 18; Social Work (Scotland) Act 1968, s 16; Education (Scotland) Act 1981, s 1; Public Health (Scotland) Act 1897, s 69(1) (as amended); Housing (Scotland) Act 1987 ss 129 and 324; Control of Pollution Act 1974, s 13(6) (as amended).
8. As inserted by s 1 of the Education (Scotland) Act 1981.
9. See *The Laws of Scotland op cit* note 1 *supra* para 202 footnote 8, and of particular relevance to sheriffs *Brown v Hamilton District Council*, 1983 SLT 397 (HL), which established that common law judicial review is competent only in the Court of Session.
10. *Glasgow Corporation v Glasgow Churches' Council*, 1944 SC 97.
11. See *The Laws of Scotland op cit* para 338, based on C.M.G. Himsworth *'Administrative Appeals to the Sheriff'* (unpublished).
12. I.D. Macphail *op cit* note 6 *supra* at para 26–13.
13. I.A. Milne in the *Introduction to Scottish Legal History* Stair Society (1958) Vol 20 at 350–351.
14. C.A. Malcolm in *op cit* note 13 *supra* at 360.
15. Green's *Encyclopaedia of Scots Law* (1899) Vol 11 at 320.
16. J.S. Shaw *The Management of Scottish Society, 1707–1764* John Donald (1983), at 18 and ch 2.
17. Green's *Encyclopaedia of Scots Law* (1899) Vol 11 at 320.
18. Since the Sheriff Courts (Scotland) Act 1971 s 4 'Sheriffs Depute' are referred to as 'Sheriffs Principal', and 'Sheriffs substitute' are known as 'Sheriffs'.
19. A.E. Whetstone *Scottish County Government in the 18th and 19th Centuries* John Donald (1981) ch 1.
20. *Ibid* at X and 116–117. See also O. Checkland *Philanthropy in Victorian Scotland* John Donald (1980) Parts III–V.
21. Checkland *ibid*, and R.E. Wraith and P.G. Hutchesson 'Administrative Tribunals' Allen and Unwin (1973) at 29; 'Scottish legal history points to a much closer relationship between the administration of justice and the conduct of government than a superficial understanding of the separation of powers doctrine would admit.'
22. The Report of the Commission on the Court of Session and Office of Sheriff Principal Cmd 2801 (1927).

23. Report *op cit* note 22 *supra* at para 1181.
24. Cmnd 3248 (1967) ch VIII.
25. 1976 SLT (Sh Ct) 3.
26. *Ibid* at 6, and see also C.M.G. Himsworth 'Scottish Local Authorities and the Sheriff' (1984) *Jur Rev* at 75–77.
27. A.E. Whetstone *op cit* note 19 *supra* at X and Lord Cooper of Culross *Selected Papers* Oliver & Boyd (1957) at 180–181.
28. The Grant Report on the Sheriff Court Cmnd 3248 (1967) para 268.
29. I.D. Macphail *op cit* note 6 *supra* at para 26–08.
30. SLC Memorandum No. 14 *Remedies in Administrative Law* para 10.2.
31. See *ibid* note 28 and Cmd 2801 (1927) para 2775 C (Oral evidence presented by the Association of Sheriffs Substitute: 'The office of sheriff substitute was never intended to be an administrative one. It has only grown to be so . . . by the customary habit of the legislature when putting down administrative duties of allowing them to be performed by the Sheriff Substitute.').
32. 1988 SCLR 327.
33. *Ibid* at 331.
34. *Op cit* note 1 *supra*.
35. D.N. MacCormick, *H.L.A. Hart*, Edward Arnold (1981) 129 quoted in C. Harlow and R. Rawlings *Law and Administration* Weidenfeld & Nicolson (1984) 316.
36. Lord Hailsham *The Dilemma of Democracy: Diagnosis and Prescription* (1978) 106–7, quoted in Harlow and Rawlings *op cit* note 35 *supra* at 315.
37. Principally C.M.G. Himsworth in 'Scottish Local Authorities and the Sheriff' (1984) *Jur Rev* at 80–86, and I.D. Macphail *op cit* note 6 *supra*.
38. See note 1 *supra*.
39. W. Jennings 'The Report on Ministers' Powers' (1932) 10 *Public Admin* 333.
40. *Ibid* at 345–346.
41. G. Marshall 'Justiciability' in A.G. Guest (Ed) *Oxford Essays in Jurisprudence* Clarendon Press (1961).
42. *Carvana v Glasgow Corporation*, 1976 SLT (Sh Ct) 3 at 7.
43. See C.M.G. Himsworth *op cit* note 37 *supra* at 78–80.
44. L. Fuller *op cit* note 5 *supra* at 397–398.
45. T.C. Hartley and J.A.G. Griffith *Government and Law* (2nd ed) Weidenfeld & Nicolson (1981) 334, and see also Harlow and Rawlings *op cit* note 35 *supra* at 81.
46. D.J. Mullan 'Fairness: The New Natural Justice?' (1975) 25 *University of Toronto L J* 281 at 300 and Harlow and Rawlings, *ibid*.
47. (1898) 14 Sh Ct Rep 189 at 192 and C.M.G. Himsworth *op cit* note 37 *supra* at 79.
48. But not always: see C.M.G. Himsworth *ibid* at 79–80.
49. D.J. Galligan *Discretionary Powers* Clarendon Press (1986) 216.
50. *Ibid* at 239.
51. *Ibid* at 240.
52. E. de Bono *The Mechanism of Mind*, Simon and Schuster (1969) 7.
53. See *Portobello Magistrates v Edinburgh Magistrates* (1882) 10 R 130; *Neill's Trs v Macfarlane's Trs* 1952 SC 356; and *Director-General of Fair Trading v Boswell* 1979 SLT (Sh Ct) 9.
54. E.g. Agricultural Holdings (Scotland) Act 1949 ss 74 and 75, Sched 6, paras 16 and 18, and Merchant Shipping Act 1894 s 668.
55. Licensing (Scotland) Act 1976 s 117(2).
56. Cmnd 3248 (1967) para 305.
57. Oral Evidence presented to the Grant Committee by Edinburgh University on 18th January 1967 at 20 (unpublished).
58. Oral Evidence presented to the Grant Committee by Sheriffs-Depute on 5 February 1965 at 24 (unpublished).
59. *Ibid* at 19.

60. Ss 18–21.
61. 1989 SLT 3 at 49; see also *T v Secretary of State for Scotland* 1987 SCLR 65.
62. S 8.
63. See *ibid* ss 3, 5, 7, as amended by the Lunacy (Scotland) Act 1857, and the Mental Health (Scotland) Act 1960.
64. SLC *op cit* note 2 *supra* para 10.2.
65. *Associated Provincial Picture Houses Ltd v Wednesbury Corporation* [1948] 1 KB 223.
66. (Sheriff Dean) (Glasgow Sheriff Court) 23 June 1989, unreported.
67. *Ibid* (transcript) at 1.
68. *Ibid* at 4.
69. *The Laws of Scotland op cit* note 1 *supra* at para 338.
70. S 28A, as inserted by Education (Scotland) Act 1981 s 1.
71. M. Adler, A. Petch and J. Tweedie, 'Parental Choice and Educational Policy', Edinburgh U P (1989) 159–160.
72. *Ibid.*
73. (Sheriff Maguire) (Glasgow Sheriff Court), 17 August 1983, unreported (transcript) 4.
74. Adler, Petch and Tweedie *op cit* note 71 *supra.*
75. *Ibid* and (Sheriff McVicar) (Edinburgh Sheriff Court), 20 October, 1982, unreported (transcript) 7.
76. See also the Civic Government (Scotland) Act 1982, Schedule 1, para 18(7).
77. L. Fuller *op cit* note 5 *supra* at 43.
78. Cmnd 2021 (1963).
79. 'If what is appealed to the Sheriff is in a real sense a true *lis* between the parties, so that the sheriff has to pronounce a judgement between the respective claimants, then the appeal involves invoking the sheriff in his judicial capacity.' See *Kaye v Hunter* 1958 SC 208 at 211, and I.D. Macphail *op cit* note 6 *supra* paras 26–38.
80. See *Strathclyde R C v Hunter*, (Sheriff Principal Dick), (Glasgow Sheriff Court), 23 December 1981, unreported.
81. *Child Care Law Review, Consultation Document 1* (1989) paras 3.9, 3.10 and 3.11.
82. Adler, Petch and Tweedie *op cit* note 71 *supra* 49–53.
83. C. Harlow and R. Rawlings *op cit* note 35 *supra* chs 1 and 2.
84. A.W. Bradley Book Review (1981) 1 *Legal Studies* 329 at 332.
85. D.C.M. Yardley *Principles of Administrative Law* Butterworths (1981) viii.
86. Licensing (Scotland) Act 1976, s 117(2) and Burial Grounds (Scotland) Act 1855, ss 4, 5.
87. A.W. Bradley *op cit* note 1 *supra* paras 213–301.
88. C.M.G. Himsworth *op cit* note 37 *supra* at 86 and I.D. Macphail *op cit* note 6 *supra* at 26–10.
89. A.W. Bradley *op cit* note 1 *supra* at paras 345–499 and *Brown v Hamilton DC* 1983 SLT 397.

Ombudsmen: the Private Sector Dimension

A.R. Mowbray

A. Introduction

In his significant contribution towards modern thought on administrative law Professor A.W. Bradley has always extended his gaze beyond the courts engaged in judicial review, important though that function may be.[1] Hence we have his writings on the role of tribunals in the field of social security adjudication.[2] One institution which provides redress for citizens' grievances outside the traditional framework of adjudication has attracted Bradley's scrutiny on several occasions during the last two decades. That institution is the Parliamentary Commissioner for Administration (PCA), more commonly referred to as the Ombudsman.[3] During the early 1970s Bradley perceived the value of the PCA's case reports as a rich vein of information for administrative lawyers regarding the internal processes and features of central government administration. He noted that 'the published reports of the Parliamentary Commissioner, despite their limitations, give a much more vivid and complete picture of the actual work of government than do the administrative law cases in the law reports'.[4] Bradley disclosed that from this source we could learn of the way in which administrative discretion was exercised in the taxation system, the payment of war pensions and the making of *ex gratia* payments by departments.[5] Later, Bradley subjected these reports to a study which resulted in the finding that

> thus, inevitably, the British Ombudsman has developed principles, standards and rules of what he believes to constitute good administration, since otherwise no notion of maladministration could have emerged . . . . And it may not be pressing this analysis too far to conclude that the individual citizen thus acquires what may properly be called new rights to the maintenance of a certain quality of administration.[6]

He also extracted specific norms governing the need to handle citizens' affairs with reasonable speed and the duty to give correct advice to citizens regarding their dealings with government, from the PCA's jurisprudence. Thus Bradley helped pioneer the academic evaluation of the Ombudsman's casework and thereby contributed towards one of the growth industries of the 1980s.[7] Additionally, he has sought to educate a wider public about the existence and workings of the PCA through his textbook[8] and via his video-recorded discussions with the last two serving Ombudsmen.

This essay seeks to extend Bradley's scrutiny of the Parliamentary Ombudsman into the sphere of private sector ombudsmen whose roles are to investigate not the workings of central government departments but those of major insurance companies, banks and building societies.[9] Can, however, the constitution, powers and functioning of such ombudsmen operating in the market-place of the financial services industry be said to fall within the legitimate concerns of public lawyers? The answer must surely be yes, as public lawyers have a duty constantly to adjust the boundaries of their subject as the nature of the state and its allocation of functions alters in accordance with changing ideological values. As McAuslan has argued, public lawyers need to recognise that currently

> the dominant administrative-cum-economic perspective is public choice, a philosophy which rejects collective consumption and takes as its basic principle the efficacy, indeed the superior moral quality, of the market, as a way of distributing public goods and services; a philosophy which goes a long way towards rejecting the notion of public goods and services when applied to education, health care, housing and utilities. Rather than collective provision, there should be private provision, rather than collective consumption there should be individual consumption based on individual choice.[10]

Consequently, the institutions which were once clearly part of the public administrative structure have now been re-allocated to the business sector through processes such as privatisation.[11] Yet, society as a whole may still claim an interest in the functions performed by such organisations. Lewis argues that developments over recent decades mean that today there is an interpenetration between government and society with the result, 'that there is no clear divide between the public and private spheres. The public interest in the general governance of the nation is extensive, in fact unlimited. We should not, in particular, be confused by the labels ordinarily attached to functions as being distinctly private or public.'[12]

Therefore, from these theoretical perspectives public lawyers should not feel constrained to limit their attentions to a contracting group of formal public institutions. Also, from a more prosaic standpoint, we should be interested in the evolution of the private sector ombudsmen in order to discover if they have borrowed any practices or concepts from their older public sector counterparts.[13] It may also be that the private sector ombudsmen have refined methods of operation which would be of relevance to the public ombudsmen.

B. The Constitutional Arrangements and Powers of the Private Sector Ombudsmen

The legal structures of all the private ombudsmen have been moulded by the actions of three major insurance companies[14] who decided in 1980 to establish a voluntary ombudsman scheme for their sector of the financial services industry.[15] They adopted the legal form of a private unlimited company[16] for their scheme. The company's Memorandum of Association provides that its objectives include the receiving of 'references in relation to complaints, disputes and claims made in connection with or arising out of policies of insurance or contracts . . . and to facilitate the satisfactory settlement or withdrawal of such complaints, disputes or claims whether by the making of awards or by such other means as shall seem expedient'. To that end the Articles of Association create three bodies. The *Board of Directors* comprises a maximum of twelve persons, three of whom may be lay members, whilst the remainder must hold senior offices in organisations belonging to the *Bureau*. The primary duties of the Board are to control the financial affairs of the Bureau and to appoint, or approve the appointment of, Council members. The *Council*, which currently has ten members, two of whom are directly appointed by the Board, has responsibility for appointing the Insurance Ombudsman; defining his powers and duties, subject to the Bureau's Memorandum of Association; receiving the Ombudsman's annual report; approving a draft budget for each financial year (which is subject to the Board's final endorsement); and instituting or defending legal proceedings brought by or against the Bureau. The *Ombudsman*[17] must be financially independent of organisations which are members of the Bureau[18] and holds office for a maximum of two years (a period which is renewable). He can investigate eligible complaints from natural persons about their insurance policies with member organisations. Several conditions govern the receivability of complaints, including prior consideration of the dispute by senior management in the relevant member organisation, the absence of previous referrals of the dispute to the Ombudsman, the abandonment of any contemporaneous legal proceedings concerning the dispute and the referral of the complaint to the Ombudsman within six months of senior management having expressed their views on the issue. During the course of an investigation the Ombudsman can request a member organisation to provide any relevant information which is in its possession. If the member fails to accede to such a request within a reasonable time the Ombudsman must refer the matter to the Council for their consideration. As a result of his inquiries the Ombudsman may make a binding award against a member and in favour of the complainant for a sum not exceeding £100,000. In making such an award the Ombudsman should, 'act in conformity with any applicable rule of law or relevant judicial authority, with general principles of good insurance, investment or marketing practice and with his terms of reference . . . [but he is not] bound by any previous decision made by him or by any other Ombudsman or by any predecessor in any such office'.[19] Hence the Insurance Ombudsman scheme represents an innovative example of the private law concept of a company being harnessed to provide the constitutional structure for a voluntary ombudsman regime.

The next sector in the financial services field to create an ombudsman was the banking industry. During 1983 the National Consumer Council published a report[20] which revealed that around one third of the bank customers who were surveyed displayed dissatisfaction with the manner in which the banks dealt with their complaints. The report suggested that an ombudsman scheme would enable these concerns to be alleviated and could also provide the banks with useful data regarding their customers' worries. Therefore, in 1985, nineteen banks, including all the major high street banks, created the Banking Ombudsman scheme.[21] They also used the registered unlimited company as the legal form for their scheme. Their tripartite constitutional arrangements of a Board, Council and Ombudsman replicated the organisation of the Insurance Bureau. However, there are some differences in the composition of the Board and Council under the banking scheme. The *Board* of the Office of the Banking Ombudsman is wholly composed of representatives of the sponsoring banks, whilst the *Council* has a lay majority of only one member, including the lay Chair. The power to appoint an independent *Ombudsman*[22] is exercised by the Council. The Ombudsman's general remit is to 'receive unresolved complaints about the provision of banking services and to facilitate the satisfaction, settlement or withdrawal of such complaints'.[23] The concept of banking services covers 'all banking services provided by banks in the ordinary course of their business to individuals'.[24] However, certain types of complaint are expressly excluded from the Ombudsman's jurisdiction, such as complaints directed at the banks' commercial judgements about lending and security, the general interest rate policies of banks and concessionary services accorded to banking employees. As with the insurance scheme, eligible complaints must have been brought to the attention of senior managers in the relevant bank and must be referred to the Banking Ombudsman within six months of that time. During an investigation the Ombudsman may request a bank to provide him with related information in its possession. If such a request is unreasonably refused by the bank it can be reported to the Council. A successful complaint can result in the Ombudsman making a binding award of up to £100,000 damages against a member bank. But, such an award must be compensatory and not punitive. Furthermore, at any time prior to the Ombudsman's making such an award the respondent bank can remove the complaint from the Ombudsman's scrutiny on the grounds that it raises an issue of important consequences for the bank or involves a novel point of law.

The last financial services ombudsman to be created was the Building Societies Ombudsman. Although this scheme has a constitutional structure broadly similar to the two ombudsmen previously examined its legal origins are, uniquely for the private sector ombudsmen, found in legislation. During the committee stage of the Building Societies Bill in 1986, cross-party back-bench opinion encouraged the Government to promise an amendment providing for a mechanism to deal with complaints against societies. That promise matured into sections 83–85 of the 1986 Act; they require all building societies to create an independent complaints mechanism which is recognised by the Building Societies Commission.[25] Subsequently, the societies agreed amongst themselves to create one common ombudsman scheme.[26]

Under the building societies' arrangements their *Board of Directors* is composed wholly of representatives from the societies, but the *Council* has a lay majority of two members (including the Chairman). The jurisdiction of the *Ombudsman* is more elaborately defined than in the other schemes. Specified activities by the societies are covered,[27] subject to the Ombudsman's discretion to decline or discontinue an investigation if certain conditions are present.[28] A complainant must, however, base his complaint on undefined grounds, which include 'maladministration' and 'unfair treatment'.[29] He is also required to allege that the society's actions have caused him 'pecuniary loss, expense or inconvenience'.[30] The Ombudsman may require the complainant or a society to provide him with relevant information in their possession. He can make an award of up to £100,000 against a society and such an award is binding unless the society refuses to pay and agrees to publish the reasons for its refusal.[31] Such a let-out clause was subject to critical back-bench comments during the report stage of the Bill, but the Minister offered the following justification:

> [W]e felt obliged to include the let-out clause by which a society may decide not to comply with the ombudsman's decision as long as it explains its reasons publicly, because we did not want to remove the legal rights of a society before the courts . . . But there is a point of principle. In requiring societies to belong to a scheme under which they must accept the directions of a third party, we should be depriving them of their rights of law before the courts.[32]

Hence the legislative basis of the scheme was invoked as a rationale for the non-binding nature of the Ombudsman's awards. However, other procedures, such as judicial review of the Ombudsman's reasoning and decision, would also have enabled building societies to seek a legal resolution of their rights.[33]

Despite the common usage of the private company concept and a basic three-organ structure the above schemes demonstrate some marked differences in their constitutional arrangements and powers. As regards the membership of the important councils, which act as the bulwarks between the industry-dominated boards and the independent ombudsmen, the lay majorities varied from six under the insurance scheme to one under the banking arrangements. Clearly, therefore, some sponsoring industries had a greater say in the oversight of their ombudsmen than had others. Likewise, the formal investigative powers of the ombudsmen varied – the Building Societies Ombudsman being able to require the production of documents, whereas his insurance and banking counterparts could only request the provision of information. This power is important because, as we shall see below, sponsoring organisations may not always willingly provide documents sought by an ombudsman. Lastly, the Insurance Ombudsman was the only one empowered to make an unconditionally binding formal award against a sponsoring company; this fact reveals the caution of some industries when drafting their ombudsman schemes.

C. The Roles of Private Sector Ombudsmen

Moving on from the formal structures of the Ombudsmen we need to consider how they actually perceive their roles and their relationships with other grievance-handling agencies. From the early years of the pioneering

insurance scheme it was made clear by the Council of the Bureau that the
Ombudsman was neutral as between the interests of consumers and the
sponsoring industry. The Council observed that

> there is a common misconception that the Ombudsman is 'the
> consumer's protagonist'. This is not so and it would be to the
> disadvantage of policyholders if it were so. It is the Ombudsman's
> impartiality guaranteed by the Council, which assures both insured and
> insurer fair consideration of their dispute. If the Insurance Ombudsman
> were to be partial in either side he would lose his credibility as an
> adjudicator.[34]

Although he is a neutral adjudicator, he has not adopted the Anglo-American
judicial umpire role;[35] instead, the Insurance Ombudsman considers that
'an Ombudsman is by nature an inquisitor, like a coroner or like a judge
in any of the European systems of law'.[36] In performing this function the
Ombudsman has sought to avoid trespassing on the territory of the ordinary
courts. This was made clear in a complaint regarding a company's refusal
to pay a death claim under a life policy. The Ombudsman articulated the
principle that a company should not make such a payment unless there was
a death certificate or judicial declaration of death. Furthermore 'although
on the face of it I have power to make an award against a company of up
to £100,000 and can thus cut across the Court's jurisdiction to inquire into
a death it is no part of my function to usurp the Court's powers and in
effect to declare the policyholder dead by finding as a fact that the event
covered by the policy has happened'.[37] Consequently, the Ombudsman
believes that the subject-matter of some complaints renders them more
suitable for resolution by other remedial mechanisms.

The Banking Ombudsman has likewise stated that he adopts a neutral
position *vis-à-vis* banks and their customers. In his first report he noted,

> the term 'Ombudsman' means 'Grievance Man' and what the Banking
> Ombudsman Scheme seeks to do is to provide an Ombudsman who
> will try to promote a satisfactory outcome to a complaint within the
> scope of the scheme when it has transpired that such cannot be achieved
> between bank and customer. Nevertheless – and it is important that
> this be understood – the Banking Ombudsman is not a 'customer's
> champion', concerned to uphold the customer 'right or wrong'. He
> is more in the nature of an umpire or referee.[38]

Clearly, therefore, a consensus among the private sector ombudsmen as to
their attitudes towards sponsoring companies and dissatisfied customers has
been evolving. This may be due, in part, to institutional links between the
separate ombudsmen. As the Banking Ombudsmen disclosed,

> [We] do also receive some complaints which are nothing to do with
> banking (e.g. matters of central and local government). All those the
> Office of the Banking Ombudsman tries to re-direct into a more
> appropriate channel, and we have informal 'two way' arrangements for
> forwarding to and from various other national bodies. For example,
> we have liaison arrangements with the Insurance Ombudsman Bureau
> under which insurance complaints more aptly falling within that scheme
> can be transferred to it, and vice-versa.[39]

He has also stated that certain types of complaints are more suited to resolution by the courts. During one year he discontinued investigations into three complaints because

> two were cases of alleged defamation involving issues of law and fact of major complexity, and the third a case involving the resolution of acutely conflicting evidence of a course of negotiations and events which took place over a period of several months – and our scheme is not a suitable forum for trials estimated to last for days if not weeks.[40]

This illustrates the limits on the fact-finding powers of some private sector ombudsmen.

The Council of the Building Societies Ombudsman has endorsed the independent role of their ombudsman,[41] who has openly acknowledged the debt his office owed to the established Insurance and Banking Ombudsmen during the period of its gestation. Their links have remained due to the fact that, 'we cooperate regularly on an informal and highly satisfactory basis'.[42] However, in elaborating the extent of his powers the Building Societies Ombudsman has also had regard to the heritage of the public sector ombudsmen. He reported that

> [a] high proportion of complaints which I receive allege maladministration, which is not defined in the 1986 Act or my terms of reference. However, a guide which is often quoted is the so-called 'Crossman Catalogue' which was part of a statement made in Parliament at the time of the passing of the Parliamentary Commissioner Act 1967. Even though this catalogue was provided in the context of the public service, I find it a useful guideline.[43]

He thus expressly recognised that similar jurisdictional concepts may govern both public and private sector ombudsmen.

Overall, the private sector ombudsmen have developed a common understanding of their roles as neutral investigators and decision-makers. Their similar understanding appears to be partly the product of a common culture derived from the newer ombudsmen building on the foundations created by the established schemes, together with their current regular exchanges. However, it may be contended that such an understanding is a universal one held by ombudsmen in both the private and public sectors. Hence the Parliamentary Commissioner has recently defined the ombudsman principle thus: '[T]he essence of that principle is, as I see it, that citizens with grievances concerning the administrative actions of government departments or public bodies are entitled to an *independent* investigation and appraisal of the justification – or otherwise – for their complaints'[44] [original emphasis]. The private sector ombudsmen have also acknowledged that the courts may have superior fact-finding abilities. In this context they should perhaps have regard to the experience of the PCA who has developed a number of techniques, such as applying a balance of probabilities test and obtaining the views of relevant third parties, in order to resolve disputes concerning questions of fact.[45] His practices could help to bolster the skills and confidence of the financial services ombudsmen.

D. The Relationship Between Supervisory Councils and their Ombudsmen

The annual reports of the three ombudsmen schemes disclose a spectrum of relationships between the councils and the ombudsmen. At one extreme the Council of the Insurance Ombudsman Bureau normally confines its brief annual comments to an endorsement of his determinations. For example, in 1984 their Chairman stated that 'furthermore the Council itself, while it appoints the Ombudsman and maintains watch over his operations, also keeps at arm's length from the Ombudsman's actual decisions. The Council backs his judgment on the basis of his overall performance, but has no part in the considerations which lead to particular decisions.'[46] And, significantly, in his retrospective comments on holding the office of Insurance Ombudsman for eight years, James Haswell made no reference to his Council.[47]

By contrast, the Council of the Banking Ombudsman Scheme have demonstrated more activism in the performance of their tasks. They have gone so far as to define what they consider amounts to maladministration in the context of bank lending: 'normally maladministration can be loosely defined as ". . . muddle or mistake . . ." but in this instance we have made it clear that it also includes undue delay'.[48] In another report the Council expressed a willingness to recommend improvements in 'good banking practice' where they considered it appropriate in the light of specific investigations by the Ombudsman.[49] They also gave their support to the Ombudsman when a bank refused to provide him with papers relating to three complaints against them. The bank claimed that the Ombudsman was acting *ultra vires*. Nevertheless, 'we – the Council – insisted that the decision on whether a particular complaint fell inside or outside the terms of reference must lie with the Ombudsman, not with the bank. The Board, representing all the member banks, accepted our view and persuaded the bank in question to submit the papers and accept the Ombudsman's adjudication.'[50]

During a relatively short existence the Building Societies Ombudsman Council have adopted a relationship with their Ombudsman which falls within the spectrum delimited by the insurance and banking councils. They have supported the Building Societies Ombudsman in his unsuccessful attempts to have his terms of reference amended to include expressly 'precompletion' matters (e.g. pre-purchase valuations or surveys).[51] Additionally, the Council have sought to publicise the situation where a building society exercised their right under the scheme not to pay an award made by the Ombudsman. In their subsequent annual report the Council declared: '[W]e are nevertheless determined that building societies should not confuse a publicity option with a soft option. The price tag attached to the required negative publicity should always be an appropriately high one, so that societies think long and hard before deciding to pay it.'[52]

It is difficult to extract from the annual reports comprehensive explanations for these differing relationships between councils and ombudsmen. Whilst personalities and their interaction may be relevant, one factor which clearly encouraged activism by councils in regard to casework was the existence of business resistence to scrutiny by ombudsmen. Consequently, where a bank refused to supply papers to the Banking Ombudsman and a building society refused to meet an award made by the Building Societies Ombudsman the appropriate councils were required, by their position in the constitutional structure of the schemes, to intervene publicly to support their ombudsmen. In giving this support the councils were following the established practice of the Select Committee on the PCA, which carefully monitors the Parliamentary Commissioner's powers and Departmental responses to his conclusions in specific cases.[53] By way of contrast the Representative Body, to whom the Local Ombudsmen in England report, have demonstrated a much less positive attitude. Indeed their primary concern with budgetary matters and retaining the jurisdictional status quo is more reflective of the attitude shown by some of the Boards of Directors under the private ombudsman schemes.[54]

E. The Ombudsmen's Processes of Investigation and Decision-Making

In his first annual report, the Insurance Ombudsman distinguished the process of providing summary advice from that of investigating complaints. Of the former he stated: '[S]ome of the enquiries which reach the Bureau concern issues based on the interpretation of a member company's standard policy where the facts are essentially simple and accepted by both sides. In some such cases I will offer 'summary advice' to the policyholder because I have a counselling function written into my terms of reference.'[55] The main rationale for the abbreviated process of decision-making was to provide a speedy answer to the enquirer's query without having to wait for the production of case files by the relevant company. He then elaborated on the methods by which complaints were fully investigated. As all complaints are unique the Insurance Ombudsman cannot adopt a single method of investigation; instead, he has evolved three processes which vary according to the substance of the complaint.

First, where the complaint revolves around an issue of fact he will employ an expert to give his opinion on the matter. For example, a structural engineer may be able to explain what caused damage to a building. If an expert's opinion cannot resolve a serious conflict of evidence then the Ombudsman will himself investigate the matter. These investigations will not normally be conducted on adversarial lines.[56] Instead he adopts an inquisitorial procedure which he explained thus,

[I]t is based on the judicial inquiry and is closely analogous to the civil and criminal systems of trial on the continent of Europe. I observe the rules of natural justice all right, but they are wider and more flexible than those applicable to the courts in this country. Essentially, they do not require me to question any set of facts which seem on the face of it to be unchallenged and therefore I do not have to seek many policyholders. I can and do give to anyone who is likely to be adversely affected by a decision of mine an opportunity to produce further facts or to be heard on points of law or insurance practice before I make it.[57]

If this practice is unable to facilitate the determination of fundamental questions of fact then the Insurance Ombudsman can hold an adversarial hearing with legal representation for the parties and cross-examination of witnesses modelled on a High Court trial.[58]

Secondly, the Insurance Ombudsman has to deal with complaints about issues of law normally involving the interpretation of insurance policies. Where the language of the policy is of a traditional form this frequently obliges the Ombudsman to apply rulings of the courts.[59] However, the modern tendency is for the insurance industry to use 'plain English' when drafting its policies. The Ombudsman stressed in his first report that, 'in cases where new wording is involved it is extremely important to observe the proper principles of interpretation and I have access to counsel when necessary to assist me'.[60] By 1988 he was also utilising a more basic approach:

> '[W]hen considering the extraordinary meanings which some aggrieved policyholders have put on words used in policies, I have devised a very simple test: could the claimant reasonably have used the particular word in the policy when describing the incident to a friend? To take a rather dotty example from an old case, would he have said to his friend: 'Squirrels got into my roof space and their teeth made an *impact* on the electric wiring up there'? . . . [D]amage by vermin cannot reasonably be brought within [the scope of the insured peril of 'impact'] by twisting the language out of shape.[61]

Thirdly, the Insurance Ombudsman investigates complaints about the exercise of discretion by insurance companies to affirm or avoid a contract, to allow or repudiate a claim or to make an *ex gratia* payment. In such a review, he states 'I would only interfere with the exercise of discretion if on examination of the company's claims file I felt that insufficient facts were available for a fair decision or the company had been misinformed or an error of principle had been perpetrated and that there had been injustice towards the policyholder'.[62]

Errors of principle cover the situation where a company acts contrary to established good insurance practice. The Ombudsman discovers the substance of these norms by making enquiries of experienced claims staff and having regard to current textbooks.

The Banking Ombudsman has developed a two-stage process for handling complaints. During the first stage, termed 'Informal Assessment', he seeks to act as a conciliator between the complainant and the bank with the objective of securing an agreed resolution of the dispute. If such an outcome is not achieved then he will reach his own findings and issue a 'Formal Recommendation'. The Ombudsman has explained that he attempts to follow a procedure of investigation which is 'flexible and as informal as possible'. It appears that this process is primarily focused on the scrutiny of documents because

> banking matters do normally involve a legal relationship between banker and customer to which established legal principles apply. And the vast majority of complaints under the Scheme do turn to a very substantial extent upon written records of one sort or another. For those reasons

it is the exception rather than the rule to arrange oral hearings in connection with any aspect of a complaint.[63]

The Ombudsman is, however, willing to send one of his staff to visit the home of complainants if such a method of obtaining information is necessary.[64]

The Building Societies Ombudsman also uses an inquisitorial procedure which relies heavily upon documentary evidence. Complainants must file a standard complaints form with his office and he then seeks a written response from the appropriate society. The complainant is then given an opportunity to comment on the society's submission. At this stage he, like the Banking Ombudsman, tries to effect a negotiated settlement, because, he reports, 'I welcome the resolution of disputes by agreement. I consider that a compromise is often likely to be more satisfactory than a formal decision. I do what I can to encourage them in appropriate cases.'[65] Where such an agreement cannot be reached the Ombudsman will then draft his determination. He considers 'whether the Society is in breach of its obligations under the 1986 Act or any contract, or is guilty of unfair treatment or maladministration'.[66] In arriving at such a conclusion he may call upon the advice of experts in fields as diverse as automatic teller machines (i.e. cash dispensers) and the forgery of documents. The Ombudsman then faces a task of 'great difficulty' in calculating what financial loss the complainant has suffered as a result of the society's failings. When the Ombudsman has completed his draft report he will send it to the parties for their comments and then formally issue his decision.

Comparing the decision-making procedures of the three ombudsmen we can once again observe a substantial degree of uniformity of practice among them. They all demonstrated a marked reluctance to convene adversarial oral hearings and a preference for the inquisitorial method. And, in ascertaining facts, they primarily relied upon documentary evidence supplemented by the opinions of expert advisors. The ombudsmen were also active promoters of bilaterally agreed settlements of disputes which pre-empted the need for formal determinations of the complaints. By way of contrast, the PCA historically used a labour-intensive method of investigation which was, according to Stacey, of high quality because, 'in the great majority of cases the Parliamentary Commissioner's investigators go to the department to examine the files once an investigation has been decided upon, and in about 50% of cases also interview the civil servant concerned.'[67] More recently, though, Rawlings alleged that the PCA has become complacent in his investigations: 'quite often the PCA's staff did not even bother to talk to the complainant before reaching a conclusion.'[68] Nor does the PCA act as a conciliator. This is because the MP filter[69] is designed to ensure that disputes capable of bilateral solution are not referred on to the PCA, whereas the Local Ombudsmen in England are keen supporters of conciliated settlements,[70] the explanation being, in the words of their Chairman, that their primary task is to obtain 'a remedy for any person whose complaint is substantiated and a local settlement does precisely this.'[71]

Another facet of the private sector ombudsmen's decision-making is the status and weight attached to their earlier decisions by the ombudsmen themselves and by members of the industries subject to their scrutiny. The Insurance Ombudsman confronted this issue in 1985 when he warned loss adjustors not to treat his statements as binding rules of law:

> [C]ertainly I have expressed views on points of principle and on procedures and practices generally, sometimes illustrating the point by reference to cases I have decided. However, there is one enormous difference which is being overlooked when decisions of mine are quoted. I am an ombudsman, not a judge! I operate in the area of discretion, not solely that of strict law. There is therefore, no guarantee that I will apply any principle I have derived from my earlier cases to any particular claim. There may be overwhelming reasons why I should not do so and that is why I am quite specifically not bound by my terms of reference to follow previous decisions.[72]

He repeated a similar warning in his next annual report.[73] However, a later report suggests that he is gradually beginning to increase the significance of earlier determinations as a factor in subsequent decision-making:

> As Ombudsman, I am not bound by precedent and am thus free to deal individually with the hard cases which would otherwise proverbially make bad law. However, I am now receiving references on some topics in such numbers that various sets of principles have emerged. It is the more important of those principles which are regularly published in my Annual Reports and treated with reasonable caution give an indication of how mainstream cases are likely to be decided.[74]

The Building Societies Ombudsman has also expressly endorsed the above statement.[75] On the other hand, the Banking Ombudsman has tended to minimise the originality and significance of his earlier decision-making:

> [A]part from the circumstance that the Terms of Reference expressly relieve me of any obligation to follow my own previous decisions in later cases I have in my Formal Recommendations consciously reached a conclusion breaking any new legal ground in only one instance – an esoteric point of trust law of not the remotest importance to bank customers generally. For the rest I have merely applied existing authorities to the facts of the particular case as I have found them to be.[76]

As we have already seen, Bradley has revealed how the PCA has developed principles of good administration through his investigation of individual cases. To a lesser extent the same phenomenon can be found in the casework of the English Local Ombudsmen. In a major study, Lewis and his colleagues concluded: '[O]ur reading through many hundreds of reports suggests that some broad themes indicating maladministration can be detected but that it is dangerous to regard them as more than that.'[77] These findings suggest that where ombudsmen are confronted with an extensive case load over a number of years they inevitably begin to articulate general norms regarding particular types of behaviour by those institutions and persons subject to their scrutiny. Hence the willingness of the Insurance and Building Societies Ombudsmen to refine statements of principle out of their casework. But the constitutions establishing the private sector ombudsmen expressly prevent them from treating these principles as binding precedents. Furthermore, the private sector ombudsmen, unlike the PCA, do not publish their individual determinations, thereby depriving external commentators of an opportunity to analyse their determinations in order to discover the degree of consistency, if any, in their treatment of analogous complaints.

F. The Outcome of Investigations by the Ombudsmen

We can now consider the statistics regarding the determination of complaints by the three ombudsmen in order to discover how complainants fared under the different schemes. Inevitably, each ombudsman utilises a distinct system of recording statistics together with varied terminology to describe the results, thereby rendering the making of comparisons an imprecise science. Nevertheless, during 1988 the Insurance Ombudsman processed 4,661 enquiries.[78] But, in 1935 of these cases the policyholder subsequently failed to respond to the Ombudsman's correspondence. Therefore, the Ombudsman reached a formal determination in only 1,354 cases. The complainant was successful in 274 cases and the insurance companies' decisions were upheld by the Ombudsman in 1,080 cases. Consequently the Ombudsman reached a determination favourable to the complainant in just under 20 per cent of cases subject to a formal adjudication. In the course of 1988 the Ombudsman also received 2,541 enquiries about insurance companies which did not belong to the scheme and 640 which concerned matters outside his jurisdiction.

In his annual cycle covering 1987–88, the Banking Ombudsman dealt with 1,792 complaints.[79] Of this total 557 were rejected as relating to matters outside his jurisdiction. The Ombudsman interpreted his remaining cases as disclosing 299 consumer 'winners'. However, only 17 of these complainants actually received a determination by the Ombudsman which was in their favour: whilst the remaining 282 were achieved via his role as a conciliator. He also gave a formal determination against the complainant in 47 cases. Therefore, in terms of formal adjudications, complainants were successful in approximately 26% of cases.

Under the Building Societies Scheme the Ombudsman processed 1,217 enquiries during the year 1988–89.[80] Of these, 241 related to matters outside his jurisdiction. In 22 cases he determined that the complainant was wholly successful and in a further 27 cases that the complainant was partly successful, whereas he confirmed the actions of societies in 117 cases. Consequently, complainants were to varying degrees successful in approximately 29 per cent of cases reaching a formal adjudication. Additionally, 36 cases were settled by agreement between the parties.

From the above overview it is apparent that as regards formal determinations the private sector ombudsmen find in favour of complainants in between 20 and 30 per cent of cases. Although these figures might appear rather low they should be interpreted in the context of the ombudsmens' jurisdictions which expressly require the exhaustion of internal complaints mechanisms prior to investigation by the ombudsmen. If these internal processes are working satisfactorily one would expect the overwhelming majority of valid complaints to be settled at that stage. Therefore, it may be that only extremely complex and/or hopeless cases would be brought to the Ombudsmen by persistent complainants. Furthermore, as we now know, the ombudsmen seek to achieve conciliated settlements before proceeding to formal adjudications; therefore, at this stage the industries are given another opportunity to agree a satisfactory solution to justifiable complaints which have slipped through their internal complaints mechanisms. So, only a small proportion of valid complaints should ever filter through to a final determination by the ombudsmen.

It seems that the ombudsmen have not needed to have recourse to their constitutional powers to require the payment of compensatory awards by businesses where a complaint has been upheld. As the Banking Ombudsman reported, in all those cases where he found against a company they voluntarily paid any sum recommended by him.[81] Likewise, although James Haswell made explicit reference to this power in his retrospective review of the Insurance Ombudsman's work, he did not provide any examples of its actual usage.[82] Compliance with their findings and proposed remedies is not, therefore, a problem for the ombudsmen at the present time.[83] However, this conclusion is subject to banks and building societies continuing to refrain from exercising their rights to remove individual complaints from the ambit of the schemes.

The annual reports of the ombudsmen do not reveal many instances where businesses have made a general change to their practices as a result of recommendations derived from an ombudsman's investigation. One would expect to find the greatest number of these developments in the Insurance Ombudsman's reports, because his office has the longest history. He has indeed recorded the occasional modification of general business practices;[84] but more frequently his reports contain regular exhortations for specific changes which suggests that the industry is reluctant to alter its established behaviour at his behest.[85] It seems, therefore, that the financial services ombudsmen, like their public sector counterparts,[86] are more suited to securing justice for individual complainants than to achieving major administrative reforms.

G. External Assessments of the Ombudsmen

During the 1980s two official review bodies examined aspects of the functioning of the private sector ombudsmen. Professor L.C.B. Gower in his Review of Investor Protection noted the creation of the Insurance Ombudsman and expressed the view that 'this is an admirable move which might well be followed by other branches of investment business'.[87] However, he was concerned about the coverage of the scheme and in particular the absence of many life insurance companies at that time.

Later, the Jack Committee devoted a whole chapter of their Report on Banking Services to the operation of the Banking Ombudsman.[88] They also were in favour of the creation of an ombudsman to deal with consumer complaints, because

the Ombudsman process with its informality and accessibility is particularly well suited to the resolution of disputes between banker and personal customer. These disputes usually concern relatively small amounts of money, not worth the expense and inevitable delay of court action, yet sometimes giving rise to an intense personal sense of grievance.[89]

Nevertheless, the Committee reported that three major criticisms had been levelled against the existing scheme. First, the fairness of the scheme has been attacked. The Committee accepted that some features of the schemes were unfair, including the inability of the Ombudsman to compel the production of documents by banks and the right of banks to withdraw individual complaints from the Ombudsman's scrutiny. Secondly, the scheme could appear to lay persons to be unfair:

[T]he doubt on the score of credibility stems from its basic structure . . . [t]he undoubted remoteness of the Board from specific cases and decisions does not alter the fact that its role in approving both the original terms of reference, and any amendments to them, is absolutely crucial . . . We consider this matter of credibility a potentially serious flaw.[90]

Thirdly, the scheme was said to be inefficient because it did not cover every bank operating in the UK: 'indeed it is claimed that the Scheme covers about 99% of all private bank customers. Yet it has been represented to us that the omission of some smaller banks (especially ethnic banks) is a defect in the Scheme'.[91]

Although the Committee made no criticisms of the way in which the Ombudsman exercised his powers and reached determinations in particular cases, they were so dissatisfied with the structure of the scheme that they recommended its replacement with a statutory mechanism modelled on the building societies' arrangements. They felt that a statutory system would enable an external agency to establish the precise jurisdiction of the ombudsman, thereby alleviating public fears of unfairness (the Committee suggested that the Bank of England perform this role); a legislative mandate could ensure that all banks were parties to the scheme.

In the light of these major offical criticisms of the banking scheme, we can ask whether the voluntary insurance scheme is equally vulnerable to such a critical analysis? Taking first the criteria of the Ombudsman's powers it is apparent that he too can merely request the provision of documents held by companies.[92] Likewise, it is the Board of the Insurance Ombudsman Bureau who have the final say over the Ombudsman's terms of reference.[93] Thirdly, as regards the coverage of the scheme, we have already noted the concerns of Professor Gower and discovered that during 1988 the Ombudsman received 2,541 enquiries involving companies which were not members of the scheme.[94] Therefore, the structure of the insurance scheme demonstrates many of the weaknesses found in the banking scheme.

How then might future institutional reforms of the various ombudsmen schemes overcome the structural weaknesses elaborated by the Jack Committee? In their report the Committee raised the possibility of a merger between the Banking and Building Societies Ombudsmen Schemes. They believed that such a development would enable the ombudsmen to pool their knowledge on common topics (e.g. regarding Automatic Teller Machines which currently represent the most popular subject matter of *intra vires* complaints to both ombudsmen). Furthermore, the Committee recognised that the commercial activities of banks and building societies were increasingly overlapping,[95] with the likelihood that the two ombudsmen would be facing even greater similarity in the types of complaints referred to them. However, the Committee was worried about 'the difficulty of finding a generally acceptable organisational solution . . . and doubtless workload problems would intrude'.[96] Here the experience of public sector ombudsmen can provide a ready answer in the organisational form of the commission, which is utilised by the Local Ombudsmen in England. The commission structure enables one body collectively to handle many thousands of cases[97] with the combined virtue of a single commissioner/ombudsman retaining specific responsibility for the investigation of each complaint. The allocation of complaints between the commissioners/ombudsmen could be on the basis of geographical factors (e.g. the three English Local Ombudsmen each deal with complaints originating from a separate part of England) or subject matter (e.g. one ombudsman could specialise in ATM complaints). But the individual commissioners/ombudsmen can regularly meet together as a collegiate body to share their wisdom and determine important questions of policy. In addition the commission system has organisational advantages as the individual commissioners/ombudsmen can be serviced by one integrated body of support staff providing administrative and technical facilities. Complainants would also find it easier to refer their financial services queries to one commission and then let that body allocate their complaints to the appropriate commissioner/ombudsman. The structure of a commission is also flexible enough to allow the Insurance Ombudsman to participate in discussions of strategic policy questions affecting all the financial service ombudsmen (e.g. on measures to increase public awareness of the ombudsmen) by means of ex-officio membership of the new commission. For example, the PCA is able to participate in similar deliberations of the Commission for Local Administration by virtue of his ex-officio membership status.

G. Conclusions

It is now possible to answer the general questions that were posed at the beginning of our study. As to the manner in which the ombudsmen have evolved, we have seen that the three schemes have taken a similar legal form – the private company. But the supervisory boards and councils created under these schemes contain different ratios of lay and industry members. Similarly, the jurisdictions and powers of the ombudsmen vary according to the willingness of the sponsoring industries to delegate authority to their ombudsmen. The ombudsmen themselves have developed both personal and institutional relationships. From these associations a common culture has emerged which extends over their methods of investigation (e.g. a dislike of oral hearings and a preference for the scrutiny of written documents supplemented by the advice of experts), their status as neutral adjudicators between consumers and industries, together with their support for the conciliated settlement of complaints.

Generally, therefore, the financial services ombudsmen have developed without making many overt references to the established heritage of public sector ombudsmen in the United Kingdom, although the Building Societies Ombudsman has expressly adopted the 'Crossman Catalogue' as a source of guidance in defining the concept of maladministration. Despite this limited interchange between the private and public ombudsmen it is clear that they have reached an identical view of their role as independent investigators and decision-makers. Such a parallel development provides further evidence that there is a distinct function of dispute resolution through the offices of an ombudsman which can be distinguished from other modes of determination, such as arbitration or submission to a court of law. If there are to be institutional reforms of the financial services ombudsmen in the light of the Jack Committee's deliberations, then Parliament and the affected industries should take note of the virtues associated with the structural form of the commission, which has proved to be so useful in the context of the Local Ombudsmen in England.

The public sector ombudsmen could benefit from examining the methods by which the financial services ombudsmen have created distinct modes of investigation and determination according to the subject-matter and complexity of the complaint. It is obvious that the PCA needs to approach a straightforward complaint about the provision of advice to a citizen by a local social security office[98] differently from his investigation into the Barlow Clowes affair.[99] Yet the contrasting views of Stacey and Rawlings indicate that there is uncertainty as to the standard method of investigation followed by the Parliamentary Commissioner. Therefore, the PCA might profitably contemplate whether he should officially devise a range of investigative processes that varies according to the substance of the complaint.

This essay has shown that public lawyers still have much work to undertake during the 1990s in continuing Bradley's research into the workings of ombudsmen. There remains a need to examine the virtues of creating a legislative foundation for private sector ombudsmen, allied with the designing of institutional structures which promote both the independence and efficiency of these ombudsmen. Finally, a more detailed study of the casework determinations of the financial services ombudsmen is essential in order to increase our general knowlege regarding decision-making by ombudsmen. We must seek to grasp these challenges vigorously because, as Borrie recently observed, 'the ombudsman idea has proved itself a valuable independent complaints investigation instrument right across the boundary of the private and public sectors'.[100]

Notes

1. See his regular 'Comments' in *Public Law*, e.g. 'Judicial Review, the Prison Rules and the Segregation of Prisoners' [1989] PL 521.
2. E.g. 'Recent Reforms of Social Security Adjudication in Great Britain' (1985) 26 *Les Cahiers du Droit* 403.

3. Created by the Parliamentary Commissioner Act 1967, as amended by the Parliamentary and Health Service Commissioners Act 1987.

4. 'Research and Reform in Administrative law' 13 JSPTL 35 at 36.

5. See further C. Harlow *Compensation and Government Torts* Sweet & Maxwell (1982) Part 4.

6. 'The Role of the Ombudsman in Relation to the Protection of Citizens' Rights' [1980] CLJ 304 at 310–311.

7. See e.g. C. Harlow and R. Rawlings *Law and Administration* Weidenfeld & Nicolson (1984) chs 7, 8; A.R. Mowbray 'The Parliamentary Commissioner and Administrative Guidance' [1987] PL 570 and 'The Compounding of Proceedings by the Customs and Excise: Calculating the Legal Implications' [1988] BTR 290.

8. E.C.S. Wade and A.W. Bradley *Constitutional and Administrative Law* (10th ed) Longman (1985).

9. Other private sector ombudsmen exist (e.g. the ombudsman created by the *Sun* newspaper to deal with complaints about the paper); however, the constraints of space necessitates a concentration solely upon the above three ombudsmen in this essay.

10. P. McAuslan 'Administrative Justice – A Necessary Report?' [1988] PL 402 at 403. For a further development of these ideas see his 'Public Law and Public Choice' (1988) 51 MLR 681.

11. E.g. the privatisation of the Trustee Savings Banks (see *Ross v Lord Advocate* [1986] 3 All ER 79) and the National Giro Bank. On some of the legal issues raised by privatisation see T. Prosser and C. Graham 'Privatising Nationalised Industries: Constitutional Issues and New Legal Techniques' (1987) 50 MLR 16.

12. N. Lewis 'Regulating Non-Government Bodies: Privatisation Accountability and the Public–Private Divide' in J. Jowell and D. Oliver (Eds) *The Changing Constitution* (2nd ed) Clarendon Press (1989) 244–245.

13. These include not only the Parliamentary Commissioner but also the National Health Service Ombudsmen (National Health Service Act 1977 and National Health Service (Scotland) Act 1978) and the various local government ombudsmen operating throughout the UK – the English and Welsh Commissions for Local Administration (Local Government Act 1974), the Scottish Commissioner for Local Administration (Local Government (Scotland) Act 1975) and the Northern Ireland Commissioner for Complaints (Northern Ireland Commissioner for Complaints Act 1969).

14. They were: Guardian Royal Exchange Assurance Ltd., General Accident Fire & Life Assurance Co Ltd. and Royal Insurance Co Ltd.

15. For further details see M. Stone 'Ombudsman for Policyholders' *The Times* 21 March 1981.

16. Named 'The Insurance Ombudsman Bureau'.

17. At present there are two such office holders: an Ombudsman and a Deputy Ombudsman.

18. 308 insurance companies together with Lloyd's were members on 1 February 1989.

19. Articles of Association para 66(b)(ii).

20. 'Banking Services and the Consumer'.

21. For a valuable discussion of the background to the scheme and its constitutional arrangements see P.E. Morris 'The Banking Ombudsman' (1987) *Journal of Business Law* 131–136 and 199–210.

22. Currently there are two banking ombudsmen (the Banking Ombudsman and the Assistant Banking Ombudsman).

23. Naturally, this jurisdiction only extends over banks which are members of the Office (as of 30 Sept 1988) 19 banks and 19 designated associated companies were members).

24. Banking Ombudsman: Terms of Reference.

25. The detailed provisions are elaborated in Schedules 12 and 13 to the Building Societies Act 1986.
26. The Building Societies Ombudsman Co Ltd.
27. Terms of Reference para 17, e.g. Share Accounts.
28. *Ibid* para 16, e.g. the society's internal complaints mechanism has not been exhausted.
29. *Ibid* para 18.
30. *Ibid* para 14.
31. *Ibid* para 33.
32. 4 June 1986 HC Debs col 932.
33. For the possibility of judicial review of such an institution see *R v Panel on Take-overs and Mergers, ex p Datafin plc* [1987] 1 All ER 564 and note the approval of Sir Gordon Borrie 'The Regulation of Public and Private Power' [1989] PL 552.
34. Insurance Ombudsman Bureau, *Annual Report 1982* at 22 (hereinafter abbreviated to A.R. in respect of each Ombudsman referred to in the text).
35. See M. Zander *Cases and Materials on the English Legal System* (5th ed) Sweet & Maxwell (1988) ch 4.
36. A.R. 1988 at 13.
37. A.R. 1986 at 16.
38. Banking Ombudsman Scheme, *Annual Report 1985–86* at 7–8.
39. *Ibid* at 6.
40. A.R. 1986–87 at 8.
41. A.R. 1988–89 at 6.
42. A.R. 1987–88 at 16.
43. A.R. 1988–89 at 18. For a further discussion of this concept see G. Marshall 'Maladministration' (1973) PL 32.
44. PCA Annual Report 1988 (1988–89) HC 301 1.
45. For a more detailed discussion see A.R. Mowbray 'A Right to Official Advice: The Parliamentary Commissioner's Perspective' [1990] PL 68.
46. A.R. 1984 at iii.
47. A.R. 1988 at 33–35.
48. A.R. 1987 at 14.
49. A.R. 1986–87 at 21.
50. *Ibid* at 18.
51. A.R. 1987–88 at 7–9.
52. A.R. 1988–89 at 5.
53. See further R. Gregory 'The Select Committee on the P.C.A. 1967–80' [1982] PL 49.
54. E.g. see the Representative Body's comments on the English Local Ombudsmens' review of their powers conducted during 1984, *The Local Ombudsman Annual Report 1986* Appendix 4.
55. A.R. 1981 at 10.
56. A.R. 1983 at 3.
57. A.R. 1986 at 30.
58. The first such hearing was held during 1988: A.R. 1988 at 2.
59. E.g. applying *Austin v Drew* (1816) 2 Marsh 130 in A.R. 1983 at 12–13.
60. A.R. 1981 at 11.
61. A.R. 1988 at 8–9.
62. A.R. 1983 at 12.
63. A.R 1985–86 at 6.
64. The Banking Ombudsman Scheme: General Guide 5.
65. A.R. 1987–88 at 11.
66. *Ibid* at 9.
67. F. Stacey *Ombudsmen Compared* Clarendon Press (1978) 137.
68. R. Rawlings 'The Legacy of a Lawyer Ombudsman' June 1985 *Legal Action* 11.
69. S 5(1)(b) of the Parliamentary Commissioner Act 1967.

70. During 1987–88, 565 out of 4128 complaints considered were settled by agreement: *Annual Report 1987–88* Appendix 3(b).
71. D.C.M. Yardley 'Local Ombudsmen in England: Recent Trends and Developments' [1983] PL 522 at 526.
72. A.R. 1985 at 3.
73. A.R. 1986 at 1.
74. A.R. 1987 at 1.
75. A.R. 1987–88 at 12.
76. A.R 1986–87 at 12.
77. N. Lewis et al *Complaints Procedures in Local Government* Centre for Criminological and Socio-Legal Studies, University of Sheffield (1987) vol 1 p.43.
78. A.R. 1988.
79. A.R. 1987–88 Appendices 1, 2, 3.
80. A.R. 1988–89 Appendices A, B.
81. A.R. 1987–88 at 4.
82. A.R 1988 at 33.
83. Compare the difficulties faced by the English Local Ombudsmen; in 5 per cent of their cases local authorities fail to provide a satisfactory remedy: 1987–88 A.R. at 14.
84. E.g. regarding the drafting of accident report forms: A.R. 1983 at 18.
85. E.g. recommendations concerning the form and content of renewal notices contained in A.R. 1986 at 26 and A.R. 1987 at 2.
86. See the Whyatt Report, *The Citizen and the Administration* published by JUSTICE in 1961 and C. Harlow 'Ombudsmen in Search of a Role' (1978) 41 MLR 446.
87. Cmnd 9125 (1984) 92.
88. *Banking Services: Law & Practice*, Cm 622 (1989) ch 15.
89. *Ibid* at 131.
90. *Ibid* at 133–134.
91. *Ibid* at 134.
92. Articles of Association para 66(e).
93. *Ibid* para 64.
94. *Op cit* note 78 *supra*.
95. This development prompted the decision of the former Abbey National Building Society to convert to the status of a plc.
96. *Op cit* note 88 *supra* at 135.
97. E.g. during 1987–88 the Commission for Local Administration in England dealt with 7,924 complaints; *1987–88 Annual Report* Appendix 3(b).
98. See *op cit* note 45 *supra*.
99. See *The Times* 20 Dec 1989.
100. *Op cit* note 33 *supra* at 565.

Social Security Appeals: in Need of Review?*

Roy Sainsbury

A. Introduction

In an article[1] in 1985 Tony Bradley reviewed the changes that had been made to the social security adjudication system since the Social Security Act 1975, and in particular as a result of the Health and Social Services and Social Security Adjudication Act 1983.[2] At the time, the effects of HASSASSA had yet to be felt, which led him to urge caution in the pursuit of further reforms to the adjudication system. As he wrote, 'At present it would be premature to attempt further changes.'[3]

In the five years since that article was written the seemingly never-ending series of changes to the social security system has continued, some of which have had an important bearing on the system of appeals adjudication. The largest number of reforms were contained in the Social Security Act 1986, which followed the so-called 'Fowler reviews' in 1984.[4] Supplementary benefit was abolished and replaced by income support, single payments were replaced by the social fund, family income supplement became family credit, and the rules of housing benefit were changed to bring them into line with income support and family credit. The changes have not stopped there, however. In 1989 (in Scotland) and 1990 (in England and Wales) the introduction of the community charge replacing domestic rates necessitated a new benefit, the community charge benefit, to replace rate rebates. And more changes are imminent. The government's White Paper[5] on benefits for the disabled proposes two new benefits; a disability allowance, to replace attendance allowance and mobility allowance for people under 65, and a disability employment credit, for which disabled people in low-paid part-time work would be eligible. Furthermore, the government has clearly indicated that the new disability allowance will require new adjudication arrangements.[6]

It was common in the 1980s for the appeals arrangements for new benefits to be hurriedly considered in the late stages of a Bill's passage through Parliament. For example, the arrangements for hearing appeals concerning housing benefit were first introduced only at the sixteenth sitting of the Standing Committee on the Social Security and Housing Benefits Bill 1982.[7] If such a situation is not to be repeated for the new disability allowance then the most appropriate adjudication mechanisms need to be considered well in advance. As well as the recent and prospective legislative changes, research is being carried out on the housing benefit appeals system[8] and on the social fund review sytem.[9] It seems, then, that it is no longer premature to consider the appellate arrangements but indeed an ideal time.

The aim of this essay, therefore, is to consider the state of the appeals systems at the beginning of the 1990s, and to discuss what principles might be appropriate to underpin their structures, procedures and practices. In part B of the essay I will provide a brief description of the main appellate arrangements which currently operate in the social security system. This will include a description of the evolution of the Social Security Appeal Tribunal (SSAT) and Medical Appeal Tribunal (MAT) systems, which deal with appeals on the majority of social security benefits, and a discussion of the appeal arrangements that the HASSASSA reforms left unchanged (for attendance allowance and for mobility allowance) and the benefits introduced in the 1980s that have superseded HASSASSA (housing benefit, community charge benefit and the social fund). The aim of part C of the essay is to address directly the question of what principles appellate systems ought to embody and to discuss appropriate criteria for evaluating the performance of appeal bodies. Starting with the Franks Report and its famous trinity of openness, fairness and impartiality,[10] I will argue that, commendable though these ideals are, they do not necessarily allow us to decide between the competing claims of different appeal arrangements. By using the concept of administrative justice and elaborating and adding to the Franks criteria, a critique (in part D of the essay) of the SSAT system and particularly of the exclusion of appeals concerning some benefits from it becomes possible.

B. The mainstream of social security adjudication

Prior to the HASSASSA reforms there was a clear distinction between the administration and adjudication of supplementary benefit on the one hand and of national insurance benefits on the other. Decisions under the national insurance scheme lay with the statutorily independent insurance officer in the first instance, and with the National Insurance Local Tribunal (NILT) on appeal. Thence, there was a further right of appeal to the Social Security Commissioner.[11] In contrast, initial decisions on the main means-tested benefit, supplementary benefit, were made by DHSS officials on behalf of the Supplementary Benefits Commission. Appeals were possible to Supplementary Benefit Appeals Tribunals (SBATs) but there was no right of appeal to the Social Security Commissioner. Under the industrial injuries scheme, 'disablement questions' were (until 1983) decided by a medical board of two doctors, from which an appeal was possible to a Medical Appeal Tribunal.[12] Medical boards also heard appeals on mobility allowance on medical questions. Further appeal was allowed to the MAT, comprising a legally-qualified chairman and two doctors of consultant status.

Although NILTs were generally regarded as working satisfactorily,[13]

SBATs were subject to repeated criticisms in the 1970s.[14] The strong current of dissatisfaction with SBATs led the DHSS to commission research by Professor Kathleen Bell of Newcastle University into their operation.[15] Bell's research revealed numerous shortcomings in the SBAT system; tribunal chairmen, most of whom were not legally qualified, were found to have a limited knowledge and understanding of supplementary benefits; proceedings were unsystematic; there was an over-reliance on the clerk (an official seconded from the DHSS); decisions were not recorded satisfactorily; and discretion was not exercised in a disciplined or systematic way. Bell concluded that a comprehensive review was required as a matter of urgency and proposed a number of reforms to be achieved in three stages. Immediate improvements could be secured by providing training for chairmen and members; other changes would take longer to implement (such as the introduction of legally-qualified chairmen); whilst other changes were structural in nature, such as the provision of a further stage of appeal after the SBAT, and the merging of SBATs with NILTs.

Changes within the existing SBAT structure began to be implemented in 1977. More legally-qualified chairmen were appointed, training was instigated, a procedure manual produced, and a right of appeal from SBATs to the High Court in England and the Court of Session in Scotland was provided. Later, in the Social Security Act 1979, full-time senior chairmen were introduced, to have some responsibility for organising tribunals in addition to hearing cases.

Bell's structural reforms took longer to achieve. In 1980 the supplementary benefits scheme, which until then had been based largely on administrative discretion, was replaced by a scheme conferring legal entitlement to benefits. The case for merging SBATs and NILTs therefore became stronger, and the desirability of change was accepted by the government.

The culmination of the reforms which had begun in the late 1970s was HASSASSA, which in 1983 introduced a unified three-tier adjudication system comprised of adjudication officers (replacing insurance officers and supplementary benefit officers), a unified Social Security Appeal Tribunal (replacing SBATs and NILTs), and the Social Security Commissioner (whose jurisdiction now extended to supplementary benefit). Furthermore, the posts of Chief Insurance Officer and Chief Supplementary Benefits Officer (DHSS officials who had previously issued guidance to insurance officers and supplementary benefit officers respectively) were replaced by the statutorily independent Chief Adjudication Officer (whose primary tasks were to advise adjudication officers and to monitor the standards of their decision-making). Finally, the SSAT system was brought within a presidential organisation similar to that of other tribunals.[16] The President is a barrister, advocate or solicitor of not less than ten years' standing[17] appointed by the Lord Chancellor. As well as being responsible for the management of SSATs and MATs, the President also has a responsibility for training tribunal chairmen and members, and for ensuring that they have access to appropriate social security texts. To assist him, the President has seven Regional Chairmen of Tribunals to whom he can delegate appropriate duties. The rationale behind the presidential system is to remove _ any direct and obvious link between social security tribunals and the Department, and to concentrate experience and expertise relevant to both types of tribunal.[18]

HASSASSA also made changes to the medical adjudication system. Medical boards comprising of two doctors were, except in specified instances, replaced by a single doctor, now called an 'adjudicating medical practitioner', but they continued to hear appeals against mobility allowance decisions. Whilst the constitution of MATs remained the same they were also brought within the presidential system already discussed.

The SSAT and MAT systems cover the majority of social security benefits. There are exceptions, however, which fall into two main groups. First, there are those benefits that were untouched by the HASSASSA reforms (attendance allowance and mobility allowance), and secondly there are those benefits which were introduced in the 1980s and whose appeals arrangements could have been brought within the existing tribunal system but were not (housing benefit, community charge benefit and the social fund).

Apart from a few non-medical questions (for example, whether a claimant satisfies the residence conditions) which fall within the normal social security adjudication system, decisions on eligibility for attendance allowance are made by the Attendance Allowance Board.[19] More accurately, the Board empowers 'delegated medical practitioners', who are in practice salaried medical officers of the DSS, to make decisions on its behalf. They do this by considering a report prepared by a specially-trained doctor called an 'examining medical officer', usually a practising or retired General Practitioner. Claimants who are refused attendance allowance or have it awarded at only the lower of the two possible rates, may apply for a 'review' of their decision by the Attendance Allowance Board. In practice, another examining medical officer will examine the claimant and provide a fresh report to be adjudicated upon by a different delegated medical practitioner. There is a right to further appeal on points of law only to the Social Security Commissioner.

The second exception is the mobility allowance medical board. Initial decisions for mobility allowance are made by adjudication officers on the basis of a medical report prepared by another specially-trained doctor, the 'examining medical practitioner'. As with the attendance allowance, there are certain non-medical questions to be determined (such as age and residence) which are decided by adjudication officers and which can be appealed against to an SSAT. However, there are also a number of medical questions to be decided (such as the claimant's walking ability) from which appeal lies initially not to an MAT but to a medical board. This board is made up of two doctors (who are also trained as examining medical practitioners). They have no independent status comparable to MATs nor do they have a legally-qualified chairman. Appellants are not allowed to call witnesses or to ask questions of either of the board's members, and may be represented only with the board's approval.[20] This two-tier system appears to be unique amongst the benefits administered by the DSS.

The appeal arrangements for housing benefit reflect the tensions inherent in the administration by autonomous local authorities of a national social security benefit. The passage of the Social Security and Housing Benefits Bill through Parliament in 1981 and early 1982 is well-documented by Partington and Bolderson[21] and reveals how the appellate rights of claimants were not considered until late in the parliamentary process. The arrangements which eventually emerged were a government attempt to reconcile the demands of the welfare rights lobby, which had pressed for housing benefits to be brought within the jurisdiction of the then SBAT structure, and the representatives of local authority interests, who argued that such an independent body would be an infringement of local democracy if they could overrule the decisions of the publicly accountable local authority. What emerged was a two-tier system of internal administrative review by local authority officers, followed by a hearing before a review board composed of local authority councillors.[22] There is no right of appeal to the Social Security Commissioner from a housing benefit review board, although aggrieved appellants may seek judicial review.

Community charge benefit was introduced in Scotland in 1989 and in England and Wales in 1990. Effectively it replaced the rate rebate element of housing benefit when domestic rates were abolished and the community charge (or poll tax) was introduced. The same two-tier appeal structure that is in place for housing benefit deals with appeals against community charge benefit decisions. Similarly there is no further right of appeal, although judicial review may again be available.

The social fund replaced single payments under the supplementary benefit scheme in April 1988.[23] The entitlement to payments for items such as furniture, cookers and refrigerators under regulations was replaced with a discretionary scheme of loans and grants which would be administered not by the statutory authorities, (i.e. the adjudication officer in the local office) but by social fund officers acting within the directions and guidance of the Secretary of State. Applicants dissatisfied with the decision of a social fund officer can obtain a review of the decision[24] if they apply in writing giving the grounds for their request. The social fund officer who made the original decision will either grant the appeal in full or invite the claimant for an interview, at which the decision will be discussed. If the social fund officer is not prepared to change the decision, the case is passed on to a senior member of the local office management, who will again review the original decision. Claimants who are still dissatisfied may then request a further review by a social fund inspector.[25] The inspectors have three possible courses of action. They can substitute their own decision, uphold the original decision or refer the decision back to the social fund officer. There is no right of appeal to the Social Security Commissioner. The quality of decision-making by social fund inspectors is monitored by the Social Fund Commissioner who has a statutory responsibility to report annually to the Secretary of State.[26] Reminiscent of the genesis of housing benefit review boards, the provision of a right of appeal to a social fund inspector was added to review by local office management only following the considerable opposition that the original proposals provoked.[27]

C. Appeals and administrative justice

The brief history of the evolution of social security appeals described above
shows how the march towards greater legalisation and independence which
began in the 1970s seemed to have come to a halt with HASSASSA. Since
then the preferred method of dispute resolution has been to review decisions,
initially within the organisation that was responsible for making the original
decision. The question now arises of whether one system is better than the
other. To answer this question we must address a series of other related
questions.

What is it that appeals tribunals should be expected to provide? Should
they display certain characteristics, and if so, which? What yardsticks are
appropriate in judging their performance? Finally, as a way of bringing all
these concerns together, in designing a new appeals system (which will be
required for the new disability allowance) what should it look like? The
models on offer, as we have seen, are varied.

Griffith, in his introduction to *Tribunals Practice and Procedures* suggests
one approach: '[W]hat is needed is, first, research to analyse and evaluate
the practice in different tribunals, and then the establishment of uniform
basic principles – not necessarily uniform provision – which can be applied
consistently'.[28] Unfortunately, social security tribunal research has largely
been confined to SSATs. However, another approach would be to turn
Griffith's approach round and attempt first to articulate the basic principles
which can then be used as evaluation criteria in judging the performance
of tribunals, or more generally, of all the stages of an appeals system.

In looking for principles I was attracted by the notion that the problem
was really to identify what constitutes justice in administration, or
administrative justice. The American lawyer Mashaw provides what I think
is a useful characterisation of administrative justice when he writes that the
'justice' of an administrative system means 'those qualities of a decision
process that provide arguments for the acceptibility of its decisions'.[29] In
other words, the decisions which emerge from a decision-making system
will be considered acceptable by the recipients or those responsible for the
system if they display certain characteristics. Trying to identify the desirable
characteristics of an appeals system is by no means a recent endeavour, but
as the quotation from Griffith suggests, it is still necessary. The search
certainly predates the Franks enquiry but this is a convenient place to join
the pursuit.[30]

The advantages of administrative tribunals according to Franks were
'cheapness, accessibility, freedom from technicality, expedition, and expert
knowledge of their particular subjects'.[31] Apart from these attributes, the
Franks Committee expected administrative tribunals to demonstrate the
qualities of 'openness, fairness and impartiality' in their procedures and
practice. The Report explains the terms thus:

> [O]penness appears to us to require the publicity of proceedings and
> knowledge of the essential reasoning underlying the decisions; fairness
> to require the adoption of a clear procedure which enables parties to
> know their rights, to present their case fully and to know the case which

they have to meet, and impartiality to require the freedom of tribunals from the influence, real or apparent, of Departments concerned with the subject matter of their decisions.[32]

In the evaluation of social security appeal tribunals these criteria have proved extremely influential and have attained a near-sacrosanct status. As Birkinshaw comments, because there have been 'many beneficent effects of Franks . . . it might appear churlish to stand back and make a critique of its overall impact'.[33] Nevertheless, as Bradley argues, Franks should not be treated as the definitive statement on administrative tribunals: '[T]he Franks Report was a product of its time and restricted in the depths of its findings . . . [I]n the light of development in the social security system since 1957 the views of the . . . Committee on the structure and purpose of these tribunals should not be accepted today without thorough examination.'[34]

To take up Bradley's challenge, one could examine specifically the Franks criteria in turn. However, I wish to take a different path and return to the definition of administrative justice quoted earlier and suggest a number of characteristics which might be thought of as providing arguments for the acceptability of the decisions emerging from an appeals system. The characteristics discussed below are intended as a response to Griffith's exhortation to identify principles which can be used in the assessment of tribunal procedures and practice, whilst conceding that there will never be consensus on what should be included since 'administrative justice' is what Dworkin describes as an 'interpretive concept', one that can encompass a wide variety of meanings.[35] The principles (or characteristics) that I wish to discuss are drawn from studies of the theory and practice of administrative justice. Briefly, they can be described as accuracy of decision-making, impartiality, participation, accountability, independence, and promptness.

By definition, claimants who make an appeal against the decision of a social security officer disagree with that decision. To put it another way, claimants want to be sure that they have received the full amount of benefit that they are entitled to, and will therefore accept the decision of an appeal system only if they are convinced that it is an accurate assessment of their entitlement. The Franks Report did not discuss accurate decision-making as a desirable feature of administrative tribunals. However, Mashaw provides a useful definition of accuracy in relation to social security when he describes it as 'the correspondence of the substantive outcome of an adjudication with the true facts of the claimant's situation and with an appropriate application of the relevant legal rules to those facts'.[36] This definition illustrates well how an 'accurate' decision relies on what might be considered to be the two activities of decision-making: the collection of information, and the application of a set of decision-making criteria, in this instance social security legislation.

In the Franks Report, impartiality is narrowly defined as freedom from departmental influences. However, impartiality can be regarded in a broader sense as the requirement that decision-makers do not allow feelings of bias or prejudice to impinge upon decision-making. Bias and prejudice can arise from a number of sources, and intrude at all stages of the decision-making process; for example, in the collection of information, in the sifting of the evidence, in the application of the decision-making criteria, or in the personal treatment of the individual. By remaining impartial, decision-makers should be able to reach accurate decisions since these would be more likely to be based solely on the relevant advice and decision-making criteria, and not extraneous considerations or personal judgements.

Participation reflects aspects of the Franks criterion of fairness. The suggestion is that individuals should be able to take an active role in decision-making by being given an opportunity to present all the evidence they wish to support their position, and to respond to evidence supplied by others. Like impartiality, participation can promote accurate decision-making. Mashaw's definition of accuracy presupposes that the 'true facts' of a case can be established. Possible difficulties about incomplete, unclear or contradictory evidence can be overcome, in part, through the active involvement of claimants when information is being gathered, since they are likely to be the principal source of that information. Claimants may be in a vulnerable position if they do not understand fully the requirements of the decision-maker or the significance of certain pieces of evidence, and hence may unintentionally give unhelpful or misleading answers to enquiries about evidence. Participation in the process should help overcome such problems and ensure a higher quality of evidence on which to base a decision. This will also serve to convince individuals that a decision is accurate in their particular circumstances (i.e. increase the 'acceptability of the decision process'). The active participation of the appellant will also encourage decision-makers to explain the reasoning behind decisions and hence enhance accountability.

Accountability requires that individuals receive a comprehensible explanation of the decision-making process and of the final decisions reached. The Franks Report captures the essence of acountability in its definition of openness. Robson has eloquently expressed its importance: 'There is a lack of conviction, an apparent arbitrariness, about a decision which is unsupported by an account of the reasoning process on which it was based.'[37] The argument for accountability is also made strongly in an unreported Social Security Commissioner's decision:

> [I]n an administrative quasi-judicial decision the minimum requirement must at least be that the claimant looking at the decision should be able to discern on the face of it the reasons why the evidence has failed to satisfy the authority; . . . a decision based, and only based, on a conclusion that the total effect of the evidence fails to satisfy, without reasons being given for reaching that conclusion, will in many cases be no adequate decision at all.[38]

Like impartiality and participation, accountability serves a dual purpose. First, it is desirable, *per se*, that individuals understand why certain decisions have been taken about them in order that they can be convinced of their acceptability. And secondly, if decision-makers carry out the decision-making process in the knowledge that they must account for their decisions, then they will be encouraged to be diligent and assiduous in the task.

In considering the desirability of administrative tribunals the Franks

Committee concluded that their decisions should be made independently of the minister: 'We consider that tribunals should properly be regarded as machinery provided by Parliament for adjudication rather than as part of the machinery of administration'.[39] The recent JUSTICE-All Souls report commented similarly: '[T]he visible independence of the tribunals is the cornerstone of the system. In the matter of adjudication appearance is crucial.'[40] The first President of SSATs, Judge John Byrt QC also considered the independence of the tribunal system to be of great importance: 'First, it must establish credibility as an independent system – independent not only of the Secretary of State, but also of the poverty lobby and of the politicians.'[41]

Next in importance to the demand that appeal mechanisms produce accurate decisions is probably the demand that they produce them quickly, even though the speed of the decision may not, in Mashaw's terms, 'provide an argument for the acceptability of the decision'. Nevertheless, the maxim quoted by Nonet has a simple and persuasive force: 'Justice delayed is justice denied.'[42] A possible interpretation of this maxim is that a decision should be made as soon as possible and without delay, where 'delay' implies an interval of time where a case is receiving no positive attention either within the administrative agency or outside. Again, though, avoiding delay applies both to the collection of information and to the application of the decision-making criteria, and it is frequently in the former activity that most delay actually occurs.

In the final part of this essay I wish to apply the criteria of accuracy, impartiality, participation, accountability, independence and promptness to the structures, procedures, and performance of the range of appeals mechanisms operating within the social security system. These criteria, with the exception of promptness, do not readily lend themselves to quantitative assessment. Accuracy can be measured to some extent by judging whether a decision is justified on the evidence, and the Chief Adjudication Officer carries out this task in respect of adjudication officers, but he stops short of declaring that individual decisions are either right or wrong. Rather, he will identify where the adjudicatory process is deficient in some way.[43]

In applying the criteria, therefore, one is looking for elements of the structure and procedures that promote their achievement, as well as more tangible and objective measures.

D. Scrutinising social security appeals

SSATs have come a long way since their predecessors, the SBATs, attracted universal criticism, and were labelled the 'slum of the English Tribunal system'.[44] In 1985 Bradley reviewed the potential benefits which might accrue from the merging of tribunals and the presidential system; five years later, it appears that many of those benefits have indeed been realised.[45] The introduction of the presidential organisation has led to an improvement in the quality of chairmen and of members through better selection and training. The quality of decision-making is monitored by the full-time regional chairmen. The principle of accountability is given force through the requirement that tribunal chairmen record their decisions, reasons and findings of fact and supply these to appellants and their representatives. Hearings are not held in DSS premises, clerks are no longer provided by DSS local offices, and the headquarters office employs an increasing number of staff directly recruited rather than on secondment from the Department. In the drive for independence the SSAT organisation is now almost completely separate from the DSS.

Participation has always been a feature of tribunals at which appellants and their representatives attend oral hearings, and the DSS now encourages attendance in its appeal forms and publicity. The one weakness of the SSAT system at present, though this is not a criticism of its structure and procedures, is the time taken to hear appeals.[46] In 1984, cases took an average of 13.5 weeks to be heard,[47] but this had reached 24.7 weeks by 1988.[48] This was partly due to the increase in appeals towards the end of the life of the single payments scheme in 1988 but the trend in the five years from 1984 to 1988 was nevertheless upwards.

The strengths of the structure and procedures of MATs are similar to those for SSATs, and the same criticism about delays applies, although no national statistics are published.

The review arrangements for attendance allowance were examined in a report in 1983 by P.R. Oglesby, a senior civil servant. Though the conclusion of the report was that decision-making on review was of a high quality, this was overshadowed by the emphasis given to the lack of independence of the arrangements. The author commented ruefully: 'It has to be admitted that this system . . . doesn't look good.' The report continues:

> I considered whether, despite its apparent imperfections, the system does in practice produce satisfactory results. The Department has always maintained that it does and I must say that my investigations bore this out. Dissatisfaction reviews, which are really appeals, receive what I can only describe as 'Rolls Royce' treatment. The officers concerned take immense pains and trouble to ensure that any possible grounds for amending a rejection of an allowance, or for increasing the rate awarded, are investigated, and where this does not result in a more favourable decision, the reasons for this are set out in 'reasoned decisions' that are among the best I have seen under any system.
>
> Nevertheless, it cannot be ignored that the public, or at least those who protest the loudest, remain unconvinced that justice is in fact done, despite the Department's best endeavours. Moreover, there is a strong feeling in this country that 'justice must be seen to be done' and under the present system it is not and is never likely to be possible to satisfy that feeling. Ministers will always have trouble on this score under the present system and for that reason I have come to the conclusion that it should be changed, even though a different system may not in practice produce better (or even sometimes as good) results for the claimants. At least they should feel better about the outcome.[49]

This analysis of attendance allowance reviews is a powerful illustration (the relevance of which will be reinforced in the discussion of the social fund, below) of the tensions between the principle of independence and the desire for high-quality decision-making. Contrary to the received wisdom that independence is the cornerstone of a tribunal system, the author's conclusions suggest that independence, in the sense of a complete separation from the DSS along the lines of SSATs, may not be necessary for an acceptable appeals system.

In contrast with appellants in some other appeal systems, those appealing against attendance allowance decisions are afforded a degree of limited participation in the sense that they are re-examined by an examining medical officer, but they do not have the opportunity of challenging the assessment on which the delegated medical practitioner will make a decision.

Medical boards which hear appeals against mobility allowance decisions are unusual in that they do not have the status, nor do they adopt the procedures of MATs, and yet they are not comparable to an internal administrative review. Their claim to independence might come from the fact that two doctors who have had no connection with the original decision sit to hear the appeal. However, this independence is undermined since the board is drawn from the panel of examining medical practitioners who have been selected and trained by departmental officials. Furthermore, as was described earlier, medical boards do not allow the appellant the same degree of participation that is afforded the MAT appellant. They are, however, required to record, and send to the appellant, their decision, including a summary of findings of fact.[50]

The internal review stage of the housing benefit appeal system holds no promise of independence since the original decision is reviewed within the same local authority office. Furthermore, there is no element of participation built in to what is essentially a paper exercise and there is no statutory requirement for local authorities to provide explanations of the reviewed decision. The quality of review decisions is not subject to any monitoring outside the local authority. Nevertheless, the holding of an internal administrative review holds the promise of a comparatively quick decision. In contrast review boards, by holding an oral hearing, allow for the participation of appellants and their representatives. Review boards, like SSATs, are required to record their decisions, reasons, and findings of fact.[51] By contrast with SSATs, there is no organisation responsible for training or for overseeing standards of decision-making. Some of the criticisms that were made of SBATs in the 1970s now seem to apply equally to review boards: they have no legally-qualified chairman; they can rely too heavily on the clerk (who is a local authority employee); and there is no common procedure.[52]

The internal review of decisions by social fund officers attracts criticisms similar to those levelled at housing benefit internal reviews, particularly concerning the lack of independence. Participation is served to a degree by the requirement that, if the social fund officer refuses to change the original decision, then the claimant must be offered an interview. At the second stage of the review process, the alleged lack of independence of social fund inspectors has been challenged by the Social Fund Commissioner, although the problem of convincing others is recognised:

[O]ne of my main priorities has been to confirm the unit's independence and to ensure that everyone with an interest in the social fund review process is aware of the inspector's role. As the review process becomes established and it is recognised that inspectors are not 'rubber-stamping' the decisions of social fund officers, the worth of the inspectors' review will become apparent . . . I remain firmly convinced that inspectors must be truly independent, and be seen to be so, if the review process is to be accepted and respected.[53]

Of course, one might have expected the Social Fund Commissioner to write in such terms but an early review of the social fund, including the activities of social fund inspectors, confirms that there may also be some substance to the rhetoric. As Drabble and Lynes comment: 'It seems . . . that the inspectors, guided by the Commissioner, are displaying a degree of independence which could hardly have been predicted from the statutory framework in which they operate.'[54] The conclusion that can be tentatively drawn, therefore, is that although review by a social fund inspector does not provide the opportunity for participation, it can provide high quality decision-making (which is overseen by the Commissioner) and provide reasoned decisions. Furthermore, the process takes less time to complete than an appeal to an SSAT. Up to December 1988 only seven cases had taken longer than six weeks to clear.[55]

E. Conclusion

In this essay I have attempted to identify principles of administrative justice which can be used, first, to assess the existing appeal arrangements in the social security system and, secondly, to guide reforms and influence the design of new appeals systems. In the process, the slippery concept of administrative justice has generated a further set of slippery concepts: accuracy, impartiality, participation, accountability, independence and promptness. This is not, perhaps, surprising but the result is that the task of evaluation is made more difficult.

For example, it is rarely possible to say that an appeal system is totally independent. Instead there are only degrees of independence. This is illustrated by the HASSASSA reforms, which were justified in part because they promoted, or increased, the independence of the adjudication system. However, even the presidential system, which placed SSATs at a greater distance from the DSS than in the past, still relies on the Department to channel appeals to the tribunals rather than on receiving appeals directly and still employs officers seconded from the Department. Independence lies not only in the organisational distance between the DSS and the appeals system but also in the distance between the officer who made the initial decision which is at issue in an appeal, and the person or people who hear the appeal. For example, as I have explained earlier, the Social Fund Commissioner claims that inspectors are able to make decisions independently even though they are still officials of the Department. Similarly, housing benefit review boards can never be truly independent of the officials who make the initial decisions since, as members of the local authority, they have an indirect responsibility for the administration of housing benefit. However, if they are in practice able to divorce themselves from the wider concerns of the council (such as its housing or finance policies), then they may be able to claim a degree of independence similar to that claimed on behalf of social fund inspectors. There is little in the appeal structures discussed above that can demonstrate high-quality or accurate decision-making, even though this was promised by the HASSASSA reforms. Whilst first-tier adjudication is monitored by the Chief Adjudication Officer (even though his jurisdiction does not extend to housing benefit or community charge benefit), there is no comparable system for second-tier decision-making. Instead there are features of the appeal system which can promote better decision-making, such as the training of SSAT chairmen and members, and the participation of appellants in oral hearings, which increases the likelihood that the 'true facts' of their circumstances will emerge.

The comparisons to be made within the range of social security appeal mechanisms reveal an important inconsistency in that, for some benefits, claimants need appeal only once to have their case heard by a (more or less) independent person or body whilst, for other benefits, the claimant must first negotiate the hurdle of an internal administrative review. For most benefits an appeal against the decision of an adjudication officer is sufficient to ensure that the case is heard by an SSAT. Similarly, a single appeal against a decision on attendance allowance will result in the 'Rolls Royce' treatment of a review described by Oglesby. However, to reach the housing benefit review board or the social fund inspector the claimant must first apply for internal review and, if still dissatisfied, appeal again. This might be considered an advantage in that the claimant gets two bites at the cherry were it not for the limitations of internal review identified earlier in the light of the principles of administrative justice.

Whilst many of the developments in social security provision and in appeals mechanisms are incremental there are occasions when more of a quantum leap is possible. The HASSASSA reforms were the last such leap but in the early 1990s there seems to be a further opportunity to make radical changes. With the likely imminent abolition of attendance allowance and mobility allowance, two of the anomalies of the present appeal arrangements will disappear. In addition, two of the other exceptions, housing benefit and the social fund, are under scrutiny. However, there is no conclusive argument that the SSAT and MAT systems should take over responsibility for appeals on these benefits. As Griffith argued, it is not uniform provision that is required but uniform principles applied consistently. Whatever arrangements are chosen, they should reflect the principles of administrative justice as outlined above in their structures and procedures, and regular monitoring (perhaps by the Council on Tribunals) should be used as a means of ensuring that these principles are carried through into practice.

* Earlier versions of this essay were presented to the Centre for Criminology and the Social and Philosophical Study of Law, University of Edinburgh, in October 1988, and at the Socio-Legal Group Annual Conference at the University of Edinburgh in April 1989. My thanks to

those who contributed to the useful discussions which followed both presentations.

Notes

1. A.W. Bradley 'Recent Reform of Social Security Adjudication in Great Britain' (1985) 26 *Les Cahiers de Droit* 403.
2. Throughout this essay the Act is abbreviated to HASSASSA.
3. A.W. Bradley *op cit* note 1 *supra* 445.
4. See M. Adler 'Lending a Deaf Ear: The Government's Response to Consultation on the Reform of Social Security' in R. Davidson and P. White (Eds) *Information and Government* Edinburgh U P (1988).
5. *The Way Ahead. Benefits for Disabled People* Cm 917 (1990).
6. *Ibid* para 7.4.
7. See M. Partington and H. Bolderson *Housing Benefit Review Procedures: A Preliminary Analysis* Brunel University (1984).
8. This research is being carried out by the Social Policy Research Unit at York University.
9. This research is being carried out by the Policy Studies Institute.
10. Committee on Administrative Tribunals and Enquiries *Report* (The Franks Report) Cmnd 218 (1957).
11. Social Security Commissioners must be barristers, advocates or solicitors of at least ten years' standing. They now decide appeals on points of law from either the claimant or the adjudication officer against the decision of an SSAT or MAT. The Commissioners' decisions constitute the case-law of social security. The more important of them are published as 'reported' decisions. Under certain circumstances (on a point of law only) there lies a further right of appeal to the Court of Appeal or the Court of Session.
12. Special arrangements exist for hearing cases which involve serious chest diseases such as pneumoconiosis and asbestosis. See N.J. Wikely 'Social Security Adjudication and Occupational Lung Diseases' (1988) 17 *Industrial Law Journal* 92.
13. See K. Bell, P. Collison, S. Turner and S. Webber 'National Insurance Local Tribunals' (1974) 3 *Journal of Social Policy* 289.
14. See, for example, N. Lewis 'Supplementary Benefit Appeal Tribunals' [1973] PL 257; J. Farmer *Tribunals and Government* Weidenfeld and Nicolson (1974); M. Adler and A.W. Bradley (Eds) *Justice, Discretion and Poverty* Professional Books (1976); J. Fulbrook *Administrative Justice and the Unemployed* Mansell (1978).
15. K. Bell *Research Study on Supplementary Benefit Appeal Tribunals: Review of Main Findings; Conclusions; Recommendations* HMSO (1975).
16. Presidential systems operate in connection with *inter alia* Mental Health Review Tribunals, Industrial Tribunals Immigration Appeal Tribunals, VAT Tribunals, the Lands Tribunal and the Lands Tribunal for Scotland.
17. HASSASSA sch 8 para 8 Judge John Byrt QC the first President, retired from the office in 1990 and was replaced by Judge Derek Holden QC.
18. W.A. Robson '*Justice and Administrative Law* Reconsidered' in (1979) 32 *Current Legal Problems* 107.
19. See A. Ogus and E. Barendt *The Law of Social Security* (3rd ed) Butterworths (1988) 578.
20. Social Security (Adjudication) Regulations 1986 SI 1986/2218 regs 29(7) and 29(9).
21. Partington and Bolderson, *op cit* note 7 *supra*.
22. The rules governing the housing benefit claimant's rights of appeal are contained in the Housing Benefit (General) Regulations 1987 SI 1987/1971.
23. Social Security Act 1986, Part III.
24. *Ibid* s 34(1).
25. *Ibid* s 34(3).

26. *Ibid* s 35.
27. Particularly vehement were the Council on Tribunals who took the unusual step of publishing a special report on the subject: *Social Security – Abolition of independent appeals under the proposed Social Fund*, Special Report by the Council on Tribunals, Cmnd 9722 (1986). See also *The Draft Social Fund Manual – Report by the Social Security Advisory Committee*, 1987.
28. J. Griffith 'Introduction' to J. Bowers (Ed) *Tribunals Practice and Procedures* Hemstal (1985). For an excellent example of applying principles (in this case the Franks criteria) to practice, see M. Sayers and A. Webb 'Franks Revisited: A Model of the Ideal Tribunal' (1990) 9 CJQ 36.
29. J. Mashaw *Bureaucratic Justice* Yale U P (1983) 24–25.
30. See, for example, W.A. Robson *Justice and Administrative Law* Macmillan (1928); and Committee on Ministers' Powers *Report* (The Donoughmore Report) Cmd 4060 (1932).
31. Franks Report *op cit* note 10 *supra* para 38.
32. *Ibid* para 42.
33. P. Birkinshaw *Grievances, Remedies and the State* Sweet & Maxwell (1985).
34. A.W. Bradley 'National Assistance Tribunals and the Franks Report' in M. Adler and A.W. Bradley *Justice, Discretion and Poverty* Professional Books (1975) 50.
35. R. Dworkin *Law's Empire* Fontana (1986) 73–76.
36. J. Mashaw 'The Management Side of Due Process: Some Theoretical and Litigation Notes on the Assurance of Accuracy, Fairness and Timeliness in the Adjudication of Social Welfare Claims' (1974) 59 *Cornell L R* 772 at 774.
37. W.A. Robson *Justice and Administrative Law* Macmillan (1928) 208–210.
38. CA 1/72, quoted by R. Lister *Justice for the Claimant* CPAG Poverty Research Series No. 4 (1974).
39. Franks Report, *op cit* note 10 *supra* para 40.
40. JUSTICE-All Souls Review of Administrative Law in the United Kingdom *Administrative Justice – Some Necessary Reforms* Clarendon Press (1988).
41. From an interview in *Legal Action*, September 1989 at 7 'Five Years of Tribunals'.
42. P. Nonet *Administrative Justice* Russell Sage Foundation (1969) 211.
43. See the Annual Reports of the Chief Adjudication Officer, and also R. Sainsbury 'The Social Security Chief Adjudication Officer: the First Four Years [1989] PL 323.
44. H. Rose 'Who Can De-label the Claimant?' in M. Adler and A.W. Bradley (Eds) *op cit* note 14 *supra* 150.
45. See A.W. Bradley *op cit* note 1 *supra*; J. Fulbrook 'HASSASSA and Judge Byrt – Five Years On' (1989) 18 *Industrial L J* 177.
46. See, for example, the Annual Reports of the Council on Tribunals.
47. *Social Security Statistics* HMSO (1986).
48. *Social Security Statistics* HMSO (1989).
49. P.R. Oglesby *Review of Attendance Allowance and Mobility Allowance Procedures, and of Medical Adjudication* DHSS (1983) 36–37.
50. Social Security (Adjudication) Regulations 1986, SI 1986/2218 reg 30.
51. Housing Benefit (General) Regulations 1987, SI 1987/1971 reg 83.
52. N.J. Wikeley 'Housing Benefit Review Boards: The New Slum?' (1986) 5 CJQ 18.
53. *Annual Report of the Social Fund Commissioner for 1988–89 on the standards of reviews by Social Fund Inspectors* HMSO (1990).
54. R. Drabble and T. Lynes (1989) 'Decision-making in Social Security. The Social Fund – Discretion or Control' [1989] PL 317.
55. *Annual Report of the Social Fund Commissioner for 1988–89 on the standards of reviews by Social Fund Inspectors* HMSO (1990) para 3.14.

Crown and Prerogative in Scots Law

W. James Wolffe

A. Introduction

The Crown is the spider at the centre of the British constitutional web. The courts of justice act in its name. On its behalf, executive government is carried on. Legislation is formally enacted on receipt of the Royal Assent. The Crown's special position is recognised by that body of rules, principles and doctrines broadly described as the prerogative. The Crown has many powers, privileges and immunities. It makes war, commands armies, enters into treaties and dispatches ambassadors abroad. It recognises governments.[1] It is the ultimate superior of all land held on feudal tenure and is the last heir of those who die intestate. It holds various rights in the seashore on behalf of the people at large. Statutes restrict it only if this is expressly set out or necessarily implied. The Crown cannot be the subject of an interdict. It may claim privilege for certain documents in its hands. It appoints governments and judges, and summons and dissolves Parliament. Much is obscure about the nature of both the Crown and its prerogatives in modern law. This is perhaps more true of Scots law than of English law, for reasons discussed below. This essay seeks to cast some light into the gloom, by exploring a number of themes which arise when the Crown and its prerogatives are at issue before a Scottish court. Detailed exposition of the rules encompassed under the broad heading 'prerogative' is beyond the scope of this paper, but they are of course drawn on throughout.

In treading this ground, one cannot but be conscious of debts to two great Professors of Constitutional Law at Edinburgh University: Professors Mitchell and Bradley. The late Professor J.D.B. Mitchell, who did so much to assert the autonomy of Scottish constitutional law as a subject of study, wrote an article, 'The Royal Prerogative in Modern Scots Law',[2] which is a seminal treatment of the subject-matter of this essay. A fresh look at the subject is justified only because, since the publication of Mitchell's paper a number of significant decisions have considered the position of the Crown in Scotland. In particular, the House of Lords has pronounced in *Burmah Oil v LA*,[3] *British Medical Association v Greater Glasgow Health Board*[4] and *LA v Strathclyde RC and Dumbarton DC*.[5] If Professor Mitchell reminded us that constitutional law has a Scottish dimension, Tony Bradley has shown

us that this is also true of administrative law, in his work for the Scottish
Law Commission's *Memorandum on Remedies in Administrative Law*[6] and
in his work ('article' does not convey its significance) on administrative law
for the *Stair Memorial Encyclopaedia*. Teachers and writers of high calibre
are essential to the legal profession. Without good teaching, practitioners
never learn – or understand – the law. Without good writing, they cannot
ascertain it. Tony Bradley's contribution in both areas has been outstanding,
and on his departure to London the profession in Scotland has suffered
a great loss.

B. What is a Prerogative?

The term 'prerogative' – wrote Dicey – 'has caused more perplexity to
students than any other expression referring to the constitution'.[7] In large
part this is because it is used by different writers in different senses. In
particular, the definitions of Blackstone and Dicey, both oft-cited, and
neither entirely satisfactory, are inconsistent with one another. Blackstone
described 'prerogative' as 'that special pre-eminence which the King hath,
over and above all other persons, and out of the ordinary course of the
common law, in right of his royal dignity'.[8] In other words it is unique
to the Crown.[9] Dicey called it 'the residue of discretionary or arbitrary
authority, which at any given time is legally left in the hands of the
Crown'.[10] His definition has two elements: the power must be residual
(and therefore presumably non-statutory); it must also be 'discretionary
or arbitrary'. The confusion is perhaps compounded by a failure to analyse
with care the sources of the Crown's powers to act, which are in fact various.

1. *Legal capacity*

The Crown is a person.[11] Subject to any special limitations, it therefore
has all the powers of action of a person.[12] It can buy and sell, distribute
information,[13] make contracts,[14] lend, borrow, and give away money.[15] Of
increasing practical importance though these are,[16] they are merely aspects
of the Crown's ordinary legal capacity. These powers fall within Dicey's
definition: they are residual and non-statutory. They are not included in
Blackstone's, for they are shared with all other legal and natural persons.

   It follows that any general legal doctrines which in special circumstances
entitle persons to act in a particular way apply to the Crown as they apply
to others. The most important example in this context is the doctrine of
necessity, in its strict sense,[17] where the Crown's hand is truly forced by
events. The application of this doctrine to the Crown became an important
question in the *Burmah Oil* case. When it became clear in 1942 that the
British Army could no longer hold Burma, Burmah Oil's installations there
were destroyed, to prevent their falling into Japanese hands. If this was
truly done under compulsion of necessity, Burmah Oil would have had no
right to compensation. In the event, the House of Lords held that this strict
doctrine of necessity did not apply, and that the destruction had been carried
out under a different sort of non-statutory power, which did entail a duty
to compensate. It is clear, however, that although the Crown has additional

rights it, too, may act in cases of necessity. This doctrine does not fall within Blackstone's definition. Dicey, perhaps, would not recognise it as prerogative either, since, *ex hypothesi*, discretion is eliminated.

2. *Statute*

The Crown is given many special powers by statute. Dicey's definition would exclude such powers from the prerogative, and this would accord with most usages of the word. This is not, however, entirely satisfactory. In historical terms, many rules which are thought of as 'prerogatives' in fact have statutory origins. This is true of the rule that the Crown cannot be prejudiced by the neglect of its servants and of the modern rule that the Crown is immune from taxation.[18] The Crown's role in criminal prosecutions in Scotland is likewise founded on statute.[19] Indeed, the Scottish Parliament on numerous occasions formally recognised all the existing prerogatives of the Crown.[20] Does this mean that the prerogative in the 'true' sense is abolished?

3. *Special non-statutory powers*

The Crown has a number of further powers which derive neither from statute nor from its legal personality. These are the powers which are normally described as prerogative powers. They include such powers as the 'war power' discussed in *Burmah Oil*, the power to grant honours, and the power to make treaties. These powers are heterogeneous. They can be further classified in a number of ways:

(a) Powers which affect legal rights, duties or status can be distinguished from powers which do not. Into the latter class would fall powers such as the power to proclaim the royal style and titles, and the power to regulate precedence. There is judicial authority for describing these as 'prerogative' powers.[21] Wade argues that only the former are true prerogative powers.[22] The terminology does not matter much, provided it is clear what is being described.

(b) An important subcategory of special non-statutory powers consists of those which derive from the Crown's special property rights, for example in the foreshore and the seabed. In relation to these, subject to a number of specific limitations for the benefit of the public at large, the Crown has the powers incident to ownership. There is judicial authority for restricting the term 'prerogative' to its *other* special non-statutory powers, i.e. those not deriving from ownership.[23] Once again, the terminology is not important provided the meaning is clear.

(c) The Crown's special non-statutory powers can also be classified according to the justification given for them. A number can be derived from its position in the feudal system, and indeed one can argue that this is the historical basis for its special legal position.[24] As examples, it is possible to argue that the prerogative right to call on the citizens in time of war is analogous to, if not derived from, a superior's right to call on the assistance of his vassals.[25] Likewise, it has been observed that membership of the

Scottish Parliament was restricted almost exclusively to the King's vassals, and that Parliament was summoned by virtue of the King's authority as ultimate superior.[26] It may be possible to distinguish such powers from powers which are based on governmental needs and requirements, such as the power to destroy property in the face of advancing enemy forces. It is of course difficult to draw the line, and powers which have been justified historically by reference to feudal theory may today be more satisfactorily explained by reference to government need.[27]

(d) There is an important practical distinction between those prerogatives which are exercised personally by the monarch, and those which have in fact, by convention, become powers of the government.[28]

Like statutory powers, these non-statutory special powers may or may not grant wide discretion. Viscount Radcliffe noted in *Burmah Oil* that the war prerogative relied on in that case was 'not discretionary or arbitrary in any typical sense'.[29] Such powers do not necessarily, therefore, fit into Dicey's definition. This reflects the general truth that the source of a power is not necessarily related to the degree of discretion which it allows.

The above classification divides government *powers* according to their source. The Crown has in addition special immunities. These too may be created by statute (e.g. the immunity from interdict proceedings), or be non-statutory. One of the most important non-statutory immunities is the rule that the Crown is not bound or restricted by any statutory provisions, unless this is expressly stated, or necessarily implied.[30] Such immunities are habitually ascribed to the prerogative. It may be important, however, to distinguish these from prerogative *powers*. They do not empower the Crown to do anything in particular, but merely leave it free to act to the extent that it has the power to do so, whether as part of its ordinary capacity, by statute or under a special non-statutory, or 'prerogative', power of the sort just described. Just as it has special immunities, so also are there special rules applying only to the Crown, which *restrict* the Crown's exercise of its various powers. These too may be statutory restrictions, or they may arise at common law. An historically important example of the latter was the restriction on alienation of Crown patrimony.[31]

It is clear that use of the term 'prerogative' is liable to confuse all sorts of distinctions which can be made between different sorts of government powers. Moreover, a categorisation such as the above, based on the legal sources of government powers may tell us very little about those things which are practically important about it: how politically significant it is; how frequently used; and how much discretion it gives to the Crown. Thus, in contrasting statutory and non-statutory powers, one must recognise that the boundary between statutory and non-statutory powers of the Crown is contingent and arbitrary. Important government powers lie on both sides of it. So do trivial ones. There are statutory powers which limit the Crown, and others which free it from common law limits.[32] Statutes often grant the Crown wide discretion. Some of its common law powers are quite limited. All that being so, it is extraordinary that significant practical consquences should flow, as they did prior to *CCSU v Minister for the Civil*

Service,[33] from the location of the line between statutory and non-statutory powers.

C. Does the Prerogative Claimed Exist?

A court, faced with an appeal to the prerogative by the Crown, must decide whether the privilege, immunity or power claimed in fact exists. How does it do this? This is really a question about the sources of law. What materials or evidence do Scottish courts look at in order to answer the question?

1. *Statute*

If the privilege is granted by statute (and hence is not a prerogative in the normal sense), the task is essentially one of statutory construction. The immunity from interdict in the Crown Proceedings Act 1947 is a good example. There are many others. Interestingly, the courts have in at least two instances used a statute as a starting-point for development of an immunity going well beyond the statutory terms.

(a) The King cannot be prejudiced by actions of his servants

This doctrine started life as a statutory rule in an Act of 1600,[34] expressly limited to the context of litigation. The King was not to be prejudiced in the conduct of litigation by the 'sloth and negligence' of his officers. This is how the Act was interpreted by Mackenzie,[35] who in other contexts promoted a wide prerogative. In the nineteenth century, however, the courts restated the doctrine as a general principle.[36] In *Advocate General v Garioch*, in considering the liability of Crown lands to certain taxes, it was argued that taxes had in fact been paid in respect of the land in question. Lord Ivory stated that such a practice would not avail against a clear right: 'The Crown cannot be affected by the negligence or omission of its officers.'[37] Similarly, *Somerville v LA* decided that the Crown was not subject to the jurisdiction of the Dean of Guild. The Crown had apparently in fact applied to the Dean of Guild for warrant in the past. Lord Trayner said, '[N]or can the inadvertence or error of the Crown officials in making such applications affect the rights of the Crown. The Crown's rights cannot be prejudiced by the inadvertence, error or neglect of its officials.'[38] Similar remarks are found in a series of cases in which the Inland Revenue was allowed to reopen claims for tax which had previously been settled: for example, '[i]t is the privilege of the Crown not to be bound by the omission, neglect and blunders of their officers';[39] and 'it is settled law that the Crown is not barred by the neglect or omission of its officers'.[40] The doctrine has been repeated in this century.[41] It is not at all clear how far it goes. It did not protect the Crown from the running of prescription.[42] An extraordinary extension of it is found in *Advocate General v Commissioners of Police*,[43] where Lord Jeffrey suggested that one could draw no inference from enumeration in a statute of properties exempt from tax, that other Crown property was subject to tax, because 'the Crown is not to suffer by the laches of its officers'. This opens up the startling possibility that the government may plead its own inability to control the passage of legislation whenever a statute affects it adversely.

356 W. James Wolffe

(b) **The Crown is not subject to taxation, or bound by general statutory words unless expressly or by necessary implication named**

The development of these doctrines from the Exchequer (Scotland) Act 1707 has been fully described by Mitchell and by J.T. Cameron.[44] In brief, it has been recognised that prior to 1707 the Crown had no general immunity from taxation[45] or statutory burdens.[46] The 1707 Act set up the Exchequer Court, and required it to apply English law and procedure. Cases in that Court[47] quite properly applied the general English law doctrine that the Crown was not subject to taxation. After the abolition of the Exchequer Court, the Court of Session applied it in cases analogous to taxation.[48] Eventually it was applied in a non-tax context, but *obiter*, with some reluctance, and subject to important restrictions.[49] Meanwhile, the suggestion that it imported all the English rules, giving the Crown preference in competition with other creditors,[49] was firmly rejected.[50] In *LA v Strathclyde RC and Dumbarton DC*, any doubt was laid to rest in favour of the Crown. The Property Services Agency, carrying out work to the perimeter fence at Faslane, caused an obstruction of the road without permission of the roads authority or the planning authority. Both these authorities took enforcement action. The Crown argued that it was not subject to the restrictions in the relevant legislation, although it was not expressly exempted in respect of activity, such as the work in question, not on Crown land. The House of Lords applied the clear English doctrine that the Crown is not bound by statutory restrictions unless named or by necessary implication. It thus overrode the limits which could have been placed on the doctrine based on its historical statutory context and the previous Scottish cases.

2. *Caselaw*

If a non-statutory privilege which is not merely an incident of the Crown's legal capacity is claimed, the court must look, as it would in any common law case, at other sources. The Scots lawyer has particular difficulties. Sources are scanty. The institutional writers wrote little about constitutional matters. Stair's treatise on the prerogative[51] is now lost. In his Institutions and in the works of Erskine and Bell references to the Crown arise only incidentally in the exposition of private law. Mackenzie's *Jus Regium*, although it has been relied on in the courts[52] was essentially a polemical response to Buchanan's *De Jure Regni Apud Scotos*[53] (which did not pretend to be a legal text). It employed unfashionable modes of reasoning, described the law only in general terms and was written prior to the fundamental changes of 1689. It was easy for post-Union writers to assume that in constitutional matters the law was the same north and south of the border. For example, Bankton, who did devote part of his *Institutes* to public law, relied heavily on English law.[54] He is not wholly reliable.[55] This was exacerbated, as noted above, by the wholesale importation of English exchequer law. There were – and remain – few Scottish textbooks.[56] Being a small jurisdiction, there is relatively little case-law. It is extraordinary how long it was before some matters came before the courts. Only in 1918 was it established in Scotland that the Crown cannot change the law by proclamation[57] and only in 1921 was it finally clear that the Crown could not be sued in delict.[58] Such case-law as exists is often elderly. The courts could respond to such absence of authority in one of two ways. One, probably the more constitutionally correct, would be to hold that where no privilege had been established in the existing case-law, no such privilege should now be recognised. As Lord Diplock said in *BBC v Johns*,[59] it is 350 years and a Civil War too late for the prerogative to enlarge. Lord Reid made a similar suggestion in *Burmah Oil*,[60] and long ago Lord Jeffrey deprecated 'the high deference paid . . . to the prerogative of the sovereign'.[61] If there is to be an extension of Crown privilege it is for Parliament to bestow it. The alternative would be to treat silence in the authorities as permitting development of privileges and immunities by reference to sources other than Scottish case-law. As the two examples already mentioned indicate, the Scottish courts have been willing to follow the latter course, on the basis of statutory clues. Another source which they have relied on regularly as a basis for expanding the prerogative is English case-law.

The relevance of English case-law is a particular issue for Scottish judges in this context. Scots law was historically sceptical of Crown claims. As we have seen, it regarded the Crown as bound by general statutory words. It had no general preference in competition with other creditors. It was subject to interdict proceedings and probably to diligence.[62] It could sue and be sued,[63] in contract, and possibly in delict.[64] The courts did not regard a ministerial claim of privilege in relation to disclosure of documents as conclusive.[65] English law was in many situations diametrically opposite. The Scottish courts have thus been faced from time to time with a conflict between the rules of the two systems. Their attitude has vacillated. On the one hand, one finds *dicta* to the effect that English law on the prerogative is 'irrelevant' to the Scottish position;[66] the House of Lords, in *Glasgow Corporation v Central Land Board*, affirmed a distinctive Scottish position. On the other hand, there are statements that the 1707 Union rendered the law almost necessarily the same;[67] in the Faslane case the House of Lords harmonised the two jurisdictions on the basis of the English rule. A number of observations can be made.

(a) There can be no doubt that what one might call the high governmental prerogatives of the Crown – such as those relating to the summoning and dissolution of Parliament, the appointment of a Prime Minister, and the granting of the Royal Assent – are identical. Indeed, these are rules of Scots law (or English law for that matter) only in the analytical sense that there is no United Kingdom legal system as such. Although pre-Union Scottish monarchs had analogous powers, the current rules (which are in any case much overlain by constitutional convention) do not derive from them. They are rules which relate to the workings of institutions which are common to both legal systems, and in a real sense form British constitutional law (although so to characterise them involves some interesting questions about the nature of a legal system). It would perhaps not only be constitutionally unworkable, but logically impossible, for these rules to differ, depending from which side of the border they are viewed.

(b) It would, however, be a mistake to take this further than necessary. The mere fact that the Crown of the United Kingdom is one Crown does *not* imply that it is logically impossible for it to have different rights and privileges under Scots and English law. Just as any other legal person may find that its powers and capacity may change from jurisdiction to jurisdiction, so might the Crown's. It is Scots law which, in Scotland, determines how the Crown may acquire property or make contracts, for example. Likewise, it is Scots law which determines the limits of any immunities which the Crown may enjoy in Scotland, and the limits of any prerogatives (in the sense of special non-statutory powers) which it enjoys. The courts have properly denied that the Treaty of Union, which (with the Acts of Union) created a unified Crown, in itself harmonised the Crown's legal position in the jurisdictions.[68]

(c) Harmonisation is often desirable, but for the following reason and on the following basis. If there is a justification for any particular privilege to be granted to the Crown, that justification will probably hold good for both jurisdictions. This follows from the sharing of common political institutions. In addition, in relation to particular privileges, there may be specific arguments for a common approach. For example, the rule that the Crown is not bound by general statutory words should probably be the same in both jurisdictions because statutes are enacted by the same institutions and often apply throughout Great Britain or the United Kingdom. Lord Keith stated this strongly in the Faslane case, and it played a key part in his conclusion in that case. A similar approach is found in *King's Printer v Buchan* where, although English law was said to be 'irrelevant', the court found that Scots law was in conformity with English law because the same underlying rationale applied in both jurisdictions. What is probably more important than harmony for its own sake is that the best or most appropriate rule be selected and applied in both jurisdictions. It is by no means obvious that this is always the English rule.[69] The history of the courts' approach to ministerial certificates in relation to public interest immunity in the two jurisdictions from *Duncan v Cammell Laird*[70] to *Glasgow Corporation v Central Land Board* to *Conway v Rimmer*[71] is clear evidence of that. There continues to be potential for reciprocally beneficial influence in this particular area of law. English law has moved on, recognising that the public interest in non-disclosure of documents is not exhausted by the interests of the Crown.[72] Scottish case-law still suggests that it is restricted to central government.[73] Scots law probably should follow English law in this respect.[74] This is a lesson in *discriminating* consideration and application of the most appropriate rule.

(d) As far as the weight to be attributed to English case-law is concerned, any cursory examination of the Scottish cases, right back into the eighteenth century, reveals regular citation of and reliance on English authority. In one case, the Court even suggested that parties should obtain the opinion of English counsel.[75] Of recent cases, *British Medical Association* is notable for exclusive reliance on English authority, and the Faslane case for accepting

English case-law to the exclusion of Scottish. Such citation is often crucial to the decision. Where there is no Scottish authority to speak of, and a clear English rule, it is apparent that the Scottish courts are inclined to adopt the English solution. The adoption of the rule that the Crown cannot be sued in delict (later reversed by statute) is the prime example. Where there is Scottish authority, and it appears to conflict with the English approach, much probably depends on how certain the rules in the two jurisdictions are. For example, in *Central Land Board* it was the existence of a consistent tract of Scottish authority which allowed the House of Lords to decline to follow its own decision in the previous English case of *Cammell Laird*.[76] Likewise, in the Faslane case, a clear English law rule was contrasted with, and preferred to, what was perceived to be a rather weaker series of Scottish cases. By contrast, in *Burmah Oil*, although Lord Reid admitted that there was a current of English authority against any right to compensation, and there was certainly no obvious Scottish authority on the matter at all, he held that there was a right to compensation. The House of Lords was probably, in that case, anxious to find the best rule, which it was accepted would apply to both jurisdictions.

3. *Other sources*

Because of the paucity of authority, the courts occasionally resort to somewhat unusual sources. Grotius, Bynkershoek, Vattel, Pufendorf and Burlamaqui were relied on in *Burmah Oil*, along with a number of United States decisions. That case also contains a rare citation of a political philosopher: John Locke. In *LA v University of Aberdeen*,[77] the court resorted – although the Orcadian context was important – to ancient Norse laws to help ascertain the Crown's rights to treasure hidden in the ground. Apart from particular unusual authorities, the courts have also looked from time to time at the following:

(a) **Usage and practice**

Usage has on occasion been relied on by the courts to ascertain whether or not a privilege exists. In 1789, the obligation to pay for the quartering of troops,[78] and in 1817 the right to press-gang seamen,[79] were defined by usage. More recently, 'constitutional usage' was relied on to define the right to take property in defence of the realm.[80] The Crown practice of paying compensation was noted in *Burmah Oil*,[81] as was the *absence* of any recorded instances of land being taken under the prerogative.[82] While the law must take account of constitutional developments, there is a danger in relying on mere practice alone: it allows the government to legitimise its own activities merely by being consistent.

(b) **The aura of majesty**

In the past, the courts have relied on alleged attributes of kingship, in particular the maxim, 'The King can do no wrong'[83] in order to justify a particular prerogative. This maxim was relied on in *Macgregor v LA* to support the rejection of a right to sue the Crown in delict. For most purposes, this case has been overturned by the Crown Proceedings Act 1947 and Crown Proceedings (Armed Forces) Act 1987, and this casts doubt on the general relevance of the maxim.[84] The First Division in the Faslane case deprecated reliance on such maxims. Whatever place they had in the theory of medieval kingship, they have none in relation to modern government privileges.

(c) **Reason**

Occasionally the courts have considered whether or not the functions of government are such as to require a particular prerogative. In *King's Printers v Buchan* the court had to decide whether the Crown had a monopoly on the printing of bibles. It held that it did. The Lord President stated that '[e]very First Magistrate . . . must as a duty furnish to the public the sources whence instruction is to be derived as to the religion of the state', while Lord Balgray relied on the duty of the monarch of 'preserving the purity of the sacred text'. Such reasoning is attractive. It bases government privileges on the requirements of government. If such privileges can be justified, it must be by reference to those requirements. A criticism which can be levied at many of the decisions on Crown prerogatives is that they fail to consider *why* any particular privilege should be accorded to the Crown. Without considering that question, the court has no rational basis on which to grant, refuse, restrict or expand the privilege claimed. *King's Printers* is also, however, a good example of the difficulties of such a functional approach. It demonstrates – if current political debate about privatisation did not – that the functions of governments are often controversial. Moreover, agreement on the functions of government does not necessarily lead to agreement on whether government requires a prerogative power to assist it in those functions. The courts should always remember that the government has ready (and, when required, speedy)[85] access to Parliament to obtain required powers. A striking example of the danger of such reasoning is the recent English case, *R v Secretary of State for the Home Department ex parte Northumbria Police Authority*,[86] in which the Court of Appeal discovered a general prerogative power, exercisable by the Secretary of State, 'to do all that is reasonably necessary to preserve the peace of the realm'. Discovery by the courts of generally expressed prerogative powers, based on alleged government requirements or functions, is not the best way to deal with complex and controversial matters. However, provided the courts retain an anchor in precedent, and observe the presumption against expanding the prerogative stated by Lords Diplock and Reid, it would be instructive if they were to take into account such functional considerations.

D. Who is the Crown?

Having ascertained that a particular privilege exists, the courts must decide who is entitled to claim it. Since government privileges are equated in our law with Crown prerogatives, this in effect means that they must identify the Crown. This is not easy. As Maitland said, the Crown is 'a chattel, lying in the Tower and partaking of the nature of an heirloom'.[87] Any other use of the term is metaphorical. In law such metaphorical use is well-established. One can start with the premise that, if a prerogative attaches to anyone, it attaches to the monarch. This follows from the feudal origin of prerogatives in Scotland. Active prerogative powers may, as noted above, either be exercised personally by the monarch, or by particular ministers or bodies (such as the Crown Estate Commissioners). Provided the body which exercises such a prerogative power is properly authorised, it will usually be unnecessary to consider whether it forms part of the Crown. In the case of immunities, on the other hand, the courts may well have to consider whether a particular immunity is enjoyed by a particular body, in effect whether that body forms part of the Crown for that purpose. It is reasonably clear that government ministers and civil servants acting under their direction are part of the Crown.[88] The question is much more difficult in relation to the plethora of public boards and quasi-governmental bodies which make up so much of the governmental machine. We are sometimes assisted by statutes which expressly state that a public body carries out its functions 'on behalf of the Crown':[89] it is presumably intended that such bodies are entitled to Crown prerogatives. In *Glasgow Corporation*, in addition to this statutory assistance which weighed heavily with the House of Lords, a number of other factors, both institutional and functional, were taken into account: the Central Land Board operated in England as well as Scotland, and for the purposes of English law was entitled to the benefit of the Crown Proceedings Act 1947; it had a duty to comply with directions of the Secretary of State; it was not a commercial corporation; it was funded by the Treasury; and its substantial function was to fix charges and collect them for the Crown. All these taken together indicated a sufficiently substantial connection with central government to entitle the Board to claim Crown privilege. Non-governmental bodies may also be clothed with the protection of the Crown, if they are carrying out work on the instructions of the Crown. Thus the private contractors carrying out the work at Faslane on behalf of the Property Services Agency were not subject to planning and roads legislation any more than was the Agency itself. In addition, persons and bodies which do have immunity in some contexts do not have it in others. Thus pre-1947, a Crown employee, driving a Crown vehicle, did not have protection from negligence actions when off on a frolic of his own.[90]

In its most recent pronouncement on the subject, *British Medical Association v Greater Glasgow Health Board*, the House of Lords took an approach rather different from that taken in *Central Land Board*. The pursuers wished to obtain an interdict against the defenders. The defenders argued that such a remedy was incompetent, in terms of section 21 of the Crown Proceedings Act 1947. That section (amended for Scotland by section 43) provides that 'where in any proceedings against the Crown any such relief is sought as might in proceedings between subjects be granted by way of interdict . . ., the court shall not grant an interdict'. The defenders' case was supported by an earlier decision of the House of Lords that the use of drugs by the National Health Service was, for the purposes of the Patents Act 1949, 'for the services of the Crown'. It was also supported by the express statutory exclusion of Crown privilege in relation to disclosure of documents, which suggested that without such statutory provision, this privilege would be available to health boards. The House of Lords focused on the interpretation of the words 'proceedings against the Crown' and decided that, whatever other claims health boards might have to Crown privileges, the proceedings against them were not 'proceedings against the Crown'. They did not consider factors of the sort looked at in *Central Land Board* in order to decide what sort of body a health board is or what connection it has with central government. They reviewed the statutory background, and relied on the fact that the 1947 Act was intended to broaden rights against the government. They thus avoided the underlying and conceptually inescapable question: is a health board part of the Crown? The case signalled a departure from the logic of Crown privilege in another respect. While it is apparent from the reference to the Crown Proceedings Act 1947 in *Central Land Board* that the fact that a body enjoys one Crown privilege is *relevant* to whether it should enjoy another, *British Medical Association* indicates that this does not necessarily follow. Lord Jauncey suggests as much:

> [T]he critical question . . . is not whether health boards perform functions on behalf of the Crown . . . nor whether health boards for the purposes of statutory immunity or other purposes fall to be treated as the Crown or as agents so clearly identified with the Crown that they are for all practical purposes indistinguishable therefrom, but whether the respondents' petition amounted to 'proceedings against the Crown' within the meaning of s. 21(1).[92]

It appears, then, that any particular body may enjoy some Crown privileges but not others, and indeed may enjoy some privileges in relation to certain activities but not in relation to others. This is not surprising, given the diverse nature of these privileges. There is no obvious reason why the bodies which can refuse to disclose documents on grounds of public interest should be the same bodies which are immune from interdict proceedings, or why either of these should coincide with the bodies to which legislation applies only if expressly referred to. After all, the policy reasons (to the extent that there *are* policy reasons) justifying each privilege are different. It is therefore welcome to find that the courts grant or withhold them selectively and flexibly. Because, however, they must talk in terms of Crown prerogatives, this means that the term 'Crown' is not used consistently. This is likely only to cause confusion.

Should the use of the term be avoided? The law has available other terms such as 'the State', 'public authority' and 'government' which overlap with the Crown.[93] A change of terminology would perhaps be difficult in such matters as Crown rights in the *regalia*, and as ultimate superior, and in other cases where the rights can be seen as personal to the monarch. In relation to privileges which are in truth being claimed by an arm of the government (as in the Faslane case, *British Medical Association*, *Central Land Board* and *Burmah Oil*) it could only promote clearer understanding of what is in truth going on. As Lord Diplock has said, 'to use the expression "the Crown" as personifying the executive government of the country tends to conceal the fact that the executive functions of sovereignty are of necessity performed through the agency of persons other than the Queen herself'.[94] Further, '[w]here . . . we are concerned with the legal nature of the exercise of executive powers of government, . . . some of the more Athanasian-like features of the debate . . . could have been eliminated if instead of speaking of "the Crown" we were to speak of "the government"'.[95]

This would also eliminate the confusion and real practical difficulty which can arise from the variety of overlapping terms. Abandoning the use of 'the Crown' would not of course immediately solve all difficulties. Cognate terms are also prone to a good deal of uncertainty, which derives inevitably from the diversity of quasi-governmental bodies. For example, in *LA v Argyll CC*,[96] the court had to decide whether or not the Forestry Commission was a 'public department' for the purposes of section 1 of the Crown Suits Act 1857, and a 'department of the government' in terms of the Public Authorities Protection Act 1893. Its approach was akin to that adopted in *Central Land Board*, considering institutional and functional factors which indicated the Commission's place in relation to government. This does at least direct the court to practically relevant considerations, and such terms do remove the rhetorical power and mystique with which talk of 'the Crown' tends to clothe the executive. Such talk is, after all, only metaphorical.

These considerations lead naturally to a further question: do bodies other than the Crown (however that is defined) have 'prerogatives' too? Other public bodies certainly have special statutory powers and immunities. They also have legal capacity, subject to their incorporating document (Charter, Act of Parliament, or whatever). Do they also have non-statutory special powers or immunities arising from the nature of their activities, or do they also share in some of the Crown's special powers? A good example is public interest immunity, which, as has been noted above, has burst out of Crown privilege in England. This is a case where, given the policy behind the rule, it is difficult to resist its extension to bodies other than the Crown. The risk in considering policy is that the courts are forced to engage on the controversial assessment of what is the government's business, as discussed above. For example, in the nineteenth century the Court of Session tried to grant Edinburgh University exemption from poor-rates, essentially because these existed for public or national objects, to fulfil 'the duty of the State or Sovereign to educate the people'.[97] This was overruled by the House of Lords. The Lords resorted to the same sort of policy-based arguments, taking the view that 'it is impossible . . . to bring the functions of a University within the proper meaning of government purposes'.[98] It is nonetheless possible that, in an appropriate case, the courts might recognise that bodies other than central government have certain special non-statutory powers. Hume in his Lectures[99] suggested that local authorities might well have the power to override private property rights in an emergency. This might be regarded as a species of necessity. Even if it is, it appears likely that the governmental nature of such a body might well entitle it to take steps to effect or co-ordinate the response to a local disaster (a major rail collision, a widespread city fire, a Lockerbie-scale air disaster), going beyond those steps which a private individual might be justified in taking. It is more correct to see such a power as more than just an aspect of necessity: the authority's hand is not forced. They may also have special non-statutory immunities. In *Phin v Magistrates of Auchtermuchty*,[100] the Crown successfully objected to sale by the creditors of a Royal Burgh of its town-house, jail and town bell, in effect because these were essential for the burgh to perform its public duties.

This issue is likely to become of importance as government functions are hived off to private organisations. The possible implications of privatisation were highlighted in the recent case of *Bank of Scotland v IMRO*.[101] The Bank of Scotland sought judicial review of decisions of the Investment Management Regulatory Organisation Limited, one of the regulatory bodies operating within the framework of the Financial Services Act 1986. IMRO is in law a private company, with its registered office in London. Its relationship with the Bank is regulated in law by contract. Under the jurisdiction rules applying to contractual obligations, the court had no jurisdiction. It was further observed by Lord Dunpark that it may not be possible for the Court of Session to review a decision of a body based outside Scotland. This decision would almost certainly have been different if IMRO had been a traditional government regulator, because the Crown is domiciled throughout the United Kingdom.[102] Likewise, privatisation may, by severing the institutional link to the Crown, involve the loss of governmental privileges and immunities which previously applied to the activities privatised.

E. Control of the Prerogative

It is a mistake to think of the prerogative as unbridled. There are various mechanisms of control, both political and legal. Most prerogatives are in fact exercised by the government, rather than by the monarch. This is true, perhaps as a matter not of law, but of constitutional convention. This exposes such exercises of the prerogative to the processes of political accountability. It does seem, however, that in practice political scrutiny is more difficult in relation to prerogative powers.[103] This makes legal mechanisms of control of particular importance. The Courts have a number of tools.

First, the courts define the limits of government powers and immunities (as in the Faslane case), particularly those non-statutory special powers and immunities normally described as 'prerogatives', and may require compensation to be paid in respect of their exercise (as in *Burmah Oil*). They also determine whether any particular body is entitled to claim or enjoy a particular prerogative, as in *British Medical Association*. The conceptual uncertainty surrounding the words 'prerogative' and 'Crown', and the relative absence of authority give them considerable latitude in these respects. Their role in expanding the prerogative shows this. Second, they determine whether and to what extent prerogatives have been superseded. They can certainly be superseded by statute.[104] This is perhaps just a particular example of a general principle that, if the requirement expressed in a particular prerogative is satisfied by some other means, there is no need for the courts to recognise that prerogative. For example, in *Smith v Jeffrey*,[105] it was suggested that the Crown could no longer resort to the prerogative power to requisition ships for the defence of the realm, except perhaps in a case of urgent necessity, because of the existence of the Royal

Navy. If special non-statutory powers and immunities are restricted to those truly necessary for the proper functioning of government, this general principle makes sense. It also confirms that, in the event that a statute which supersedes a prerogative is repealed, the prerogative *should* revive, provided that it still reflects a manifest requirement of good government. Third, the courts may find limits implied in the way in which the government chooses to exercise its prerogative. Thus, in *Smith v Jeffrey*, the Admiralty issued instructions empowering its agents to impress seamen. That power was restricted by express limitations in those instructions. Fourth, some prerogatives are subject to specific limitations. A good example is the way in which the Crown's rights in the *regalia* are hedged with its obligations to the public at large. It may be important to examine carefully what sort of right is at issue in any particular case, in order to determine the limits applicable to it.

To this armoury, the courts can now add judicial review of actions carried out under the prerogative. This was confirmed in *CCSU v Minister for the Civil Service*.[106] Prior to that case, although the position was not completely free from doubt,[107] the orthodox view was that while the courts could fix the boundaries of the prerogative they could not review its exercise. In this case, the Minister for the Civil Service (who happened also to be the Prime Minister) removed from Civil Service employees working at Government Communications Headquarters (GCHQ) the right to belong to a trade union. This was done under powers conferred by a prerogative instrument, the Civil Service Order in Council Act 1982. No consultation took place. The House of Lords held that this exercise of prerogative power was reviewable on the ground of procedural unfairness – although they declined to review it in this case because national security requirements prevailed over procedural propriety. This decision is perhaps the most important recent example of a formal approach giving way to a functional one. The House of Lords denied that the court's power to review government action depended on the legal basis of that action. Review was not confined to acts done under statutory powers. The courts are not merely guardians of Parliament's will. They apply general principles of review to both statutory and non-statutory powers. Review will not, however, be exercised over some powers – defined by reference to their subject-matter. Lord Roskill gave a list of such non-reviewable powers. They included the making of treaties, the defence of the realm, and the dissolution of Parliament. These are not 'susceptible to judicial review because their *nature and subject matter* is such as not to be amenable to the judicial process'.

There are numerous issues arising from the GCHQ case which still remain to be settled.[108] Which powers are unreviewable? Will the courts in fact apply the same standards as they apply to statute-based administrative action? In Scotland, it still in theory perhaps remains open whether the GCHQ case will be applied so as to allow the courts to review the exercise of the prerogative. It probably will. It certainly should.[109] The Scottish courts have already regularly cited (albeit in the context of judicial review of statutory powers) Lord Diplock's threefold classification of the *grounds* of review enunciated in *CCSU*.[110] They have historically been unsympathetic to Crown claims. They have also been willing to accept English authority and, on occasion, to take a functional approach to definition and attribution of prerogative rights. Judicial review of the prerogative therefore fits readily into the Scottish tradition. Most importantly, the reasons for the courts to review prerogative acts are equally cogent north and south of the border.

F. Conclusion

In any organised society, the institutions charged with government probably require powers going beyond the ordinary capacity of other persons. In our society most of those powers are bestowed upon the government by Parliament. Government may, however, require additional powers in order effectively to fulfil its functions. Thus, in the United States, it has been held that the President, as the constitutional repository of the executive power, has those powers which are regarded as necessary incidents of sovereignty,[111] in particular relating to foreign affairs and control of the armed forces. His power, like the Crown's prerogative power, increases in time of war.[112] The President, like the monarch, has immunities from suit and the executive has privileges in the law of evidence.[113] Moreover, even the active US judiciary regards itself as constrained in dealing with 'political questions'.[114] It is, therefore, a mistake to regard government privileges as unusual, or indeed unjustifiable. What is unfortunate in the British context is that such privileges are considered in terms of Crown prerogatives. Crown prerogative is a metaphor shackled to an ambiguity. Consideration of government claims in those terms does not assist the courts to address the issues rationally, and hinders a sensible appreciation both of true government requirements and of the arguments against the grant of a particular privilege. This has perhaps been one factor in the apparent willingness of the courts to expand the scope of government privileges. It is to be hoped that in the wake of *CCSU* the courts will take a more critical look at the claims of the government. They should scrutinise closely the nature of the privilege claimed by analysing strictly its legal basis, by applying a presumption against expansion of the prerogative, and finally by applying the principles of judicial review. Metaphor and mystique are marvellous in romantic mysteries. The constitution, however, is not romantic; nor should it be mysterious.

Notes

1. See *Government of the Republic of Spain v National Bank of Scotland* 1939 SC 413.
2. [1957] PL 304.
3. 1963 SC 410, 1964 SC (HL) 117; see (1965-66) 79 *Harv L R* 614.
4. 1988 SLT 538, 1989 SLT 493.
5. 1987 SCCR 171, 1988 SLT 546 (noted [1988] PL 339), 1990 SLT 158 (noted [1990] PL 14).
6. No. 14 (1971).
7. A.V. Dicey, *Introduction to the Study of the Constitution* (4th ed) Macmillan (1893) 352.
8. Comm I. 239.

9. *Cf. Somerville v LA* (1893) 20R 1050 at 1073.
10. *Op cit* note 8 *supra*.
11. Probably a legal person. In English law it is called a corporation sole. The monarch is presumably (also?) a natural person.
12. See H.W.R. Wade *Constitutional Fundamentals* Stevens (1980) 48.
13. E.g. *Jenkins v A – G* (1971) *Current Law* 1628.
14. See C. Turpin *Government Contracts* Penguin (1972).
15. E.g. *R v Criminal Injuries Compensation Board ex parte Lain* [1967] 2 QB 864.
16. See T. Daintith 'The Executive Power Today: Bargaining and Economic Control' ch 8 of J. Jowell and D. Oliver *The Changing Constitution* Clarendon Press (1985).
17. See W.D. Prosser 'The Burmah Oil Case' [1963] PL 12.
18. Both of which are further discussed *infra*.
19. Especially 1587 c 77; see Normand 'The Public Prosecutor in Scotland' (1938) 54 LQR 345.
20. E.g. Acts of 1597 c 255, 1606 c 1, 1609 c 8, 1612 c 1, 1633 c 3.
21. *The Royal College of Physicians v The Royal College of Surgeons* 1911 SC 1054; *MacCormick v LA* 1953 SC 395.
22. *Op cit* note 12 *supra* 46 – 53.
23. *Parker v LA* (1902) 4F 698.
24. See J.T. Cameron 'Crown Exemption from Statute and Tax in Scotland' (1962) 7 *Jur Rev* 191; Mitchell, *op cit* 308 – 310.
25. *Smith v Jeffrey* 24 Jan 1817 FC.
26. E.g. Kames *Essays upon Several Subjects Concerning British Antiquities* Edinburgh (1747) Essay II.
27. Mitchell *Constitutional Law* (2nd ed) W. Green & Son (1968) 185.
28. *Ibid* at 175 – 184.
29. *Burmah Oil* 1964 SC HL 117 at 135.
30. This was established in the Faslane case. For the previous Scottish position see *infra*.
31. See Cameron *op cit* note 24 *supra*.
32. E.g. until the enactment of s 21 Crown Proceedings Act 1947 the Crown could be subject to an interdict in Scotland: *Russell v Mags of Hamilton* (1897) 25R 350; *Bell v Secretary of State* 1933 SLT 519.
33. *CCSU v Minister for Civil Service* [1984] 3 All ER 935; *infra*.
34. Act of 1600 c 14; see H.R. Buchanan 'Some Aspects of the Royal Prerogative' (1923) 35 *Jur Rev* 49. This rule does not permit the Crown to ignore ordinary rules of pleading: *Ramsay v McLaren* 1936 SLT 35.
35. *Observations upon the Statutes and Acts of the Scots Parliament*; see also Erskine I.2.27.
36. Stair IV.35.2 also seems to state the rule in general terms.
37. *Advocate General v Garioch* (1850) 12D 447.
38. (1893) 20R 1050 at 1061.
39. *LA v Miller's Trs* (1884) 11R 1046 *per* Lord Fraser.
40. *Alston's Trs v LA* (1896) 33 SLR 278; see also *LA v Duke of Hamilton* (1891) 29 SLR 213 *per* Lord President Robertson; *LA v Meiklam* (1860) 22D 1427 *per* Lord Justice Clerk Inglis.
41. *LA v Merrielees' Trustees* 1943 SC 587 at 594 per Lord Keith; *cf* 1945 SC (HL) 1.
42. See Buchanan *op cit* note 34 *supra*.
43. (1850) 12 D 456.
44. J.D.B. Mitchell 'The Royal Prerogative in Modern Scots Law' [1957] PL 304; Cameron *op cit* note 24 *supra*.
45. *LA v Strathclyde RC and Dumbarton DC* 1990 SLT 158 at 161.
46. *Advocate General v Garioch* (1850) 12D 447; *Advocate General v Commissioners of Police for the City of Edinburgh* (1850) 12D 456; *Advocate General v Oliver* (1852) 14D 356; *Advocate General v Magistrates of Inverness* (1956) 18D 366.
47. *LA v Barbour and Lang* (1866) 5M 84.

48. *Somerville v LA op cit* note 9 *supra*; *Magistrates of Edinburgh v LA* 1912 SC 1085; see also *Burnet v Barclay* 1955 JC 34.
49. *LA v Galbraith* (1910) 47 SLR 529.
50. *Admiralty v Blair's Tr* 1916 SC 247. It is true to say, however, that in this case the Crown sought to rely on pre-Union English law: the court was fortified in its resolve by the fact that its decision in fact accorded with contemporary English law.
51. Mentioned in his Apology, published with *The Institutions of the Law of Scotland* (1681) (More ed 1832) xxi.
52. *Burmah Oil* 1963 SC 410 at 424 per Lord Kilbrandon, 453 *per* Lord President Clyde, 464–5 *per* Lord Sorn, 473 *per* Lord Guthrie.
53. (1579); published in a translation by D.H. McNeil as *The Art and Science of Government among the Scots*, MacLellan (1964).
54. See e.g. IV.1.44, 46.
55. See Mitchell, *op cit* note 44 306.
56. The texts remain Green's *Encyclopaedia of the Laws of Scotland* (2nd Ed) Vol 4 1910 s.v. 'Crown'; W.I.R. Fraser *An Outline of Constitutional Law* (2nd ed) W. Green & Son (1948) chs VII, X, XI: J.D.B. Mitchell, *Constitutional Law* ch 9.
57. *Grieve v Edinburgh and District Water Trs* 1918 SC 700.
58. *MacGregor v LA* 1921 SC 847.
59. [1965] Ch 32.
60. 1964 SC (HL) 117 at 127.
61. *Common Agent in Prestonkirk Locality v Ferguson* (1846) 9D 61.
62. *LA v Matheson* (1986) 1 SLR 174; J.G. Stewart *A Treatise on the Law of Diligence* W. Green & Son (1898) at 328; overruled by s 45 Crown Proceedings Act 1947.
63. See *King's Advocate v Dunglas* (1836) 15S 314. Special rules relating to Crown litigation are contained in the Crown Suits (Scotland) Act 1857 and the Crown Proceedings Act 1947.
64. See J.R. Philips 'The Crown as Litigant in Scotland' (1928) 40 *Jur Rev* 238 at 245–9; Lord Murray: 'Rex Non Potest Peccare' (1939) 55 *Sc L Rev* 1, 40. It has to be said that the position is obscure. Lord Murray relied heavily on *Bruce v Hamilton* (1946) 58 *Jur Rev* 83, which in fact has nothing to do with delictual liability of the Crown: see Cooper 'The King versus the Court of Session' (1946) 58 *Jur Rev* 83.
65. *Glasgow Corporation v Central Land Board* 1956 SC (HL) 1.
66. *King's Printer v Buchan* (1826) 49 559.
67. *MacGregor v LA* 1921 SC 847 at 851 *per* Lord Justice Clerk Scott-Dickson.
68. *Glasgow Corporation v Central Land Board* at 21 *per* Lord Keith; *Parker v LA* (1902) 4F 698.
69. *Cf MacCormick v LA* 1953 SC 396 at 411 *per* Lord President Cooper.
70. [1942] AC 624.
71. [1969] AC 910.
72. See especially *D v NSPCC* [1978] AC 171.
73. *Higgin v Burton* 1968 SLT (Notes) 52; see also *Strathclyde RC v B* unreported, Glasgow Sheriff Court, 17 Feb 1984, mentioned in I.D. McPhail *Evidence* Law Society of Scotland (1987) S 18 54C.
74. See *Conway v Rimmer* [1968] AC 910 per Lord Reid and Lord Upjohn; I.D. MacPhail *op cit* note 73 18.54; A.B. Wilkinson *The Scottish Law of Evidence*, Butterworths (1986) at 107–115; D. Field *The Law of Evidence in Scotland* W. Green & Son (1988) 265–8.
75. *Robertson v Jardine* (1802) M 7891.
76. *Somerville v LA op cit* note 7 *supra* at 1073 per Lord McLaren; approved in *Smith v LA* 1932 SLT 374 at 379.
77. 1963 SC 533.
78. *Wemyss v Magistrates of Canongate* 6 February 1789 FD.
79. See note 25 *supra*.

80. *The Moffat Hydropathic Co Limited v LA* (1919) 1 SLT 82.
81. 1963 SC 410 at 449 per Lord President Clyde; 1964 SC (HL) 117 at 167 *per* Lord Pearce.
82. 1963 SC 410 at 430 *per* Lord Kilbrandon; 1964 SC (HL) 117 at 122 *per* Lord Reid.
83. See Lord Murray, *op cit* note 64 *supra*.
84. *Cf Cameron v LA* 1952 SC 165 at 171.
85. E.g. the enactment of the Prevention of Terrorism (Temporary Provisions) Act 1974 in the space of a few hours after the Birmingham bomb outrage. The relevance of the accessibility of Parliament was acknowledged by Viscount Radcliffe in *Burmah Oil* 1964 SC (HL) 117 at 133.
86. [1988] 1 All ER 556; see A.W. Bradley 'Police Powers and the Prerogative' [1988] PL 298.
87. F.W. Maitland 'The Crown as Corporation' *Selected Essays* H.D. Hazeltine, G. Lapsley and P.H. Winfield (Eds) Cambridge U P (1936) 104, 116.
88. *British Medical Association v Greater Glasgow Health Board* 1988 SLT 538; *Griffin v LA* 1950 SC 448.
89. E.g. *Glasgow Corporation v Central Land Board* 1956 SC (HL) 1. Statutes also sometimes deal with the monarch in her private capacity expressly: e.g. s 40 Crown Proceedings Act 1947.
90. *Salt v McKnight* 1947 JC 99.
91. *Pfizer v Minister of Health* [1965] AC 512.
92. *British Medical Association v Greater Glasgow Health Board* 1989 SLT 493 at 497.
93. See G. Marshall 'The State, the Crown and the Executive' in his *Constitutional Theory* Oxford U P (1971) 13; see also *Burmah Oil* 1963 SC 410 at 469 *per* Lord Sorn.
94. *BBC v Johns* [1965] Ch 32.
95. *Town Investments v Department of the Environment* [1978] AC 359; see also Lord Simon of Glaisdale's speech; and the opinions of the Second Division in *British Medical Association v Greater Glasgow Health Board* 1988 SLT 538.
96. 1950 SC 304; see also *Smith v LA* 1932 SLT 374; *Ronson Nominees Limited v Mitchell* 1982 SLT (Sh Ct) 18.
97. *Edinburgh University v Greig* (1865) 3M 1151.
98. *Greig v Edinburgh University* (1868) 6M (HL) 97 at 100 *per* Lord Westbury; see also *Commissioners for the Harbour and Docks of Leith v Miles* (1866) 4M (HL) 14; and contrast *Glasgow Court Houses Commissioners v Glasgow Parish Council* 1912 SC 194.
99. III. 205.
100. (1827) 5S 690.
101. 1989 SCLR 386.
102. Section 46(1), (3)(a), Civil Jurisdiction and Judgements Act 1982.
103. C. Munro *Studies in Constitutional Law* Butterworths (1987) 166–9, 172–4.
104. *A–G v de Keyser's Royal Hotel Limited* [1920] AC 508.
105. *Op cit* note 25 *supra*.
106. *Op cit* note 33 *supra*.
107. Munro *op cit* at 175–182.
108. C. Walker 'Review of the Prerogative: The Remaining Issues' [1987] PL 62.
109. See also 1985 SLT (News) 101.
110. E.g. *City of Edinburgh DC v Secretary of State for Scotland* 1985 SLT 551, *Connor v Strathclyde Regional Council* 1986 SLT 530; *O'Neill v Scottish Joint Negotiating Committee* 1987 SLT 649; *Lakin v Secretary of State for Scotland* 1988 SLT 780.
111. *United States v Curtiss–Wright Export Corp* 299 US 304 (1936).
112. L.H. Tribe *American Constitutional Law* (2nd ed) The Foundation Press 1989 at 238.
113. *Ibid* at 268–285.
114. *Ibid* at 96–107.

Index